GOETHE

He has to live in the midst of the incomprehensible, which is also detestable. And it has a fascination, too, that goes to work on him. The fascination of the abomination – you know, imagine the growing regrets, the longing to escape, the powerless disgust, the surrender, the hate.

Joseph Conrad, *Heart of Darkness*

GOETHE

HIS FAUSTIAN LIFE

A.N. WILSON

BLOOMSBURY CONTINUUM
LONDON · OXFORD · NEW YORK · NEW DELHI · SYDNEY

BLOOMSBURY CONTINUUM
Bloomsbury Publishing Plc
50 Bedford Square, London, WC1B 3DP, UK
29 Earlsfort Terrace, Dublin 2, Ireland

BLOOMSBURY, BLOOMSBURY CONTINUUM and the Diana logo are trademarks
of Bloomsbury Publishing Plc

First published in Great Britain 2024

A catalogue record for this book is available from the British Library

Library of Congress Cataloging-in-Publication data has been applied for

ISBN: HB: 978-1-4729-9486-8; eBook: 978-1-47299-485-1; ePDF: 978-1-4729-9484-4;

2 4 6 8 10 9 7 5 3 1

Typeset by Deanta Global Publishing Services, Chennai, India
Printed and bound in Great Britain by CPI Group (UK) Ltd, Croydon CR0 4YY

MIX
Paper | Supporting
responsible forestry
FSC® C171272

To find out more about our authors and books visit www.bloomsbury.com
and sign up for our newsletters

CONTENTS

To my beloved daughters, Emily, Bee and Georgie

A NOTE ON TRANSLATIONS

I owe much to all the translated versions of Goethe that I have read. The translations given here of his poetry are my own. Deep apologies if I have not been consistent here and inadvertently quoted from someone else's translations, but I do not believe myself to have done so. In the case of other sources – for example, Thomas Mann's *Lotte in Weimar* – I have quoted from English-language sources, which are noted in the Bibliography. From Eckermann I have used my own translations.

TIMELINE

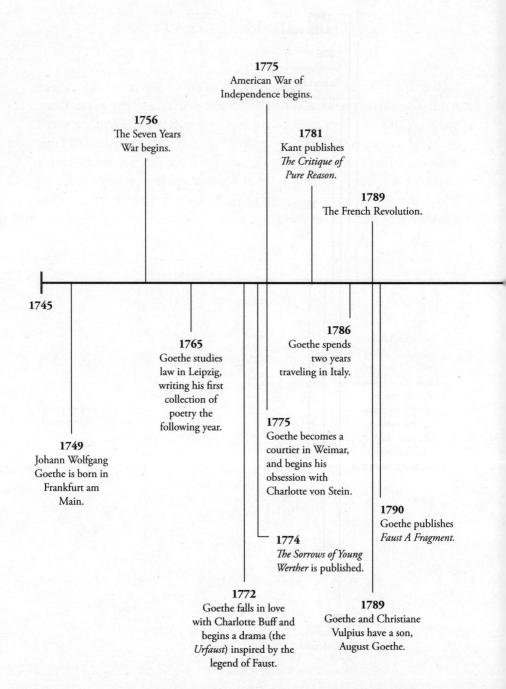

1775
American War of
Independence begins.

1756
The Seven Years
War begins.

1781
Kant publishes
*The Critique of
Pure Reason*.

1789
The French Revolution.

1745

1765
Goethe studies
law in Leipzig,
writing his first
collection of
poetry the
following year.

1786
Goethe spends
two years
traveling in Italy.

1775
Goethe becomes a
courtier in Weimar,
and begins his
obsession with
Charlotte von Stein.

1749
Johann Wolfgang
Goethe is born in
Frankfurt am
Main.

1774
*The Sorrows of Young
Werther* is published.

1790
Goethe publishes
Faust A Fragment.

1772
Goethe falls in love
with Charlotte Buff and
begins a drama (the
Urfaust) inspired by the
legend of Faust.

1789
Goethe and Christiane
Vulpius have a son,
August Goethe.

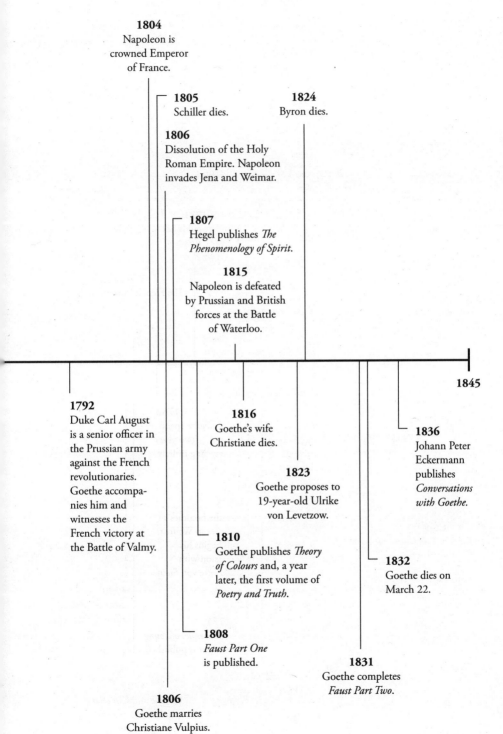

1804
Napoleon is
crowned Emperor
of France.

1805
Schiller dies.

1824
Byron dies.

1806
Dissolution of the Holy
Roman Empire. Napoleon
invades Jena and Weimar.

1807
Hegel publishes *The
Phenomenology of Spirit*.

1815
Napoleon is defeated
by Prussian and British
forces at the Battle
of Waterloo.

1845

1792
Duke Carl August
is a senior officer in
the Prussian army
against the French
revolutionaries.
Goethe accompa-
nies him and
witnesses the
French victory at
the Battle of Valmy.

1816
Goethe's wife
Christiane dies.

1836
Johann Peter
Eckermann
publishes
*Conversations
with Goethe*.

1823
Goethe proposes to
19-year-old Ulrike
von Levetzow.

1810
Goethe publishes *Theory
of Colours* and, a year
later, the first volume of
Poetry and Truth.

1832
Goethe dies on
March 22.

1808
Faust Part One
is published.

1831
Goethe completes
Faust Part Two.

1806
Goethe marries
Christiane Vulpius.

I

THESE VERY SERIOUS JOKES

He is the man in whom for the first time there dawned the consciousness that human life is man's struggle with his intimate and individual destiny – that is, that human life is made up of the problem of itself, that its substance consists not in something that already is ... but in something which has to make itself, which, therefore, is not a thing, but an absolute and problematical task.
José Ortega y Gasset, 'In Search of Goethe from Within'

The little delegation, arriving at Goethe's house in the second half of November 1828, was assembled to bring momentous news. Sixty or more years after the great poet had begun to write his *Faust*, they were proposing, in honour of his eightieth birthday in the following year, to stage a production in the Court Theatre at Weimar. It was a theatre where Goethe had himself directed innumerable productions, and plays and operas, during the decades he had lived in the little town. Here he had played Orestes in his own drama, *Iphigenia in Tauris*. Here he had directed Mozart operas, Schiller's great three-part masterpiece *Wallenstein*, and countless bad, but highly popular, plays by his *bête noire* Kotzebue, and many another entertainment. He had, indeed, grown disillusioned with the theatre, the boorishness and stupidity of the audiences, the temperament of actors, the sheer grind of getting a production off the ground.

But a staging of *Faust*? In Weimar! This would surely be something different. He had first started to write a drama based on the *Faust* legend when he was a law student in Strasbourg. He had begun to write it in a different world, a world where the Old Regime was more or less in place: there was a Holy Roman Empire; Louis XVI and Marie Antoinette sat on the throne of France; they were still executing witches in Germany.

The project had been laid to one side many times. Once he had arrived in Weimar, fifty-three years earlier, in 1775, to take up his position as a courtier and administrator to the young Duke, later Grand Duke, Carl August, his writing had to be squeezed between the all-consuming business of administration. As well as attendance at frequent Privy Council meetings, his duties had included the supervision of road building, the organization of the mines at Ilmenau, the running of the university at nearby Jena, the mustering and pay of the tiny ducal army. But all through these years, he had periodically worked on *Faust*, so that it had changed and expanded many times. Now, they were in a new world. There was a clamour among the young intellectuals for a united Germany, a republican Germany. Over in England, they had built something called the Stockton and Darlington Railway. There were clever people over there, as he sometimes remarked.

The first part of the *Faust* play is one with which most modern audiences are familiar: it tells the story of how a scholar-mage of Renaissance times, thirsty for knowledge and the power which knowledge brings with it, resorts to magic; how he encounters a strange poodle, who turns out to be an embodiment of Mephistopheles; how the devil offers him a kind of pact, though one rather different from the pact known to earlier audiences of such versions of the story as Christopher Marlowe's *The Tragicall History of Doctor Faustus*.

True, in the original sketched-out version, penned in student days, Goethe appears to have retained the idea that Faust would be damned for his presumptuous pride and ambition. But as the story developed in his mind, Goethe emended and eventually abandoned this idea, making the scholar and the devil, in some ways, two sides of a conglomerate personality: good and evil perceptions flying like sparks from the hectic pace of their enterprise and their dialogue, which, by the time he completed it, had embraced a satire on the contemporary European political situation, reflections on the development of modern science, and a dazzlingly original retelling of the Helen myth from classical times.

Goethe, from the first, had introduced an entirely new strand into the legend: that Faust should meet, fall in love with and seduce an innocent teenager called Gretchen (Margaret); that their union would produce a child whom Gretchen, in her panic and shame, drowns, a crime for which she is condemned to death. Faust, meanwhile, who when first seen by the audience seems to be consumed with spiritual thirst for higher things, an insatiable devotion to science, theology and philosophy, now only seems interested in the pursuit of power, and in self-advancement. And yet, there is a part of him which strives for a better life – not only for himself, sometimes even for humanity itself, but, as he admits, in one of his finest monologues,[1] the devil becomes a companion he cannot do without.

The original Faust story, which Goethe had come to know through puppet shows as a child in Frankfurt, was very close to what we find in Marlowe's play. In that early, primitive version, it was true to say, as did C. S. Lewis, 'You will read in some critics that Faustus has a thirst for knowledge. In reality, he hardly mentions it. It is not truth that he wants from the devil, but gold and guns and girls.'[2]

Goethe's expanded and transmogrified *Faust* was a much bigger thing than this. Much more morally complicated. For, in the years since he first conceived of the play, Goethe realized that he had been drawing out of the Faust legend a parable of his own: he had been writing about the emergence of modern humanity itself.

A key aspect of what we mean by 'modern' here is ambiguity. Goethe was one of the most fascinating characters in history; Faust is one of the most fascinating characters in literature: because they are both so ambivalent – cold, yet passionate; cynical, yet intensely serious and devoted to Love, to Nature, and to the spiritual quest.

Zwei Seelen wohnen, ach! in meiner Brust[3]
There are two souls/selves dwelling in my breast.

Faust is not an imitation of Hamlet, but he grows, in part, out of Goethe's preoccupation with Hamlet; and both Hamlet and Faust anticipate modern humanity adrift from all the old certainties of faith and tradition.

As a volume in the Collected Works demanded by an eager publisher, between 1787 and 1790, Goethe had published *Faust A Fragment*. It was a poem – play – reflection – on its own times. It had been conceived long before the French Revolution.

By the time he had finished the play now known as *Faust Part One*, first published in 1808, Europe had moved from that revolution to a period of war and social upheaval without previous parallel. By the time *Faust Part One* was finished in 1797, two immense developments had taken place in Goethe's life, on the one hand, and in the history of Europe on the other. On the personal level, he had formed his friendship with the greatest playwright in the history of German literature, Friedrich Schiller. On the public scale, Napoleon had appeared. The 'whiff of grapeshot', in Carlyle's famous phrase, had on Napoleon's decisive command cleared the Parisian streets of the mob on 13 Vendémiaire 1795. In March 1796, this young Corsican officer had married Josephine Beauharnais. The following year, 1797, saw his triumphant Italian campaign in which he routed the strength of the Austrians – hence of the Holy Roman Empire itself – and defeated the proud republic of Venice. Having established hegemony in France – defeating the hopes of the royalists, and subduing the revolutionaries to his will – Napoleon was well on the way to 18 Brumaire 1799, when, as First Consul, he would become the French dictator, and would soon become the Emperor. Friedrich Nietzsche was surely right to say that Napoleon was the demonic inspiration for the developed and completed *Faust*.

By the time Goethe published *Faust Part One*, Napoleon, at the height of his powers, had invaded Germany, slaughtered tens of thousands of Goethe's fellow countrymen, reduced the university town of Jena to rubble and requisitioned Goethe's house for occupation by the French military top brass.

None of this seemed to have diminished Goethe's admiration for the man he called 'mon empereur'. Throughout the Napoleonic times, while Goethe was at work on his colour theory, in which he attempted to refute Newton, and during which he had been deeply, and embarrassingly, at odds with his Duke in Weimar, who was actually at war with Napoleon, Goethe was visiting and revisiting the literature and philosophy of the Greeks, a journey which would involve a recovery of truths and perceptions which had been explored by the pre-Christian Grecian tragedians, as well as by Homer. Was their cult of female divinities an intuitive pursuit of the centrality of imagination in human life? Was this properly understood as the Eternal Feminine? Was this what lay behind the Catholic cult of female saints and of the Blessed Virgin herself?

These ideas, which Goethe would explore in the conversations of old age with his many visitors, were all fomenting and changing into *Faust Part Two*. But it was not of this second play that the little delegation, in November 1828, wanted to speak.

They knew that he was at work on a continuation, but it was the finished *Faust*, ending with poor Gretchen calling out Faust's name, and a voice from Heaven pronouncing her redemption, that they wished to stage. *Faust Part One*.

Although audiences had seen other plays by Goethe – his *Iphigenia*, his *Egmont* (for which Beethoven wrote incidental music which Goethe scorned), his *Torquato Tasso*, his *Götz von Berlichingen* – these plays had never been especially popular with theatre-goers. He sadly admitted that in Weimar the audiences had the chance to see *Iphigenia* or *Tasso* only once every three or four years, and that they obviously found them boring.[4] These plays were literary productions to be read, more than they were compelling stage plays. They lacked his friend Schiller's capacity to hold an audience in thrall.

An exception might be *Faust*, which was full of dramatic incidents if they could be successfully enacted – the appearance of the Earth Spirit – a gigantic fiery head symbolizing Nature in all its amoral power and energy; the appearance of the poodle-devil; the pathos and beauty of Gretchen's love for Faust; and the disturbing movement of Faust's from tender – even rather soppy – 'love' for Gretchen to his orgiastic hours on the mountains on Walpurgis Night, utterly forgetting the fact that he has allowed the devil to drug, and kill, Gretchen's mother, to enable the seduction to take place; followed by the murder of Gretchen's brother Valentine, who turns up at an awkward moment to accuse her of being a whore.

It is strong meat, even before the theatrical director asks how it is conceivably possible to stage the orgy of Walpurgis Night. Highly understandable was the fact that, in none of the cities of Germany, had theatres risked the obloquy of the censors.[5]

Goethe had always doubted whether *Faust* was stageable.[6] When it was known, in 1806, that he had finished *Part One*, his admirers assumed that, as director of the Weimar Court Theatre, he would make the attempt to mount a production, but there was a long silence. In 1812, the composer Prince Anton Heinrich Radziwill composed music for the piece and made it into a part-opera, part-oratorio, but these versions, delightful as Goethe found them, were only privately performed. Between 1810 and 1812, Goethe had discussed the possibility of a stage production with his secretary, Professor Riemer, and, one of Goethe's favourite actors, Pius Alexander Wolff, but on each occasion August Wilhelm Schlegel's judgement seemed to be borne out, that 'to put Goethe's *Faust* on stage, you would need Faust's book of magic and his magic spells to make it work'.[7] A very much cut version of the play had been performed in Berlin at the Schloss Monbijou. This production, amounting to no more than a few select scenes, was directed by Carl Friedrich Moritz Paul, Count of Brühl, for an invited audience.

But Goethe was the great German genius. France, Britain or the fledgling United States of America, could define themselves in terms of national identity. What it meant to be German was a very different thing – the sprawling territories which had been the Holy Roman Empire (until Napoleon abolished it) and the various duchies, states, electorates and kingdoms had yet to find a national unity which could forge Germany itself into a nation. The German unity was a cultural one: it was found in a shared language, in shared poets and philosophers and in its musicians. To adopt the role of the great German genius, a role which suited Goethe just fine, was to be more than a famous writer. It was almost as though he held the German soul in his hands. And yet, much as he might like being the Great Man of Weimar and the great Genius of the German Language, the role also disgusted him, and he despised German nationalism – one reason why he so controversially was proud to wear the *Légion d'honneur* which had been bestowed upon him by 'mon empereur' in Erfurt, when Napoleon – having abolished the Holy Roman Empire – had bullied the Russians into a carve-up of Europe, with France dominating the West, the Tsar being ruler of the East.

That was all long in the past. And now, here we were, in 1828. And here they were, the little delegation arriving at the Privy

Councillor's house in the central square of the beautiful little town, the Frauenplan, the legendary Weimar address to which pilgrims had been flocking for decades. There was Chancellor Friedrich von Müller (aged forty-eight), a highly cultivated figure, much loved by Goethe, not least because he had lived in Paris and was steeped in French culture and literature; there was the put-upon Professor Friedrich Wilhelm Riemer, in his early fifties, a distinguished philologist, author of a Greek–German dictionary, but whom Goethe had enlisted as a tutor for his oafish son, August, now aged thirty-nine, and later as a harmless drudge, putting his papers in order and taking down Goethe's words and works at dictation speed; and there was the oafish son himself. Had he not been a bit drunk, or very drunk, as he accompanied the others into his father's presence, it would have been a rare occasion – drink would finish off August von Goethe in not more than a year after the fateful interview. There was also, of the party, the actor who hoped to play Mephistopheles, Karl August La Roche; and there was Eckermann – Johann Peter Eckermann, thirty-six-year-old secretary to the poet, who with his long, sleek hair covering his ears like those of a spaniel, was the devoted, the slavish follower, destined to write down Goethe's celebrated conversations.

This particular conversation, however, between Goethe and the delegation, in late November 1828, did not find its way into Eckermann's book. Eckermann the intelligent, sharp-nosed, faithful spaniel wants his great German genius to appear to us in the best possible light, and, although he records those moments when he allows the reader to see that Goethe was moody, short-tempered, occasionally unwilling to perform his conversational feats for the secretary-recording-machine Johann Peter, Goethe always retains his dignity, and he is, on the whole, in Eckermann's pages, a benign figure.

It was the indiscreet thespian La Roche who recollected the pompous, petulant way in which they were received that day. Chancellor von Müller had also most entertainingly recorded his many conversations with Goethe – they are less formal than Eckermann's memories: Müller was the Minister of Justice at Weimar, a Cabinet member with Goethe and his social equal – they spoke freely together – often denigrating colleagues and friends – Oh I can be beastly too, said Goethe on one occasion. It was Müller who nervously began.

Müller was aware of Goethe's 'protean disposition to transform himself into every shape, to play with everything, to adopt diametrically opposite viewpoints and oppose them'.[8] He also knew, as Eckermann did – though Eckermann would never have shared the information with the public – that Goethe was a (controlled) alcoholic, whose moods could never be relied upon by visitors. Müller knew, moreover, that the staging of *Faust* was a delicate subject, not least because – unlike the Perfect Man who would be the subject of Eckermann's creative conversations – Goethe was only human, and minded terribly that pot-boiling plays by Kotzebue were performed over and over again to rapturous acclaim, whereas his own dramas were unpopular with audiences. Müller must have sensed that what they were to disclose would not be altogether agreeable to Goethe. Perhaps he even realized, in advance, that what Goethe would find disagreeable was that he himself had not been involved from the outset with this project. The faithful spaniel Johann Peter had been engaged in large part because he was sycophantic and studiously obedient. Together, Eckermann, as an assistant, and the master were putting together, in Goethe's old age, an image which was scrupulously edited. Together they had finished his autobiography, *Poetry and Truth* – which could perhaps have been entitled *At Best, a Version of the Truth*. The famous 'love affairs', which had inspired his most celebrated novel and so many poems, were all platonic crushes on women, and could be crafted into stories, whereas his undoubted bisexuality could be airbrushed out of the story. Goethe's celebrated *Italian Journey* had also, forty years after it had taken place, been carefully edited, with his solemn reflections on the antiquities rather prosaically masking the erotic and emotional awakening which happened in the city – the only scene of *Faust* written in Rome (Sigmund Freud's favourite bit of the play) was that of the Witch's Kitchen where Faust is given the love potion to make him irresistible to women. (Interesting that he needs a potion to make heterosexuality work for him.) The surviving letters and correspondences between Goethe, his family, his friends, and between him and so many of the great and famous men and women of the age, were likewise carefully edited and arranged so that posterity was given little chance to form an independent version of the story.

It was the Goethe who was fashioned by old Goethe, as obediently crafted by Eckermann, Goethe as a Grand Old Man, that later generations were to be allowed to meet. And yet now, here he stood, the for once disobedient spaniel, with the hulking oaf son and the others, while Chancellor von Müller stumbled out the words.

'It's been decided,' Müller began, after a nervous clearing of the throat, 'in honour of the Privy Councillor, Herr von Goethe's eightieth birthday, August 1829 ... it has been *decided* to stage a production of *Faust* on stage at Weimar.'

It was, La Roche remembered, as if Goethe had been stung by a gadfly, and in a fury, he began to pace up and down the room.

'Oh, so it's been decided, has it? Does anyone think that if I had wanted, I might have been able to put on a production of *Faust* myself? *Decided*, eh? It has been decided, without so much as asking *me*?'

The fit of rage passed, like smoke evaporating into the air. When the visitors expressed their embarrassment at having caused the explosion, Goethe's daughter-in-law, Ottilie, tried to put them at their ease. If the production takes place, she assured them, she would make sure he attended it. She knew that he had 'form'. When they'd revived his *Iphigenia*, in March 1827, he had admitted to Eckermann, 'I must admit that I have never succeeded in witnessing a perfect representation of my *Iphigenia*. That was the reason I did not go yesterday.'[9]

In the event, when *Faust* was first staged at Weimar, Goethe behaved very characteristically in the matter. He allowed the director of the Weimar Court Theatre, Herr von Spiegel, and the director of the play, Klingemann, and the principal actors, to consult him frequently. The surviving prompt book for the 1829 Weimar production contains seventeen marginal notes, written in pencil by the poet himself. Riemer frequently came to consult him.

They divided the play into eight sections, greatly reducing the text to make the whole performance including interval last no more than three hours. (It would begin at six and end at nine.)

As it happens, the actual premiere of *Faust* was performed, not on Goethe's birthday at Weimar, but on the stage at Braunschweig (Brunswick) on 19 January 1829 for the Grand Duke Carl. It was in effect a dummy run for the Weimar production later in the year.

Goethe's diary on the occasion of his eightieth birthday is not without a sort of ridiculous pathos. He had, after all, devoted his adult life to being a public servant in Weimar. He was its most highly esteemed citizen. And *Faust* was his great, his masterwork. But on the big night we find him at home, and alone. Having made his stand the previous November, and expressed his objections to others staging *his* play, he stuck to his guns and refused to see what they made of it. So he did not see what was evidently a successful production, nor hear the music – some of it by Radziwill, and some written for this production specially by Eberwein. If we turn to read what Eckermann has to say about his hero's eightieth birthday, we discover that the famous *Conversations* have a yawning gap between April and September 1829.

But they contain many considerations of *Faust*.

Goethe's lifetime – 1749–1832 – witnessed the birth pang of the Modern – the arrival of democracy as a political possibility in the United States; attempts to replicate this republican experiment in Europe; coming to terms with the growth and eventual dominance of the rising commercial class. Merchants replaced marquises as the most powerful men in England, Scotland, France and Germany. Men and women began to doubt the old religious certainties. And against this background of vital change, literature reflected the fact that this was an age when the Individual, the Private Personality, emerged as a subject of consideration. Novels came into being – stories not, like previous romances or myths, about knights or dragons or kings and queens, but about women, with sexual feelings, falling in love. Many of the novels pretended to be in the form of letters, and letters themselves, in the improved postal services of Britain and Europe – with great programmes of roadbuilding facilitating the speed with which mail could be delivered and exchanged – could be seen as works of art. They were a long way away from inventing microphones, tape recorders or television cameras, but in such works as Boswell's *Life of Johnson* you could buy a book and have the illusion of listening to a great conversation.

Goethe, one of the most receptive as well as one of the most influential imaginations of his time, tapped into all these phenomena and many more. It was inevitable, as he and Eckermann compiled the picture of himself as the Completed Man, the *vollendete Mensch* (it could also mean, or almost mean, the 'perfect man'), that he should appear in so many autobiographical modes. His early life was edited as *Poetry and Truth* (*Dichtung und Wahrheit*). His emotional Courtly Love for Charlotte von Stein, during his first ten years in Weimar, became a deliberately teasing point of interest – he had made her into an object to be read about in the same way that Richardson's Pamela or Rousseau's Emile might be a fictional heroine. She shrank from being used in this way and destroyed her side of the correspondence when she had managed to get it back from him, but he retained the letters which he treasured the most – his own – and they are part of the Collected Works, sitting on the shelves beside his poems, his scientific work, his novels.

Wilhelm Meister, the prototype of what came to be known in literature as the Novel of Education or the *Bildungsroman*, was a three-part book which, like *Faust*, he spent a lifetime perfecting. It was not an autobiography but it was autobiographical, for he poured himself into it, his protean nature animating every page. It is an immensely attractive book, improving on each rereading. In this book, paradoxically, which is furthest away in some respects from the outward realities of Goethe's life, we nonetheless often feel ourselves closest to the core which he was attempting to … not conceal, exactly, but to dress up, to reinvent.

By listing his letters to Charlotte von Stein, *Wilhelm Meister*, *Italian Journey*, *Poetry and Truth*, we have described a great proportion of Goethe's works. The prodigious size of his poetic output is, or purports to be, very largely lyric compositions about his own yearning for impossible loves, his passionate curiosity about the natural world, his inner life as a philosopher and a scientist.

All this – and *Faust*. The pages which follow are not a narrow account of how Goethe wrote *Faust*, in the sense of being a close reading of the text, or a comparison of where this or that Goethe scholar might differ about points of interpretation. That is not, I believe, where the majority of non-German-speaking readers are, in relation to *Faust*. What follows is the story of Goethe's life, but it is written very much from the perspective of Goethe the author of *Faust*. It is written with the conviction that *Faust* is the first great modern work of literature which, as well as being a supreme poetic masterpiece, reveals us to ourselves, challenges and disturbs and consoles us, seeing, sometimes as if by magic, into the preoccupations of a generation which worries about the way in which the world is governed – and it means the world, not just Europe; how we respond to Nature; what we are doing to the planet; how the economy of the nineteenth century, the capitalist development of investment economics, paper money, fiscal borrowing, growing side by side with industry and the exploitation of the earth for the purposes of human enrichment – these are all here in this dramatic poem. So too is the place played in our lives by love, sex, the exploitation of the weak by the powerful in the sexual realm. The pursuit of the Imagination in Life, the holding sacred of the Imagination and its power to redeem and explain our predicament, these, and so much more are the creation of that strange old man, in a strop, sitting alone in his museum of a house while the rest of Weimar flocked to the theatre to see the first staging of this play.

However much you insist on Goethe's rewriting of the myth, Faust remains the man who sold his soul to the devil. In Goethe's version, he does not quite do this, and by the end of *Part Two* Faust is redeemed, or 'redeemed', in so far as a non-Christian man in a non-Christian play can be said to be redeemed. It is not even clear whether Faust believes in life after death, even though, by the time he finished the work, Goethe said that he did so.

We go on speaking of Faustian pacts and Faustian apocalypses and Faustian climaxes as if Goethe's play leads to the same sort of conclusion as the older versions of the story – the version known to audiences of Marlowe's *Doctor Faustus*, for example. One reason for this, of course, is that many people have never read Goethe – or at any rate, have not been able to make much of *Faust Part Two* which – let us admit at the outset – while being a masterpiece, is a very difficult book to understand.

But the clichéd use of 'Faustian' to mean dabbling with the devil – and dabbling with catastrophic consequences – is not entirely inappropriate when we think either of Goethe's literary output, or of his life, or of his influence. The Germany in which he grew up was the place where much of the intellectual drama of the Enlightenment would be played out. Immanuel Kant, having explored the limits of human Reason, inspired a generation of philosophers which would fire off in fascinating directions: the intense personalism of German Idealism, the 'Ich' of Fichte and of Hegel's *Phenomenology of Spirit*, also giving birth to quite different notions of how the modern political state could be reinterpreted as a sort of rewrite of the Old Testament, only an Old Testament without God. The inevitability, the ineluctability of world events, would, for Karl Marx, be the story of the Materialist Dialogue. Nietzsche, who conceived the poetic idea that human pity had killed the human beings' God, lived in an emotional territory which grew out of *Faust*, and which was 'beyond good and evil'. So did Sigmund Freud, who was steeped in Goethe.

Faust, in the second part of the drama, cynically manipulates the politicians. He is also, in the most extraordinarily prophetic way, an embodiment of that contradictory human tendency which is both in love with 'Nature' and wants to exploit and rape the earth; which revives the bogus economy of the Empire with paper currency, but also by mining; which dreams of driving back the sea itself to reclaim land for the purposes of industry and agriculture, while at the same time extolling Nature and its beauties in a mysticism which parallels that of William Wordsworth.

When, at the end of Goethe's century, we read of the horror story unfolding – industrial and technological ingenuity perfecting the arms race, a godless capitalist humanity exploiting the industrialized poor and getting its inevitable comeuppance, in the wars and revolutions – it does not seem entirely fanciful to describe the coming catastrophes as 'Faustian'. This is not to say that Goethe was, by the smallest stretch of the imagination, a proto-Nazi, or a proto-Communist, even though, throughout the first half of the twentieth century, German governments would try to enlist him as a supporter of their ideologies. But when the stupendous (1998) history of Berlin by Alexandra Richie was subtitled *Faust's Metropolis*, any intelligent reader would see why the author selected that title – even though Goethe himself scarcely ever visited Berlin. The account of Goethe's reputation during the Third Reich and, in particular, the relationship between the German Goethe Society and the Hitler regime was entitled *Der Faustische Pakt* (2019). The author, W. Daniel Wilson, was not accusing Goethe of being a Nazi, but the story of Germany from 1919 to 1945 inevitably tugs us back to the memory of *Faust*. This is, not least, because Goethe himself depicts the story of an energetic human aspiration which quickly gets out of control. That is why, later in this book, I explore the kinship between Goethe's *Faust* and his much simpler story of 'The Sorcerer's Apprentice', which, in the century of the Common Man which produced Hitler, was also superbly brought to life on the silver screen by Walt Disney. Mickey Mouse and Hitler, both rapturously popular at the same historical period, were in a sense comparable figures.

Faust is not damned in Goethe's version – the angel in the final scene says there is always redemption for one who 'strives'. He is saved, then, not through Grace, as Christian theology understands it, but because God gives him the benefit of the doubt. Also, surely, there is a hope, breathing through all the fire, despair and chaos, that the eternal values explored, glimpsed, celebrated by the ancient Greeks will overpower the barbaric consequences of modern greed, fear and selfishness. (Wilson ended his book about the Faustian Pact between National Socialism and the most important literary society in Germany with recognition that the post-war life of the Society and of its officers was like the fate of Faust himself.) While he was stricken with conscience for his misdeeds, he was pardoned by his author.[10] Nevertheless, an awful lot of destruction happens along the way, and most of it – like the poisoning of Gretchen's mother in *Part One* – was unintentional (on Faust's part at least, if not of the devil's). Even by the end, the old man Faust's hunger to possess the last bit of coast for his land reclamation scheme leads to a terrible act of triple murder by Mephistopheles/Faust's henchmen. Faust did not intend it, but he did not do anything which was going to prevent it – and the same could be said of those Germans who found themselves with Adolf Hitler as their Führer, the Sorcerer's Apprentice who could begin, but not staunch, the floods of calamity which he unleashed.

No wonder – we shall enter into this at the appropriate time – that Klaus Mann, in his devastating novel about his lover, Gustaf Gründgens, entitled the book *Mephisto*. The journey from lefty-idealist Hamburg actor to Goering's toady is unforgettably tragi-comic. So is Gründgens' rendition of Mephistopheles in Goethe's drama – and a few years before his drug-related end, possible suicide, he made the performance on celluloid, so we can watch it again and again – camp, cruel, florid and, even in 1963, when the film was made, Nazi to the core. What could be called the Concentration of Camp.

Klaus Mann's novel – what other title could it have had than *Mephisto*? – inspired his father Thomas to write his *Doktor*

Faustus – a book which is in part about Wagner, in part about Nietzsche, but also – as these fateful intellectual ancestors imply – about the German twentieth-century catastrophe. No one who reads, in *Part Two* of Faust, authorizing the torching of the old people's cottage and chapel can fail to see it as a dreadful foreshadowing of Kristallnacht. And it would be an insensitive tourist indeed who delighted in the olde-tyme beauties of Weimar not to remember who coined the phrase 'the Weimar Republic';[11] nor to forget that, not so far out of town, in the very place where Eckermann and Goethe enjoyed their picnics, was the beechwood which gave its name to one of the most gruesome of the labour camps. Beechwood or Buchenwald. This place, now with everlastingly horrible associations, is said to have fed Goethe with the inspiration for so many of his most perfect lyrics, such as the love poem to Charlotte von Stein, 'To the Moon' (*An den Mond*).

Faust touches us because it is about us. It is not just a supremely great poem, studded with insights into the human condition, into science, into love, religion, politics, even into economics. It is both a history and a prophecy of how Western humanity has viewed itself since the early modern period to our own. Goethe, a man of the Enlightenment, mythologized Faust, a man of the Renaissance. He used Faust's inner journeyings as a way of exploring his own contemporaries' attitudes – to science, to philosophy, to the structure of society, to revolution, to war, to Nature. The great figures of Goethe's time – Napoleon, Byron, Kant, Hegel – might not be named in *Faust*, but they are all there. What makes Goethe different from any of them is that he saw the way that their actions and attitudes were going to shape later worlds – the world of newspapers and mass media, the world of international power politics, the world which had taken leave of God but did not know how to live – to understand its most fundamental ethical concerns – without him. Faust, moreover, a man-in-Nature – to this extent a figure as materialist as any produced in the eighteenth century – is not happy to be so. The thought of the sheer pointlessness of his attempts to master science – in the sense of understand, in the sense of control the world of Nature – drives him close to suicide.

Yet he remains as acutely conscious as any contemporary poet – as conscious as Shelley and Wordsworth in English – of Nature, of the human absorption in Nature as a spiritual power. In the largely secularized world of the twenty-first century, Faust the devout servant of Nature, and its wrecker; Faust the man who tries to make industrial use of the very movement of the ocean; Faust the money man who exploits the vulnerability of the poor people who are powerless to resist him – foresees the destruction and enslavement of the planet by globalization; just as Faust and Mephistopheles have introduced to 'the Emperor', i.e. the governing powers, the concept of enriching themselves by mining minerals and by creating the illusions of 'magic money' – paper currency with an often notional relation to what is perhaps itself an illusion, actual wealth.

That is Goethe's achievement – to see the mythological potential of the old Faust story, to translate it into a picture of what had happened in his lifetime, and to convey imaginatively a prophecy of our own preoccupations and concerns.

The historical Faust (if there was one – see below) was a representative of that new breed of figures at the time of the Reformation and the Renaissance, struggling to make sense of Nature by the means of science. This was the period when modern science began its birth pangs. Copernicus, confirmed by Galileo, told us that we are not in a geocentric, but a heliocentric universe. The pattern of the skies which had been accepted by humankind throughout the Middle Ages – the Heavens through which Dante had travelled to visit Heaven Itself – was a construct based on a fundamental mistake. The earth – and perhaps, by extension, humankind itself – was not the centre of the universe.

But Goethe and his contemporaries were living in a world which had moved on from those early modern concerns. Modern science – real science – chemistry, physics, botany, astronomy – was beginning. Philosophers, moreover, were asking the questions which both made a modern scientific outlook possible and which challenged its possibilities. How can we claim that we know anything? What is the role of Reason in our drawing a picture of the universe?

Epistemology – the philosophy of how we know things – began, for modern people, with René Descartes (1596–1650) – locating the self as the arbiter of what can be known. I think, therefore I am. In the century which followed Descartes, Europe entered the Enlightenment. It is a catch-all term but a useful one. For the Enlightenment, the universe was the astronomical machine revealed to the learned by the works of Isaac Newton (1642/3–1727), who displayed how the machine worked (by Newton's laws of motion) and how we may perceive it – by the power of Reason. Enlightenment philosophers wanted to know how far Reason could go, both in giving us an accurate picture of the universe, and of experience; and how Reason could help us come to terms with some of the older certainties – about ethics and religion, for example. Reason could lead us to believe in the laws of gravity, but could it make us certain of the existence of the biblical God? It could perhaps persuade us that Newton's mechanical universe, the place 'where in the end, we find our happiness, or not at all'[12] was a process started by some 'blind watchmaker'. (This was Deism – the mindset of many figures of the Enlightenment – a belief that God had started his machine, and then left it to its own laws and devices.) This was a very different thing from the Bible's belief that God could and did intervene in his creation, even to the point where he chose, for the salvation of souls, actually to become incarnate as a human being. It was a very different thing from the belief of Thomas Aquinas (1225?–74), the great medieval philosopher who taught that God was Being Itself, *esse seipsum*. A point of view much closer to the twentieth-century existentialist thinker Martin Heidegger (1889–1976) in *Sein und Zeit* (1927) and the Indian philosophers of the Bhagavad Gita.

The Enlightenment attempted, by its most articulate trailblazers – Descartes, Locke, (1632–1704), Hume (1711–76) – to provide a rational foundation for the emergence of natural science. Its philosophers, however, soon found that they were being led into problems which seemed insoluble. Reason is a faculty of criticism, the power to examine evidence. Reason is also the power to provide an explanation for things. The problem, especially for Hume, the ultimate sceptic about our capacity to know anything, was that the critical faculty undermined our capacity to make sense of the world, the universe, in terms of scientific naturalism. If all we have to give us a reliable guide to truth are our sense-impressions, if we are ourselves the products of Nature, we must be led ineluctably to a reductionist materialism. Everything, including human rationality, is thus to be seen as the product of material forces.

Some Enlightenment thinkers, most notably the Baron d'Holbach (1723–89), boldly threw out any attempt to maintain the older ways of thinking. For d'Holbach, we live in a godless, materialist, mechanized universe, and religion could – in his own salons at least – be smilingly discarded. It was the ease with which the materialist d'Holbach and his followers could reach this conclusion which horrified not only the Christian Churches, Protestant and Catholic, but the great majority of thinking people in the eighteenth century, which was not ready to discard its religious tradition and who feared, intensely, what might replace it.

The hidden patron saint of the materialist outlook was Baruch Spinoza (1632–77). His views got him expelled from the synagogue in Amsterdam, where he was born and lived; and his work was placed on the Index of Forbidden Books of the Catholic Church. A century or so after his death, he was enlisted by Enlightenment exponents of materialism. God, that is Nature – *Deus sive Natura* – is the only phrase of his work known to many, but it is enough to undermine Christianity and Judaism as traditionally believed. Is what men and women had been accustomed to call 'God' simply another way of describing what *is* – a way of talking about the nature of things?

Goethe was in the thick of this debate, and his *Faust* is an attempt to come to grips with it. His own understanding of Spinoza was rather different from that of his contemporaries – his was too fizzing, too overwhelming an imaginative response to experience to buy into the glib confinements of materialism.

Faust, as Goethe told Eckermann in old age, cannot be summarized or grasped: it is *incommensurable*, to use his word. It must not be supposed that this is because it was conceived in a muddle, nor that the mists in which it enshrouds its readers are the creation of a random accident. Quite the reverse. Goethe was a scientist; for much of his life he conceived the scientific writing as being the most important part of his oeuvre. He was also a man of the Enlightenment. But *Faust* is also a careful challenge to some of the Enlightenment's presuppositions. One of its central messages is that we cannot presume to certainty about very much. That is why Goethe both embraced and sat light to Kant, and to all the philosophers who contributed to the phenomenon sometimes known as German Idealism, all those thinkers who were cast into an agony by the scepticism of Hume, or by the supposed scepticism of Spinoza.

For Goethe, it was axiomatic that 'we all walk in mysteries. We do not know what is stirring in the atmosphere around us.'[13] It is hard for us to grasp, perhaps, that this acceptance of mystery stemmed from the fact that Goethe, like his great friend Schiller (1759–1805), represented a unified vision of reality, which is totally at odds with the current views of the modern academy, which emphasizes fissure and the non-availability of meaning. For Goethe, meaning *is* available, in myth, in poetry, and in the acceptance of mystery.

We all walk in mysteries. *Wir wandeln Alle in Geheimnissen.* *Heim* means home. The *heimlisch* is the familiar. Yet *heimlich* means secret, and *unheimlich* is uncanny. We carry all these meanings around in our walk through the mysteries.[14] *Heilig*, which means holy, also means set apart. The sacred and the secret share the same semantic roots. Faust says that in awe, humanity is at its best. The shudder is the man's best part.[15] Karl Jung (1865–1961), who owed so much to Goethe, said that we depend on having secrets, we need them. This is because there are some things which we cannot possibly know, and we must live with the knowledge of their hiddenness from us. Above all, since we only see death as something happening to others, we cannot truly be said to understand death. We know it will happen to us, but we cannot, by definition, experience it. *We need secrets.* We need to walk in a life which cannot be explained, which does not have cut-and-dried empirical answers to the experiences and manifestations which puzzle us. 'A word speaks when it is bearing the weight of what is not spoken. This is when the word/language secretes something, as a perfume secretes nectar,' says the French philosopher Bertrand Vergely (b. 1954).[16] As Goethe himself once said of poetry, 'only insufficient knowledge is productive'.[17] He would surely have echoed words which Rilke (1875–1926) wrote to his Polish translator, Witold Hulewicz (1895–1941): 'We are the bees of the invisible. We wildly collect the honey of the visible to store it in the great golden hive of the invisible.'[18]

Finally, a word to answer an almost impossible question: why does Goethe matter? Or, to put it another way, what are the millions of non-German-language readers missing by not knowing Goethe? (For he is, surely, among all the truly great writers of this world, the least read in the English-speaking world.) My answer is, read on! I am writing this book in order to provide that answer. But if I had to boil things down to a few short paragraphs, I'd say this.

Neuroscience, historians of ideas, pop-philosophers and psychologists have all been interested, for the last few decades, in the hemispherical nature of the human brain.[19]

Some of the scientists want us to approach this subject very gingerly, some would even go so far as to deny there is any point in the laity barging into this area. Others, the pop-philosophers and pop-purveyors of the history of ideas, make wildly broad and largely false generalizations – that the left hemisphere is the side which manages, orders and classifies, and the right is that which feels, emotes. Some have seen the left hemisphere as that which leads to the human *Logos* – Reason, Rationality; the right hemisphere suggesting *Mythos* – the human capacity to make sense of life through myths and rituals.

It is furthermore often said that during the eighteenth century, the phenomenon which, for shorthand, is called the Enlightenment was guided by the Logos, by the left hemisphere. During this period, philosophy boxed itself into a rationalistic corner. Isaiah Berlin (1909–97), in his book *The Roots of Romanticism*, referred to 'the three propositions ... upon which the whole Western tradition rested'. These were 'that all genuine questions can be answered, that if a question cannot be answered it is not a question' and that 'all these answers are knowable, that they can be discovered by means which can be learnt and taught to other persons'.[20]

Even when Western humanity tried to react against the conscriptions of these beliefs, it was saddled with them, not merely when attempting to answer philosophical problems, but also in practical, technological, political ways. The absolutely anthropocentric world view of the Enlightenment had taken over from the Hebrew Bible the idea that this planet was created primarily or solely for the use of humankind, rather than embracing the views which would be found in many Asiatic thought systems and philosophies, that human beings are part of the Natural order, part of the ecosystem. Many of the catastrophes which the Western human race brought upon itself, and on the planet, during the phase of the Industrial Revolution came about directly as a result of embracing the three propositions which Berlin identified as characteristic of Descartes, Locke, Hume. Not merely the rape of the planet, the plundering of its natural resources without regard for the ecosystem – foreseen and condemned by that great prophet John Ruskin (1819–1900) in 'The Storm Cloud of the Nineteenth Century' – a century before the Green Movement, Ruskin noticed that the very clouds in the sky were changing shape as a result of the burning of fossil fuels – but also the political systems of oppression which the human race devised in the next two centuries – Communism, mechanized mass warfare, Fascism – came about as the unforeseen and yet direct consequence of being a left-hemisphere planet, ignoring the intuitive, the capacity for metaphor, the ability to find 'meaning' in Mythos and ritual, which lasted longer in such places as India and China and Japan, until they too followed Western patterns of thinking and behaviour.

Tolstoy (1828–1910) defined Ruskin as a man who thought with his heart. Tolstoy too was such a man. Goethe – here is my initial answer to the questions 'why does he matter and what are we missing if we do not read him?' – is that Goethe thought with the heart. The left-hemisphere/right-hemisphere distinctions which we have mentioned, and which fell into such an imbalance at the time of Goethe's lifetime, were in his finest imaginative achievements perfectly balanced, as we feel them to have been in the bisexual, ambivalent imagination of Shakespeare. Left hemisphere/right hemisphere? Yin or Yang? It is not a distinction which we find in Goethe's mighty brain, his scientifically analytical intelligence, in his abundant capacity for intelligent emotional responses to experience.[21]

Some thinkers – most notably Nietzsche (1844–1900) in his first great book, *The Birth of Tragedy* – would think that the rot set in long before the Enlightenment. Nietzsche saw in the great tragedians of the fifth-century BCE in Athens – the draining away of their capacity to hold Logos and Mythos in tandem. Their Dionysian response to the human condition was lost in the Apollonian attempts to control instinct by (deliberate) misunderstanding. Socrates (469–399 BCE), by making Reason the paramount factor in a human armoury, and by dismissing Homer (eighth-century BCE) and the poets, thereby destroyed the instinctive, the daimonic, the many responses to human life which are necessary, life-enhancing but, as he would have thought, irrational.

The distinction took its name from the god Apollo, of Light, Reason, Logic, and the cult of Dionysus/Bacchus. Both gods were invoked by the Greek poets, and worshipped by the population of Greek-speaking Mediterranean lands; and it is to the poets that we look to restore, first, the fractured, soiled, cliché-battered language, which has been appropriated by political and commercial slogan-makers; by fake ideologues, by fanaticisms and by tawdry purveyors of popular culture. Then, we look to the poets to return us to a world and a world view where Mythos and Logos are held in balance. There is no writer, in my reading experience, certainly no Western writer, who does this more than Goethe. In *Faust*, he made a myth of modern humanity, which was percipient, prophetic. He did so partly by returning to the source of so much Western truth, the Greek mythologies. He was endowed with the most prodigious linguistic and imaginative gift. One of his twentieth-century English translators has written, 'Not by calculation, but by a profound creative instinct, he was already, in his youth, performing his historic linguistic role: that of being (with Luther and perhaps Nietzsche) one of the two or three greatest originators and perfectors of Modern High German as a literary medium.'[22] In common with Chaucer and Shakespeare in English he invented or introduced dozens, hundreds of neologisms into his language. But these were not simply verbal tricks. He was expanding and deepening the way we could all think, and respond to the world. Whether he was writing about God (or the gods), whether he was writing about the human experience of sexual love, or of yearning, *Sehnsucht*, which defines so much of intellectual and spiritual, as well as of sexual life; whether he was expanding the borders of our scientific knowledge, Goethe was writing things which

22

are as burningly alive today as when he wrote them. I reach the point later in this book of believing that there are senses in which ours, the post-postmodern generation, is the first which is in a position, fully, to receive what he had to say. He was the pioneer scientist of evolution, and his reflections on the 'metamorphosis' of plants and animals retained a sense which got lost, in some of the cruder reductionism of so-called modern Darwinism, of our becoming better scientists the more we retain our capacity for wonder, and a sense of Nature's holiness.

'Rejoice,' he exhorts the reader. 'The highest product of Nature, in your capacity to rethink her supreme thought.'[23] This, from the *Metamorphosis* [or Evolution] *of Animals*. We share our planet with the other animals, with plants, with the atmosphere and weather conditions, all of which fascinated him and about all of which he had things to say. We alone among our brothers and sisters the beetles, baboons and buzzards have the capacity to be aware of our own awareness; and aware of our place in the whole.

This whole, this vast Everything, is not, as Newton and the proto-mathematicians and scientists of the Enlightenment supposed, best seen as a mighty machine. It is better seen as a living organism. Goethe, who studied the Indian mystics and as much of the Chinese philosophy as was available to Europeans at the time, would have echoed Laozi, the fourth-century BCE founder of Daoism. 'The Dao begets one; the Dao begets two; the Dao begets three, three begets the myriad creatures.' The Dao is not, like the Deist God of 1600s and 1700s Europe, a crazy inventor in a laboratory who 'creates' a universe and then sits back to watch it working, like an electric toy train set. As Goethe would do, Laozi used the metaphor of motherhood. 'The world has a source: the world's mother. Once you have the mother, you know the children. Once you know the children, return to the mother.'[24]

It is the discovery of the principle of the Eternal Feminine which would become Faust's quest – first, in his clumsy and catastrophic late venture into heterosexual love, later in his exploitative 'use' of Nature, for mineral wealth, for political gain. 'The Lord' speaks rather airily to Mephistopheles, at the beginning of the poem, of humanity's basic decency, its capacity not to go too far, to pull itself back from wasted chances and abused relationships both with one another and with the planet. 'A good man, in his dark stressful life, knows deep down what's right.'[25]

One of Goethe's best translators and most fervent champions in the nineteenth century was Thomas Carlyle (1795–1881), whose injunction to the reader was 'Close thy Byron! Open thy Goethe!' There was deliberate irony in the proclamation, as in so much of what that wry Scot wrote, since, as he knew better than anyone, Goethe himself had idolized Byron. In the twenty-first century, the phrase needs adaptation – close thy Wikipedia, close thy Google, close thy Bible Fundamentalism and thy Richard Dawkins's reductionism, close thy Culture Warriors on either side, close thy popular press and thy unpopular press, close thy BBC and thy *New York Times*, close thy mad distortions (both by Islamophobes and by the radicalized fanatics) of the beautiful sayings of Islam, and open thy Goethe who so revered the Prophet and his writings! Open thy Goethe, who wrote so feelingly about so wide a range of subjects from botany to casual sex, from cloud formations to Napoleon, from Greek mythology to Persian poetry to zoology to the comedies of Molière. Open not merely thy poems and novels and plays by Goethe but attune thine ear to his letters, and to what must be the most scintillating conversations ever heard since the death of Socrates. Absorb, above all, some of his most covetable negative qualities – his refusal to be impressed, especially by political systems, his refusal to be fashionable, and, perhaps his most impressive quality of all, his refusal to take anything (for very long, that is) completely seriously.

In a letter he wrote, as a very old man, some five days before he died, to Wilhelm von Humboldt, the inventor of the modern university system and the founder of Berlin University, Goethe spoke of *Faust* which, after sixty years in the making, he had finally accomplished. 'Beyond question, it would give me infinite joy if, while I live, I were able to dedicate these very serious jokes to my valued friends everywhere.' Non-Germans too easily seize on the famous phrase *diese sehr ernsten Scherze* ('these very serious jokes'), to groan that, for the German intellectual, humour itself is a subject to be taken earnestly. On the contrary, Goethe will resist any attempt to force him into a stereotypical straitjacket. His conversations continually caught interlocutors off guard because they never knew which way he would jump, nor, indeed, whether opinions he had expressed earlier would be upended, mocked, undermined. One of the deepest analysts of Goethe has maintained that he lacked a tragic sense.[26] Another, no less profound has written the complete opposite: 'For *Faust* is, as its full title insists, basically a tragedy. Heroic tragedy in the great tradition of Aeschylus, Sophocles, Euripides, Shakespeare, and Calderon, the drama of man destroyed by the larger force than himself which is life, yet enjoying triumph in inevitable defeat.'[27] And … '*Faust* is in the last analysis the expression of a profoundly tragic view of life.'[28]

How is it that two deeply intelligent and observant readers could come to such different conclusions? Maybe we have gone beyond tragedy, as well as beyond a joke. The world which produced *Oedipus Tyrannus* or *King Lear* had not known Stalin, the Third Reich, the nuclear bombardment of Japan; not known the visible, palpable prospect of the human race frying the entire planet because of its addiction to fossil fuels. 'This present age is really so absurd and confused, that I know I shall only be very poorly repaid for my many years of sincere effort in erecting this strange building.'[29]

One absurd and confused reader – me – knows when he is being put in his place by a great Master. But he is going to attempt the impossible – to read *Faust* and persuade you to do so too.

2

TURNING LIFE INTO A PICTURE

*'I suppose that is the difference between an author and an
ordinary man,' said Emily. 'Because, of course, there must be
some difference. An author does things from a new self or an old
self, and an ordinary man just from his ordinary self, as if he were
doing an ordinary thing, which, of course, he is'*
Ivy Compton-Burnett, Pastors and Masters

The visitor to Frankfurt airport is confronted by a larger-than-life
three-dimensional version of a celebrated German painting – the
portrait of Goethe in the Roman Campagna by Johann Wilhelm
Heinrich Tischbein (1751–1829).

It is a strange picture by any standards, not least because the
sitter appears to be possessed of two left legs. Multiplied in size and
translated into a (fibreglass?) sculpture which looms over the Goethe
Bar, it is overwhelming, like its great original, Goethe himself.

For those for whom Frankfurt is home, there is something
appropriate about the fact that the figure is larger than life. The
greatness is something which those take for granted who have heard
his lyrics, in their own language, studied *Faust* at school, and heard,
in concerts or around the piano at home, the settings by Beethoven,
Schubert or Schumann of the better-known Goethe lyrics, such as
'Der Erlkönig', 'Der Fischer' and 'Der König in Thule'. These songs
echo in every German-speaker's head, and most of them have read
The Sorrows of Young Werther and *Faust Part One*.

For the non-German-speaker, things are a little different, not least because Goethe's poetry is more sublime than it is easy to describe, and next to impossible to translate into English. He loses in translation more than any poet I have ever tried to read. And it is on his poetry that his reputation for greatness rests, his poetry into which he imported all his other polymathic concerns.

The foreigner, therefore, walking through the airport in the city of Goethe's birth, who sees this fibreglass monstrosity with its slightly sinister fixity of expression, its lurid colouring and its two left feet, does not quite know what to make of it. The bafflement is not unlike the feelings of the non-German-speaker in a library who surveys the multitudinous spines of Goethe's Collected Works: poems, plays, novels, science, autobiographical works, letters (innumerable), conversations (apparently interminable). Any reader who begins the adventure of opening these works might come to feel that the editors could apply the term 'Autobiographical Writings' – found on the spine of just some of these volumes – to nearly all, even the science. And yet, it would be a naïf reader of Goethe who, for example, saw his play about a court poet who burned with love for his Duchess and resented the restraints of court life (*Torquato Tasso*) as a straight account of his own experience after ten years in Weimar, as a Privy Councillor, nursing what appear to have been platonic passions for one of the ladies of the court. As well as being a professional self-revealer, Goethe was also a self-concealer on the grand scale, an editor of his own experience and of the versions of experience which have been handed down to us.

He knew whereof he spoke when he gave to Mephistopheles the lines 'The best thing you can know is what you don't say'.[1]

The title of Goethe's autobiography, *Poetry and Truth*, turns out to be tautology. Poetry in the Age of Goethe, perhaps always, is more than the quest to find the best language in which to encapsulate experience. It is the attempt, through the correct use of words, to arrive at truth itself, scientific truth which, in Goethe, is discovered inwardly. He does not distinguish between different kinds of truth – scientific, emotional, spiritual. Truth is truth. His contemporary Immanuel Kant (1724–1804) devoted his career to seeing whether language/philosophy can get beyond the tool of language to penetrate the thing-in-itself. Goethe revered Kant, but in important respects

27

disagreed with him. Kant's concept of 'representation', the thought that we can only know representations of reality, rather than the thing-in-itself was not one which Goethe found useful, and by the end of his life it would seem that he did not find it necessary. Poetry and science, in Goethe's concept of both, do provide us with Knowledge, as Kant's Reason felt itself powerless to do.

Wallace Stevens (1879–1955), alluding to Kant ('Not Ideas about the Thing but the Thing Itself'), asked whether writing can ever step outside the role of describing the world, and actually glimpse the *thing*: share with the reader reality itself.

> That scrawny cry – it was
> A chorister whose c preceded the choir,
> It was part of the colossal sun.
> Surrounded by its choral rings,
> Still far away. It was like
> A new knowledge of reality.

Goethe delivered a new knowledge of reality over and over again, especially in his poetry, and above all in his long, very difficult, but incomparable *Faust*. Another American poet, Robinson Jeffers (1887–1962), speaks of humanity as 'nature dreaming', and the phrase takes us very close to what we learn from Goethe. The over-hearer of Goethe's sublime conversations, the reader of his letters, the puzzler over his copious scientific work, is entering into an appreciation of reality itself, of Nature's dream. Like Lear in his momentary drift into wisdom with Cordelia, Goethe invites us to 'take upon us the mystery of things'.

When Goethe was in his mid-twenties, his friend Johann Heinrich Merck (1741–91) wrote to him, praising him because 'your dim but unswerving endeavour is to give a poetic form to the real; others seek to give reality to the so-called poetic, to the imagination, and of that nothing will ever come but stupid stuff. Whoever apprehends the immense difference between these two modes of procedure, whoever insists upon and acts upon this conviction, has gained enlightenment on a thousand other things.'[2]

Goethe lived for most of his adult life in a tiny little duchy in the now-vanished Holy Roman Empire. He was completely a man of his time, and he was in many respects a conservative, even a reactionary.

28

Yet such is his clarity of vision, and his interest in absolutely everything, he is also our contemporary.

Without wishing to push the point too clumsily, we can find in his writings a vision of things which anticipates our world. The present concern of environmentalists and of holistic scientists, who are aware of the intimate kinship of all natural phenomena, is something which animated the whole of Goethe's life as a writer. The arid debates, of a few decades ago, between 'Creationists' and 'Materialist Atheists' need never have taken place had those so vociferously at odds with one another appreciated Goethe's science. This is not to say that he got everything right – no scientist does, and there would be many who question his colour theory. In the great debate, in his times, about the geological origins of the earth – Vulcanists versus Neptunists – he was simply wrong. (Did the geological formations of prehistory have their origin through the movement of waters or the subterranean volcanic eruption? He was a Neptunist.) But where he was consistently right was in his sense that human beings are part of Nature, and that their scientific endeavours make no sense until they appreciate this.

He is our contemporary in so many other respects too – in his scorn for nationalism, his sense of the essential unity of European culture and politics, tempered by the knowledge that the world is not, and should not be, Eurocentric. Goethe was the great pioneer of what he called World Literature, and he was indebted to the Persian poets and the Chinese philosophers.

In some ways, Goethe is best seen as a religious poet. But his 'religion' was post-Christian, and in this, too, he seems more modern than eighteenth century. His attitude to love – which was so central to his poetry, his fiction and his life – owed nothing to conventional Christianity, nor to middle-class conventions. Like so many in the modern world of today, he shared his love with a 'partner' whom he married only after more than two decades together. She was of a completely different class and income bracket. Neither in life nor in his writings was he 'respectable' – one reason for his reputation, especially in nineteenth-century England, as a 'wicked' writer: another being his apparently ambivalent attitude to suicide. Samuel Taylor Coleridge, who translated *Faust*, grossly distorted it by omitting the Prologue in Heaven on the grounds that it was (in Coleridge's, by then, Anglican view of things) a blasphemous parody of the Bible. In his introduction, Coleridge stated, 'the prologue has been passed over … It is repugnant to notions of propriety such as are entertained in this country' (i.e. Britain).[3]

Goethe is understandably regarded by German-speakers as the embodiment of everything the Western world describes as the Enlightenment. Such is the paradox imposed upon the reading experience by language, however, that Goethe is chiefly known among those who speak and read his language. Books about him, even when they are written in English, are largely addressed to students of German literature and culture.

This book, perhaps with an ambition which borders on the foolhardy, is addressed both to those who know and speak German, and to those who do not.

Yet, even as Tischbein painted him in his extraordinary wide-brimmed hat and his mantle wrapped around him, in the countryside outside Rome a few years before the French Revolution, Goethe was being seen, and was content to be seen, as a figure bigger than his times, a messiah of what the Germans could teach the rest of the planet.

What, after the collapse of the Holy Roman Empire, during and after the rise and fall of Bonapartism, what was Germany, what was Europe, to become? Germany as a nation did not exist as France, or Britain, or the United States existed, and whatever the dreams of German-speaking liberals, it was hard to see how it could, quite, exist. There could be no compromise between two incompatible visions of what Germany might be, between the militaristic power of Prussia, and the desire, even after the Empire ceased to exist, of the Austrian Empire, to hold the German-speaking lands in her embrace. Germany, with its many quasi-independent city-states, electorates, duchies, principalities and kingdoms, was held together by something other than political cohesion. In his Jubilee poem at the start of 1815, he wonders whether the world's great powers will ever be able to come to peace. He sees the optimistic German, in his own intimate circle, freed from worry, and, both at home, and afar, able to sustain a new, better organized world.[4]

The union could only be one of language and culture. The first great work of German literature in the early modern period was Martin

Luther's Bible (1534). Nietzsche believed that the history of German literature began with it, and for the Protestant German-speaking world this was clearly true. Goethe, both as a poet and as a human being, is of a magnitude comparable with Luther's. The modern crisis of Christianity – concerning the status and plausibility of the Bible – had its origin in German universities, especially Tübingen. Goethe had never really believed the Bible, as Christians are meant to do. But, such is his fondness for paradox, and his essential conservatism, he rather deplored the beginning of the dismantling of Christian orthodoxy, which was being played out by the theologians in his old age. He was friends with those for whom the Enlightenment crisis-in-Christianity was of paramount importance – philosophers, theologians, preachers; and his Faust was – he sighed and said Alas![5] as he admitted it – a theologian. But Goethe himself wrote as if he lived in a post-Christian age. He had had a brief dose of evangelical piety during a phase of illness in late adolescence. Apart from this he showed no signs of anxiety about faith.

> Well, name it then, and call it Joy, or Heart –
> Or Love or God – for my own part
> I have no need a name to call –:
> For my own part – Feeling is all.[6]

He began to write the great dramatic poem while he was a law student at Strasbourg. He often laid it aside, but it remained the great work of his life for the next sixty years and he was still engaged upon it when, as the grand old 'Sage of Weimar', he had passed his eightieth birthday. It was not an autobiography, but it grew out of his life-experience, and became an allegory of his life and times.

In the autobiography *Poetry and Truth*, he speaks of the delight of his grandmother arranging for a puppet show in their house in Frankfurt am Main, as a Christmas treat.[7] Children need puppets and a theatre. So says the grandmother in one of the many versions of autobiography which Goethe wrote[8] – this, a novel called *Wilhelm Meister's Journeyman Years*. She remembered, in her own childhood, spending her pocket money on seeing puppet shows of Doctor Faustus, and of the Moorish Ballet.[9]

In the novel, a young lieutenant in the artillery is prevailed upon to build Wilhelm Meister his own puppet theatre, which is where his passion for theatre began.

The remarkable puppet-show fable of Faust made an answering echo in my breast. I too had ranged through the whole round of knowledge, and was early enough led to see its vanity.

Certainly, in the Frankfurt where Goethe was born – on 28 August 1749 – and where he grew up, there was no shortage of puppet shows, at the fairs and in the marketplaces of this prosperous medieval town. The story of Faust was one of the most popular in the repertoire. Faust was a story which had been in Goethe's head since childhood, and he would use it, in his endless reworkings of the legend, and his inability to finish the drama, as a vehicle for working out what had happened to himself, and to the world, in his long decades on this planet.

Robin Hood (fl.1180?) and Don Juan Tenoiro (fl.1350) are figures comparable to Faust, who began life as historical characters and quickly became the stuff of legend. Faust, though he would become the hero of an English dramatic masterpiece – Marlowe's *The Tragicall History of Doctor Faustus* (c.1589–93) – was German born and bred. He stems from that moment when Renaissance and Reformation were beginning – very tentatively – to develop a scientific outlook. He is the contemporary of Paracelsus (?–1541), who was both alchemist-mage and pioneer of the use of modern chemistry in medicine. At roughly the same time Copernicus (1473–1543), Polish mathematician and astronomer, had worked out that the part of the universe inhabited by human beings – what we now rightly call the solar system – was not geocentric but heliocentric.

The story of Faust had its origin at the beginning of the sixteenth century. One George Sabellicus obtained the post of schoolmaster at Kreuznach, through the offices of one Franz von Sickingen, 'a man very fond of mystical lore'. He was neither the first, nor the last, schoolteacher in history to make a sexual nuisance of himself with his pupils. Hounded out of his post, we find him again, two years later, now calling himself Johannes Faust, achieving the degree of BA in theology at the University of Heidelberg. Although we cannot be certain that 'George Sabellicus' and 'Johannes Faust' were one and the same, it looks likely. In October 1513, we find George Faust, 'Helmitheus Hedebergensis', the demigod of Heidelberg, has made a name for himself as a caster of horoscopes. In today's world, horoscopes belong to the back pages of cheap newspapers, and form the mental furniture of the uneducated. In the early modern period, however, a belief in astrology and magic were all but universal, and it is hard to find a public figure – whether a pope, a king or a queen – who did not dabble in it.

In 1520, Faust was paid 10 gulden for casting the horoscope of the Bishop of Bamberg. His bragging about his achievements was believed in some quarters, and he was spoken of as 'as remarkable a sorcerer as could be found in German lands in our times'. On 15 June, Dr George Faust of Heidelberg was banished from the town of Ingolstadt for sorcery. On 10 May 1532, the city of Nuremberg refused 'the great sodomite and necromancer' safe passage through its gates. 1535 found him in Münster, correctly prophesying that the city would be recaptured by its bishop, who had been exiled in the religious wars following the Reformation.[10]

Before the historical Faust vanishes into the shadows, we notice that he has achieved a mention in Wier's *De Praestigiis Daemonium*. It is Wier who tells us that Faust actually boasted that he was in league with the devil. Wier was interested in mages who had a serious claim to have acquired secret knowledge or be, like Paracelsus or Giordano Bruno (1548–1600), adepts of secret knowledge. The Renaissance was a time, not so much when magic was in decline as when it was transforming itself into the branches of knowledge which would eventually go by the names of philosophy and science. The real Faust played no part in the history of magic, nor in that alternative intellectual world of the occult, of the gnostic or Neoplatonic thought which existed sometimes side by side, sometimes beneath the surface of contemporary theology.

Faust, however, by chance, entered legend. Pass a generation from the time of the original Faust, braggart and charlatan, and we find Spiess, a Frankfurt am Main bookseller, publishing the first of many *Faust Books*, the story of a man whose inquiring mind led him to offer himself to the devil in exchange for forbidden knowledge. It is easy to see how this Renaissance trope transforms itself into the myth of our modern quest for knowledge, and for new ways of understanding – 'mastering' in all senses – the universe.

As a reward for his compact with Mephistopheles, signed with his own blood, Faust would be able to perform magical tricks and miraculous journeys into space. He could summon up Helen of Troy. Although overcome at the end of his life journey by remorse, the legendary Faust, though he came to birth in a Christian country, and a country whose most famous prophet, Martin Luther (1483–1546), preached Justification by Faith only, he could find no salvation. The Damnation of Faust is an essential part of the story.

Luther's greatest literary achievement was to translate the Bible into German, and thereby to make possible his ambition that every ploughboy might hold a copy of the Scriptures in his own hand. One of the first great stories in that monumental book is that of our ancestors, in the Garden of Eden, being offered something very tempting by the devil, who took the form of a serpent. Knowledge is what is on offer, not merely scientific knowledge, but also moral responsibility, the ability to distinguish between what we consider to be wrong and what we consider to be right. God has attempted to keep these two fundamental human capacities for himself. The forbidden tree symbolizes Knowledge, moral and scientific, and God has told the man and the woman that if they eat of it, they will die.

> And the serpent said unto the woman, Ye shall not surely die: For God doth know, that in the day ye eat thereof, then your eyes shall be opened, and Ye shall be as gods, knowing good and evil.[11]

Since the sixteenth century, when men and women – first, historically speaking, German, then English – could read these words in their own tongues, this story has resonated as a symbolic version of what was happening to them, collectively and individually, vis-à-vis the authority of the State, the Church and the Academy. Luther led the breakaway from the notion of papal authority. In Goethe's day, which would see the French Revolution breaking out when he was forty years old, and the whole world changing in consequence, the origins of modern science went hand in hand with the development of empirical philosophy and scepticism. Joseph Priestley (1733–1804) in England and Antoine Lavoisier (1743–94) in France were at work discovering the properties of hydrogen, oxygen and the compound H_2O, which were the foundations, first of chemistry, then of the forward rush of scientific knowledge and of technology, since, once the property of water was known, steam power would soon be developed.

Goethe, at many points of his life, would probably have seen himself primarily as a scientist – a pioneer in the field of anatomy; an obsessive in the area of optics; an early evolutionary theorist, with views on the history of plants and animals; a contributor to the contemporary debate about the geological history and origins of the earth itself. Like his Faust, he was both a scholar-scientist and a symbol of humanity at that point in history when it was learning to see the universe in a new way, in all its complexity, in all its mystery.

The first Fausts of which he became aware, however, were almost certainly, like the Faust known to the granny in *Wilhelm Meister*, figures in a puppet theatre. Successful puppet shows, whether of Faust or of Punch and Judy, rely on a simplicity of plot line, and there is something satisfying about the bad guy getting his comeuppance. That is why the early Faust books and the early Faust puppet plays forget all that Christian theology about the infinite mercy, and hold the mage firmly to his bargain with the devil. (In this, of course, the story cohered with that determinist strand of Reformation theology which departed from Luther and followed Calvin into the view that the fate of individuals was pre-ordained, and most of them were elected to damnation.)

The critic for the *Morgenblatt für gebildete Stände* described a puppet performance of *Faust* in Frankfurt during the month of April 1824, and there is no reason to suppose that things had changed much in the traditional medium of marionette theatre. This particular performance was put together by the marionette-impresario Lorgee.

A rather narrow, gloomy and smokily illuminated hall had accommodated a relatively enormous crowd of onlookers, who were staring at the curtain in tense expectation. It was brick-red, painted in boldly draped folds, ornamented with rather fantastic emblems of dramatic art and seemed undoubtedly to be concealing something unusual behind its mysterious veil. It must be confessed that the majority of the audience belonged to the rising generation and that nursemaids represented the higher grades of the middle-classes. But there was also a sprinkling of haute volée. We saw several gifted ladies of our acquaintance, who waved to us with smiles and shrugs; the literary profession was adequately represented, and curiosity had impelled some artists to attend. After a far from classically executed overture – as far as I remember it was the one to Spohr's Faust – the curtain rose, and the black-clad doctor, jaded with learning, stood upon the stage. What ought one to say, and what can one say about the acting and eloquence of these three-foot wooden personages, about the gaily magnificent decorations and the expenditure of gunpowder and fireworks? It should all be seen and experienced, not written about and read. In a word, the impression was on the grand scale. Not only the youthful element in the audience, but we grown-up children were enchanted and clapped until our hands were sore.[12]

In old age – by now Privy Councillor Johann Wolfgang *von* Goethe (the 'von' a sign that he had been ennobled by the Holy Roman Emperor) – he expressed gratitude that he felt happy in his own skin:

and I felt myself so distinguished, that I could not have been considered more remarkable if I had been made into a prince. Indeed, when I became a peer of the Empire, many people supposed that I would feel as if I had been elevated. Between ourselves, it meant nothing to me – absolutely nothing. We Frankfurt Patricians always considered ourselves to be nobility, and when I held the diploma in my hand – the diploma making me a peer – I did not think I had gained anything which I had not possessed for a long time.[13]

It is true that the eighteen-year-old woman who gave birth to Goethe was the daughter of the *Schultheiss*, Johann Wolfgang

Textor (1693–1771). He was the senior civil servant in the old 'Free Imperial City', responsible for all the ceremonial at the coronations of the Emperors which, time out of mind, had always taken place in Frankfurt. The Gothe or Goethe family, however, were less elevated and by no stretch of the imagination could they be described as 'patrician'. Goethe's father Johann Caspar (1710–82) was a successful lawyer, who was 'self-made'. His own father had been a tailor, and the paternal grandmother, Cornelia (1668–1754), had started a highly respectable inn called the Weidenhof. It had prospered, and Goethe's father had been a rich man even before making money from his law work.

Frankfurt in the eighteenth, as in the twenty-first, century was a hub of commercial life. In many respects – its streets narrow, its half-timbered houses higgledy-piggledy squashed together, its gallows at street corners, where women were hanged for abortion or infanticide, its church towers and bells – it was the same city it had been since the Middle Ages; its many inns deriving their roaring business from the frequent trade fairs or *Messe* which took place there. Goethe's father owned two of the houses so described, and much of the poet's childhood was dominated by the noise and disruption of building work, as his father converted these architectural throwbacks to the time of the Thirty Years War into the appropriate backdrop to his large collection, brought from a visit to Italy in young manhood. The (pre-Piranesi) engravings and prints of Rome – of the Piazza del Popolo, the Colosseum, the Piazza of St Peter's – which his father hung on the walls of the well-furnished rooms made an indelible impression on Goethe's mind. As well as the house, with its library and its artistic reminders of a greater European world, Goethe grew up with a large garden, airy views from the back windows and a daily sense of Nature's proximity.

He and his sister Cornelia (1750–77, born one year after himself) were the only surviving children, and they had an upbringing largely cut off from the outside world. After a short spell at an elementary school, Goethe and his sister were taught almost entirely at home, with writing master, Latin master, French master, drawing master all brought in. As far as the outside world was concerned, the children were only aware of it as a political battleground between his father and their paternal grandfather, the old *Schultheiss* Textor. Naturally, given his role in the centuries-old Imperial traditions of coronation, Textor was passionate in his defence of the Empire and in his reverence for the Emperor in Vienna. Johann Caspar Goethe, by contrast, hero-worshipped the Emperor's enemy, the King of Prussia – Frederick the Great (1712–86).

When Goethe was seven years old, this rivalry between Frederick and the Habsburgs became something more serious than a matter which German-speaking families disputed over the dinner table. The Seven Years War broke out. Maria Theresa of Austria (1717–80) and Frederick of Prussia had recast the decades-old European alliances. Maria Theresa had united with her old enemy, Bourbon France, to resist the Prussian power. In 1757, a year after the war broke out, the Empress of Russia, Elisabeth (1709–62), formally joined the anti-Prussian alliance.

Frederick in turn had allied with Great Britain. It would quickly become a world war, in which Britain and France fought for dominion of territory in Canada and India. As far as Europe was concerned, the initial point of territorial contention was Silesia, which, in conclusion with her previous war against Frederick, Maria Theresa had conceded to Prussia. She now wanted it back. Silesia, with its mines, weaving trade and industry, could finance armies, as both Maria Theresa and Fritz, from their aggressive perspectives, knew very well.[14]

It was a bloody war. In the Battle of Prague alone 30,000 were killed in just five hours. Europe was being redrawn. In Vienna, it was said that ladies were poring over atlases rather than reading their prayer books. As far as Britain was concerned, it ended with the British laying claim to Canada and large tracts of India. The European picture was much fuzzier, Frederick the Great feeling that the only major concession he was forced to make to the Empire was to accept the succession of Maria Theresa's son Joseph (1741–90) as the next Holy Roman Emperor. (The description of his election, and the procession of the Imperial regalia from Aachen to Frankfurt, the assembly of the electors and the rites of coronation occupy many pages of Goethe's autobiography, since he witnessed it all as a youth of sixteen.)

The Goethe household could not stand aloof from the war, since, much to Johann Caspar's chagrin, they had a French officer, and his retinue of servants, billeted on them from 1759 to 1761. Count Thoranc (1719–94), a pockmarked, thin native of Grasse, in Provence, was a source of perpetual irritation to Goethe's father. News came of a French victory over Prussia. When passing his host on the stairs, Count Thoranc said to Johann Caspar, 'You must congratulate both yourselves, and us, that this affair has ended so happily.' Johann Caspar growled that he wished it had taken the Frenchman to the devil, even if it had meant him joining him on the journey. The Count momentarily lost his cool, and threatened to have Goethe's father arrested.

But for the son, the presence in the house of a cultivated Frenchman was a benefit. Thoranc set up a French theatre in the city, and the pro-Austrian (hence, now pro-French) grandfather, old *Schultheiss* Textor, gave Goethe a free ticket to attend performances whenever he liked. Goethe had a deep knowledge of the French repertoire. His favourite playwright was Molière (?–1673) whom he read and reread every year of his life. He knew Racine (1639–99) well and came to know most of Corneille (1606–84) as a boy. Neither during this juvenile experience of French occupation, nor in Weimar, when the city was not merely occupied but severely bombarded by the French, did Goethe feel drawn to patriotic or nationalistic sentiments. He was always a European more than he was simply a German.

From an early age he was haunted by poetry. His father had the belief that poetry must be something which rhymed, but even as a young boy, Goethe had been transfixed by the *Messias* of Friedrich Gottlieb Klopstock (1724–1803), written in non-rhyming hexameters; the first three cantos had been published in Leipzig in the year before Goethe was born, in the *Bremer Beiträge* magazine.

The *Messias* is an epic of truly cosmic proportions, longer than the *Iliad*; it begins with Christ's entry into Jerusalem on Palm Sunday and takes us on journeys through space, to pursue the destinies of the demons in hell and hear the discourse of angels in Heaven. Their family friend Councillor Schneider, 'a dry man of business', read the poem each year, and it became a favourite of Goethe's mother, though his father was never persuaded. Goethe and his sister Cornelia vied with one another in who could recite the most of it.

Klopstock had been inspired to write his epic – which would absorb decades of his life, only finishing it in 1773 – by reading the translation of Milton's *Paradise Lost* by the Swiss professor, theologue and man of letters Johann Jacob Bodmer (1698–1783). There had been no figure in German literature who occupied a position comparable to that of John Milton (1608–74) in England, where generations, down to and including the Romantic poets, grew up in his shadow, and where every literate person knew his work intimately. In his autobiography, Goethe noted the fact that, in German-speaking lands, while honours were heaped on the nobility and on men of science, poets were not esteemed. They were poor sprigs of humanity, forced to crawl painfully through life, little better than a court jester or a parasite.[15]

Klopstock changed the status of the German poet overnight. In Goethe's sense of his own life story, Klopstock is seen as one of the great masters, because he made it seem possible that one could be a great writer in the German language. Hitherto, to be a great writer implied that you would write in French or English.

Three German geniuses, within twenty years of one another, made works of art out of the story of Jesus, and his redeeming death: Johann Sebastian Bach (1685–1750) wrote the *St Matthew Passion* in 1727; Handel's (1685–1759) *Messiah* had its first performance in Dublin in 1742; and Klopstock's *Der Messias*, the first three cantos, six years later.

One of the most remarkable things about Klopstock's poem is Satan's speech to the other fallen angels, whom he addresses as gods. Clearly, it is in some ways an echo of Satan's speeches to the other devils in Milton's Pandemonium (*Paradise Lost*, Book One), but it is much more specifically related to the person of Jesus, whom he has in his sights as the frustrater of their devilish work. The bloodthirsty delight in which he reminds them of the massacre of the innocents in Bethlehem is utterly horrific. A speech to the Nuremberg Rally. And when we think of Goethe and Cornelia trying to learn more and more of it by heart, and then we turn back to his version of the *Faust* legend, we see how completely detached his version is from the traditional Gospel narrative, which informed Bach, Handel and Klopstock, and from the Lutheran exegesis of the Scriptures which underlay all three of them. For the three, humanity is lost, irrecoverably estranged from the Good, without the Redeemer's Sacrifice, without Grace; whereas

Goethe's Faust is humanity striving to better himself. His devil, unlike the sinister King of Hell in Klopstock, is much of the time genial, and sometimes almost endearingly silly.

Since we are writing the story of Goethe's *Faust* and how it evolved, and how it related to the poet's own day-to-day existence, we note that Klopstock's *Der Messias* is a depiction, an overwhelming depiction, of the strength of the angelic powers. True, he derives this from Milton, but in the German epic, even more than in *Paradise Lost*, the devil has a sinister power and malice which cannot be read without a feeling of horror.

There is, of course, an extreme paradox, or mystery, for the modern reader either of Klopstock or of Milton, two fervently devout Christian men who almost certainly believed in the literal truth of angels, archangels, the heavenly and the infernal realms, and yet who had the temerity to invent speeches exchanged between archangels and the Almighty Himself. Does this mean that on some level – intuited by many of the post-Miltonic Romantic poets such as Blake or Shelley – the older writers did in fact regard the Christian story as mythological, or the Bible as a mythological representation of inner truth? Goethe, who would conclude *Faust* with the choral assurance that everything is parable, every phenomenon is a representation of reality, must have always, with a part of his mind, assumed this to be the case.

It is, in origin and essence, a very Protestant issue. For the Orthodox and Catholic Christians of the first 1,500 years of the religion's existence, the story was kept alive by liturgy, by ritual enactments, in which the written story itself, the Bible, was divided into snippets and sung as something which had a dramatic, visual form. You did not have to be literate to grasp it. For the Protestant after Luther, the Bible was something to be read, and Christianity was a literary event or experience.

Goethe's own poetic efforts were at this stage more modest but he was drawn to write a drama based on the classical Pantheon found in Ovid's *Metamorphoses*,[16] and the compulsion to compose verse was well established by the time he was in his early teens. However we interpret Goethe, and whatever we find him doing from year to year, it must be remembered that there was almost never a time when he was not composing lyric verse, and he was, in terms of sheer technicality, one of the most productive and proficient poets in European history. No judgement could be less true than that of T. S. Eliot (1888–1965) who wrote, in 1933, with quite staggering folly, 'Goethe ... dabbled in both philosophy and poetry and made no great success of either' (he recanted the error!).[17] By the time he left Frankfurt, aged sixteen, to start his law studies at the University of Leipzig, Goethe left behind with his father 'numerous quarto volumes of manuscript'.

So that habit began from which, my whole life through I have not been able to deviate, of turning into a picture or a poem whatever rejoiced, troubled or occupied me: it was a way of directing my understanding of outward things, as well as bringing calm to my inward being.[18]

The Spirit of Nature – Where are you, Faust?

*Everything in it [Faust] is saturated with life. Thought is never
presented in it in an abstract form, just as sentiment is never
separated from thought, so that what is most individual is still
heavy with meaning, and, so to speak, exemplary.*

André Gide, *Journals*, 26 June 1940

Not much of Goethe's Leipzig remains, though his bewigged,
elegant statue stands in the street; and Auerbachs Keller, where
Mephistopheles and Faust tease the boozers, still survives; its huge
cavernous space panelled with wood, its cheap brown tables and
chairs occupied by Leipzigers who in youth seem to start mousey,
thin and bespectacled and then, after a decade or so of grown-up life,
respond to the diet of beer, dumplings and potatoes by turning into
Michelin men and women. Though more than thirty-five years have
elapsed since *die Wende*, you feel you could still be in a Communist
state. In the vaulted cavern, scenes from *Faust* were painted, very
amateurishly, in the twentieth century – the death of Valentin, the
soliloquy to Nature, the wooing of Gretchen in Marthe's garden. As
the rotund waitress, who has already brought me a complimentary
gallon of fizzy beer, tries to make me have 'Noch ein Weinchen'
while I await my salmon (served on a bed of cabbage and mashed
potatoes in a kind of jam sauce with three gargantuan spuds in a
saucer as a 'side'), I look about and think on the nature of things,

43

and of the German experience. Child of the English Midlands, born in peacetime, coming to Central Europe makes one aware, for the umpteenth time, that by the comparison of those living in this place for the last three centuries, one has not lived: the Thirty Years War, the Seven Years War, the invasion of Napoleon, and his murderous marches through these parts, with tens of thousands dead, the revolutions and counter-revolutions of the nineteenth century ... And all this before the First World War, the hyperinflation time of the Weimar Republic, the Third Reich disaster, the forty miserable years of the German Democratic Republic.

Goethe, who came to a city which had only just lost Bach (after his twenty-seven-year stint at the Thomaskirche), could not possibly have foreseen what was going to happen to his country in the twentieth century, and yet, as the crudely painted scenes from *Faust* around the restaurant remind any reader of the poem, he sort of did, he sort of intuited and imagined it all, which is what makes the poem a text to which generations of readers return again and again and – as with biblical exegesis – find things which are there, but had been invisible to earlier generations, miss things which had been obvious to its first readers, and, bringing their own baggage and their own preoccupations, their own distortions and misreadings, mysteriously change the text for the next generation who can come along and read it afresh, but never quite afresh.

1767, the year Goethe went to Leipzig as a student, was the 250th anniversary of the moment – in history, or in legend – when Martin Luther nailed his Theses to the church door in Wittenberg and so began the Reformation. There is a biographical irony in the fact that young Goethe thereby missed a notorious performance of a Faust play in his native city. Some strolling players enacted *The Vicious Life and Terrible End of Dr John Faust of Wittenberg*. Great offence was taken by Luther's university at setting this not entirely serious treatment of the theme in their alma mater. The city burghers of Frankfurt felt the need to calm things down by apologizing to the theological faculty at Wittenberg, for associating their illustrious and scholarly traditions with the adept of infernal arts.[1]

There was a marked contrast between medieval Frankfurt, with its narrow winding streets and half-timbered buildings, and Leipzig, the most populous city in Saxony, which was a modern trade and university town.

Far from meditating on the so-German legend of Faust, with its Teutonic witches and Northern demonology, in Leipzig Goethe was absorbing an altogether different aesthetic, and a Southern, classical outlook. Devoting a minimum amount of time to the law, he enlisted in the drawing classes of Adam Friedrich Oeser (1717–99). There was to be an everlasting contrast in Goethe's imagination between the Germanic, loosely speaking Romantic, primitive collection of tales, superstitions and attitudes, and the sunlit Hellenistic world. One of the things which happened in *Faust Part Two* was that these two traditions were amorously conjoined. They literally mate, Faust the German and Helen of Troy, the Eternal Feminine symbol of Hellas.

His father's Roman prints had excited in Goethe a love of Italy and the classical past. He was a good schoolboy Latinist, and he had passable Greek. But it was Oeser who introduced him to the full blast of contemporary classicism. Oeser, the friend of art historian Johann Joachim Winckelmann (1717–68), had illustrated this pivotal figure's works – *Thoughts on the Imitation of Greek Work in Painting and Architecture* (1755) and *The History of Art in Antiquity* (1759). Winckelmann and Oeser were the sworn enemies of French rococo, and 'scroll and shell' design.[2] The robust formal simplicity of the Greek temple, and the god-like form of young male naked Greek athletes, immortalized in their sculpture, were their models. Winckelmann converted to Catholicism and became the librarian in turn to two cardinals – Archinto and Albani. In his sojourn in Rome, he built up an unrivalled knowledge of the sculptures of antiquity, as of the temples at Paestum.

Goethe reached Oeser's rooms up a winding stair in the Castle Pleissenburg. He walked through a room hung with Italian Old Masters, and came into an apartment where furniture, the presses, the books and portfolios were all maintained with the maximum of simplicity. With his portfolios of copperplate engravings, reproducing works of classical sculpture and Renaissance painting, Oeser began Goethe's formal education. When he came to have his own would-be grand residence in Weimar, Goethe would recall Oeser's apartment, with its portfolios.

Oeser introduced Goethe to an essay which had been published the previous year, 1766, entitled 'Laokoön, or the Border between the Plastic Arts and Poetry'. The author, Gotthold Ephraim Lessing (1729–81), took issue with Winckelmann over the celebrated statue of Laocoön. Readers of Virgil's *Aeneid* Book Two, which concerns the Fall of Troy, will remember a series of ill omens, before the tricksy Greeks manage to intrude their wooden horse into the besieged city. One such incident of hideous painfulness occurs when Laocoön the priest tries to expose the Greek ruse by shoving a spear into the wooden horse. As a punishment the sea god Poseidon/Neptune summons up a sea serpent who comes out of the ocean and wraps itself round the bodies of two young men, Laocoön's sons. It was in Renaissance times, 1506, that the sculpture (older than Virgil's poem) was excavated in a Roman vineyard and set up in the Vatican by Pope Julius II, the patron of Michelangelo. It was seen at once as one of the most powerful expressions of pure human suffering. The face of the desperate priest influenced countless Renaissance paintings of Christ's Passion.

It had been Winckelmann's contention that the sculpture was a supreme example of the superiority of Greek art to Roman, since, he maintained, the Greek statue of Laocoön suffers silently, whereas in Virgil's poem he bellows like an ox being sacrificed on an altar. 'His roaring fills the flitting air around,' as Dryden translated it. Lessing, however, disagreed. The statue could not *but* be silent! And the demands of plastic and poetic art are different.

Both Lessing and Winckelmann, however, had an enormous effect on the generation who read them. Goethe said the Laocoön essay led him into the open fields of thought, and we shall still find him in those open fields, moving now towards Winckelmann's adulation of Greece, now towards Lessing's realization that literature makes different demands from those of sculpture, deep into his old age.

Oeser held out to his young pupils the exciting prospect of Winckelmann coming back to Germany. He was due to visit one of his patrons, the young Prince of Dessau, and he would surely visit Oeser at Leipzig. Alas, as he made plans for the journey, Winckelmann found himself in an inn at Trieste, where he was murdered by one Francesco Arcangeli – his taste for the beauty of the male form perhaps having led him into dangerous territory.

Goethe and his young student contemporaries did not set their sights so high as to hope they would actually converse with Winckelmann, but they set up an observation post in some beautiful countryside near Dessau, certain that his carriage would pass that way, and hopeful that they might sometimes see him walking with Oeser and conversing with their tutor. Then, one day, as he approached the winding staircase to Oeser's room, Goethe was met by one of his fellow students and told not to call on their master that day. The hideous news had arrived. Goethe speculated, in later life, about the powerful influence of Winckelmann and wondered whether the murder, and the untimely end, had not increased the potency of his influence.[3]

Presumably, Goethe would have continued his studies at Leipzig, and passed a few law exams, as he deepened his friendship with Oeser. He was there for nearly three years, during which time he wrote poetry, most of which he subsequently destroyed, pursued a number of crushes or love affairs and made some friends. It is impossible to know the extent of his sexual experiences since this was part of the story which he was extremely successful in editing. The impression given to some was that, although he was frequently in love, he would wait until middle age before actually having the full experience. Given the prevalence of venereal disease in the eighteenth century, this is perfectly possible. There is really no point in speculating about it, though, as we shall see in subsequent chapters, the carefully edited versions of his girl-crushes and the poems and fiction which they inspired are part of the story which he allowed us, or wanted us, to consider.

Fate, however, would cut short his Leipzig years, when, in the summer of 1768, he suffered what appears to have been a tubercular haemorrhage, which necessitated his return home. Recovery was slow. His father longed for him to finish his studies and begin to be a useful member of society – i.e. a practising lawyer.

It was a serious illness, and for some weeks he hovered between life and death. In her despair, his mother opened her bible for inspiration and came upon the verse in the Prophet Jeremiah: 'Thou shalt plant vines upon the mountains of Samaria: the planters shall plant and shall eat them as common things' (Jeremiah 31.5). It appeared to be a hopeful omen.

Fräulein Susanna von Klettenberg (1723–74) was an old family friend, distantly related to Goethe's mother. The relationship formed between the sick adolescent and the rather beautiful forty-five-year-old would be replicated on a number of occasions, not least in Weimar, where his devotion to the Dowager Duchess Anna Amalia (1739–1807) and his near worship of Charlotte von Stein (1742–1827) coloured the whole of life for a decade. He tells us that when he came to write *Wilhelm Meister*, the section known as 'The Confessions of a Beautiful Soul' were directly based on the words of Fräulein von Klettenberg. Surely one of the most memorable of the Beautiful Soul's confessions is that she intervened to prevent two men killing one another with swords. By the time rescue had arrived, she was covered in blood – some hers, some theirs – and the mistress of the house takes her off to an adjoining bedroom to change her into clean clothes. It involves a full strip in front of the mirror – 'and for the first time, I saw with some pleasure that I might be regarded as beautiful without the assistance of dress'.[4]

The 'Beautiful Soul's consciousness of sin leads her to an evangelical conversion experience. In the depth of depression, she prayed to God for faith. A magnetic force drew her to the cross where Jesus died. 'It was a force – I can't describe it in any other way – exactly like what draws us to an absent someone with whom we are in love, a drawing near which is probably more real and more true than we can possibly imagine.'[5]

Goethe says that in dress you could have taken her for one of the Moravian sect – the same group who, in England, converted the Wesley brothers. This passionate woman, Fräulein von Klettenberg, was, like so many Germans of the period, what is called a Pietist. Nicholas Boyle tells us that there were some 250 'awakened souls' in Frankfurt at the time, belonging to one evangelical group or another.[6]

This was the only time in Goethe's life that he embraced Christian faith, and it did not outlast the illness. Once he was better, he would return to his Nature-worshipping pantheism. One of the interesting things about the Pietists – and this makes Klettenberg one of the godparents of *Faust* – is their interest in the esoteric knowledge of Renaissance Platonists. She had read Georg von Welling's *Opus Mago-cabbalisticum* (1719), a compendium of magical and alchemical rituals that still dominates the way in which the subject has been viewed. Fascinated by his denunciations of the 'secret knowledge' of Paracelsus and others, she had turned to those very works which he had abominated. She was providing Goethe with Faust's reading list.

Moreover, since Klettenberg was a rich woman who lived in a large house, she had room for a laboratory, and with her alembics and retorts, and little air furnace, she conducted experiments on the qualities of iron, believing it possible to extract the healing powers hidden in base metals. When he had firmly lost any belief in Klettenberg's theology, Goethe would continue to enjoy chemical experiments and to dabble in those regions where science and magic meet. What is science, after all, but the harnessing of natural forces and an attempt to control or manipulate the processes of Nature? The Renaissance alchemist with his alembic and the physicists on the Manhattan Project were following the same paths.

> *That is why I have devoted myself to Magic.*[7]
> *Was it a God who wrote these signs?*
> Which bring peace to my inner violent feelings[8]
> And fill my poor heart with joy?
> That work their will with secret power,
> Revealing the power of great Nature?

He would never choose to answer the question, nor to name the God who wrote these 'signs' in Nature and the universe. Attending a meeting of the so-called *Herrnhuter* (Moravian Brotherhood) shortly before he left Frankfurt to continue his university studies, he was totally repelled. What chiefly disgusted him was their capacity to confuse their own whims with God's purpose, 'their will with secret power'.[9]

Faust would pass through so many revisions in Goethe's imagination before its completion, that it is sometimes easy to forget that, in its origin, it was a meditation on an actual or semi-historical figure; or at least, a figure fixed in the early modern period, when European humanity was preparing for two monumental revolutions in thought: the Reformation, and the casting off of a papalist idea of the Christian Church; and the beginnings of what we call science – though to Goethe's generation it was always natural philosophy.

A key figure in the early modern understanding of this fundamental shift in collective human consciousness was Pico de Mirandola (b. 1463), the first to bring Cabbala into Christian philosophy and to unite it with Neoplatonism.[10]

The fragmentary early version of Goethe's play, written when he was a student at Strasbourg, and known to scholarship as the original, or *Urfaust*, contains the discussion between Gretchen and Faust on the subject of whether he is a religious believer and Goethe's idea that his own life, his own life-experience, and indeed the whole of human experience is to be understood in symbolic terms. The origin of this viewpoint is Platonic, and the conduit through which he picked it up was through the Neoplatonism of the Renaissance.

'I have always regarded everything I have done as symbolic, and it is more or less a matter of indifference to me whether I made pots or dishes.' Goethe said this as an old man, as a man by then, of the nineteenth century, whose Enlightenment rationalism had always been tempered by mysticism, and who seemed rather to enjoy misty uncertainties. In its historical origin, as he was well aware after reading cabbalistic texts with Fräulein von Klettenberg, the connection was close between Neoplatonic mysticism and – hence the importance for *Faust* – magic. Pico saw a natural kinship between magic and Cabbala. 'There is no natural science which makes us so certain of the divinity of Christ as Magic and the Cabbala,' he wrote in his *Apology*, and the passage in the *Apology* from which this is drawn could be an extended prose version of the first part of Goethe's drama:

> One of the chief charges against me is that I am a magician. Have I not myself distinguished two kinds of magic? One, which the Greeks call goeteia, depends entirely on alliance with evil spirits, and deserves to be regarded with horror, and to be punished; the other is magic in the proper sense of the word. The former subjects man to the evil spirits, the latter makes them serve him.

This is central to *Faust*, since, of course, Faust himself is never sure – nor are we? – whether, after the pact, Mephistopheles is his servant or his master. Pico went on, 'The former is neither an art nor a science; the latter embraces the deepest mysteries, and the knowledge of the whole of Nature with her powers.'

Here we have an early modern man expounding what would become the modern scientific outlook; it is completely central not only to *Faust* but to Goethe's entire life's work as a scientist and as a poet, whether he was making pots or bowls.

In *Poetry and Truth*, Goethe says that it was at this stage of his life that he discovered Spinoza.

> After vainly looking around for a means of educating [Bildungsmittel] my peculiar nature, I finally chanced upon the Ethics of this man. It would not be possible to say exactly how much I gained from that work ... It is enough to say that I found in him a sedative for my passions, and he seemed to me to open up a large and free outlook on the material and moral world.[11]

He claims to have learned 'disinterestedness', and quotes an epigram from his own *Wilhelm Meister's Apprenticeship* (Book IV, Chapter 9): 'If I love you, what is that to you?'

The epigram was written years later than the period 1773–4, when he was supposedly enraptured with Spinoza. There is one letter from this period, in which he writes to a friend, who has lent him a volume of Spinoza, 'May I keep it a little longer? I will only see how far I may follow this chap [*Menschen*] in his subterranean tunnellings'[12] – which suggests that he has *not* yet read Spinoza. We see here that Goethe's autobiographies are not to be taken as especially scrupulous records of the truth – more as impressions, formed years after the event, of the state of his mind when he wrote down the 'memories'.

Spinoza did play a part, a large part, in Goethe's inner life – but much later on. Moreover, there is Spinoza, the actual Dutch lens-maker-philosopher who penned the *Ethics* and other philosophical works, and there is the Spinoza who was taken up by the Enlightenment as the sponsor of materialist-atheist views. In the

1780s onwards, the word 'Spinoza' was a dog whistle to readers of *les philosophes* – such as Goethe's friend Friedrich Heinrich Jacobi (1743–1819): it was a call to reject the 'unnecessary hypothesis' of a Creator when attempting to account for the existence of natural phenomena.

It is possible, however, that the young Goethe formed an impression of Spinoza, and that this contributed to his unfinished fragment *Der Ewige Jude*. We do know, however, that one book which he most definitely did read and absorb as a teenager, when he was recovering from the severe illness after Leipzig, was Gottfried Arnold's *Impartial History of the Church and its Heresies* and we also know that in preparing his thesis for his Doctorate of Law at Strasbourg, he had looked into Spinoza's *Tractatus Theologico-Politicus*, and its scathing criticisms of the perversions of Christ's teaching by generations of Christians.

Der Ewige Jude, in Goethe's version of the Wandering Jew myth, was said to have been a shoemaker, who would hold conversations with passers-by – with Sadducees, Pharisees, with Jesus himself – examining their beliefs by Socratic, jokey cynicism, framed in a *Knittelvers* verse meter which is very similar to some of the metrical mockery placed on the lips of Mephistopheles in *Faust*. Only, the fragment is not really cynical. Returning to earth and landing on the very mountain where he had been tempted by the devil, the Son of God expresses boundless pity for the human race, and for the world, where truth and error, happiness and misery, are so inextricably bound up. The fragment was never finished, and Goethe did not risk publishing it in his lifetime. It appeared in print four years after he had died.

———

With the return of health came a yearning to be out of his father's presence. The charming rooms and pleasant scenes where he had suffered so much now caused him pain. In short, home was unendurable. He resumed his law studies, not in Leipzig, but in the Alsatian city of Strasbourg.

To read his account in *Poetry and Truth*, of climbing the cathedral tower and surveying the beauty of the surrounding countryside, is to hear Goethe's Pastoral Symphony. The Rhine wove its way through a pre-industrial, lightly inhabited country. The eye took in the distant mountains, its fertile groves, farmsteads, hamlets: a paradise.

Not long after he had established himself in lodgings on the south side of the Fish Market, he witnessed the passage through the city of Maria Antonia, Archduchess of Austria-Lorraine (1755–93), on her way to becoming Queen Marie Antoinette of France. Raphael's Cartoons of Jason, Medea and Creusa had been woven into tapestries to decorate the great city hall – inapposite figures, as they seemed to Goethe, since Jason and Medea would hardly be held up as models of happy marriage (she would murder their children in revenge for his adulteries). Before Maria Antonia's arrival, disabled people had been cleared from the streets so that her eyes need not fall upon the lame or the sick. Goethe wrote a poem (in French) contrasting the arrival of Christ, who came to this earth specifically to meet such people, and the new French Queen who scared such unfortunates away.[13] It was vaguely prophetic – seeming to intuit the sad future of playing at the Dresden shepherdess of Le Petit Trianon.

He spent a little over a year in Strasbourg. Contrary to his father's wishes, he would not manage to become a Doctor of Law, but he scraped through enough examinations to allow him to practise. Although he had been lazy in his studies, Goethe was quick-witted enough to become a highly competent lawyer.

It was a seed-time. As in Leipzig, and back home in Frankfurt, he would fall in love. During the Strasbourg year, the girl was called Frederika. Riding out into the country with friends, he had come to the village/small town of Sesenheim and visited the parsonage. It felt like stepping into a novel – indeed, he compared the pastor with Goldsmith's *Vicar of Wakefield*, which remained one of Goethe's favourite books.

The parson's daughter, Frederika, wore the old-fashioned 'German costume' – a white skirt, short enough to reveal her ankles; a tight white bodice and a black taffeta apron. It was not long before they were walking together in the moonlight. Goethe had the surely rather tedious fondness for incognitos and joke identity. He and the friend accompanying him on this trip pretended to be shabby theological students. He brushed his hair differently.

The infatuation with Frederika was one of many which punctuated his life. It inspired one of his most beautiful early lyrics – 'Welcome and Farewell' – which, of course, had written into it the bittersweet guarantee that the would-be lovers must part.

But oh, already with the rising sun,
The farewell-pain had pressed against my heart.
How happy were your kisses – every one –
But how your eyes were sad that we must part.
I'm off, you stand and gaze towards the ground –
Then, you look up, your eyes with tears are wet:
But – to be loved – what happiness we've found!
And, more, to love, oh Gods! What happiness is that!

In September 1770, at the entrance to the Zum Geist inn, Strasbourg, Goethe saw a man in a black frock coat who could have been an elegant, aristocratic abbé. It was in fact Johann Gottfried Herder (1744–1803), who had come to Strasbourg for a painful eye operation on his lacrimal sac. (The surgeon Johann Friedrich Lobstein [1736–84] had perfected this operation, which involved the bottom of the sac being cut open and a hole bored in the bone behind it. A horse hair was then passed through the hole to prevent it from closing before a new duct formed itself.)

Herder, a clergyman some five years older than Goethe, was already a celebrated literary man. His relationship with Goethe was not always easy, but it would last until Herder's death. The two men did not merely spar, but sparked – their wide range of interests were often complementary and, when they disagreed, about theology, or science, or philosophy, it was often a creative disagreement.

Herder was raised a poor man who had become literate by steeping himself in Luther's Bible. He grew up in East Prussia – now Poland – and was a pupil of Immanuel Kant at Königsberg – now Kaliningrad, Russia – though long before Kant 'awoke from his dogmatic slumbers' and wrote *Critique of Pure Reason* (1781).

Herder's own philosophical development was interesting. He was one of the first people to equate cognition with language itself. You can trace a thread between Herder's view that human beings are of their essence linguistic, that the stuff of philosophy, and many of its apparent problems, are linguistic stuff and linguistic problems – this – and Wittgenstein's 'Language Games'.

Of more immediate influence on Goethe and on the development of German literature, Herder's 1772 *Treatise on the Origin of Language* urged the Germans to shake off their inferiority complex vis-à-vis France. They should 'spew out the ugly slime of the Seine' and 'Speak German, O, you German!' He urged the recovery of German folk traditions, and an interest in the old Germanic legends and poems of the North – the *Edda* in Old Norse, the poetry of the Middle Ages in the *Nibelungenlied*. He urged Germans to treasure Dürer. The 'times of the Swabian Emperors' deserved to be studied, and made the subject of literature, quite as much as those of the classical Greeks.

Moreover, rather than idolizing Racine and Corneille, Herder was the first really influential German man of letters to urge the excellence of Shakespeare.

All of this was to have the profoundest influence in the life of the young Goethe. His early sketches for the *Faust* play, begun at the time when he first got to know Herder, are the depiction of a German mage in a German setting. The Germanness of *Faust*, and his Gothic, cobwebby study, and even the Germanness of Mephistopheles, which contrasts in *Faust Part Two* with the magic and legends of the Greeks, are essential.

Goethe had been taught by Oeser and Winckelmann to think of the Roman poets and the austerity of classical style as his ideal. The discovery of Shakespeare he owed to Herder's essay 'On German Character and Art' – *Von Deutscher Art und Kunst* – in which he expounded the centrality of *character*, rather than formal verse or dramatic unity to Shakespeare's art.

There was another dimension to Herder's reading of world literature. He invented the term 'folk song', which was subsequently to become a loan word in other European languages. He taught Goethe and his young protégés in Strasbourg to see the virtue of the great Gothic cathedral, and the organic aesthetic of the Middle Ages, which did not follow the stiffer Greek conventions beloved of Winckelmann but could exuberantly soar into an architecture of mystery. So, too, he could find in the anonymous music and lyrics of the folk song a freedom and an expressiveness which was denied to Racine or Voltaire. Goethe was soon imitating 'folk songs', as would the English poets of the Romantic movement over the next decades.

All these things – the discovery of 'the Gothic', the enjoyment of earthy folk lyrics – fed into the earliest drafts of *Faust*. He would also, before long, have begun to write a 'Shakespearean' drama of his own. In the autumn of 1771, Goethe sat down and in six weeks drafted a play then entitled *The History of Gottfried von Berlichen with the Iron Hand. Dramatised*. It was later known to the world as *Götz von Berlichingen*. 'Whoever is not a Hungarian ox, shouldn't come too near me. From my iron right hand he would receive such a biff on the ear that he would cure him of a headache, a toothache and every kind of other ache on earth.'

The play was a publishing sensation when it appeared in 1773. It made Goethe the rising star of the new literary firmament. Its fame even reached the sceptical ears of Frederick the Great himself, the Enlightened Despot of Prussia whose boast was that his enormous library did not contain a single German book. (Only French and Latin for him.) When he read *Götz* – which was to be enthusiastically translated into English by Walter Scott – 'Fritz' proclaimed it 'a revolting imitation of bad English plays'.[14]

Götz did not impress Herder, either. Naturally, Goethe sent him a copy of the play, and received the reply that Shakespeare had 'spoiled him'. It was not the first and certainly not the last put-down which Herder would deliver in the course of a stormy friendship, which would eventually break through mutual acrimony. Herder was not for nothing a preacher. Before the eye trouble which brought him to Strasbourg, he had been the court preacher at Riga and there was always something censorious about him. At this stage, Goethe was prepared to take the rough with the smooth.

'Jacob wrestled with the angel, and thanks to this I shall always be lame!' Goethe wrote in August 1771, in reference to one of Herder's gruelling criticisms.

The readings in Paracelsus with Fräulein von Kettenberg had awakened Goethe's interest in Renaissance science-magic-hermetic lore. At some time, either at the end of his time at Strasbourg or shortly thereafter, he began to write a play about Faust.

———

It would seem[15] that Goethe knew Rembrandt's 1652 etching[16] of Faust gazing at a mysterious magic disc shining near his tall study window. This perhaps is what he had in mind when, in the first long monologue, Faust opens the volume of Nostradamus and sees the sign of the Makrokosmos. He had certainly looked into Welling's influential *Opus Mago-Caballisticum*.

One problem for the modern reader of the Faust story, whether in Goethe's versions or others, is to discern how seriously we are meant to take the magic, how literally, do we suppose, did Goethe – for example – believe in it all? Further to this conundrum, there is the interpretative academic question: how far do modern historians of science consider that early modern scientists practised, or were influenced by, occult theory?

From the mid-1960s to the mid-1980s, the academic history of science in Britain was dominated by the divisive and distinctive figure of Frances Yates.[17] Deeply read in the occult texts of the Renaissance, and herself a little bit witchy, Yates contended that the scientific revolution of the seventeenth century grew out of magic. A potent cocktail of Neoplatonic philosophy and Christian Cabbala led to the 'Hermetic Tradition'. The more sobersides historians of science – in part, it must surely be said, stung by discovering their ignorance of many of the texts unearthed by Yates – rejected her utterly. Others, more measured, felt that she had grossly exaggerated the extent to which science and mathematics proper had 'grown out of' magical or occult rituals. In the work of Dr John Dee, for example, the famous 'mage' of the time of Queen Elizabeth I in England, it is possible to distinguish between his development of 'catoptrics' – the use of mirrors, both in optics and astronomy as modernly understood – and his belief in astrology and planetary influence. What the duller modern historians perhaps miss is the obvious fact that Dee, on one level recognizable by us as a scholar, mathematician and scientist, was regarded by contemporaries, including the Queen herself, as endowed with singular powers. (Elizabeth on more than one occasion asked Dee to cast her horoscope, using this information, for example, to decide on a propitious date for the coronation.) Yates revealed to us the extent to which the 'Hermetic Tradition' was widely believed and read as a sort of underground alternative to Catholic and Protestant theology of the time. Giordano Bruno was hung upside down naked in the Campo dei Fiori in Rome before being burned at the stake in 1600 – regarded by some as a 'martyr to science', and to others, such as Yates, as an apostle of the Hermetic Secret. There seems no doubt that some of his 'heresies' – such as his insistence on the heliocentric universe – were dictated by scientific attention to truth; that he believed in magic also seems beyond question. According to Yates, he derived much of his astronomical knowledge from Islamic texts. His theories about the Art of Memory inspired Yates's two best books.[18] Goethe had not only read him, but also alludes to his death in *Faust Part Two*.

The so-called Yates thesis is not something on which I am qualified to speak, but it throws into relief the continuing intertwine between what the post-Enlightenment world called science, and what the in-between times, from the Renaissance to the Age of Goethe, might have seen as magic, or secret knowledge. What concerns us, in telling the story of Goethe's *Faust*, is what the young poet saw in all this.

Centrally, very early on – probably in Goethe's twenty-fifth year of life – we find his Faust dwelling on the 'Sign' or image of the Makrokosmos.

How everything weaves together in a Whole,
Each individual thing working and living in another.
How the forces of Heaven surge and swoop,
Each holding out to the other the Golden Pail.[19]

It is almost what could be called nature-mysticism, but Faust, like Goethe, was not content to see it merely as a pageant, a play, a *Schauspiel*. He wants to be able to do what we should call science; he wants, in both senses of the term, to master it, and this is one of the ways in which *Faust* is the foreshadowing of the modern world, modern science in all its glory, wonder, terror and power to destroy.

> *Wo fass ich dich, unendliche Natur?*
> Eternal Nature, how can I grasp thee?[20]

Faust summons up the Spirit of Earth, who, when he makes his gigantic, fiery appearance, is a Terrible Sight, or a truly terrifying face. He is the 'anima terrae' of Giordano, the 'archeus terrae' of Paracelsus.[21] It is the Order of Things, the Spirit of organic actual Life on Earth. 'The great Spirit has scorned me,' Faust complains later in the drama. Nature has shut up her secrets and won't disclose them.[22] It is not going to be enough for Faust to immerse himself in 'Nature' like a Wordsworthian nature-lover or mystic. He wants to know. This is the Enlightenment embracing the scientific spirit. As the Spirit himself says to Faust in *Urfaust*:

> Gasping, you prayed to see me,
> To hear my voice, to see my face.
> So, your great prayer compelled me,
> And here I am! What pitiful funk
> Takes hold of you, Superman? [Übermensch?]
> Where is the soul that cried out?
> Where is the Breast that created and bore inside itself a whole
> World?
> That, trembling with joy, could nurse such pride
> In your capacity to make yourself the equal of us spirits?
> Where are you, Faust?

The Spirit, with disdain for the Kantian yearning to grasp the thing-in-itself, dismisses Faust/Humanity as merely the mind which observes, not the spirit itself. The Spirit – the elusive phenomenon of Nature in its Whole, its entirety, which poetry and science would, in the breast of Goethe, spend a lifetime trying to understand – pursues its own mysterious life:

> In the deluge of Life, in the storm of action,
> I weave and surge,

From birth to grave
An eternal Sea
An everchanging Life.[23]

Sometime after his sixtieth birthday, Goethe doodled a sketch of the Earth Spirit:

prompting literary critic Friedrich Kittler to describe it as the first instance in the history of German drama of an impracticable stage direction.

The unfinished fragment which is *Urfaust* has been described as 'the concentrated expression of what had most intensely engaged Goethe's mind and heart previous to the period when it was produced'.[24] It contains many of the lines and passages which 'everyone knows' from the finished play *Faust Part One*: the song of the Earth Spirit, the lines commenting on man's vain endeavour to comprehend the past; the dreariness of theory – 'Dear Friend, all Theory is just grey' – contrasted with the freshness and colour of life; and Margaret's songs ('Mein Ruh is hin,/Mein Herz ist schwer' 'My peace of mind is gone, my heart is heavy' and 'There was a King in Thule' 'Es war ein König in Thule'). It also has to be admitted that two of the unfunniest 'funny' scenes in world drama – Mephistopheles hoodwinking the student by dressing up in Faust's academic gown, and the drunken debauch in Auerbach's Cellar – both made the final cut and appeared in the completed *Faust*.

Still, it was a long, long way from being a finished play, and probably he did not conceive of it as a play to be acted. What he had sketched out, in a number of as yet disconnected scenes, was the skeleton of what would one day be *Faust Part One*. It starts – as does *Part One* – with the scholar-mage in his study, monologuing about his intellectual and spiritual frustrations. Immediately there follows the encounter with the World Spirit.

Goethe had not written, had perhaps not worked out, how he was to introduce the devil into the story, so we have none of the cynical bet, which we know from the finished version between 'the Lord' and Mephistopheles, about the temptation of Faust. Nor had he written any scene about the bargain between the pair. The first we see of Mephistopheles in *Urfaust* is of the devil, masquerading as Faust himself, and interviewing the student about his choices of faculty, culminating in the young man deciding to opt for Medicine. It was a subject which Goethe considered pursuing while at Strasbourg. His motives may or may not have been purer than those of Mephistopheles and the student, who dwell on the professional pleasures of feeling, first the pulse of female patients and then, as they allow you to unlace their stays, their hips and beyond. Given his pioneering work on anatomy during his late twenties and early thirties, it is not surprising to find a serious academic interest in scientific medicine dawning in the younger Goethe.

Readers of *Urfaust* will find no Walpurgis Night, and no transformation scene of the aged scholar into a young dude as a result of drinking potions in the Witch's Kitchen.

The chief innovation which Goethe brought to the Faust story is found in the earliest version: namely the catastrophic love affair with a young woman, Gretchen (Margaret), whom he met casually in the street. Listen, Faust says urgently to the devil, 'you've got to procure me that broad' (*die Dirne* – it is the word for a girl, but it is also a term of contempt, and can mean tart). Disturbingly, to modern tastes at least, Faust urges the devil to get to work, observing that she must be at least fourteen.

So here we have a middle-aged man, deliberately setting out to seduce a person who is little more than a child. The devil warns Faust that he, Mephistopheles, will have difficulty corrupting her – she has just come from confession, even though she had been completely innocent and had no real sins to confess.[25] There is something more than unsettling about the scene when Faust slips into Gretchen's bedroom to plant the casket of jewels in her closet, and imagines the innocent life she has led there:

Here the kid lay, her delicate bosom filled
With warm life.[26]

The prison scene, with which the first part of the play ends, is much shorter in *Urfaust* than in *Part One*. It is infinitely, even horrifically, touching. Gretchen is still in love with Faust, if anything even more so, since the series of calamities. 'I have killed my mother' – she does not add – 'with the sleeping draught *you* gave me to give to her' – 'I've drowned my child. *Your* child, Henry. Great God in Heaven, this is no dream! You're moist – wipe it – it is blood – Put your dagger away – my God, I'm going mad.' Faust: 'You are killing me.' Gretchen: 'No, you've got to survive. You, above all things, have to survive.'

This is a terrible 'love' story, and one has seen replications of it in many 'true crime' stories, of a woman, sexually bewitched by a man even though, between them, they have committed terrible crimes. The difference here between such low-life stories in a modern newspaper and the draft of *Faust* is that Gretchen is destined to die a penitent Christian who, we must hope, is redeemed; but Faust, far from getting any kind of comeuppance, as he would have done in the old puppet-play versions, must survive, must go on to greater and greater triumphs, his sentimentalizing of his feelings for Gretchen developing into a quasi-mystical pursuit of the Eternal Feminine, before the great work is done.

The disturbing thing from a biographical point of view is that, while Faust is clearly *not* Goethe, nor even a version of Goethe, he is the creation of Goethe and it is difficult to know to what extent we are meant to sympathize with Faust. He has seduced a girl who is not much older than fourteen. He has given a sleeping draught to her mother, to ensure that the seduction will not be interrupted. (Perhaps Mephistopheles is to blame for the dosage being deadly.) He then runs a dagger through her soldier brother, who is denouncing her for becoming a whore. She has then killed their baby. She pays the price in prison, where she awaits the death penalty, and he gets off scot-free.

In the fragment, there is no knowing whether Goethe has planned some plot development in which Faust will suffer appalling pangs of conscience, or whether there is a part of the story in which we – 'we' the readers – are meant to think Gretchen was 'only' a 'Dirne', a broad, and that 'these things happen'.

Two more features of the *Urfaust* which deserve a mention.

Firstly, the snatch of dialogue in which Gretchen elicits from Faust his creed. She quizzes him about his religious belief and says that it is not good enough simply to say one honours Christianity, it is necessary to believe in it, to practise it, to go to confession and take the sacraments.

Gretchen: Do you believe in God?
Faust: My child, who can say
I believe in a God?
You can ask Priests and Sages: their replies
Seem only to mock the questioner.
Gretchen: So you believe not?
Faust: Don't get me wrong, you beautiful baby-face!
Who can be allowed to name him,
Or who could admit
I believe in him?
Who can really feel
And dare to say
I don't believe in him?
The All-embracing

The All-sustaining
Does he not embrace and hold
You, me, himself?
Does not the vaulted Heaven stretch above
Does not the Earth lie firm beneath our feet?
The eternal stars,
Do they not cast their friendly gaze on us?
Do we not gaze into one another's eyes?
And don't things crowd into our heart and head
Invisibly and visibly weaving
An ineffable mystery around you?
Fill up your heart with this – it's all so great,
And when you are at the peak of bliss with all this feeling,
Then name it if you want ...

At a slightly later point, Faust claims that this is, in fact, not merely what all theologies have at their basis. It is what all hearts believe 'under the heavenly day, each expressing it in their own way'.[27]

This Catechism of Wishy-washy-dom would sustain many a Victorian sage, from Carlyle to Emerson, through the nineteenth century. It is what Goethe in his autobiography calls Natural Religion.

Secondly, another scene worth noting in *Urfaust*, which would be carried through into three later versions, is the very short scene called Night in the Open Country. It is one of the most atmospheric things Goethe ever wrote, worth quoting in full:

Faust and Mephistopheles, on black horses, racing back
Faust: What are they doing there under Ravens' Rock?
Meph: Don't know – what they are doing or brewing.
Faust: They hover, up and down, they swoop, they dive ...
Meph: It's a witches' crew.
Faust: They strew, and bless.
Meph: Come on! Come past, come past! ...

You feel that much of the second part of Wagner's *The Valkyrie* is suggested by this fragment. Gothic, witchy Germany in all its spookiness and mystery is borne past on the wild wind.

4

Some Notes on Suicide

Of course, people do kill themselves a good deal, between fourteen and nineteen. It's an age in life when things are very much out of proportion. Schoolboys kill themselves because they don't think they can pass examinations and girls kill themselves because their mothers won't let them go to the pictures with unsuitable boyfriends. It's a kind of period where everything appears to be in glorious technicolour.

Agatha Christie, *Ordeal by Innocence*

It is difficult to think of any cultural difference more profound than that between societies which approve, and those which abhor, suicide. Imperial Japan, or ancient Rome, saw suicide as noble – certainly more noble than allowing yourself to be humiliated, or to die in disgraceful circumstances. Hence, Seneca, rather than be executed by his pupil Nero, underwent the Stoic's end, slitting his wrists in the bath, while discoursing on the wisdom of his life and his end.

Christians who believe that life is the gift of God have traditionally seen the wilful taking of one's own life as a blasphemous rejection of his bounty. Suicides in the past would be forbidden Christian burial, buried at crossroads, even impaled in some countries. I have attended funerals of those who committed suicide where the coffin was not permitted to be brought into the church for the service.

For this reason, in the post-Christian countries of the West, suicide is seen as a manifestation of disease, the result of depression or other mental illness which should be prevented at all costs. Suicide is the twelfth leading cause of death in the United States, with approximately 47,000 deaths per year. In England and Wales, an average of eighteen people kill themselves every day.[1] In Scotland, for reasons which have not been fully discovered, the statistics are higher – is this because of the shorter days in a Scottish winter, the severity of the winter, the dangerously depressing effect of whisky drinking, as opposed to wine or beer consumption in other countries?

Any article on the subject, whether in specific medical journals or in regular journalism, speaks, understandably enough, of the phenomenon as an undesirable one, something which should be treated as a grave social problem.

But, what if suicide were to be seen in quite different terms, as something reasonable? Sophocles expresses the thought, in *Oedipus at Colonus*, that not to have been born is best. (Admittedly a different thing from justifying suicide, but one thought could lead to the other.)

We do not know how many of the 47,000 Americans who will commit suicide this year have done so as a result of mental illness, or intolerable sadness of one kind or another, and how many have decided that, from an intellectual standpoint, life is simply not worth living.

Goethe returned to the question at various points in his life and, paradoxically, for a man who held onto existence for over eight decades, he never seems to have varied his Senecan view that suicide is a potentially noble thing. His most famous novel, however, *The Sorrows of Young Werther*, was accused (on flimsy evidence) of having created an epidemic of suicides in Europe; here the situation is murkier, and harder to disentangle. In this story what begins as a pastoral of unrequited love becomes an anguished cry of fury against life itself. Goethe himself spoke in retrospect of Werther having gone mad.

The origins of the story are well known, and clearly illustrate the manner in which Goethe made use of personal experience and transformed it into art. In his autobiography, he made no apology for this. He recalled being so depressed, as a twenty-three-year-old, that he slept with a dagger beside his pillow and felt tempted to plunge it into himself. With the retrospect of middle age he was able to say that it was a lack of occupation which led to his depression. He was able to 'laugh off' thoughts of suicide, once he had transformed the incidents of that summer into art. There is a breezy callousness in this memory of an earlier self which is not present in the novel, where the raw emotions of a man who is governed by passions and violent mood swings is captured with unforgettable sympathy and sharpness.

When Goethe finished studying law at Strasbourg University, he went, at his father's behest, to continue his legal studies at Wetzlar, 50 kilometres or so north of Frankfurt, seat of the Supreme Court of the Holy Roman Empire. The little town, of no more than 5,000 inhabitants, was Jarndyce-and-Jarndyce-ville. The place was awash with lawyers, all deep in abstruse cases, some of which had been going on for decades: disputes over tax, debts, ownership of land, inheritance, all nice work for the lawyers. To Wetzlar also resorted ambassadors of the numerous states of the Empire. Goethe was soon a byword for non-interest in their deliberations; the slim Doctor of Law who was studying every subject other than the law; the bright-eyed poet scornfully known as 'the Frankfurt newspaper-writer'. One of his contemporaries there noted that while in Wetzlar he spent more time reading Homer, Pindar etc., than he did pursuing his legal affairs.[2]

The man who dubbed Goethe 'the Frankfurt newspaper-writer' was a young legation secretary, Wilhelm Jerusalem, who had been a student contemporary of Goethe's spell at Leipzig. Jerusalem's grisly fate and Goethe's stratospheric success as a writer were soon to be gruesomely entwined. One of the articles Goethe wrote at this time for the *Frankfurter Gelehrten Anzeigen* was a favourable review of an epistolary novel – in the manner of Samuel Richardson's *Clarissa* – by Frau Sophie von La Roche, to whom he had been introduced by his friend Johann Heinrich Merck. More of Merck in a moment.

Goethe said that Richardson (c.1689–1761) had 'opened the eyes of the middle classes to a more refined morality'. These novels – above all *Clarissa*, but also *Pamela* and *Sir Charles Grandison* – explore the mysteries of the human heart, and – for the first time in literature – primarily the secrets of a woman's heart, the narrative being pursued by letter. This formula makes them hypnotically readable, other people's letters being surely among the most tempting possible reading matter. Young Clarissa Harlowe's misfortunes extend over many volumes. This child of nouveau-riche parents who want to force her into an arranged marriage is beguiled by a libertine, Lovelace, and eventually kidnapped and raped by him. Samuel Johnson, a personal friend of Richardson, was an enormous admirer, claiming that Richardson 'had enlarged the knowledge of human nature, and taught the passions to move at the command of virtue'.[3] Certainly, novels in the form of letters, exploring the turmoil of love life, were manifestos for the continental cult of *Empfindlichkeit*, the cultivation of Feeling as all-important.

It was from England that the epistolary novel was born. Goethe tells us[4] that it was the popularity of these books, by Richardson and Goldsmith, which explained the upsurge of interest in learning English among his young contemporaries.

The epigramist Georg Christoph Lichtenberg (1742–99), who was at school with Merck in Darmstadt, joked that the reason that Richardson's novels could not be imitated in Germany was the appalling condition of the roads. If a girl went through the streets of London in an evening to meet her lover, she could be in France before her father awoke. By contrast, in Germany, even if the father only noticed her departure after three days, he would know that, 'if she'd gone with the Post coach, he only had to trot after her and catch up with her at the third stage along the road'.[5]

Even in the 1770s, the posts in the Holy Roman Empire were swifter than Lichtenberg's joke implies. Certainly by 1808, for example, a letter from Goethe's son in Weimar to the Bohemian spa town of Karlsbad took just over a week. In the height of the summer season, when spa-goers and holidaymakers of the upper and courtly classes were letter-thirsty (to use Goethe's vivid adjective), and when intrigues and love affairs were one way of passing the time, letters could travel from spa to spa much faster.[6] A postilion between two nearby spa towns could give customers next-day delivery of billets-doux and locks of hair.

When he accepted his position as a Privy Councillor at Weimar in 1775 under the young Duke Carl August, one of the many portfolios which Goethe was to undertake would be the responsibility for roadbuilding in the Duchy, and in Weimar there was much to be done. Things were better between Strasbourg, Wetzlar and Frankfurt, where, of necessity, trade and administration required the possibility of fast communication. So when Goethe set *The Sorrows of Young Werther* in Wetzlar and its environs, he could hope that Werther's confidant, Wilhelm, will receive relatively speedy blow-by-blow accounts of the young man's loves and sorrows.

Perhaps almost as important as efficient road surfaces in the development of the epistolary novel was the Protestantism of the lands in which the form first flourished. The letter was a substitute for the confessional. Although Goethe often used Catholic language in an emblematic sense, he was a dyed-in-the-wool Protestant, both in upbringing and in prejudice, and even heroes such as Winckelmann were censured for their Catholicism. The Catholic setting of the *Faust* play, and the intensity of Gretchen's Catholic piety, is never for an instant shared by Faust himself, nor by the author. In fact, one of the first things we overhear Faust doing is him wrestling with his new translation of the Fourth Gospel; he is clearly, like his contemporary Luther, one of the first Protestants.

Goethe's literary education began with the Luther version of the Bible and Klopstock, and the only dabbling he had with Christianity was with the Pietism of Fräulein Klettenberg. The letter, as a form in its own right or as a vehicle for fiction, was both an art form at which he excelled, and his confessional.

Goethe described one of his correspondents, Ernst Wolfgang Behrisch, as his confessor and soul-doctor[7] – and it is probably no accident that the epistolary novel flourished in Protestant lands as a confessional-substitute. Equally, however, for a generation which was Richardson-obsessed, it was easy to make your own life into an epistolary novel when writing to friends. Certainly Goethe, one of the most creative and prolific of letter writers, had a tendency from his teenage years onwards, and right through his life, to treat his correspondents as readers of his own life as love story, or as philosophical or scientific dialogue. His enormous correspondence can be seen as a part of the creative output, the letters themselves often halfway to becoming novels.

As a young teenager, starting study at the University of Leipzig, Goethe had begun a novel, later abandoned, called *The Story of a Heart*. It grew out of his intense relationship with his sister Cornelia. Their mother had lost all her other children, as was so common in the past. Their father hid his feelings of affection behind an 'iron sternness'. Cornelia and Johann Wolfgang, very close in age, had grown up almost as twins, and because most of their teaching was done at home, it was not surprising that – when the brother went away to study in Leipzig, Cornelia was bereft, not least because strict middle-class conventions scarcely allowed her out of the house.

Though he abandoned his novel about the sorrows of young Cornelia, it was inevitable that it had been written in the epistolary form, and, equally, it was inevitable that when he came to write of his Wetzlar experiences, the same genre should have been the channel of his *Sturm und Drang* – 'Storm and Stress'.

The phrase, applied to Goethe in his extreme youth and to those of his contemporaries who imitated him, speaks of an emotional rather than a narrowly political or philosophical revolution. Faust's exclamation to Gretchen, in reply to her quizzing about his religious orthodoxy, was by way of being a manifesto or rallying cry, not only against the rigours of religious orthodoxy but against the intellectual and imaginative constraints of the Enlightenment. Feeling is Everything!

What has been called the Crisis of the Enlightenment spawned two systems of thought which, if taken to their logical conclusions, threatened to defeat both the possibilities of knowledge or of personal optimism.

In the areas of what can be known, epistemology, the British empiricist philosophers, above all David Hume – *A Treatise of Human Nature* (1739–40) and other writings – appeared to have taken rational criticism as far as it could go. If sense-impressions – what we actually experience as objects of sight, touch, etc. – are the only reliable guides to what can be known, then the logical conclusion would appear to be idealist scepticism – that is to say, that very little can be known: certainly nothing can be predicted, and induction becomes all but impossible. By a supreme paradox, therefore, the sceptical principle of Hume, as of Descartes, Locke, Hobbes and the other precursors of the critical scientific spirit – which aimed to make a scientific view of the world possible – actually ended by devouring its own child, and making even scientific statements problematic.

It would be for Immanuel Kant, in *Critique of Pure Reason*, to try to address this problem, and, as we shall see, Goethe, both as one of the most luminous imaginations of the age, but also as a scientist who was by then in effect helping to run the University of Jena, where so many philosophical issues were being aired, was at the forefront of puzzling out the tangles of this Enlightenment Crisis.

If the epistemological problem was one driver towards the Crisis of the Enlightenment, the other was a system of thought which was highly congenial to Goethe, especially as expounded by Spinoza. This was naturalism, the belief that Nature, the observable universe, which followed the laws discovered by Copernicus, Newton and others, was the only world in which we lived: there was no supernatural world beyond the worlds, no need, when discovering sublimity or divinity in Nature, to posit the kind of higher spirit-world imagined by Plato, of which the natural world was but an image or a shadow.

Just as David Hume's rational scepticism would lead to the epistemological impasse – how can we be said to know anything at all, beyond what is indicated by our sense-impression? – so, naturalism, which, as it is discovered in Spinoza, for example, seems modest, reverent, appreciative of Nature, and of the limitations of our knowledge of and our experience within Nature, can become, when taken to its logical conclusion, a pure materialism.

The famous exemplar of this viewpoint was the Baron d'Holbach, an out-and-out anti-Christian materialist who conceived of the universe as a giant machine, of human beings as pre-programmed machines within the machine, entities for whom the concept of free will was utterly illusory. The material was all that there is. His *Le Système de la nature* (1770) was something which, Goethe tells us, he and his contemporaries read as students. 'We did not grasp how such a book could be dangerous. It seemed to us so gloomy-grey, so Cimmerian, so deathlike, that we found it difficult to abide its presence, and shuddered at it as at a ghost.'[8]

One hundred and twenty years before Edvard Munch immortalized a scream, the 'Storm and Stress' made a comparable response to the vision of the world offered by its elders. D'Holbach, who was not in fact ancient, represented *Le Système de la nature*, in his preface, as the testimony of a wizened old man about to go into the nothingness of death, hopeful that he could hand on to the younger generation a truthful picture of their place in the universe of material things.

Determinism, whether it takes the form of materialism, Calvinism or Marxism or Darwinism, is sometimes difficult to argue against with the weapons which it uses of itself: easier sometimes to respond with a scream, a howl of protest – similar imaginative revulsions would produce the Aesthetic Movement of the 1890s, Dada, Heavy Metal. Although Goethe as an old man, recalling the effects of d'Holbach, remembered that 'we laughed at him; because we thought we had seen that old people were not able to appreciate whatever is loveable in the world'.[9] Easy to *say* from the perspective of his own old age, and to write down when he was older than d'Holbach had been when he died. Less easy to absorb when you are yourself young, vulnerable, uncertain.

Sturm und Drang, Methodism in England, Pietism in Germany, what would become Romanticism in poetry and painting, were all in their way reactions against the materialism of which d'Holbach was the relentless spokesman. Frederick the Great went into battle with the materialist Lucretius' *De Rerum Natura* in his pocket, describing it as his breviary. And it was a key text for d'Holbach. Enlightenment scientists disputed his atomism – the belief, sometimes called Epicureanism, that everything is reducible to atoms, that the material world/universe came into being as a matter of pure chance, that there is no need for a Creator or a First Cause to explain the existence of matter – summarized by Lucretius in the lines:

Hunc igitur terrorem animi, tenebrasque necesse est
Non radii solis, neque lucida tela diei
Discutiant, sed Naturae species, ratioque
This dread and darkness of the mind therefore need not the rays
of the sun, the bright darts of day; only knowledge of nature's
forms dispels them.[10]

For d'Holbach the lines were a tag which enabled him to keep up his relentless war against the Christian faith, which fed on darkness of mind and superstition (in his view). For Goethe, however, the scientific study of Nature would be central to his existence, central to his philosophic journey, central to his poetry. Lucretius believed he had removed the necessity for finding a First Cause. It was the ultimate argument against Creationism or Intelligent Design.

Yet, the soul can see and perceive as well as the body, so that Hume's epistemology seems defective. Sense perception is not our only way of having experiences – we have experiences of the soul as well as of the body, of the imagination as well as of the reason. But further to this, the Enlightenment had bought in its entirety Newton's picture of a mechanical universe which ran like a machine. In its initial phases, the Enlightenment philosophers could describe themselves as 'Deists' – technically believing that God had started off this machine and then allowed it to run on its own. The next generation after Newton, d'Holbach could discard the polite fiction that this 'God' was necessary at all.

Newton's model for the universe was the beginning of mechanical and industrial ingenuity which was flourishing in Europe as he wrote. Clocks, mills, mechanical fountains – the universe was like this. But in other parts of the world, philosophy did not make such crude analogies. Shamanic cultures, for example, could remind those who belonged to them of their kinship with the natural world, their kinship with plants, animals and the unseen. Goethe's 'paganism' would always have more in common with this, even before his discovery of Indian philosophy, than it would have with the mechanics of the Newtonian world-vision.

In a letter to his fellow councillor at Weimar, Friedrich von Müller (1779–1849), Goethe said that Lucretius was embittered by the prevailing superstitions of his day. 'Through the whole didactic poem, we sense a dark, grim spirit.'[11] It's worth remembering that, as Karen Armstrong has written,

> People in early civilisations did not experience the power that governed the cosmos as a supernatural, distant and distinct 'God'. It was rather an intrinsic presence that they, like the shaman, experienced in ritual and contemplation ... In India the Brahman, the ultimate reality, was indefinable; it was a sacred energy that was deeper, higher, and more fundamental than the devas, the gods who were present in nature but had no control over the natural order.[12]

It has been said that, for most of human history, there have been two ways of acquiring knowledge about the world, by Logos and by Mythos; the latter is an early branch of psychology. It celebrates and explores the way in which human beings respond to experience, sex, Nature. Logos, on the other hand, deals with objective facts. Logos supposedly comes from the left hemisphere of the brain; from the right sphere comes religion, music, poetry. The Enlightenment saw no use for Mythos, and celebrated Reason, Logos. But Goethe – by instinct, but partly through the example and encouragement of Herder – was trying, both in his scientific attempts to refute Newton, and in his lifelong creation of his own version of the Faust myth, to draw poetry from *both* sides of the brain.

Faust would sigh with regret that he had ever become a theologian – *und, leider auch Theologie!* – but he remained one, nevertheless, and Goethe's great dramatic poem is, among other things, a work of theology. Goethe would cheerfully adopt the 'paganism' of the Enlightenment, but not its crude materialism. This was not for sentimental reasons, but for intellectual ones. He would have agreed with the Neoplatonist Proclus that *esti de Psychis*, the soul can perceive and see. That is why, while rejecting Christianity, and being happy to use terms such as polytheist, or pagan or pantheist, at various stages of his life to describe his position, he never went into the gloomy, Cimmerian deathlike shades of Baron d'Holbach.

—————

Materialism has its own self-contradictions – since if the human mind is no more than the strands and tissues which make up the brain, if the word mind is synonymous with brain and consciousness a sort of fiction, by what criterion can one say that anything is true or false, including materialism itself? As an imaginative force, however, it is able to cast its Cimmerian gloom. Arguments against it, from those who, for example, believe in some form of Platonism – Nature being a mirror of a spiritual realm elsewhere – or from the Deist point of view of philosophers such as Leibniz or popular theologians like Paley, who thought the universe was so complex and well organized that it must have a maker or a mind behind it, were doomed to fail in their attempts to persuade the materialists. This is because the meeting between these contrasting sets is impossible, it would be a conversation between two persons who did not know a single word of the other's language. The cult of *Empfindlichkeit*, or the movement known as Storm and Stress, are not *arguments* against d'Holbach, but they are reactions against him and his elder generation.

The paradox was that d'Holbach – suavely aristocratic, Parisian (though of largely German origin), presiding over a famous salon – was seen by Goethe's generation as just as much part of the Old Regime as were the King of France or his bishops. There is undoubtedly a revolutionary underbelly to *The Sorrows of Young Werther*, though the political elements of the novel are not close to its surface.

One of the reasons Goethe, the conservative-minded Privy Councillor of Weimar, chose to wave aside memories of his early literary success with *The Sorrows of Young Werther*, was the extent to which the novella revealed his youthful impatience with the Empire, and its creaking hierarchies and traditions. When Werther gets the position of assistant to the ambassador (a job rather similar to that of poor Jerusalem, who was under-secretary to the ambassador for Brunswick (Braunschweig)), he is disgusted by the pettiness and snobbery of Wetzlar, and the absurdities of those who would boast of their aristocratic blood and their country estates.[13] It is passages such as this, as well as Werther/Goethe's disregard for conventional morality, which enabled Thomas Mann to see the novella as one of those books which were the forerunners of the French Revolution.[14] Equally, one can regard Mann's view as mistaken. Werther never calls for social or political upheaval. He recognized that the classes were unlike, and could not become like one another. 'I well know that we are not all the same and never can be.' But the fact that the novel could be seen as a forerunner of revolutionary ideas would have been one reason why Privy Councillor Goethe might have found memory of it embarrassing.

———

A delightful distraction from the unsympathetic company of the Wetzlar diplomats and lawyers was Goethe's encounter with Lotte Buff, eighteen-year-old daughter of a bailiff out of town in the country at something known as the Deutsches Haus, the headquarters of the old Order of Teutonic Knights. Lotte's father was recently widowed and Lotte, when first encountered, was acting as nursemaid to her younger brothers and sisters. When he met her at first, Goethe did not realize she was already engaged to be married to Johann Christian Kestner, a young lawyer with the Hanoverian Legation at Wetzlar.

Johann Heinrich Merck, eight years Goethe's senior, and an enthusiastic encourager of his early work, had been bombarded with letters from Goethe describing the beautiful Lotte. When he came down to meet her, he wrote in French to another friend, 'Oh, I've also found the beloved of Goethe, that girl he talks about with such enthusiasm in all his letters. She really does justify anything he can find to say about her.'[15]

Goethe had fallen in love, as he so easily and so often did. Lotte's blonde hair, blue eyes, musicality, fondness for children, enjoyment of poetry, and willingness both to flirt and to listen to Goethe's monologues all endeared her to the poet. In real life, there was never any suggestion that he might have broken up her relationship with her fiancé, nor that he would have wanted to. When he realized that his crush on Lotte was cascading out of control, and that study of the intricacies of property and inheritance law at Wetzlar was going nowhere, Goethe went home to his father's house in Frankfurt.

It was there that Frau Sophie de La Roche introduced him to her daughter Maximiliane, a beautiful woman with jet-black eyes, who had been persuaded by her mother to betroth herself to a much older, and duller merchant by the name of Peter Anton Brentano. Unlike the compliant Kestner, who had regarded Goethe's passion for his fiancée as annoying, but basically an absurdity which he decided to tolerate, Brentano reacted more heavily to the flirtation, and forbade Goethe to enter his house. (Maximiliane married him on 9 January 1774.) It was after this event that Goethe sat down and, very rapidly, in a matter of weeks, wrote *The Sorrows of Young Werther*. The two young women he had loved – Lotte and Maximiliane – were conflated. He gave to Lotte Maximiliane's jet-black eyes, but for the most part Lotte is a portrait of Fräulein Buff.

The central, and terrible drama, however, was suggested by an event which had taken place over a year before, only weeks after Goethe had left Wetzlar. Wilhelm Jerusalem, the young lawyer who had dismissed Goethe as the Frankfurt newspaper-writer, was the son of a well-known religious writer. He had been hopelessly in love with a married woman. The affair had reached an impossible crisis, and young Jerusalem had shot himself.

It was a shock to Goethe, but the manner in which he pumped Kestner for details of the case had something ghoulish about it. What is more, some of the most memorable things about the story – such as the pregnant short line 'No clergyman accompanied him', describing the 'maimed rites' of the suicide's funeral – were taken straight from Kestner's letter describing the funeral, to provide the last line of the novel.

Goethe wrote to the novelist mother of his new beloved Maximiliane – Frau Sophie von La Roche – she who had translated Richardson and penned Richardsonian romances herself in the epistolary mode:

> Merck told me that you wanted to know some of the circumstances surrounding Jerusalem's death. For four months in Wetzlar, we hung out together, and I was there just eight days ago, after his death. Baron Kielmansegg, one of the few he was close to, said that few people would believe this, but he felt Jerusalem's a man who has been so anxious striving after Truth and moral goodness that it had undermined his heart, that he was driven to his sad decision by a failure in striving towards life and passion A noble heart and a piercing intelligence – how easily they turn from extraordinary strength of feeling and life ... but what can I say to you about it? To the unfortunate, secluded fellow, who has been torn from the world by this deed, I have erected for you this monument in your heart.[16]

Already, over a year before he wrote the novel, his letter about the suicide has turned the sad incident into an event, a work of art to share with a novelist.

Goethe was a prolific letter writer and some of his best writing is to be found in his letters. A month after he wrote to Sophie von La Roche, grateful that a man's suicide had given him the opportunity to begin a literary memorial, he wrote to Kestner:

> Christmas Day. Early. It is still dark, dear Kestner, but I have got up and by the light of morning I am going to write down my memories of former times as I summon them back. I have had coffee made and I shall write to you until the dawn breaks. The church towers have sung their hymn, woke up to the tune of 'Praised be Thou, O Jesu Christ'. I always love this time of year and the songs people sing, and the cold makes it completely delightful. I had such a nice

day yesterday that I was afraid for today, but it has begun well and I have no more fears. Yesterday night I promise my two dearest shadow faces that I would write to you, they hover over my bed like God's angels: Since coming here I have cut out Lottchen's silhouette: in Darmstadt I had her image by my bed and, Lotte's [picture] remains beside my head. That pleases me so much ...[17]

How much it pleased her husband-to-be (they married on Palm Sunday the next year, 1773) to receive this letter does not matter much, apparently, since Goethe used the letter form as a vehicle for trying out half-finished concepts, which could turn into poems or fiction.

In his autobiography, he tells us that he had no sooner heard of Jerusalem's suicide than he at once sat down to write *Werther*. In fact, about a year elapsed between the tragedy and the novel. It was the marriage of Maximiliane which triggered the book.

It may well have been the case, however, that, as he said, once Jerusalem shot himself, the book had formed itself almost instantaneously in Goethe's mind. We know from other examples, and most notably of *Faust*, that he could carry in his brain ideas for poems, plays and other compositions for long periods without writing them down.

The question which at first occurred to him was whether to make it a play or a novel. Having decided upon a novel, he chose, in the tradition favoured by Sophie von La Roche, the epistolary form, though unlike the English eighteenth-century novelists who pioneered novels in the form of letters, *Werther* is not an exchange of letters. The first part of the story is told by Werther's letters; the gruesome conclusion is finished by a narrative from his surviving friend.

Faust is a story about power. It is an everlastingly troubling story because the power which is exercised and abused seems to have no moral parameter. No sooner has the scholar-mage made his bet with Mephistopheles than he appears to use power in a completely frivolous way. The man who, before the pact, had been aspiring to high scientific knowledge and an insight into the life of things, devotes his intelligence and energies to rejuvenating his appearance and seducing a young girl and doing nothing to help her when she is condemned to death for killing their baby in an attempt to hide her shame. It is not, at first glance, a particularly elevating story. In its older versions – as we shall see – Faust gets his comeuppance. He is punished for his deal with the devil, and in the famous operatic versions he goes to hell as sure as Don Giovanni goes to hell.

But Goethe's Faust shares with his creator an extraordinary capacity to ride above conventional morality. He is not a self-portrait. He is, rather, the most disturbing and authentic projection in literature of what it would mean to be a modern human being: on the one hand scientifically curious, insatiably so; on the other sex-obsessed and, beyond sex-obsessed, mystic in his pursuit, not of love, but of the Eternal Feminine. Whether we ever find out what that is, the patient reader will eventually discover. Faust the man, and *Faust*, the long, sprawling, two-part drama on which Goethe was working for his whole life, is the story of us, the story of the post-Christian world. The forward thrust of scientific curiosity has been accompanied by a backward glance at an idealized Hellenic world of philosophy and pagan Beauty-worship unshackled by Christian guilt. It is also a poem about the new world order, following the break-up of the Holy Roman Empire in Europe, after the French Revolution and the rise of Napoleon.

The French Emperor claimed he had read *The Sorrows of Young Werther* many times. It was because of this book that Goethe enjoyed – and he did enjoy it – a reputation for wickedness in the eighteenth century, which was only rivalled in the next century by the reputations of Byron and Baudelaire. For *The Sorrows of Young Werther* seemed to many of its first readers an apology for suicide. With suicide as easily the most common cause of death in the Western word for those who die under the age of forty, the matter is of relevance today, even though the story, told in letters in the manner of English novels of the 1740s, and quintessentially 'eighteenth-century' in flavour, seems, like so much Goethe wrote, to be disturbingly contemporary.

But first, the fascinating figure of Napoleon who in many respects seems so much more like the demonically energetic Faust than the self-destroying Werther.

In 1806, Napoleon visited a devastating defeat on the Prussian army at the Battle of Jena – over 10,000 Germans killed, 15,000 taken prisoner. Jena was a university town, under the jurisdiction of

Weimar, 32 kilometres away. It was here that, thanks to Goethe, a Privy Councillor to the Duke of Weimar, Schiller had become Professor of History. It was here that Schiller wrote some of his best plays, such as *Wallenstein*. Here, Hegel wrote *The Phenomenology of Spirit*. Here, the flower of German literary and intellectual life gathered – the von Humboldt brothers (Alexander, 1769–1859; Wilhelm, 1767–1835), the Schlegels (August Wilhelm, 1767–1845; Friedrich, 1772–1829), the poets Hölderlin (1770–1843) and Novalis (1772–1801) – had all spent time. And now, in that fateful year, it was being bombarded by the Corsican conqueror. Though Napoleon himself took no part in the battle, it has been described as the greatest triumph in his career.[18] So, too, Weimar had suffered heavy bombardment. Goethe noted in his diary, on 14 October, that cannonballs were coming through his roof. Napoleon eventually abandoned his idea of reducing the entire city of Weimar to rubble, and he billeted the victor of Jena, Marshal Ney, in Goethe's famous house in Frauenplan.

When the Emperor summoned the Weimar Privy Councillors, on 16 October, Goethe excused himself on the grounds of illness. Goethe's behaviour during the war exasperated the patriots. The singer Mariane Ambrosch was appalled, for example, that on the eve of the Battle of Jena he had insisted that his court theatre go ahead with his production of an absurd comedy called *Fanchon the Hurdy Gurdy Girl*, in which she was expected to sing. She said it would be more appropriate to be holding a prayer vigil. The Austrian poet Friedrich Gentz (1764–1832), who was visiting Weimar, spluttered, 'He is shamefully egotistical and indifferent.' It was at this time that he offended almost everyone by writing his poem 'Vanitas Vanitatum', with its mocking refrain, 'I put my trust in ...' or, perhaps, 'I stake my shirt on.' As the song unfolds, the poet has put his trust in money, worldly goods, women, fame, honour and eventually concludes it is better to put his trust in nothing. 'Nun habe ich mein Sach auf Nichts gestellt. Juchhe!' Hooray!

We'll return to this moment of war later in our story. His apparent indifference to outward events perhaps achieved no more insouciant a chill than when he wrote in his diary, upon the dissolution by Napoleon of the Holy Roman Empire, that the event excited less passion in 'us' – meaning the German people? Or himself? – than a quarrel between the servant and the coachman.

The ways in which Goethe did, and did not, engage with contemporary events will occupy us later. So, too, will Goethe's affectations of indifference to matters which were in fact of the deepest concern to him. These all feed into the masterpiece which is *Faust*. In this chapter, we are concerned with Goethe's most famous novel, *The Sorrows of Young Werther*. And there could be few better examples of its fame than the conversation which its author was eventually to hold with its most famous reader, Napoleon Bonaparte. In the Jena literary periodical *Jenaische Allgemeine Literatur-Zeitung*, in 1804, Goethe had described Napoleon as 'this extraordinary man who, through his enterprises, his deeds, and his good fortune, has set the whole world in a state of astonishment and confusion'.[19] In 1813, in Teplitz, Goethe described Napoleon as 'the gigantic hero of our saeculum'.[20]

Many Germans who had idolized Napoleon at his first emergence on the historical stage – because he appeared to have tamed the monster of the French Revolution, and to have an enlightened view of Europe – changed their minds when Bonaparte invaded their country, and inflicted such heavy loss of life as was seen at Jena. Beethoven, for example, had toyed with the idea of naming the Eroica Symphony after Napoleon ('Sinfonia intitolata Bonaparte' had been written on the score in 1804), but when Napoleon, that same year, had declared himself the Emperor of France, the composer had flown into a rage and exclaimed, 'So, he is no more than a mortal. Now he will tread underfoot all the rights of man and indulge only his ambition.' He strode across his room and scratched out the 'Sinfonia intitolata Bonaparte' and named his work the Heroic or Eroica Symphony.

Goethe, whose obsessions with the Will to Power would feed into *Faust*, undoubtedly found in Napoleon one of the most potent examples of the phenomenon. Faust is Modern Man, who wants to know everything, to penetrate the mysteries of Nature, and to be the Master of the World, as of his own destiny. Science, political power, sexual conquest, the capacity to reorder societies and, finally, to harness Nature for the good of human society, all these are part of the poem. Far from losing his respect for Napoleon, the Goethe who wrote *Faust* remained loyal to it. Yet, when the two men came face to face, Napoleon insisted, as did almost every stranger Goethe ever met, on bringing the subject round to the novella he had written when he was a very young man, the book which made his name.

Napoleon had convened a conference of the German Princes at Erfurt, to which the Duke of Weimar, Goethe's patron and boss, took him along. At the theatre, the Comédie-Française had been brought along to perform Racine's *Britannicus*. The famous actor François-Joseph Talma (1763–1826) played the tyrant Nero. Two days later, when Napoleon and Goethe met, the issue of power and powerful men in literature came immediately to the fore. Napoleon spoke of Voltaire's play *Mahomet*, which Goethe had translated into German. It wasn't a good play, Napoleon asserted. Voltaire had not known how to depict the world-conqueror. It would have been interesting to pursue this conversation. But though Goethe was deeply versed in French drama, it was of his own fiction that the Emperor wished to speak.

Remembering the encounter in his old age, Goethe said to his secretary Eckermann, who recorded so many of his conversations, that Napoleon's progress had been to stride from battle to battle, from victory to victory 'like a demigod'.[21] Meaning it as a compliment, Goethe had praised the 'demonic' element of Napoleon's makeup, 'always lit up, always clear and decisive, and always gifted with enough energy to undertake what needed to be done'.[22] He was, Goethe thought, beyond morality. 'Extraordinary men like Napoleon have stepped outside the boundaries of morality.'[23] He was, in the Nietzschean phrase, beyond good and evil, just as Faust is.

It is clear that Goethe had in fact been displeased by the Emperor's wishing to harp on his early work. And, moreover, that – being Napoleon, his praise had not been undiluted, but that he had suggested an area where the novella could be improved. Napoleon told Goethe that he had studied the book intensely, and that there was one part of the story which did not cohere. Goethe was vague, as he recollected this, and asked Eckermann to guess which part that was. Goethe had smilingly conceded that the Emperor was right in his criticism, but he did not tell Eckermann, or us, which part of the book was at fault. Müller afterwards speculated that Napoleon had criticized the combination of erotic passion and frustrated professional ambition which led to the tragic denouement of the book – which is a young man's suicide.

As is well known, Goethe afterwards basked in being told, by a French diplomat, Karl Friedrich von Reinhard, that Napoleon had exclaimed, on seeing the great German, 'Voilà un homme!'

———

The word *Weltschmerz*, World Pain, is as eloquent a description as any of the condition of mind which leads people to take their own life. 'There is only one really serious philosophical problem,' Albert Camus (1913–60) wrote in his 1942 essay 'The Myth of Sisyphus', 'and that is suicide. Deciding whether or not life is worth living is to answer the fundamental question in philosophy. All other questions follow from that.'[24] One might object that suicide is neither a 'problem' nor a 'question', but an act.

A proper, philosophical question might, rather, be: 'Under what conditions is suicide warranted?' And a philosophical answer might explore the question, 'What does it mean to ask whether life is worth living?' as William James (1842–1910) did in *The Will to Believe*. For the Camus of 'The Myth of Sisyphus', however, 'Should I kill myself?' is *the* essential philosophical question. For him, it seems clear that the primary result of philosophy is action, not comprehension. His concern about 'the most urgent of questions' is less a theoretical one than it is the life-and-death problem of whether and how to live.

Camus's opinion, that people commit suicide because they find the universe 'absurd', meaningless, godless, without explanation or structure, is probably one which would be shared by those who work with contemporary young people who are suicidal. From 2002 to 2018 in the United Kingdom, suicide or injury caused by self-harm was by far the leading cause of death for both males and females aged between twenty and thirty-four.[25] The Western media is frequently made aware, by the testimony of distraught, bereaved family members, usually the parents of the suicides, that their children, hidden away in their bedrooms with a laptop, have been secretly feasting on websites and online propaganda openly defending or even advocating self-harm and suicide. Goethe himself was often accused of this, and his novella *The Sorrows of Young Werther* was seen as a defence of suicide.

As an old man, adopting – in his callow secretary's eyes – the manner and tone of his own Mephistopheles, Goethe expressed regret that he had not been born in England, when he could have become a bishop and been enabled to stash away an income of £30,000 a year (millions in today's money). He would have enjoyed, he said, astonishing the simple multitude with his interpretation of the Thirty-nine Articles. (This was the list of thirty-nine items of faith to which the clergy of the Church of England had to subscribe. You also had to swear faith in the Articles if you wished to attend a university in England – hence, no Catholics at any university in the eighteenth century, and hence Dr Johnson's explanation of why he approved of expelling the Methodists from Oxford – 'You keep a cow in a field but drive her out of the garden.')

One of the reasons that Eckermann's conversations with the ancient Goethe made such an enjoyable book is that there are often moments when the younger man either fails to catch the old man's mocking tone, or only half senses that a joke is in progress. Surely, he suggested, Goethe, had he been an Englishman, could have commented on the Thirty-nine Articles without being a bishop. Goethe replied that without the privilege of wearing a bishop's cap, and pocketing the generous salary he would have enjoyed expounding the Articles, especially Article Number Nine.

We can be reasonably sure that few German readers would have recognized which Article this was. Probably no modern reader, whatever their language, would know this without consulting Google (or, if they possessed such a thing, the Book of Common Prayer). Article Nine states: 'Original Sin standeth not in the following of *Adam* (as the Pelagians do vainly talk;) but it is the fault and corruption of the Nature of every man, that naturally is ingendered of the offspring of *Adam*; whereby man is very far gone from original righteousness, and is of his own nature inclined to evil, so that the flesh lusteth always contrary to the spirit.'

Probably the Thirty-nine Articles had their origin in Germany, and their insistence on the essentially fallen nature of humanity is certainly at one with the Lutheranism which had coloured Goethe's Frankfurt childhood. The extent to which his Faust, and his Mephistopheles, remain part of this theological mindset, and the extent to which they step outside it and embrace a very different set of values, is one which all readers of *Faust* will decide for themselves. In the delightful way that one conversational theme leads to another, Eckermann recorded Goethe moving from the fantasy that he himself might have become an English bishop, to his memory of a visit he had received on 10 June 1797 from one of the most celebrated contemporary bishops – Frederick Augustus Hervey, Earl of Bristol and Bishop of Derry, the so-called mitred earl.

Goethe was getting on for fifty when this visit took place, and he had by then written many poems, plays, scientific treatises and essays. Nevertheless, as was so often the case, when a stranger approached him, it was as the author of *The Sorrows of Young Werther*. He describes one such encounter:

Lord Bristol came through Jena and, wanting to make my acquaintance, he suggested that I should visit him one evening. It was his pleasure, on occasion, to be a little bit rude, but he was manageable if you were a little bit rude back! In the course of our conversation, he wanted to deliver a sermon to me about Werther, and to force me into the conviction that I had lured people into committing suicide. 'Werther,' he said, 'is a completely immoral, indeed damnable, book.' Stop! I cried out to him. If you are going to speak about poor Werther, what tone are we going to adopt against the great ones of the world, who with one stroke of the pen can send a hundred thousand men into the field of battle, of whom eighty thousand will be slain, and who can incite them to murder, arson and plunder? You thank God for such atrocities and sing a Te Deum for them! Furthermore, if, through your preaching about the horrors of punishment in hell, you will make the weaker souls in your congregations anxious, they might well lose their reason, and such poor creatures would end up in the madhouse. Or if, through some piece of orthodox teaching, you sow the seed of doubt in your Christian hearers by the sheer improbability of what you have to say, such souls, half strengthened and half weakened will get lost in a maze, out of which the only way out is death. What do you say to yourself then, and what denunciation will you deliver to yourself? And now you want to call a writer to account and to condemn a work which has been misunderstood by some narrow-minded types, because the world has been freed from at most a dozen idiots and good-for-nothings who could do no better than to snuff out the flickering remains of their feeble light. I should have thought I'd earned the gratitude of mankind for performing such a service. And now you come along and want me to stand trial before this little court martial as a criminal, while you others, the priests and the princes, permit yourselves to be great and strong.

After this dressing down, the mitred earl climbed down from his high horse and was as meek as a lamb.[26]

One of the things which makes *The Sorrows of Young Werther* such an alarming book to read is that the hero/narrator (the story is chiefly told in letters written by Werther to a friend) possesses what appears to be an enormous capacity for enjoyment – of the beauties of Nature, the pleasures of reading Homer or Ossian, and, even after his fateful encounter with Lotte, fondness for the family and for playing with her younger siblings, to whom the eighteen-year-old acts as a sort of mother substitute.

When Napoleon met Goethe, at Erfurt, his question was about the motivation for Werther's suicide. Was it thwarted ambition or unrequited love? Goethe, plainly slightly stung, turned the criticism into flattery by graciously remarking that no one had previously been clever enough to notice this flaw.

On the surface level, Werther committed suicide because the girl he loved was engaged to be married to another man, and he did not want to break up their relationship; but there is much more to it than that, which is why the very short novella, published when Goethe was in his mid-twenties, corresponded so immediately to the mood of so many readers.

Faust, alone in his dusty study by night at the beginning of the play, concludes that all his scholarly activity has been pointless. However powerful his scientific curiosity, he feels no wiser about Nature's secrets. When he is interrupted in his musings by the famulus, Wagner, his despair deepens, since Wagner, a caricature of the archetypical academic, seems merely capable of studying other people's books and regurgitating them. His 'research' consists of nothing better, as Faust scornfully tells him, than brewing a ragout out of other people's banquets.

The mage's strange encounter with the terrifying Earth Spirit, which the famulus had interrupted, had been the start of a vision which was in some mysterious way intolerable. Peering into the life of things, far from being consoling, was terrifying, and made him long for death. He stares with greedy longing at the phial of poison which at that moment looks very tempting. To drink of it, Faust thinks, will not, however, bring sleep and peace. Nor, Hamlet-like, does he dread punishment for committing suicide. It seems, rather, as if death will allow him to stride onward to new horizons, new experiences, new possibilities of knowledge:

> My last drink! I choose it! With my whole soul, I dedicate it, solemnly, to – the Morrow![27]

Suicide in Goethe's writings, or the related, but slightly different idea, a yearning for death, is nearly always tied up with passionate, quasi-religious feelings about love.

'Happy Yearning' – 'Selige Sehnsucht'– (quoted in the next chapter) one of his most mysterious, erotic and successful lyrics, more or less identifies the act of love with the preparedness to die, perhaps even the hope for death.

> And for as long as you don't understand this,
> This truth – Die, and you will become!
> You'll be no more than a woebegone lodger
> On the dark earth.

It is the *Liebestod* decades before *Tristan and Isolde*.

The lyric enters into the curious sensation, or awareness, that in the act of making love, when it is ecstatic, the lovers come close to feeling what it would be like to be 'out of the body', soaring in a wild dance with death. To embrace life in its thousandfold mystery and variety is to be ready for a reckless, perhaps even a self-inflicted death. We meet variations on the theme in his Prometheus-drama:

> There is a moment which is the fulfilment of all that we yearn, forearm, hope for, and fear, Pandora – it is Death![28]

Indeed, half the thrill of falling in love, in Goethe's work, consists in love's intoxicating capacity to make the love-possessed long for death, as happens to young Ottilie, who commits suicide in his profoundly disturbing novel, written in middle age, *Elective Affinities*.

Goethe was probably right to think that the numbers of those who had killed themselves with a copy of *Werther* in their pocket was much exaggerated. And he could not be blamed for the moments of despair which tipped an individual into self-destruction. Not for nothing was *Hamlet* so often quoted in his letters and conversations.

Self-slaughter was to be the end of his friend Johann Heinrich Merck. Merck had married in 1766, and he and his wife had five sons, of whom three died young, and a daughter. Whereas Goethe, who had been brought up rich, never worried about money, and was to be extremely well paid in Weimar, Merck had endless money worries – though, according to Goethe, he was never as poor as he supposed. He took any work which was offered, which included accompanying the Landgrafin Karoline of Hesse-Darmstadt (1746– 1821) to Russia in December 1773 and acting as her secretary. He met Diderot (1713–84) in St Petersburg – a friendship which would be continued in Paris. It was not, however, a happy time of his life. When he returned to Germany, he discovered his wife had had an affair in his absence, and the roaring success of *The Sorrows of Young Werther* was a difficult thing for the older, less successful, writer entirely to enjoy. He displayed his ambivalence by two contradictory gestures. On the one hand – when the novel was banned in Leipzig, on the grounds of its apparently condoning suicide – Merck wrote a satirical verse defence of Goethe, 'Paetus und Arria'. On the other hand, he thoroughly enjoyed bookseller-author Christoph Friedrich Nicolai's mocking parody, *The Joys of Young Werther*, which appeared in the *Allgemeine Deutsche Bibliothek*. Nicolai (1733–1811), the friend of Lessing and Moses Mendelssohn (1729–86), was something of a figure in the Berlin literary world, and his mockery stung. Goethe responded with a poem entitled 'On Nicolai's Grave':

Once on a day, there was a young dude
Who died of melancholy-mood.
And in his grave was laid.
Then a fair Spirit trod that Road,
Who felt like dumping a full load
The way that people need.

So, down he squats upon that mound
And dumps his load upon the ground,
And, proud, surveys his turd.
With a sigh of relief he goes his way
And thoughtful to himself, he'll say,
This meditative word:
'If this young man had cleared his head,
With a really good shit
He'd probably not be dead.'[29]

Despite his initial enjoyment of the spat, Merck tried to bring about a reconciliation between the two of them. And his letter to Nicolai, attempting to persuade him of Goethe's virtue, is of interest. From Darmstadt, 19 January 1776, he told Nicolai that Goethe was capable of great mischief but that he was never treacherous or two-faced. If only the two men could meet, and spend an evening together, they would get on well. Merck said he did not intend to play the role of the go-between. 'If you only knew how often he and I have argued about matters of art, and taste, and if you'd only seen the fellow in his pyjamas and dressing gown, you'd have loved him.'

And then – the sentence which, for Merck, confirmed that Goethe was worth defending – 'His *Faust* is drawn from nature with such absolute authenticity. I've read so many attempts to make something new of the Faust story, and I'm just amazed how the fellow is visibly growing, and is producing stuff which simply would not be possible without boundless self-belief – and maybe that's not possible to have without an element of malevolence?'

———

Goethe liked to joke that he had based the character of Mephistopheles in *Faust* on his friend Merck. Probably, behind the joke lay the sense that Merck had seen things in Goethe himself which Merck, and their friendship, drew out. In the very early days of their friendship, 1772, Goethe once observed that he and Merck 'mirrored one another'.[30] Though the older man might have been 'Mephistopheles Merck', it is perhaps striking that Goethe chose to give Merck's Christian name – Heinrich – to Faust himself.

How deep, or wide-ranging, the mirroring became, we can only guess. Merck wrote to Goethe every few months from Darmstadt, but in a great auto-da-fé Goethe destroyed most of their correspondence in 1797. We know that he shared Goethe's literary interests and he was that most useful of friends to a writer, the one who with humour but no malice was able to tell Goethe when he was writing rubbish. He also shared Goethe's scientific interests and was friends with, for example, the great anatomist Sömmerring (1755–1830). But both men, when grown-up life developed, had busy lives.

When Merck got into his periodic bouts of financial difficulty, Goethe would do what he could to persuade Duke Carl August to lend or give money to 'Mephistopheles'.

Towards the end of his life, Merck dropped (18 October 1788) the formality of addressing Goethe as 'Sie', and in that year there was an impassioned letter in which he unburdened himself. He had decided to invest in a cotton mill, which turned out to be unsuccessful, and in consequence he was bankrupt.

Three years later, on 27 June 1791, the Darmstadt newspaper carried a short item which recorded that 'the author Johann Heinrich Merck' had been found in his office, with a pistol on his desk and a bullet in his skull. The last entry in his diary was entitled 'My heart has burst.' ('Mein Herz. Es platzt.')

It would be a mistake to think that Goethe was a naturally serene person. His serenity was (as his first English biographer said) 'deliberate self-conquest'.[31] 'Had you seen as much as I've seen of the strife,' he wrote, 'you'd try, as I do, to love your life.'

'Ruhe, Ruhe, nur Ruhe' ('peace, only peace'), the old man would exclaim in talk with his friends, rather for himself than his company; and more and more in his writings he lays stress on *Heiterkeit*, cheerfulness, because it is a sign of victory. His refusal 'to give up at a miserable sixty' his determination to use to the full the last embers of the sinking fire sprang from the same deliberate choice: thus it is typical of his whole attitude to life that the last assault upon the centenarian Faust should be made by *Sorge*, care, sheer worry and also that the man should find reserves of strength to meet it.

5

BILDUNG

*A stranger who has just been staying with me has drawn the
following portrait of Goethe: He is twenty-four years old; well-
versed in jurisprudence; a good lawyer, a connoisseur, a reader
of the ancients, particularly of the Greeks; a poet; a writer;
orthodox (according to some Lutheran pastors); according to
some country clergy in Swabia, heterodox; a man who likes to
play the buffoon; a musician; a striking draughtsman; etches in
copper; sculpts in plaster; carves in wood; in short, he is a great
genius, but he is the most frightful fellow.*

Letter from J. G. von Zimmermann
to Charlotte von Stein, January 1775

Goethe was a pioneer in so many forms, not least the so-called
Bildungsroman, or Novel of Character Development. *Bildung* is the
word for education, culture generally, but in this context the genre
means a book in which a young person finds the appropriate path
in life. *Jane Eyre, Huckleberry Finn*, Herman Hesse's *Siddhartha*,
Salinger's *The Catcher in the Rye* are all *Bildungsromane*. The *Harry
Potter* stories have been seen as an example of the genre. As this
random selection of examples shows, it is a modern, post-Goethean
phenomenon, and that for a rather obvious reason. The *Bildungsroman*
describes a young person choosing a path or career. For the huge
proportion of the human race, to this day, no such choice is ever
possible. Certainly, up to, and including, Goethe's lifetime, no choices
offered themselves. The huge proportion of the human race was born

into toil and poverty, and, except when caught up in warfare, not of their making, they were concerned with labouring in order to eat, or to feed their young. Likewise, at the very top of all pre-modern societies, those born to privilege – unless they chose entirely to run away from their wealth and responsibilities, to embrace monasticism, for example – had their future career mapped out for them by destiny. Their lands and properties would determine how they would occupy themselves.

Only the emergent middle classes of the eighteenth century could choose a career. Goethe's father had inherited wealth and increased it by subsequent investment. For most of his grown-up life he did very little except rehang his pictures and rearrange his collection of prints, drawings, china and furniture. He wanted more for his son. He wanted Johann Wolfgang Goethe to be a figure in the world, and becoming a successful lawyer was an obvious means of achieving this status.

Wilhelm Meister, the long picaresque novel which was the prototype of later *Bildungsromane*, was begun in February 1777. By then, without, perhaps, the author completely realizing it, his destiny was sealed. He had begun his life in Weimar.

The years between Strasbourg and Weimar – between the ages of twenty-one and twenty-five – were the time when the shape of his own life was formed. It could be said that, while *Wilhelm Meister* (in its three shapes[1]) is the archetypal example of the form, the autobiography *Poetry and Truth* is also a sort of *Bildungsroman*, written from the perspective of maturity, finished in old age, and seeing that the friendships formed in these years, and the decision which eventually took him to Weimar, were crucial.

On one level they are the years of negative choices. He was sent to Wetzlar to register in the Supreme Imperial Court in 1772; the result was not his becoming a distinguished Chancery lawyer, but his writing *The Sorrows of Young Werther*. He returned to Frankfurt, where he would remain, frustrated, for three years under his father's roof. Here he had the by now familiar experience of falling in love; only in the case of Lili Schönemann, a pretty socialite, the storyline became dangerous. Rather than as in the satisfactory cases of Lotte Buff, Frederika and the rest, who were all conveniently unattainable, Lili, alarmingly, was available, and, indeed, became his fiancée, creating in Goethe the emotional necessity of getting away. These were also the years – not, of course, chronicled in *Poetry and Truth* – of his first, perhaps his only, serious, gay love affair, with Friedrich Heinrich Jacobi.

The quest in the real-life Novel of Self Discovery through which the young Goethe was living was How to Get Away – how to get away from Frankfurt, his father, the constraints of married life. It was also, in part, once the profound relationship with Jacobi had begun, how to get away from a self-definition which included seeing himself as one who loved his own sex. Fiona MacCarthy, in her controversial biography of Byron, pointed out that it was almost certain that the reason the poet had to leave England in a hurry was that he had a dread of the anti-homosexual laws, which were stringent at the time. (Homosexuals were often hanged.) In the Kingdom of Prussia, the gay Frederick the Great introduced less harsh measures against the crime of sodomy – *Strafmilderung* (1746) – and in the Holy Roman Empire under Emperor Joseph II the offence was not punishable by death. But it was a legal offence, and in all likelihood Goethe did not want to be labelled one way or the other for his emotional preferences.

In many ways the early twenties were a positive three or four years in Goethe's life, in which the friendships formed in Strasbourg days, with Herder and Merck, would lead to travels, to new horizons, spiritual and geographical, and new characters in his personal drama. These were the years of his friendships with the brothers Stolberg, satellites of the poet Klopstock, who would take him to Switzerland. In Switzerland – Zürich – he would visit the bizarre clergyman Johann Kaspar Lavater (1741–1801) whose theories about outward human physiognomy as a guide to inner character were widely believed. They were the years of knowing Karl Ludwig von Knebel (1744–1834). And it was Knebel, then working as the family tutor to the ducal family of Saxe-Weimar, who would introduce Goethe to his two young charges – Princes Carl August (1757–1828) and Constantin (1758–93). In the friendship which immediately blossomed with Carl August, Goethe would find his perfect Get Out of Gaol card, which would release him from the constraints of his father's house, the career as a lawyer, the engagement with Lili, the affair with Jacobi, all in one neat move.

The intense, bony face of Pastor Lavater, the prominent nose, the thick, heavy eyebrows, would all have suggested to a follower of his physiognomical theories an intellectually passionate mystic. As a young man, he and his fellow Swiss the painter Henry Fuseli (Johann Heinrich Füssli in those days; 1741–1825) were political radicals, who forced the resignation of a corrupt governor of Zürich. The family of the disgraced politician vowed revenge and Füssli escaped to England, where he became well known as a painter of such formative Romantic projections as *The Nightmare*. Both men were also clergymen, but of a fairly heterodox persuasion. Both were heavily influenced by Swedenborg. Both were keen Shakespeareans – Fuseli, as he was spelled when he settled in London, became a definitive illustrator in the Boydell Shakespeare gallery, and his depiction of *A Midsummer Night's Dream* in particular. Lavater's Shakespeare enthusiasm led to a close friendship with Herder and a keen appreciation of Goethe's Shakespearean play *Götz*.

Lavater made the pilgrimage to Frankfurt with the expressed aim of meeting the author of *Götz*. To Herder, he wrote, 'I know no greater genius among all the writers.'[2] Not everyone shared the belief that Goethe was Shakespeare *redivivus*. Cynical Lichtenberg quipped, 'Goethe has come by the name of a Shakespeare as the woodlouse by the name of a centipede – because no one could be bothered to count the legs.'[3] But no doubt it was beginning to cross Lavater's mind that Goethe might be Shakespeare reborn, since he was a keen believer in the transmigration of souls. He himself had been, by turns, King Josiah (sixteenth King of Judah; c.640–609 BCE), Joseph of Arimathea (who provided the Holy Sepulchre in which the dead Christ was lain) and Ulrich Zwingli (1484–1531), the father of the Swiss Reformation. Goethe, by the way, dabbled with the possibility of reincarnation. The view which was widely entertained by Neoplatonists – as well, of course, as by so many of the Indian philosophers – was not ruled out in the Enlightenment. David Hume himself declared that metempsychosis was 'the only doctrine of the kind worthy of attention by a philosopher' and Schopenhauer wrote, 'Never will a myth be more closely connected with philosophical truth.'[4]

Lavater had read a short theological work by Goethe, 'Letter of the Pastor in **** to the new Pastor in ***', which advocated what he called Natural Religion, in opposition to abstruse, unprovable theological squabbles.[5] In a letter to Lavater which has now been lost – we know of it because Lavater quotes it – Goethe had admitted, 'I am not a Christian.' This would ultimately separate the two men. When Goethe revisited Zürich in middle age, in 1797, he saw the stooped, aged figure of his old friend in a narrow street. Goethe had put on so much weight that Lavater did not recognize him, and the two passed without greeting. It was their final (non-) encounter.[6] In 1775, however, the two were delighted by one another, and the older man was indulgent. 'You shall become one,' the pastor predicted, meaning a Christian, 'or I will become what you are.' The two slept together when Goethe visited him in Zürich, but it is almost certain that this was simply a matter of accommodation, not eros. Sharing a bed with siblings and friends was far more common then than now.

Sharing a bed with Jacobi, however, was a different thing. Goethe met him on the way to Elberfeld in the Bergisches Land. Goethe was travelling with Lavater and the pedagogue Johann Bernhard Basedow from Dessau.

Jacobi, six years older than the poet, had a large nose, curling, rather thin lips, dark, sharp eyes, and a face of high expressiveness and humour. He was considered by all his friends to be extremely handsome.[7] He had his own estate, in Pempelfort. Starting his career as a businessman in Düsseldorf, he had been, since 1772, a financial official in the Duchy of Jülich-Berg. He had already established himself as a philosophical writer and essayist.

As often happened when Goethe fell in love, it was in a triangular relationship. In the case of Lotte Buff and Johann Christian Kestner, Goethe fell in love with *their* being in love. In the case of Jacobi, who was married, it was a simple case of loving the man, but he needed to share this information with Jacobi's wife:

Your Fritz, my Betty, your Fritz, you gloat, Betty, and I swore never to name him to his loved ones until I could name as I believed I should, and now do name … How beautiful, how wonderful, that you were not in Düsseldorf, that I did what my pure heart dictated. Not led in, marshalled in, and excused, I just dropped down from the skies at Fritz Jacobi's feet! And there we were, he and I! And before any sisterly eye had determined what we should and could be.[8]

After their first meeting, Fritz wrote to 'his' Goethe and Goethe replied in a passionate letter of 13 August 1774:

> I am dreaming, dear Fritz, the moment, I have your letter, and soar around you. You have felt that it is a joy to me to be the object of your love. Oh, it is wonderful that each believes he receives more from the other than he gives. Oh, love, love! ... Good night. I soar in ecstasy, not in the heaving waves, for is not that one which shatters us on the rocks? Fortunate are those who have tears. Do not let my letters be seen.

The two would continue to write love letters to one another for years, sometimes as long as ten pages. When he heard that Goethe was writing his memoirs, in late middle age, Jacobi wrote to him, remembering their early relationship, and the time when Goethe had stayed with him at the Schloss Bensberg. On their way to Cologne from the Schloss, they had stopped overnight at the Zum Geist inn, and watched the moon rise over the hills of the Siebenbirge. They sat at a table together, and Goethe recited poems and ballads. Then they turned in. As Jacobi recalled: 'Around midnight, you sought me in the darkness – I became as a new soul. From that moment on, I could not leave you.'[9,10]

It does not seem possible to read this letter – written so much later, when Jacobi was sixty, and remembering the passions of their youth – without acknowledging that the two men had been lovers. In terms of where Jacobi stood in relation to Goethe's development as a thinker and a writer, there is an element of paradox.[11] On the one hand, Jacobi was a sentimentalist, whose novel *Woldemar*, an imitation of *Werther*, was viewed by Goethe with some scorn. In philosophical terms, the two friends would eventually part company.

This early friendship with Jacobi symbolized the complexities and simplicities of Goethe's imaginative response to the world. It remained a bond, from Jacobi's point of view, long after Goethe had outgrown it.

Jacobi is not as famous today as many of his contemporaries. In 1786, however, when Goethe was in his late thirties (and, as it happens, in Italy), Jacobi launched a bombshell into the German intellectual world. It was a key year in the history of intellectual freedom in Germany. Frederick the Great, the Enlightenment King of Prussia who had tolerated freedom of the press and freedom of expression, died, to be replaced by an administration which was far less tolerant. European revolution was in the wings; and political revolution was seen as one of the inevitable consequences of religious doubt. Gotthold Ephraim Lessing had been seen as a pillar of the German Enlightenment but as a man who held the pass, who did not want to abandon Christianity, or the religious outlook, and who believed that a rational religion was a possible thing to entertain. His writing had an enormous influence on younger generations, whether it was in the revival of the German theatre or whether he was writing about aesthetics, the classical past, theology or philosophy.

They had all pinned their hopes on Lessing being able to hold on, not just to religion, but to the Enlightenment – to the power of Reason. Jacobi – and this is why he is of such importance to Goethe, not just because of what did or did not once pass between them when the younger poet sought the older man at midnight in the darkness – attempted to rescue Reason from rationalism.[12] Jacobi would argue, in writings which spanned decades and which twisted backwards and forwards through the skeins of his own logic and illogic, that anybody who developed 'a maximally consistent version of the rationalist conception of reasons as explanatory grounds would be led inexorably to a system that was (A) monistic, (B) atheistic, (C) fatalistic and (D) nihilistic'.[13] What makes Jacobi an interesting thinker is that, while finding these conclusions inescapable, he did not find them acceptable.

Five years after Lessing died, Jacobi upset the applecart by revealing in a periodical that Lessing had confessed to him in conversation that he was actually a Spinozist – that is, a materialist atheist.

That may sound esoteric stuff to a twenty-first-century reader, but it has been plausibly argued that 'almost every notable thinker of the 1790s developed his philosophy as a response to this controversy'.[14] Herder, Kant, Hegel (1770–1831), the Romantic poets Novalis and Hölderlin, Schleimacher (1768–1834) the religious sage, the younger Schlegel, all weighed in. Moses Mendelssohn, the great Jewish philosopher (and grandfather of Felix; 1809–47), denounced Jacobi and said that it was not true that Lessing had embraced the Spinozan heresies. For Hegel, the claim was a 'thunderbolt'; for Goethe, 'an explosion'.

It was in large part to confront and overcome these views that his long-time friend and frequent correspondent Goethe wrote *Faust*. When Jacobi developed his idea that the only way out of the problem was a *salto mortale*, a life-risking leap of faith, Moses Mendelssohn and others thought at this point he was advocating a return to fideism or simple Christian piety. ('Believing where we cannot prove,' as another poet[15] described the position.) But many forerunners or advocates of the Enlightenment had seen that there must be some imaginative, and perhaps on some level rational, exit from the constraints of rationalism.

For Jacobi, as for many of us, these tangled paths would end in an intellectual muddle. In some moods, or some frames of mind, the logical constraints of determinism are too strong to resist. In other frames of mind, such rationalism seems itself irrational, untrue to the imaginative, erotic, ecstatic, musical experience, untrue to the many occasions of life when we have been more, felt more, than such rational straitjackets would imply. This is when we are closest to what Goethe was writing about in *Faust* – and indeed in so much of his poetry, his fiction and his science.

In one of his finest lyrics, 'Selige Sehnsucht', 'Happy Yearning', two lovers, himself and another, lie in the post-coital darkness of the bedroom, with only a candle flickering on the other side of the room. It is usually assumed that the lovers are a man and a woman, but since there seems a strong likelihood that Goethe slept with Jacobi, the poem could well be a memory of when 'around midnight, you sought me in the darkness'.

This is a loose version:

The riff-raff would only deride the idea –
So tell no one. Only the wise know.
Lie in my arms and learn it:
That the beings on earth I most treasure
Are those who yearn for death by burning.
Here we lie. And a strange feeling creeps over you,
After our act of love, begetting in the place we were begotten!
In the cool of the night we lie together
And watch the flickering candle.
Suddenly, in the shadows,

You are caught up in another coupling.
The first copulation has led to a soaring –
You are no longer imprisoned,
A higher desire has snatched you
And you soar, you are weightless –
You are a moth, lusting for that candlelight,
Spellbound, flying into the flames.
And you are burned.
And for as long as anyone doesn't get this,
Doesn't see that this is the truth – we die, and we become –
They will only be stranded as a miserable lodger
On the dark earth.

The dangerous leap into the unknown, the leap of faith, is one not made only by Christian converts, but by all who use language, all who have experienced love, all who have wanted to be more than just miserable lodgers in the dosshouse Planet Earth, all who have looked up and confronted the power of Nature and its beauty, all who have plunged into despair by the impenetrable problems of human life or the wickedness of their own basest intentions. That is the leap which Goethe inspires us all to make. We die and we become.

The controversy sprang from Jacobi's claim that Lessing had confessed to being a Spinozist. Spinoza was thrown out of the synagogue in Amsterdam because of his supposed heterodoxy or even atheism, whereas he was in fact a profoundly religious thinker, believing, as Plato had done, in the timeless immutability of mathematical truth and in the eternity of mind. 'Our mind, so far as it understands, is an eternal mode of thought' – an idea which Spinoza derived from and shared with the Neoplatonists.[16]

In the eighteenth century, however, the name 'Spinoza' was a dog-whistle, signalling not merely a departure from Christian orthodoxy, but the embrace of actual materialist reductionism on the Baron d'Holbach model. For Jacobi, Lessing was the only German Enlightenment thinker (*Aufklärer*) who 'was willing to take his reason to its limits and to confess its atheistic and fatalistic consequences'. Jacobi, who had begun as a critic of the Enlightenment because it was vainly seeking for rational explanations of matters which could only be adopted as matters of faith, abandoned his fideism and 'came out' as a reductionist materialist. 'The sum and substance of Jacobi's polemic was ... to renew the threat of a radical naturalism, a materialism in Spinozistic dress.'[17]

It was largely thanks to Jacobi that the German idealist philosophers post-Kant – Fichte and Hegel in particular – felt compelled to seek a way out of the brutal logic of the 'Spinozistic' position. If external things are only appearances, and appearances are nothing but representations, as in Kant, the possibility of knowledge – knowledge of *anything* – evades the mind. It makes science, and the jobbing epistemological tasks of the philosopher, difficult. It makes the assertions of the theologian impossible.

Goethe, both as a scientist and as a theological-scientist, would share some of Jacobi's fideism, while recognizing it as inadequate. In his colour theory, for example, as in so much of his poetry, and in *Faust* above all, he would come at the 'pantheist controversy' from a very different angle.

The year following the intense relationship with Jacobi was dominated by the *Bildungsroman* question – what would come next in the young protagonist's Apprenticeship Years? Was the future to be spent in the (increasingly stultifying) parental home in Frankfurt, or would there be a let out? 1775 would be the year in which his destiny was decided.

Destiny had written a *Bildungsroman* with a surprise twist. It was the irrelevant detail, the apparently casual and unimportant encounter, which would prove decisive. Goethe, who was devoting his mornings to poetry, his afternoons to jurisprudence, his evenings either to a busy social life among people his own age in Frankfurt or returning to his writing. He also had aspirations, which would continue well into middle age, to become a painter. On 12 December 1774, he was painting as the light faded. He looked up and saw approaching a slim young man whom he thought to be the one he loved. He rose, rushed forward to embrace his Fritz – but it was not Jacobi. It was a Prussian army officer called Karl Ludwig von Knebel, who was an ADC to the young Duke of Weimar. The ducal party – the young Duke, Carl August, his younger brother Constantin, Carl August's tutor, von Görtz

(1737–1821) – were staying at the Rotes Haus inn. They were on their way to Mainz, where the eighteen-year-old Duke was to arrange his betrothal to the Princess Luise of Hesse-Darmstadt (1757–1830); they were then to go on to Paris. Carl August did not want the time in Frankfurt to go by without the chance of meeting the author of *The Sorrows of Young Werther*.

So, Goethe obliged, and went to the inn. Carl August was overwhelmed by the poet's brilliance and charm. Johann Eustachius Graf von Görtz, an aristocrat of the formal old school, was less impressed: 'This Goethe is a vulgar chap, that's for certain. Goethe and I will never find ourselves again in the same room.'[18] That prophecy was untrue.

The ducal party went on – Carl August was duly betrothed to Luise on 19 December,[19] and Goethe returned to his prime devotions, poetry and love.

'If I did not write dramas, I should soon be lost,' he wrote to a young woman with whom he professed himself to be passionately enamoured. (These were the months when he wrote the unimpressive *Stella*, and the sketch for what became *Egmont*.) His correspondent was Augusta, Countess Stolberg (1753–1835). She soon began to see the similarity between his letters to her and those of the young Werther; their correspondence had begun when she had written a fan letter to him, having admired *Werther*. She recognized that his need to write to her – she quickly became 'Du', not 'Sie' – was the need to construct a fiction of love. 'I will come to a bad end ...' 'So much happiness and misery. I don't know whether I am in the world or not ... Don't abandon me ... in the time of sorrow that might come when I can be free from you and all my loved ones ... save me from myself.' The intensity of his expressions of affection come as a surprise to the reader, when one remembers that he never met Augusta in person.

Her brothers, he did befriend – Friedrich Leopold (1750–1819) and Christian von Stolberg (1748–1821). When they passed through Frankfurt on their way to a Swiss tour, they persuaded Goethe to join them. Somewhat to their surprise, he accepted the chance to leave Frankfurt with these amiable but total strangers.

There was a reason. As Goethe admitted in a letter to Herder, 'I recently thought I was approaching the port of domestic bliss and a firm footing in the true joy and sorrow of earth but am now wretchedly cast out again on to the deep.'[20]

While pouring out his heart in letters to an essentially imaginary lover – Augusta – Goethe had also grown close, in Frankfurt, to the daughter of a Frankfurt banker. Elisabeth (Lili) Schönemann (1758–1810), pretty, flirtatious, rich, was seventeen when their romance began in January 1775. Of course, he was in love again – or 'in love'. The family were less keen. Johann Caspar Goethe was comfortably off. The Goethes did not have to worry about money. There is a world of difference, though, between the comfortable middle class and the seriously rich, which is what the Schönemanns were. Much of the courtship was conducted at the country house of Lili's uncle, Bernhard d'Orville, in Offenbach. They were formally betrothed in April, and Goethe bought, not rings, but golden hearts.

Eckermann rightly complimented Goethe on the passages of *Poetry and Truth* which spoke of Lili. 'It is all very much like a novel,' he said. And he even proposed writing it in five-sectioned arrangement as if it were a fiction.[21] By the time he was over eighty, Goethe was imagining that he could still feel her breath on his cheek. 'In reality, she was the first woman whom I loved deeply and in truth. Moreover, I can say, she was also the last.'[22] It is a good indication of the obvious fact that, when Goethe spoke of his love life, there was often more poetry than truth in the words which came so eloquently forth. If Lili was the last woman he ever loved, what are we to make of his ardent relationship, once he reached Weimar, with Charlotte von Stein? What of Christiane Vulpius, the woman he married and with whom he lived for years? What of the poems of heartbreak he wrote in his seventies when Ulrike turned down his offer of marriage?

The strong objections to the marriage by the Schönemanns would probably have saved the day. But what if Goethe – who evidently *believed* his own story when he was wooing Lili, just as he believed himself to be in love with Augusta von Stolberg, with Jacobi, with Lotte Buff, with Frederika – found himself in a situation from which there could be no selfish escape into the essential, safe solitude of the writer's life? Lili's brothers thought Goethe was oafish and not of their class. Her mother was afraid that Goethe was a heretic, perhaps even an unbeliever. Nearly all his friends opposed the match. And in the emotional chaos of the situation, he was able to describe himself as if he was an actor, dressed in the wrong costume and for the wrong role.

> If you can imagine a Goethe in braided coat, dressed from head to foot in a costume the most gallant, amid a glare of chandeliers, glued to the card table by a pair of bright eyes, surrounded by all sorts of people, driven in endless dissipation from concert to ball and with frivolous interest making love to a pretty blonde, then you will have a picture of the current Goethe Carnival.[23]

At another moment, however, swooning from the effect of Lili's love, he was taking seriously her madcap scheme – if the family tried to frustrate them – of their emigrating together to the United States.

It was definitely the moment for a break, and that was when the Stolbergs suggested he accompany them on their tour of Switzerland. There was another reason, too. The journey would enable him to pass through Emmendingen. This was where his unfortunate sister Cornelia had fetched up, having married Johann Georg Schlosser (1739–99), chief administrator to the Margrave of Baden. Cornelia was very close to her brother, and very like him in character. The utter wretchedness of her marriage tolled a reverberant tocsin in his heart.

Had the aged Goethe said to Eckermann that Cornelia was the last woman he had ever loved, there might have been some senses in which this was true. There is no need, as some biographers have done, to suggest their relationship was incestuous, but there are points of comparison to the close bonds which tied William Wordsworth to Dorothy. The pair had grown up together. Goethe was Cornelia's best love, no doubt about that. Her marriage was very unhappy. She was lonely in Emmendingen. When Goethe arrived, he found that she had been bedbound for months, plunged into psychosomatic illness and depression. She rose from her couch for her brother, and they had long walks, and conversations deep into each night. In 1777, aged twenty-six, she would die giving birth to her second child, a daughter. It seems certain that, when he visited her with the Stolbergs, she did her best to dissuade him from marrying Lili. As already suggested, Goethe's divided self, while being besotted with Lili, was searching with some desperation for an escape.

The temporary escape was their visit to Switzerland. Mountains figure large in *Faust*, as they do in so many of Goethe's shorter poems. The scenery made a deep impression, and, when they reached the St Gotthard Pass, Goethe was tempted simply to part from his friends and to travel onwards alone to Italy.

This scheme, after he had returned to Frankfurt, met with his father's heartfelt approval. Old Johann Caspar's visit to Rome, and his collection of *vedute*, was the most interesting thing which had ever happened to him, and he longed for his son to have the same experience. Moreover, this was the obvious way, as both the parents agreed, of ending the unsuitable engagement with Lili.

In a letter to the Stolbergs' sister Augusta, Goethe said he was not returning to Frankfurt for Lili's sake – 'I am fed up with the whole world!'[24]

The plans for Italy were made. Luggage was obtained, clothes bought. And as the story is told, in *Poetry and Truth*, it was at this point that the young Duke of Weimar returned to Weimar, after his visit to Paris, and issued an invitation. Why did the author of *The Sorrows of Young Werther* not come to pass the winter in Weimar? He could see the Court of the Muses, established by the Duke's mother, Anna Amalia, get to know Christoph Martin Wieland (1733–1813), playwright and man of letters, and become an ornament of their court.

> My attachment to the Duke from the first moment I saw him; my veneration for the Princess whom I had known for a long time, though only by sight; a desire to render some personal service to Wieland, who had shown himself so magnanimous towards me [Goethe had mocked the older writer's rococo versions of classicism] were reasons enough to make me anxious, no, determined, to go, even had I been free from my unhappy passion. But I had the additional incentive of being forced to flee from Lili somewhere or another.[25]

So, it was all set. Or so Goethe believed. The Duke and Duchess and their entourage were waiting for a landau which was being built for them in Strasbourg. The arrangement was that they would send it to Frankfurt to pick up the poet when it was ready.

While he waited, Goethe worked on a new play, *Egmont,* and tried not to listen to his father, who did not believe that the Weimar Prince had any intention of fulfilling his promise. He continued to urge his son to go to Italy, and, when a week had passed, and no carriage arrived, Goethe began to acknowledge that the invitation had not been meant seriously.

He set off to visit a friend in Heidelberg, with the intention of going on from there to Italy. It was after he had set out that he was overtaken with a letter, brought from the Duke's chamberlain, Johann August Alexander von Kalb (1747–1814). The landau had taken longer than expected to be completed. Von Kalb had then needed to take it to Mannheim on business, and by the time he reached Frankfurt to pick up Goethe, the poet had already departed.

The autobiography ends with the author of *Werther* setting off to become the courtier at Weimar. Storm and Stress would be replaced by another existence. Wilhelm Meister's last journey was one of Renunciation, his spiritual guides the Renunciants. Leaving Frankfurt for Weimar was not, however, a renunciation in the monkish sense. He was giving up an earlier self in favour of a new one, rather as an actor, after a successful run in a particular part, accepts the chance of something new.

The idea of making himself into a work of art, role-playing, hoping the fragments of experience would form part of a 'great Confession', was central to him. The second half of his writing life was an exercise in editing out versions of the self which he found displeasing; rewriting the past. He probably never came to the consciousness of how exploitative the artist must be, in using the events of his own life, and the characters who had meant much to him, as figurines in his art; or, if he did come to such consciousness, this did not seem to have much troubled his conscience.

This, indeed, is the great theme of one of the best books ever written about Goethe – Thomas Mann's novel *Lotte in Weimar.*

6

WEIMAR

*'The true history of my first decade in Weimar, I could only
represent in the raiment of fable or fairy-story. If one wrote down
the actual facts of the case they would never be believed'*
Goethe to Kanzler von Müller

Mann's novel *Lotte in Weimar* depicts a few days in October 1816
when Charlotte Kestner (born Buff) returned to Weimar to visit her
sister, whose husband had a government job there. From the moment of
her arrival at the chief hotel, the Elephant, where her name is instantly
recognized by the old waiter who watches her sign the register, to the
extraordinary closing scene in which, swathed in the dark of night,
and his caleche, Goethe and Lotte converse, she both is and isn't the
'Lotte' in his novel. Hearing of her arrival in the town, Goethe has
asked her to dinner just once – and to a stiff, formal dinner at that.
To the intense embarrassment of her daughter, also called Lotte, the
sixty-seven-year-old Charlotte Kestner has turned up for this occasion
wearing the very dress, white, trimmed with pink ribbons, with which
the young Werther/Goethe had fallen in love in Wetzlar all those years
previously. To this extent, she is humorously colluding in the idea that
she 'is' Lotte. But Goethe's behaviour revolts her, as does that of his
sycophantic guests. The house, with its splendid classical sculptures
and its copies of great European paintings hanging on the walls, is
more museum than home. Goethe, moreover, is the chief exhibit. He,
in his court dress and decorations, is a monster ego, holding the entire

table in thrall as he runs through anecdotes, or holds forth about his scientific theories. The sense that he is an exploitative monster, who has 'used' all the human beings in his life for the purposes of his art, is also mingled with disappointment at his cynicism, and his rather oafish drunkenness.

In her very first hours in the Elephant, Lotte had been visited by a succession of different witnesses who analyse Goethe's character and art. They include Dr Riemer (1774–1845), his sometime secretary who, having compiled a Greek–German dictionary and been a don at the University of Jena, had been enlisted in the Goethe household in Weimar as a tutor to his son, and general dogsbody; the intellectual Adele Schopenhauer (1797–1849), sister of Arthur (1788–1860); and Goethe's son August (1789–1830). Riemer and Adele Schopenhauer offer us a pretty devastating view of Goethe the man.

In her dialogue with Riemer, Charlotte Kestner asks him what sort of young man it could have been who fell in love not so much, or not only, with her, but with the love which existed between her and her fiancé. 'Despite my reluctance, and with the best will in the world, I could not get rid of a word which came back to me – parasitism.'[1] She says this while acknowledging Goethe's unquestioned genius, and Riemer responds with fervent agreement. Poetry, he says, has nothing extra-human about it, other than the fact that it is divine. For thirteen years he had been noticing, as observer and private secretary, the total egoism which was part and parcel of the poetic personality.[2] But he acknowledged that it was an incarnation of the Godly.

Fräulein Schopenhauer is in a way even more damning. The matter she wants to discuss most urgently with Lotte is the forthcoming engagement of Goethe's son to her best friend, Ottilie von Pogwisch, a fellow member of the literary and intellectual circle to which Adele Schopenhauer belongs. August von Goethe is, she reveals, an oaf – a drunken womanizer who does not have enough originality to have opinions of his own, but merely parrots his father's opinions and prejudices. He has made himself hated in the town since – in contrast to all their young male friends in Weimar – he refused to enlist with the Prussian army in the final push to defeat Napoleon. August copies his father in idolizing Napoleon, and despising German nationalism. But – and this is what troubles Adele – and, by extension clearly troubled Thomas Mann – the very faults which are so grossly on display in Goethe *fils* are recognizably inherited from the poet – or, if not inherited, they are manifest, if crude, imitations of some of his predominant personal qualities.

> Certain characteristics which are in the son unhappily and destructively developed, can be found in the illustrious father already foreshadowed. It is difficult to recognize them as being the same: indeed, reverence, piety would shrink from any such recognition. In the case of the father, they are held in such happy, fruitful, even loveable balance that the world receives them with joy, whereas in the son they reveal themselves as coarse and sensual and all their moral offensiveness is obvious.[3]

She develops – or Mann develops through her lips – the notion that the imaginative processes which gave birth to that superb novel *Elective Affinities* are recognizably the same qualities which in the talentless son appear merely as gross faults:

> I have already spoken of my scruples, which are connected to the critical investigation into Truth itself, and it throws up this problem: whether the Truth is something worth striving for, whether knowledge of it, is morally incumbent upon us, whether we are obliged to it, or whether there is such a thing as a Forbidden Truth.[4]

The fictitious conversation between the two women – his early crush on Lotte Buff and the friend of his soon-to-be-daughter-in-law – takes place in the town where Goethe's life-drama was in reality played out. It is a conversation which happens after the momentous events of his life have been largely accomplished – his establishment of himself as the Sage of Weimar, the distinguished Privy Councillor. It also takes place after those events which had convulsed the world in his lifetime. Chief among these were Napoleon's failure to achieve world domination, and the philosophical revolution which came about with the Enlightenment – especially when Kant undertook to confront the apparently unconquerable empirical scepticism of Hume, and to answer the question of how we can be said to know anything at all.

Humanity at its most monstrously super-powerful, careless of how many lives it wrecks and destroys in pursuit of its own power: Napoleon. Humanity in pursuit of knowledge, and with it, the possibilities of modern science and a true understanding of our planet and what we are doing to it, and to one another on it: these were the great dramas of Goethe's age and they were incapsulated in *his* great poetic drama, *Faust*.

Mann's novel, with humour and tenderness, demythologizes the old man of Weimar who would devote the final quarter of his life to a patient editing of his own life-experiences. Mann takes us to the heart of the creative endeavour itself, and – as one of the greatest novelists who ever lived, he knew whereof he spoke. For much of the time that he was in Weimar, Goethe left *Faust* in its folder, untouched but not unheeded. In fact, in every decade between its beginning in the 1770s until its completion in the last year or so of his long life, Goethe did make significant changes to the work. But, such was his prodigious capacity for holding his works unwritten in his head, we would be wrong to think he was not at work on *Faust* merely because he was not writing it. (He told a friend the entire plot of *Elective Affinities*, in all its intricacy and disturbing twists and turns, years before he wrote it down.)

When Goethe set out for Weimar, in autumn 1775, he went as the guest of the eighteen-year-old Duke. It was not exactly specified how long he would stay, but he could not have guessed, either that he would be taken on as a member of the Duke's Cabinet, nor that he would stay in Weimar for the rest of his life. As recently as 1773, when Lotte's husband Kestner had taken an administrative post at the court of Hanover, Goethe had grandly said, 'Kestner, I deeply need to nurture the talents and powers that I have. I am used to following my own instincts and for that reason, I cannot be the servant of any prince. To learn political subordination would make me wince.'[5]

But needs must. If he had stayed in Frankfurt, practised as a lawyer, married Lili, or someone like Lili, life would have been very different. The existence of a prosperous upper-middle-class lawyer would not have allowed that manuscript, which he carried with him to Weimar among his belongings, the unfinished *Faust*, to become the great life achievement. He was intent upon becoming Goethe, so it now seems obvious that to pursue the life of a prosperous lawyer-burgher was something that he was never going to do, even if it was not obvious at the time.

The intense, heady relationship between Carl August and the twenty-six-year-old Goethe could be described as a bromance. It was not a reciprocally homosexual thing. Carl August's sexual interests were always directed towards women (far more of them than his new young wife found quite bearable), though Goethe was bisexual in a light and not especially active way. There are ways and ways of being a courtier. The mainstream of such people – otherwise, no royal or aristocratic system, no court, could survive – are a combination of deferential and quietly superior to their royal/aristocratic employers. These are the men and women who oil the wheels of a court, and without them, such an institution could not exist. History knows little of them unless they are good diarists, like the Duc de Saint-Simon, or Tommy Lascelles (secretary, by turn, to Edward VIII, George VI and Elizabeth II), unless they somehow fall out of their constricted role and make an unsuitable splash, through treachery or scandal.

In dull courts – and most courts, to function well, have had to be dull – the courtiers run the show, and they are known to one another, but not to the outside world, nor, especially, to history. And this is all that happens. You have your King, Queen, your Grand Duke, and you have your courtiers, themselves of aristocratic lineage, who oil the wheels and keep in motion both the ceremonial life of the court and the political administration which it requires.

Any such small duchy in the Holy Roman Empire, in 1775, however conservative and obscure, was about to see cataclysmic change. We look at Fragonard's *The Swing*, painted a couple of years earlier, and realize that the young woman is quite likely to fall off her perch and be thrown into the air by fate. Beaumarchais's Barber, who first appeared that year at the Comédie-Française in the Tuileries, revealed himself as cleverer, and ultimately more powerful, than his aristocratic employers – a message not lost on the Parisian audiences. Only three years after Duke Carl August's fascination with Goethe began, the good people of Boston, Massachusetts, would throw their tea into the harbour.

The other way of being a courtier, corresponding to the role of the clown or jester in earlier ages, is to kick over the traces and to be outrageously 'oneself', thereby allowing the royal personage you serve to feel liberated by the conventions of courtly life. This is the role adopted by Mephistopheles to the Emperor in *Faust Part Two*. Goethe began as the second sort of courtier – the licensed buffoon. He fairly quickly morphed into the first sort, the conventional servant of royalty.

Goethe never bothered to join revolutionary movements. Once he had thrown in his lot with the Grand Ducal family of Weimar, he did not feel emotionally or intellectually inclined to do so. Goethe and Carl August were on some level (and by modern standards) extremely conventional. For example, although they had many a picnic together and frequented country inns, Goethe would never have been permitted to dine at the ducal table in Weimar itself since he was not an aristocrat; and it was only after he was ennobled by the Emperor in 1782 that he was allowed to the high table.

Goethe, who had cut a dash in Frankfurt and Strasbourg, large modern cities, at first seemed a bird of too exotic a plumage for this little town of Weimar, which had already had its problems. It was badly in debt. Erfurt was the nearest place of any size or substance. Weimar, cut off from any commercial or industrial centre by poor roads, was agricultural. Any luxury goods had to be imported, so the prices in the shops were high. The entire Duchy did not number more than 100,000 inhabitants in all. Weimar the town numbered no more than 6,000 inhabitants, most of them peasants. There was no one making pottery or ribbons or carriages. There was a printer but no bookbinder.

> To Weimar befell a particular Fate –
> Like Bethlehem – Judah – both small and great.[6]

Into this remote fastness, all but inaccessible in muddy weather, the Grand Duchess Anna Amalia had, with great spirit and animation, created what she (three-quarters seriously) called the Court of the Muses.

She had married the eighteen-year-old Duke of Saxe-Weimar-Eisenach – Ernst August Constantin II (1737–58) – when she was just sixteen. She was the daughter of the Duke of Brunswick and her mother was the sister of Frederick the Great. (Her brother was a general and field marshal in the Prussian army.)

She experienced a culture shock when she reached Weimar. There was a marked contrast between the impoverished provincial backwater and the Sans Souci of her Prussian uncle, Frederick the Great, where Voltaire spoke of literature and Bach accompanied the accomplished flautist Enlightenment King.

Instead, she found a duchy where the treasury was deep in debt and whose very political existence as an independent entity was imperilled. That was because the neighbouring Duke of Gotha,[7] who hovered like a bird of prey, would absorb Weimar into his domains – if she failed to produce a male heir. She did manage to do so – in 1757, Carl August, our Duke, was born, and a year later, after her husband had died of tuberculosis, another boy, Friedrich Ernst Constantin.

Weimar seemed so much the home of bumpkins that when she had first arrived in the Schloss there, her lady's maid had asked her if the gate was bolted with a carrot.[8] Deep into Goethe's old age, sheep were driven through the streets from one pasture to another on a different side of the town. One says town, but, as a visitor observed, Weimar was really just a Schloss, a ducal court, with a village attached. The day was punctuated by the cows, mooing and splatting through the streets on their way to the milking parlours and back, something that Grand Duchess Maria Pavlovna found utterly astonishing.[9] (In villagey Weimar, local prostitutes were put in a pillory and beaten with cudgels, usually followed by a few weeks in prison. The sex workers who serviced courtiers and the small standing army were brought in from Gotha, Leipzig or Coburg and were ignored by the police.[10])

Anna Amalia was determined to bring the Muses, and a bit of architecture, to provide the bucolic scene with intellectual edge. The Empress Maria Theresa and her husband Francis of Lorraine both urged her, when she was widowed, to surrender her Duchy to Gotha, and/or to the neighbouring Saxe-Coburg. She refused. Moreover, even if she could not make tiny Weimar as grand as her uncle's court in Berlin, she could at least imitate his cultural and stylistic verve. She made the bold and brilliant decision to hire as a tutor for her eldest son Christoph Martin Wieland, the first German translator of

Shakespeare and himself an accomplished poet and man of letters. Weimar was to be a *Musenhof*, a Court of the Muses.

In 1784, Kant memorably wrote, 'If someone asks are we living in an enlightened age today? The answer would be No. But we are living in an Age of Enlightenment.'[11]

Wieland had dreamed of a career writing plays and opera-libretti in Vienna, but the vogue in the Imperial capital was all for Italian libretti. He was humble enough to accept Anna Amalia's offer, settled himself into Weimar, brought the two Princes up to a level of cultivation, started a monthly literary periodical – *Der teutsche Merkur* – and wrote plays in his spare time.

Anna Amalia responded by establishing a theatre where she persuaded the highly distinguished company of Heinrich Gottfried Koch (1703–75) to put on plays. When Goethe had been established in Weimar, it was thanks to Anna Amalia that Koch and his company premiered *Götz von Berlichingen* in Berlin. It was in Weimar that Christian Felix Weisse (1726–1804) composed song-cycles and Singspiels. His operetta *The Hunt* was dedicated to her. (Goethe would later write for him.) She put on concerts. She built the stupendous rococo library of which Goethe would one day be the director. All this was in place when Carl August inherited the dukedom, aged eighteen. In that same year, he had married Luise of Hesse-Darmstadt.[12] It was not to be an especially happy marriage. The day after her wedding, she wrote to her brother-in-law in St Petersburg (he would one day be Tsar Paul; 1754–1801), 'You would have sympathized with me if you'd seen me on the day; I was in a bad way. Thank God it's all over.'

She did not have much in common with Carl August, who would have preferred to be a soldier than a minor provincial duke, and whose chief passions were hunting and wenching. He saw no reason to give up either enthusiasm simply because he had gone through the statutory – for a minor princeling – business of marriage.

Moreover – perhaps inevitably, given Anna Amalia's strength of character – Luise did not get on well with her mother-in-law. 'The two women are completely sick of one another,' reported a courtier within weeks of the marriage.[13] By the time Goethe arrived in Weimar, there were two courts, one in Anna Amalia's house – given to her by her former Prime Minister von Fritsch, who had built it for himself – and the other in the house of the Finance President, since the principal

Schloss had been devastated by fire two years earlier. The theatre had been completely gutted and the players had returned to Berlin.

The fire had begun when the principal Schloss, in which the Court of the Muses had assembled, was struck by lightning. All Germany was shocked by the extent of the blaze, and when Goethe arrived in the town a little over a year later, the castle was still a blackened ruin. It would take ten years to rebuild properly.

Goethe arrived as a winter guest. Inspired by Klopstock's poem 'The Skater', he persuaded Carl August to take to the ice. It was soon the court craze, and they had all donned their skates. The passion for Klopstock – which Werther had shared with Lotte, it will be remembered – did not last long, however. When Goethe had sent the older poet some of his own lyrics – in the Storm and Stress mode – Klopstock wrote back, in a fatherly spirit, urging Goethe to curb his behaviour. Rumours were by now flying round Germany that the friendship between Goethe and the young Duke was bringing them both 'discredit'. As the father of German poetry, Klopstock felt he had the right to tell Goethe to tell the Duke to stop drinking so much.

Johann Heinrich Voss (1751–1826) – famed as translator of Homer, and later to be Goethe's friend – told his fiancée: 'Alarming things are happening in Weimar. The Duke chases round the villages with Goethe like a wild student; he gets drunk and enjoys his girls with him, like a brother. One of his ministers, who had the temerity to advise him to stop these excesses because of his health, got the answer that he had to do it to build up his strength.'[14]

Weimar had never seen anything quite like this new arrival from Frankfurt in his bright blue frock coat with brass buttons, his yellow waistcoat and top boots. He was loud, exhibitionistic, flirtatious and, by the standards of the courtlier inhabitants, rather coarse.

Carl August began to adopt Goethe's habit of swearing and cursing and shouting. To their alarm, the courtiers and administrators began to see that this outrageous guest was not, as they had assumed and hoped, going to return to Frankfurt. There was even talk of Carl August offering him a place in the administration.

Once this became apparent – that Carl August really intended to ask Goethe to stay in Weimar – the knives were out. The Duke's former tutor, Count Görtz, attempted to warn his protégé of the dangers inherent in trusting a non-noble poetical show-off and 'celebrity' but as Görtz, and his equally furious wife, observed, Goethe had become the darling, not only of the Duke, but of his mother, Anna Amalia. 'This Goethe is a boy in daily need of being caned,' Görtz wrote. His wife noted how the upstart was 'coddled', and she was appalled that Goethe even spent evenings alone with the Dowager Duchess who, taking her snuff and playing with her pugs, appeared entirely besotted with the actual Storm and Stress which Goethe was creating around him.

One of Anna Amalia's ladies-in-waiting, Charlotte von Stein, wrote to her confidant, the court physician Johann Georg von Zimmermann (1728–95):

> There is an astonishing amount on my mind that I need to tell that young monster. It is impossible that he will make his way in the world, behaving as he does! Why does he always lampoon everyone? And now, with his indecent behaviour, with his swearing, and using vulgar, low expressions ... he ruins others. The Duke is astonishingly changed. Yesterday when he was with me, he asserted that anyone with propriety, with good manners, does not deserve the name of an honest man. He can no longer endure the company of someone who is not a bit rough round the edges. This all comes from Goethe.

Yet Zimmermann saw that the firebrand was more than a noisy show-off. He assured Frau von Stein that the Duke, young as he was, had his head screwed on. He was 'a sharp-sighted, Enlightened Prince who was going to call a Golden Age into being' through his friendship with a genius. Merck, when he came to meet the Duke, took the same view. This was not Prince Hal wasting his time with a Falstaff who would have to be discarded when the serious business of government began. This was someone who could carry through Anna Amalia's 'Court of the Muses' idea, and who would create something at Weimar which was more durable than the brocaded rococo court routines of Empire. The wild, exhibitionistic, blue-coated genius was not a fool.

Carl August himself realized that Storm and Stress could go too far. He took Goethe to the nearby court of Gotha at Christmastime to see how a more conventional court life could be established, and to give him a glimpse of what might be expected of him if he took an administrative role at Weimar. The Schloss Friedenstein at Gotha is a vast baroque barracks, stuffed with family portraits and good furniture. Goethe, head still in the clouds at this period, thanked the Duke for introducing him to the court there and to the 'simple Homeric world' of its courtly routines. He had, without saying so overtly, taken the point. If he were to stay in Weimar and work for the administration, there would be meetings to attend, books to be balanced, accounts to be settled, soldiers and retainers to be paid, roads to be mended, schools and a university – Jena – to be built up and revivified, justice to be administered and the poor to be looked after.

Immanuel Kant would make famous the difficulty of getting to the heart of things, describing a thing in-itself – as opposed to merely recognizing appearances. Appearances depend on the judgement of the observer. For example, Goethe was described as 'tall' by the Duke of Saxe-Meiningen. He was about 1.8 metres in height – 5 feet 9 inches. Most modern observers would think this was an 'average' height for a man, but the German upper class (think of Queen Victoria and her mother) were distinctly tiny.

When it became clear that Goethe was to stay, and to join the Duke's government with the title of Privy Councillor, the man who had been in effect the Prime Minister, Jacob Friedrich Freiherr von Fritsch (1731–1814), immediately tendered his resignation. He pointed out, both to Anna Amalia and to Carl August, that it was entirely inappropriate for a non-aristocrat to be appointed to such a role.

The amused Anna Amalia was far too tactful to remind the faithful, conservative von Fritsch, son though he may have been of a distinguished Saxon politician and bureaucrat, that he was the grandson of a mere bookseller-publisher from Leipzig. She persuaded von Fritsch not to resign.

Charlotte probably saw, earlier than most – and perhaps Anna Amalia had already seen it – that the dissipation, the apparent willingness to waste any amount of time with the young Duke, hunting, drinking, womanizing, were on some levels a form of *politesse*, the homage of an essentially bourgeois young man to the rake of the Old World. When his life in Weimar palled, when he found that the life at court and the administrative duties were not allowing him enough time for poetry or science, he would make efforts to flit from Weimar, as he had flitted from Frankfurt.

The Duke, and his mother, summoned him back, not just because he was the author of *Werther*, and an international literary celebrity, but because, as a member of the government, he turned out to be so good. His father had trained him up to be an efficient lawyer, and however much he tried to sow wild oats in Strasbourg and Wetzlar, he had become a highly competent constitutional lawyer who understood the workings of the Empire. The Victorian joke, on one level, tells a truth about Goethe (or, rather, about why we find his life so surprising); on another level it misses the point. It was said that watching him get sucked into work as a Weimar Privy Councillor was like imagining that Lord Byron had applied for a job in the British Civil Service. In fact, it was more surprising than this. It was as if the perfectly competent Head of the English Civil Service had surprised everyone by writing *Childe Harold*. Goethe took his place in the Council, and eventually adopted so many roles in Weimar, because he was highly efficient.

And this, inevitably, led to a feeling of great ambivalence about the boy-duke whom, at first, he had loved so well.

And so Goethe was installed as a member of the Privy Council in the little Duchy. His Duke, who had imbibed from his new friend a love of Rousseau, and Back to Nature, gave Goethe the first of one of his many gifts – the Garden House near the banks of the Ilm, just outside town.

Of all the sites on the Goethe tourist route, the *Gartenhaus* is the most evocative of the author's presence. It feels quite convincingly as if the poet has just left it. Despite the insensitive suburban houses constructed behind it, the meadow still lies in front, albeit municipalized. Here, in the groves and fields, Goethe could lead a life of sporty, outdoorsy community with Nature, when he was not hard at work in administration. He took a cold bath every morning, whatever the temperature; he frequently swam with Carl August in the Ilm, and it was here that he would write some of his sublime early lyrics. Although Carl August worked Goethe so hard, and although the distractions of office so hugely interrupted work on *Faust*, the *Gartenhaus* is a sign that the ducal family, both Carl August and his mother, saw the point of having a poet in their midst. Here he could lead a life of total simplicity, and for several months each year, deep into old age, he would live here.

For this pleasure, he was offered the staggering stipend of 1,200 talers per year. Consider that five years before, in 1770, Immanuel Kant had accepted an annual salary of 400 talers to be the Professor of Philosophy at Königsberg. Young Mozart (1756–91), as the *Conzertmeister* at Salzburg, worked for 450 gulden, about the equivalent of 300 talers, some quarter of Goethe's salary. Goethe, unlike Kant or Mozart, had never known poverty. His father was no aristocrat but the house in Frankfurt had always been comfortable and beautiful, and excepting in times of war, there had been no hunger or material want. He was undoubtedly 'spoiled', if by that is meant he never had to think about money. He always spent about twice his income, and gave much of it away. When a certain Johann Friedrich Kraft (d. 1785) approached him for money, Goethe did not refuse. For his first decade in Weimar he was sending Kraft between 100 and 200 talers each year.

The person who tamed the wild young Storm and Stress poet and made him into the Goethe we recognize – both the Privy Councillor, and the measured, wise middle-aged Goethe – was undoubtedly Charlotte von Stein, Anna Amalia's lady-in-waiting.

Goethe's life is something we watch everlastingly being turned into literature. 'L'homme c'est rien – l'oeuvre, c'est tout,' Flaubert would write to George Sand – but although writers like to say this sort of thing about themselves, and to downplay the role of biography in interpreting their work, the work is never comprehensible, fully, without a knowledge of the life: and in Goethe's case, the work and the man are inseparable; the man, and his emotional experiences, is himself a work of art.

It began with the transformation of his summer in Wetzlar with Lotte Buff and Kestner into *The Sorrows of Young Werther*. All the great works – *Torquato Tasso*, *Wilhelm Meister*, *Elective Affinities*, *Faust* itself – are, not autobiographies, but works which grow out of particular role-plays. In his old age, we will watch him, together with his faithful secretary Eckermann and others, carefully constructing actual autobiography – *Poetry and Truth*, one of the great autobiographies of the world, the *Italian Journey*, which he reconstructed forty years after it had actually taken place – from letters and diaries written at the time; and, what Nietzsche considered the finest creation of German literature, the *Conversations*. Although it may seem to be an unsatisfactory admission at the beginning of his literary career, we must admit to knowing that the 'real' Goethe is going to evade our research, just as the thing-in-itself would elude that of Kant. What we have are the representations of Goethe and his world-experience which his art so stupendously produced. And among these artworks is the collection – over 1,781 communications in all – of his letters to Charlotte von Stein. It had been his habit since student days in Leipzig to make, if not actually a novel, then at least, an artwork of his letters; his passing emotional fancies and passions were forever turning themselves into poems or epistolary fiction.

This is one reason why we will probably never know for certain exactly what passed between Goethe and Charlotte von Stein, though it strikes me as inconceivable that they were ever lovers in the physical sense of the word. In August 1776, he wrote to her:

> Dear Angel! Your relationship to me is so strangely holy, that it began at the first opportunity we could know one another – I FELT it. It cannot be expressed in words. Perhaps there might be a moment when I am able to put my sorrows, which are now ever-diminishing – into words.[15]

One of the many remarkable things about these early letters of Goethe to Frau von Stein is the way that their phraseology came to be echoed, twenty years later, in the *Prologue to Faust Part One*. There were several actual dramas, in the sense of stage plays, that grew out of his relationship with her – *Torquato Tasso*, the story of a courtier-poet tormented by the love for a Princess, is one: the stately, pious figure of Iphigenia is another. But in the letter just quoted, he anticipates, not Faust himself, but the poet of *Faust* who, in the Prologue, feels himself gripped by a strange longing 'Nach jenem stillen ernsten Geisterreich', 'for a quiet, serious spirit-world'.[16]

To Charlotte, he was writing from Ilmenau, where – like Faust and Mephistopheles at the beginning of *Faust Part Two* advising the

Emperor to exploit the mineral resources of his domains – he was urging the young Duke to solve his fiscal problems by reopening the silver mines. The administrations of the middling and smaller states of the Holy Roman Empire have been described as 'a hothouse for certain kinds of knowledge': scientific forestry, alchemy/chemistry, technology and technical sciences.[17] Silver mining, in the mountainous districts of Saxony and Bohemia, had flourished in the sixteenth century, taken a dip during the Thirty Years War, and been badly affected by the Seven Years War. There had then been a silver boom in the 1770s – in Marienberg, for example.[18] Goethe wanted Carl August, and Weimar, to imitate this success.

The north-eastern rim of the Thuringian Forest chiefly produced manganese ores, but also some fluorite and minor copper ores. Deposits of silver, lead and zinc were also discovered. It was Kalb who was in charge of administering the mines. The pioneer of mining technology at this date and in this region was Christoph Heinrich von Trebra (1694–1745), one of Carl August's courtiers.[19] He was succeeded by his son, Friedrich Wilhelm (1746–1821), who became a friend of Goethe's. After seven shining years at the University of Jena, studying natural science and mathematics, he had enrolled in the newly founded mining academy at Freiberg, Saxony. Following his success at reviving the mines at Marienberg, he was engaged by Carl August to advise Goethe about the revival of the mines at Ilmenau. For some reason, neither copper nor silver was found in sufficient quantities to make the Ilmenau mines a viable economic proposition, but it would take many years before this became clear, and by then Trebra had been 'head hunted' by Great Britain, to supervise the mines at Chausthal, in the jurisdiction of Braunschweig-Lüneburg. (The Duke of Brunswick was cousin to King George III and had close ties to Britain.) Then Trebra retired to his estates and took up farming and establishing a distillery. Trebra is only one of so many Germans of this date whose range of skills benefited from the 'small is beautiful' composition of the Holy Roman Empire. The small university of Jena had nurtured his talents. The relatively unbureaucratic, small governments with which he came into contact could target those talents in a useful direction, scientifically and economically. Seeing a career like that of Trebra helps us to see the life of Goethe in context. He was a phenomenon, by any standards; but by coming to

Weimar and enlisting in the government service of Duke Carl August, he was placing himself among people whose polymathic cleverness encouraged his own.

Ilmenau is set in the Harz Mountains, and when Goethe had turned aside from the grubby little town with its criminal, poverty-stricken workforce, he could find solitude in the mountains. In a cave, he felt moved to carve in the stone his feelings about Charlotte von Stein:

Oh, how you are to me
Oh, how I've remained to you!
The truth of it no longer makes me despair!

It was as if she was there in the cave with him, and had stooped down to write in the dust. (Readers of the New Testament will remember who wrote in the dust, though He left no recorded writings on papyrus!) Charlotte is a Christ-like figure to Goethe because she opens up the spirit-world to him – the *Geisterreich* – and this experience of being in love which had broken Werther's heart and would in many instances appear silly, or even embarrassing, to Goethe's friends was one of the ways in which he appreciated the reality of the spiritual.[20]

Although he tells her that no one could ever quite fathom the mystery of their relationship – and the wide variety of baffled interpretations by the biographers bears testimony to the truth of this statement – there are two factors which make clear its colossal significance – in his life, at least. (Her views of the matter are, of course, much harder to gauge, since she destroyed her half of the correspondence when, at her request, he returned it to her.) To Lavater, on 20 September 1780, some four years into the friendship, Goethe described it: 'She has taken over from my Mother, my Sister and my Lovers so completely, that this has woven a bond as close as Re herself weaves.' Much earlier in the friendship, he had exclaimed to her, 'O, if only my sister had such a brother as I have a sister in you!'[21]

The bond with Cornelia had been the closest love of his childhood. The separation, after he had left Frankfurt to study in Leipzig and

Strasbourg, had been painful for her, not least because she had always had a bad relationship with their father. Caspar Goethe had married his daughter off to the son of another Frankfurt legal family, J. G. Schlosser. He had secured an administrative job for him at Baden, and the two were married in 1773, the same year that Lotte Buff had married Kestner. His sister's departure from the family home was one factor, surely, in making Goethe leap at the chance, eventually, of leaving Frankfurt himself. Cornelia's marriage had made Goethe say that he 'looked forward to a deadly solitude'.[22] Her letters to Goethe in Weimar, when he had also escaped the oppressive atmosphere of home, 'tore his heart', and when she died, aged twenty-six, leaving two children, it was a bitter blow, sealing off forever the happily secret world of their shared childhood and youth.

Much of what he had felt for Cornelia was consciously and a little callously transferred to Charlotte von Stein.

'If you witnessed her theatrical skills, if you saw her dancing, you would never guess that, in the moonlit nocturnal hours, this pious woman would be at prayer.'[23] So said her doctor, Johann Georg von Zimmermann, when she was in her early thirties. Schiller, much later, unkindly remarked, when she was forty-five, that she could never have been a beauty.[24]

Catty courtiers and fellow aristocrats expressed amazement when Goethe became besotted, 'for she really seems quite ugly'.

Modern readers, had they met her, might not have agreed. One must remember that the eighteenth century did not value thinness, and Frau von Stein was almost skinny, with abundant, curly, dark hair and dark eyes. The huge eyes and the soft, beautifully modulated voice, were noted by all. Some would think that, like Goethe himself, she had more a Mediterranean than a typically Teutonic appearance.

Another ethnic stereotype which one could invoke is that she had an appearance often found in raw-boned Scots. She had very red cheeks. Her father was a *Hofmarschall* – Lord Chamberlain – in Eisenach, but her mother, Concordia Elizabeth, had been an Irving of

Drum.[25] She herself was a devoted lady-in-waiting to Anna Amalia, and she was utterly the Old Regime aristocrat.

She was married to a courtier who had been 'passed over'. They had seven children, but the *Oberstallmeister* – the Keeper of the Duke's Horse – could not have been expected to give his clever wife what she derived from a ten-year *amitié amoreuse* with the most brilliant man in Germany – devoted, even passionate, admiration, jokes, affection and talk – talk about the latest developments in science, about books old and new, about their widening circle of common acquaintance.

When he met this highly intelligent woman for the first time, Goethe had a history of adoring the Eternal Feminine. To Auguste, the sister of his chums the Stolbergs, whom he had never met, he had written: 'My dear, I won't give you a name – for what is the name of friend, sister, beloved, bride, partner, but a word, and I have the whole complex of extreme feelings for you.'[26] He described these feelings of excitement which are stirred in us by another person, as intimations of the Eternal. The love he had expressed for Lili, for Frederika, for Lotte Buff, for Maximiliane La Roche and all the others, not to mention the waitresses, barmaids and such who had haunted his dreams, and the sister who had been his dearest and closest companion since childhood – he was ready, as soon as he had stepped out of his barouche onto the Weimar cobblestones that cold morning in 1775, for a relationship of the kind which unfolded over his first decade there.

It is hugely to be regretted that Charlotte's side of the correspondence was destroyed – by her – when their love came to its painful end. Both during their lifetime and since, the speculation has been endless – was it truly platonic or were they in fact lovers – or had they been lovers, for a short while? Was it – the most fantastical suggestion of all – a pure fiction, to hide the 'fact' that he was actually having a love affair with Anna Amalia, who received the letters addressed to Charlotte, knowing that it would cause scandal if he addressed her in terms of such tenderness?

We shall never know the answer to these questions. It would seem very unlikely that Frau von Stein, who was rather strait-laced by all accounts, including those of her doctor, and who clearly felt that 'enough was enough' by the time she had seven children – should have wanted an affair with the younger man, especially since she could flatteringly set the tongues of gossips wagging, and the flow of his poems and compliments gushing, without any such commitment. Goethe, on his side, clearly had a dread of commitment, and would wait until he was over forty before, in any sense, 'settling down'. In 1782, Lavater suggested to Goethe that he had a weakness for the beautiful Marchioness Maria Branconi. She was believed at the time Goethe got to know her to be two years his junior, whereas she was, in fact, three years older. Clever, beautiful and good,[27] she was the mistress or former mistress of the Duke of Brunswick. Goethe replied that his daily duty was to erect the pyramid of his existence as high as possible into the air. This did not permit him the distraction of 'monetary desire'. As for marriage – 'God preserve us from a serious bond, with which she would wind my soul out of my members.'

As autumn turned to winter, 1777, Goethe obtained permission from the Duke to set out on a solitary ride through the Harz Mountains. Only Carl August and Charlotte von Stein knew about it. Court life, administrative business, grief for his sister Cornelia, who had died in June, all combined to make him crave a time of solitude.

Moreover, he wanted to take stock. Had he made a mistake, committing himself to the Weimar court, with its heavy administrative workload, its endless round of court life and social life, some enjoyable, some silly? By the time he set out on his journey he was suffering from mouth abscesses and toothache, so that the sorrows of life needled him with local pain.

As so often happened when he wandered alone, however – as in the journey to Wetzlar which fructified into *Werther* – the journey would become a work of art, in this case one of his most remarkable poems, 'A Winter Journey in the Harz Mountains'. And, as so often happened when a great work of art was going to take shape in his brain, a whole crowd of factors would be at play here. In addition to the self-doubt about Weimar, and his love, half tormenting, half enjoyable, for Charlotte, there were other things on his mind. There was the fact that he was journeying towards the mines of Ilmenau, potentially a source of wealth which might pay off the Duchy's catastrophic debts. The mines themselves, and the responsibility he had undertaken as director of the mines, would spark his interest, burgeoning into an obsession, with geology. And, together with this cluster of things going on in his mind, there was a correspondent whom he wanted to seek out, one Friedrich Viktor-Lebrecht Plessing, who lived at Wernigerode.

Plessing was one of the many readers of *Werther* who had found the novel more than upsetting – it had awoken in him a whole series of potentially catastrophic mental torments. These were poured out in verbose letters. Goethe himself was no stranger to melancholy; and after *Werther* had catapulted him to fame he was no stranger to the novel's power to attract unstable, miserable young people. He decided to play one of his strange tricks. Since he was travelling incognito, he announced himself at the inn as a book illustrator from Gotha and inquired about the whereabouts of Plessing's lodgings. He found the young man, who noted that Gotha was near Weimar. Did the illustrator know any of the famous people in that town? Goethe reeled off a few names, but Plessing was not satisfied. Had the illustrator met Goethe? Yes, yes, he had met Goethe, who had helped him with his illustrating work. He described the famous poet, a 'curious individual'. Then Plessing read him a copy of one of the long letters he had sent to Goethe, receiving no reply. Goethe said, in his guise as the humble illustrator, that he did not know how to answer the young man's troubles, but that perhaps the answer to his sorrows lay in activity. If he tried, literally, to get out of himself, by contemplating Nature and by taking part in some work, or some physical activity, whether as gardener, miner, hunter – the depression would surely lift.

As when he had pretended to be a poor theological student when visiting Frederika, daughter of the Vicar of Wakefield, there seems something cruel in the jape of an assumed identity – cruel and also vain. But this winter ride through the hills was to allow him some solitude, so he could not face appearing as the great Goethe and having to ward off the fans and dependants.

Of course, while sagely lecturing Plessing he was delivering a sermon to himself. His own inward griefs and torments would find an outlet in work, not simply in the composition of poetry, but in the work of science, and in the technological and administrative problems associated with the mines.

As he made his way on horseback through the hills, often in foul weather, he composed some of his finest letters to Charlotte – themselves, in part, dummy runs or rehearsals for the poems which they have almost become.

On 11 December he came to a peat house at the foot of the Brocken mountain, 1,400 metres high, invisible because of thick fog, where he found a forester. The man told Goethe that the weather conditions – fog, snow, ice – made it impossible to contemplate climbing the mountain. Goethe said he wanted to do so nonetheless. After a while, they went to the window and looked out. The weather was clearing and he could see the mountain. He repeated his desire to climb. But, protested the forester, 'Do you have no servant, no one to accompany you?' Realizing that Goethe was alone, the forester said, 'Man, I will go with you.' In an ecstasy, Goethe scratched a sign on the window 'as a testimony to my tears of joy'. He added, 'I would consider it to be a sin to write about it to anyone but yourself.' ('Sie', here, the formal 'you', though also 'Liebste', dearest.) When he and the forester reached the summit of the mountain – 'All the fog lay beneath, and above, was glorious clarity, and tonight, you could see the peak in the clear moonlight, and, with the glimmering dawn, you could see it in the darkness.'

In the poem, he addresses the mountain –

You stand, your bosom unexplored,
Mysteriously revealed
Over the astonished world
You gaze out of the clouds
At its realms and their riches
Which out of the veins of your brother-mountains
Is watered from the rocks around you.

Personal self-doubt and pain; scientific interest in what the mountains contain; a sense of destiny mysteriously manifesting itself in the mountain scene, as when Wordsworth, after a night's dancing, walked home through the hill country of his Cumberland boyhood and was visited by a strange sense:

My heart was full; I made no vows, but vows
Were then made for me[28]

or, as Goethe says in his winter journey, 'A God has pre-ordained to every man his path.' No Christian, Goethe, but the only language in which he could express his experience of the mountain journey in winter was that of religion. The mountaintop, dreaded and awesome, becomes, in the poem, an altar of sweetest thanksgiving, a place of the skull, covered in snow ...

We would misunderstand Goethe completely if we attempted to compartmentalize his experiences during the journey – or, come to that, throughout his creative life-experience. To compartmentalize would be to say, 'While he was riding in the mountain scenery, to work out what to do with his life, and to grieve for his sister, he also began a scientific interest in geology – useful for his work as a supervisor of mines.' No, all these experiences come together. And readers of *Faust*, of course, will not forget that in this spot, where Goethe rode during those winter weeks, Faust and Mephistopheles will canter on their black steeds, while in the summer of Walpurgis Night the witches will revel.[29] Witches bound for the Brocken are we ... It is a place of wonder, of magic for good or ill, and what is true of the witches' magic is also true of the use and misuse of mines and minerals.

Faust, in *Part One*, has seen the Brocken and the surrounding Harz Mountains as the scene of a midsummer orgy. The mature Faust of *Part Two* will be found, lost in wonder at dawn beside the mountain cataracts.

Colour on colour emerges in the dell
Where trembling pearls drench every leaf and flower ...[30]

Life itself becomes for the mature Faust a matter of refracted colour and light – *Am farbigen Abglanz haben wir das Leben* – 'we derive life itself from refracted colour' is, almost, the sense of this untranslatable utterance. Atkins has 'What we have as life is a many-hued reflection.' Bayard Taylor ingeniously and suggestively departs from the original enough to have 'Life is not light, but the refracted colour.'[31]

Old age gave him the perspective to look back upon his winter ride in the Harz Mountains not only as the beginnings of his interest in geology, but also the dawning of his anti-Newtonian colour theory.

On a winter journey in the Harz I was coming down from the Brocken toward evening. The broad expanses above and below me were snow-covered ... If during the day the pale violet shadows had already been noticeable against the yellowish colour of the snow, one would now have to call them deep blue, as an intensified yellow was reflected from the sunlit areas. When the sun at last began to go down, however, and its beams, very much moderated by the stronger mists, bathed the entire surroundings with the most beautiful purple colour, the colour of the shadows was transformed into a green which, in its clarity could be compared to a sea green, in its beauty to an emerald green. The manifestation of it became ever more vivid. One felt that one had found oneself in a fairy-land.[32]

To the geologist, the mountains, with their mineral seams, contained clues, which, when unlocked, could further the understanding of the earth itself – its age and its origins. To a mining engineer, armed with the geologist's knowledge, the mountains were a source of mineral wealth. (To the miners themselves, they were the chance to earn a pittance in gruelling circumstances – a chief reason why the recruitment of German miners was so difficult in the eighteenth century.) To the painter the mountains made perfect landscapes to reproduce on paper or canvas, just as to the Romantic poets the mountains were the source of inspiration, such as we can read in Shelley's 'Mont Blanc'. To the mystics, from the peaks of Horeb and Sinai to the Himalayan monastic fastnesses of Lhasa, mountains have been places to commune with the infinite, to communicate with the incommunicable. To Goethe, scientist, engineer, administrator, painter, poet and mystic, the Harz Mountains were all these things.

Rather than worrying about whether Goethe slept with Charlotte, or whether this or that poem was 'inspired' by her, we are on safer ground taking the strange relationship between poet and patroness at its surface meaning. On the one hand, he had plainly needed such a relationship in his life, as he had been creating it for himself ever since late adolescence with a whole series of representatives of the Eternal Feminine. Secondly, she was plainly devoted to him

What is on the surface, and what we can see, is the extent to which Goethe's creative imagination was stirred by this woman, and by this relationship. She inspired – or 'it', if you wish to say that it was the relationship, not the woman who inspired them – some of the most wonderful of his letters; some great poetry; at least two great plays.

But not – I would submit – *Faust* or anything to do with *Faust*. It is noticeable that for the ten years of his passion for Charlotte von Stein, *Faust* remained largely untouched. Nevertheless, you could say that, when the relationship had ended, Charlotte fed into the impulses which created *Part Two* of the great drama, both in the Helena sequence and in the grand finale at the end of Act V. But this is to leap very far ahead!

Almost the first thing which had attracted Werther to Lotte was her motherliness. A sixteen-year-old girl, she is first encountered surrounded by her gaggle of younger, now motherless, siblings, six children between the ages of eleven and two. As in Thackeray's insensitive but quite funny verse account of the meeting, she is cutting up bread and butter for the little ones.

Werther had a love for Charlotte
Such as words could never utter;
Would you know how first he met her?
She was cutting bread and butter.

Goethe would not become a father until he was in his forties, but he always loved children and wanted to be a father. When, in 1783, Charlotte von Stein became dissatisfied with the standard of the tutor she had found for her son Fritz (1772–1844) Goethe took the boy into his own household for three years – the happiest three years, Fritz would say, of his life.[33] One of the really puzzling things about the relationship between Frau von Stein and the poet was that she extracted from him a promise that he would not marry, nor have a family of his own.[34]

Even before Fritz came to live in Goethe's house, he often came to stay. Their relationship was intense. Whichever of them woke first in the morning would rouse the other with a slipper.[35] Biographers note that it was from this period (probably before August 1781)[36] that Goethe wrote one of his most disturbing, indeed horrifying, poems, in which a variety of feelings – the protective feeling of a father for his child, the little boy's bewilderment in the face of clearly erotic and predatory demands being made upon him from whence he cannot understand, and a swirling, blowy, dark sense that Nature itself is a hostile and sinister force – all boil down to the unforgettable lyric 'Der Erlkönig'.

Schubert's setting of the poem captures its eeriness, its sinisterness. There is also a suitably creepy version set to music by Carl Loewe. It is a classic trope of true-life child abuse, about which our generation has become so much wiser than our forebears, that the child cannot meaningfully *tell anyone* that he is being abused. As the little boy in the poem describes the appearance of the 'Erlkönig', his allurements, his promises of great delight if the child will submit to him and – eventually – when the child tries to resist – his threats of violence – the father dismisses all the little boy's fears. The first appearance of the elven king with his crown and his comet-like trail is seen by the father as a mere wisp of autumn mist; the king's alluring blandishments are just the rustling of dry leaves in the wind; the king's daughters, trying to seduce the child into their play, are just an old willow tree. Only by the end of the frantic night ride does the father, who has been clutching the child to his breast, discover him to be dead.

Every report one reads of the discovery of a child abduction, so often followed by a child murder – those all-too common motifs of our modern lives – recall Goethe's 'Erlkönig'. In this lyric, he is closest to the dark, folkloric underbelly of pre-Enlightenment, very specifically non-Enlightenment Germany, which would be collected and chronicled by the Brothers Grimm who began to publish their *Hausmärchen* in 1812.

The biographers differ over the question of who, if anyone, inspired Goethe's most famous lyric, the second of the Wanderer's Night Songs – is he addressing Charlotte? Or his future reader? Or himself?

Über allen Gipfeln
Ist Ruh,
In allen Wipfeln
Spürest Du

Kaum einen Hauch;
Die Vögelein schweigen im Walde.
Warte nur, balde
Ruhest Du auch
Over each peak, is stillness.
You feel scarcely a breath.
The little birds are silent in the woods.
Only, wait!
Soon – you too will be at peace.

It was on 6 September 1780, while on a tour of the Thuringian Forest, that Goethe had alighted on a charcoal burner's wooden cottage, high among the peaks near Ilmenau, where he hoped to reopen, and make profitable, the silver mines. In that hut, he wrote to his beloved. It had been a difficult summer. The beautiful Marchioness Maria Branconi had visited Weimar and Goethe had been smitten. Charlotte took it hard. Alone again, up in the hills, Goethe wrote to her to assure her of his devotion; to remind her how he valued the 'sweet conversation of my inmost heart'. He hoped, 'if only my thoughts of today were written down complete; there are some good things among them'.

The following spring, in March 1781, there was a change in the relationship. He began to write to her every day, and the use of the familiar 'Du', which had been occasional, was now habitual. Charlotte and he were closer than ever.

Du. Thou. It would appear that he had written the words of his lyric, the previous autumn, on the wooden walls of the charcoal burner's hut, that very evening. Nicholas Boyle writes:

> For the biographer one feature of the poem is very revealing: its use of the word 'you'. The word refers either to Goethe or to the reader or to both – that is in the very nature of Goethe's soul – but the 'you' is not – not specifically or by allusion – the woman to whom Goethe was writing only minutes before, and after he composed the poem. Though for years he could not acknowledge it, the sources of his poetry ran deeper and purer than the 'sweet conversation of my inmost heart' that was his mental discourse with Charlotte von Stein.[37]

Even if he had written nothing else, there is something so pure and perfect about this lyric that we would feel it was penned by one of the immortals. Undoubtedly, the infatuations, enthusiasms and loves which punctuated Goethe's life fed into his poetry, but it would be a crude reader who felt that the power, let alone an explanation of the source, of such inspiration could be named in one woman or another. The point is, Goethe needed such feelings to fuel his art.

7

ARCHBISHOP OF TITIPU

> KO-KO: *Pooh-Bah, it seems that the festivities in connection with my approaching marriage must last a week. I should like to do it handsomely, and I want to consult you as to the amount I ought to spend upon them.*
> POOH-BAH: *Certainly. In which of my capacities? As First Lord of the Treasury, Lord Chamberlain, Attorney General, Chancellor of the Exchequer, Privy Purse, or Private Secretary?*
> W. S. Gilbert, *The Mikado*

There were feuds aplenty in the great cities which gave birth to the Enlightenment – in Diderot's Paris, Hume's Edinburgh, Johnson's London – but they were feuds among equals. The backbiting of courtiers, in the Lilliputian court of Weimar, was occasioned by the very nature of the situation. The number of characters in the drama was so much smaller than in a city; and they were jockeying, not simply for fame or success but for favour. There was an inbuilt hierarchy in the courtier's life which made Envy – the second of the great threats to a writer's serenity in Johnson's unforgettable catalogue[1] – absolutely inevitable.

In January 1776,[2] the post of Superintendent General and Principal Chaplain to the Court in Weimar had become vacant. The occupant of this post was Primate of the Duchy, the Weimar equivalent of an archbishop. Goethe had persuaded Carl August to offer this job to his old mentor and friend Herder.

It was in some ways a challenging role and in others an easy one. The duties consisted in having to preach before the court, to baptize the more aristocratic children born in the Duchy, to hear confessions (should the faithful members of the courtly congregation wish to make them) and to deal with the governing body of the Weimar diocese, which was the equivalent of a cathedral chapter. The seven clergy who belonged to this body were extremely conservative, and Herder had been viewed by them all with suspicion, but in fact he soon became popular, not only with his fellow parsons, but with the court. Charlotte von Stein and Duchess Anna Amalia were regular visitors to his parsonage where they quizzed him about theological and philosophical matters, as did the Duchess Luise. But it was a simple household and he and his wife Karoline, who were to have eight children, found it difficult to cope on their modest annual income, about one sixth of the generous allowance given to Goethe.

'There is no one in Weimar worthy of Herder except Goethe,' Wieland opined, 'and he is much engaged with the Duke and business.'[3] Both Herders were hurt by Goethe's apparently studied neglect of them. Once established at Weimar, they found their younger friend 'cold as frost, like an electric cloud'.[4] And although the weather changed from time to time, and they would move into happier times when they were reconciled, by 1782, Herder had begun to find Goethe insufferable.

In 1782, Goethe had been raised to the peerage. The young Duke relied upon him more and more for help in a whole miscellaneous range of government functions. Goethe's growing fame as a German sage and his ascendant power and importance in the little court of Weimar put great strains on the friendship with Herder. When they had first met in Strasbourg, Herder had been the famous one, and the difference in their ages – Herder five years older – made a big difference. The twenty-six-year-old is fully advanced into the grown-up sphere and way of thought when the twenty-one-year-old remains in adolescence. Then had come *Götz*, *Werther*, stratospheric fame and Weimar. Even the fact that Herder owed his prestigious position at Weimar to the younger man, former protégé, put strains on the relationship. And Herder, who had hoped to build on his early fame as poet and sage, now found that his ecclesiastical duties – he was in effect a bishop running a diocese, and was in charge of all the church administration for the Duchy – was eating into time which could more valuably be spent reading, writing and thinking.

Though Herder envied Goethe, the poet found the role of court favourite wasted his own time, the time most valued by any writer – that is, time alone.

It is not easy to be an idol.

Where was the time for the inner life, the poetry, the discovery of Nature in the Harz Mountains? When was there even time to be getting on with his novel *Wilhelm Meister* which he had begun to write?

The death of his father in 1782, after some years of dementia, was not something which appeared to make much impression – even though his rise to eminence would undoubtedly have meant so much to the old man had he still been in possession of his wits. How excited Johann Caspar would have been had he known that Johann Wolfgang was on the verge of being ennobled – able to add that monosyllable to his surname which is of such moment to class-conscious German-speakers – no longer Herr Goethe, but Herr *von* Goethe.

Herder, from whom Goethe was increasingly estranged, would observe rather bitterly in a letter to a friend in Königsberg:

> So now he is Permanent Privy Councillor, President of the Chamber, President of the War Office, Inspector of Works down to roadbuilding, Director of Mines, also Directeur de Plaisirs, Court Poet, composer of lovely festivities, court operas, ballets, cabaret masques, inscriptions, works of art etc. Director of the Drawing Academy in which during the winter he delivered lectures on osteology; everywhere himself the principal actor, dancer, in short the factotum of all Weimar and, d.v., soon the Majordomo of all the houses of the Ernestine houses in Saxony,[5] round which he progresses for the benefit of worshippers. He has been made a Baron ... has moved from his garden in town and set up the household of a nobleman, arranges reading circles which will soon turn into receptions, etc., etc.[6]

In 1782, the Duke gave Goethe, for his lifetime, the rambling old house on the Frauenplan, in addition to the *Gartenhaus* in the meadows on the banks of the Ilm. It is not a grand house, but it has many rooms, linked by an enfilade on each floor. It was the stage on which the Life of Goethe, that great drama, would be enacted, and, skilled theatrical director that he was, he was forever designing, redesigning and building, to perfect its suitability for his exits and entrances. There was a grand (too grand for the German-urban modesty of the house) Italianate staircase installed, adorned with casts of classical statues. At the same time, he also installed a little staircase, which enabled him, if the guest was of sufficient importance, to skitter up and be waiting at the top of the grand one, for the moment when the grandee had made their ascent. Equally, if the visitor was not wanted, the second staircase enabled Goethe to slink downstairs and out of the house unobserved.

The extravagance of the Duke's gesture fuelled the resentment of Herder. While the Herders squidged into their much smaller parsonage, the bachelor with no dependants (apart from Fritz von Stein) wandered from room to room – this, the library, that, the chamber set apart for displaying his large collection of Italian majolica. Here a music salon, there the second, more formal, dining room. On landings and in the saloons could be seen the collections – the minerals, the classical sculptures, the paintings, the botanical drawings, the anatomical specimens.

The chief exhibit was Goethe himself. The house was a cabinet of curiosities, or, to put it differently, a stage set in which the great man could display his cleverness in legendary conversations. For the next forty years – with one significant interlude – this would be where Goethe became the Sage of Weimar. In the Garden House, he could be, for some of the time at least, alone, the young poet of Storm and Stress, bathing in the Ilm, gardening, conceiving new poems and plays. On the Frauenplan, he was the public man, and it was no sinecure. For his friends, there were dismaying moments when it seemed as if the actor who had been hired by Providence to play Hamlet was now in danger, having become a court flunkey with an obsession with a much grander court lady, of becoming Malvolio.

For much of that year, Goethe toured the Empire as the Duke's ambassador, making official visits to Erfurt, Meiningen and Gotha in May. The war over the Bavarian Succession had left him with awareness of the need for the smaller German states to unite to provide themselves with security when the big powers, Prussia and Austria, were at loggerheads. In fact, it would be twenty years – during the threats posed by Napoleonic France – that such a bond, the Confederation of the Rhine, came into being. None of these cities, or their courts, were far away, but the diplomacy, the official dinners, the discussions with other courtiers, left less and less time for his true calling, writing and research.

In addition to the diplomatic duties, he had largely taken over the running of the Weimar economy, still in dire straits. Hand in hand with Goethe's forming alliances with princely neighbours, he drastically reduced the standing army, from around 500 men to just 136. As chair of the Ilmenau mining commission, he immersed himself in the study of geology. 'Thousands and thousands of thoughts rise and fall within me. My soul is like an everlastingly restless firework,' he told Charlotte von Stein.[7]

When he came to write the opening act of *Faust Part Two*, Mephistopheles and Faust find themselves at a fictitious Imperial Court. The devil is taken on as the court jester, but he soon manages to intrude himself into the meetings of the Privy Council, where the Lord Treasurer and the Lord Seneschal are trying to impress upon their monarch the parlous state of a pre-industrial economy, dependent entirely on land ownership and rents. Subsidies to their shrivelled exchequer, promised by allies, have not materialized. The troops who promised to defend the realm have not been paid for months and the land is desolate and open to attack from organized criminals and foreign enemies.

> The city council must get ready to break camp. (Draw up its tent pegs.) We're living simply now, holding on to our beer mugs and our basins. The banquet lies scattered under the table. It's my job to settle the accounts, and the Jew won't let us off a penny of the debts. Liens and attachments will determine our spending in future years. The pigs are not going to get fat; the very pillows under our heads are mortgaged; and at table we are fed bread that has already been chewed.[8]

Mephistopheles's solution is that the government should exploit its native mineral resource.

> In underground seams and walled foundations is gold, minted and unminted.[9]

The next four years would be the period of his life when he was most preoccupied with political and administrative duty, least able to concentrate on his work, still less on his Works. When, in 1784, Goethe made a speech, which was reprinted in the literary periodical *Deutsches Museum*, the editor wrote, by way of introduction, 'It has been a long time since our readers have had anything new from their favourite author Göethe [*sic*] but he laid down his pen in order to be active.' It was in fact eight years since he had published anything at all.[10] But, as we see over and over again in *Faust*, his life-experience was being absorbed, marinated, kept in store until it came to imaginative fruition.

Herder was right to note that, more than for most courtiers or writers, life was an ego trip for his friend, almost ex-friend, and protégé. There was undoubtedly something on the verge of absurd about Goethe playing so many roles on Weimar's little stage – including, sometimes, literally acting on the stage of the Weimar theatre. But whereas his friends felt he was being an intolerable show-off, or wasting his talents, or doing both, the finished work, or works, which we can contemplate in his old age, especially when *Faust* was eventually complete, show that in the life of Goethe little was wasted. Experience was stored, often for decades, and then richly garnered.

———

The year which saw Goethe elevated to the peerage, and installed in the Frauenplan, also saw him joining the Amalia Lodge of the Freemasons, in the company of his Duke. Lessing had been a mason. Herder and Wieland were both members of the Amalia Lodge before Goethe. Probably, Goethe had been aware of the broad outlines of Masonic beliefs – the universality of mankind, a religious viewpoint which resembled the perennial philosophy – since first befriending

Herder in Strasbourg. Faust's lofty speech in which he told Gretchen his credo, written then, could have been spoken by a mason:

> It is what all hearts
> Under the light of Heaven's day
> Will say.
> Each in their own language –
> Why not I in mine?[11]

Freemasonry, in the eighteenth century, was, among other things, an excuse for men[12] – and it was an exclusively male set of secret clubs – to express Deist beliefs, in defiance of orthodox Christianity, without fear of heresy hunts. Its humanist universalism was, in some quarters, a cloak for republicanism. It was certainly egalitarian in so far as it accepted the brotherhood of man in all lands. Rudyard Kipling, who joined in Lahore in 1885, would write:

> Outside – 'Sergeant! Sir! Salute! Salaam!'
> Inside – 'Brother', an' it doesn't do no 'arm.
> We met upon the Level an' we parted on the Square,
> An' I was Junior Deacon in my Mother-Lodge out there![13]

Goethe was capable of ambivalence about anything, and it is true that, after a few weeks of belonging to an inner ring of masons called the Illuminists, he wrote: 'It is said, you can best get to know a man when he is at play. Now I have reached the Ark of the Covenant, I have no comment to make. To the wise all things are wise, to the fool, foolish.'[14]

Carlyle entitled one of the most hilarious chapters of his history of *The French Revolution* – that in which Robespierre initiated a service in Notre Dame, converting it into the Temple of Reason – 'Mumbo Jumbo'. And there was much they called Reason in the eighteenth century which to a later generation would best be described as mumbo jumbo. Georg Forster, leader of the revolution in Mainz, through and through a man of the Enlightenment, was a keen Rosicrucian. Goethe, as is shown by the very fact that Faust dabbles in magic, was drawn to mumbo jumbo, as well as finding it ridiculous. Goethe's contemporaries Mozart and George

Washington were only two among thousands who were masons. Benjamin Franklin, General Lafayette, Immanuel Kant were all masons, as well as, in later years, many powerful individuals, including Prince Albert's brother, Duke Ernst II of Saxe-Coburg, his nephew, King Edward VII of England, King Oskar II of Sweden and Abraham Lincoln.[15]

German Freemasonry, which began as an import from England, had reached something of a crisis point by the time Goethe and Carl August joined up, with fierce feuds and disputes between the Rosicrucians and the rest. The Amalia Lodge kept what was called a Rite of Strict Observance, believing themselves to be following the rubrics of the Knights Templar.

His poem 'Masonic Lodge' makes the same point as Kipling's a century and more later:

'Here eyes do regard you
'In eternity's stillness;
'Here is all fullness,
'Ye have to reward you,
'Work, and despair not.'

His poem entitled 'Divinity' is a distillation of Masonic ideas. We must all complete the cycle of our existence in accordance with divine, immutable laws. We reverence the immortals, but we cannot see them. Our duty while on earth is to work, and to exercise virtue.

The noble-hearted man
Should be helpful and good.
Tireless, let him do
What is needful and right.
May we be models of those mysterious beings
Whom we speculate.

Herder would make it plain that he was at one with Goethe in belief, however much the younger poet enraged him. He told Jacobi that he could no more believe in a personal, transcendent God than Lessing could[16] – but this was not 'atheism'. It was the sense of the universal brotherhood of mankind, reverencing God, Nature, human equality and dignity.

The doings of masons are by definition secret, though Goethe made no secret of his membership. Shortly after he joined the Amalia Lodge, it was closed, following a shake-up of the Masonic movement in Germany by the actor-manager Friedrich Ludwig Schröder.

It has been argued, by Dan Wilson, that Goethe's motive for joining the Lodge was in order to monitor secret societies which, it was feared, might be hostile to the monarchical or hierarchical principles on which the Old Regime was founded.[17] In a famous letter to Lavater, Goethe said: 'Believe me, the moral and political world is undermined by subterranean movements, cellars, hidden groups.'[18] In his great play *The Natural Daughter*, there are allusions to the hidden forces which will undermine society. It has been sagely observed that many beneficiaries took comfort in conspiracy theories to explain the French Revolution, when it came, because it enabled them to blame the catastrophe on a few malcontents working in secret, rather than addressing the huge societal and economic phenomena which led to the political earthquake in France.[19]

The jury is out, then. We cannot know to what degree Goethe or the Duke saw their membership of the Lodge as a way of keeping an eye on potential subversives.

In 1785, Emperor Joseph II issued an edict in his own hand which declared that, from all the information he had received, the activities of the Freemasons were beneficial. He also thought, however, that the existence of secret societies could be politically dangerous in revolutionary times, and he therefore had decided that only one Lodge per province of the Empire was to be allowed. When Joseph died in 1790, the French Revolution had occurred and there was widespread belief that it had come about through the secret machinations of the Illuminati.[20] In such an atmosphere, it would have been impossible to reopen the Weimar Lodge.

After the invasion of Napoleon and its aftermath, however, things changed. But when the Lodge reopened in 1808 (following the end of the French invasion) Goethe continued his membership, until his death.[21] A poem he wrote in old age (1827) – entitled simply 'Symbol' – speaks of the mason labouring all his life, to build. We go on our way. The voices of great spirits, the voices of masters, call from above:

don't omit to listen, and to perform good deeds at their prompting. Here they are crafting crowns for us, in an eternal stillness.[22]

Goethe may not have written much of *Faust* during his first ten years in Weimar, but we know that he gave readings of it aloud. He was known as the author of a new interpretation of the Faust legend, and it was received with fascination and rapture. One of the court ladies, Luise von Göchhausen, borrowed the manuscript and copied it. This was a common practice in the eighteenth century, when books were scarce. If it had not been for Fräulein von Göchhausen, we should know far less about the play's textual history. Goethe's own manuscript of the original was lost or destroyed. Only in 1887 did the literary scholar Erich Schmidt find the copy in Fräulein von Göchhausen's literary remains. He entitled it the *Urfaust*, or the primitive Faust. By comparing the *Urfaust*, which was written in 1776 (probably) with *Faust A Fragment*, which was published in 1790, we can work out which lines Goethe wrote after he came to Weimar.

Faust and Mephistopheles are interrupted in their discourse, in the scholar's study, by the arrival of a student, who wants advice about which courses to pursue at the university. Mephistopheles puts on Faust's gown and assumes the identity of the distinguished academic. When the young man says that he does not feel much inclination to study Jurisprudence, Mephistopheles says:

> For that I scarcely blame you since I know
> How, in that discipline, conditions stand.
> Still, Laws and Rights, transmitted like disease
> Are handed on from generations.
> Reason becomes sheer nonsense, good-deed Plague –
> Alas for you, that you inherit this!
> The deeper thing, the inward, truest Right –
> Alas, you'll never hear them gassing about that.[23]

Mephistopheles makes short shrift of Kant's idea of the Categorical Imperative, an impersonal but recognizable law of morality implanted in us all. The Western world has seen so many examples of this phenomenon, in which an action regarded not merely as illegal but grossly immoral in one generation becomes, after a passage of time, either permissible or positively desirable. Homosexual acts and abortion are but two examples. Bravery on the hunting field, which for a medieval knight or a Victorian squire might have been part of the moral virtue of being a gentleman, would have become, for many in the late twentieth century, a sign of barbaric cruelty to animals.

One of the grisliest of Goethe's roles was to sit in judgement upon criminals who had been found guilty of capital offences; and this included women who had, in their distress, either aborted or killed, after giving birth, an unwanted child. The law stated that such a woman should be punished by death. At the turn of 1771–2 a woman in Frankfurt called Susanna Margarethe Brandt, 'to escape the shame and condemnation of other people', had killed her own child. She was publicly executed with a sword, some two hundred yards from the Goethes' house in the Hirschgarten. Goethe was present, as the young woman was led from her prison cell, in a procession of clergy and soldiers, and the judge in a red robe accompanied her. The event would remain in Goethe's mind as he wrote the last scene of *Faust Part One*, in which another Margarethe, or Gretchen, in her prison cell waits a similar fate for the same offence.

From his first reworkings, in his earliest twenties, of the Faust story, the new ingredient which he had introduced to the myth was the story of Gretchen, the young girl who, having become pregnant by Faust, kills her child and pays the penalty of the law – execution. During the first decade in Weimar, Goethe's *Faust* was in abeyance, but in 1782 there was an episode which still has the power not merely to puzzle but to shock. The drama of Faust and Gretchen surely cannot really work unless we feel that the young woman's situation is pitiable; and, given the fact that Gretchen would eventually be more or less canonized in *Faust Part Two*, appearing not merely as an emanation of the Eternal Feminine, indistinguishable from Helen of Troy, but also at one with the Virgin Mary and the other New Testament women who sing of Faust's redemption in the Mahlerian closing scenes.

During 1782–3 in Weimar, what could have been passing through the same mind which created, and was to create, such mythologies out of the sad story of Gretchen? A young woman, Johanna Catharina Hohn, of Tannroda, was convicted of infanticide. She was an unmarried servant aged twenty-four and had killed her child with a knife, cutting the baby's throat. The murder happened on 11 April, and when the case had been investigated the Duke was informed – on 2 May. Carl August had been considering for some time waiving the death penalty for cases of infanticide. Desperate women, anxious to cover evidence of their sin, frightened of social ostracism and still suffering from post-natal mental turmoil, were surely not to be considered in the same category as cold-blooded murderers who had killed for some nefarious motive, such as robbery.

The Duke referred the case to the judicial authority, and, although the minutes of their deliberations have been lost, it is clear that they disagreed among themselves, since they referred the case back to the Duke, and asked for the matter to be decided by the Privy Council. Clearly, the discussion between these lawyers could have gone either way. The law of the Empire still decreed that infanticide was punishable by death. The Hohn baby had been murdered in an especially bloody and unpleasant way (Gretchen in Goethe's still fragmentary play-notes drowns her child). There was a case for being severe. On the other hand, Carl August, great-nephew of the Enlightened Despot Frederick the Great, surely believed that laws dating back to medieval days needed adaptation to reflect changing times. Compassion and understanding were called forth, in this instance by reason, which surely made clear that the woman's pathetic plight could not be seen as a situation where she was entirely responsible for her own actions.

The hesitant Carl August referred the matter to his Privy Council. He, and they, had read an essay written by Christian Gottlob Voigt who was, in the coming decades, to become the most important minister in Saxe-Weimar. Voigt advocated abolishing the death penalty for infanticides, but his solution to the problem of infanticide – a widespread one, given the absence of birth control, and the vulnerability of poor women who were at the mercy not only of their own class but of their employers – was a sentence of life imprisonment with hard labour.

It was argued at the time that this was a punishment less merciful than death, and those who have attempted to exonerate Goethe and the Privy Council have tried to suggest that it was mercy which led them to make their gruesome judgement.

Unfortunately, there is no evidence that these considerations affected their judgement.

Moreover, it overlooks Voigt's wide-reaching proposals, suggesting that, for example, one feature of the whole sad phenomenon was the class system. So hierarchical was the caste system in Old Regime Empire days that it was difficult to marry out of one's class, and a woman like Hohn might well have been unable to marry the father of her child even if he and she had agreed upon the matter. In the light of the fact that Goethe depicted just such a love affair across the class divide, it seems especially poignant that he responded to this case in the way that he did. And in the light of his own preparedness, four years after the Hohn case, to set up a domestic arrangement with a woman who was considered in Weimar to be his social inferior, his judgement of the Hohn case seems even stranger.

Although it is a matter of record Carl August had been proposing the abolition of the death penalty for infanticides since as far back as 13 May 1781, the Privy Council – Fritsch, Schnauss and Goethe – advocated that Johanna Hohn should die. On 28 November 1783, she was beheaded, with a sword, by the public executioner.

'Deliberately stage-managed spectacles of death,' as a modern scholar has called such executions, needed a director with a sense of theatre.[24] If they worked well, the crowd could be convinced that the governing authority was maintaining morality and order – 'for the punishment of wickedness and vice and the maintenance of … true religion and virtue', as the English Prayer Book has it. But this required the victim to express contrition. If the person about to be executed showed contempt for the authorities, or died with a display of bravado, the crowd might put the executioner, literally, off his stroke, and, more dangerously, make the government seem weak or unfair.

So, a stage was erected in the marketplace at Weimar and Johanna Hohn was put through a show trial in which she was catechized and made to admit publicly, all over again, after her trial in court, that she had killed her child deliberately.

Goethe knew that all this would happen when he agreed with his fellow Privy Councillors to have the woman executed. He knew, too, of the cases of women who had been punished by hard labour and who had later been released. Moreover, he and the Duke, since

1777 when Goethe bought a copy, had both read Carl Lessing's adaptation of Heinrich Leopold Wagner's play *The Child Murderess*, which is highly sympathetic to the remorse of the central character who has been seduced by an aristocratic soldier. Both Carl August and Goethe had admired the play, in which the harshness of the law is clearly criticized.

W. Daniel Wilson, in his article 'Goethe, His Duke and Infanticide: New Documents and Reflections on a Controversial Execution',[25] places all the facts at our disposal. It is not comfortable reading. He shows that earlier scholars have tried to let Goethe off the hook. In a way, however, it is more disturbing than simply coming to terms with the fact that Goethe took a reactionary attitude to a matter of debate in his own pre-revolutionary times: that he sided with the notion of public order against enlightenment. No, what is disturbing for those who would try to come to terms with Goethe and his genius is the demonstration, in this grim story, of his capacity for detachment. *Lotte in Weimar* had noticed it, the callousness. More than this, the exploitativeness. Faust himself lets the most terrible things happen to Gretchen – allows Mephistopheles to murder her mother, and, despite his attempt to rescue her from prison at the end, he is persuaded to escape, leaving her to her fate.

On that solitary winter ride through the Harz Mountains, Goethe had claimed, with an authority which would surprise ornithologists, to have seen a vulture hovering overhead in the Thuringian hillsides. More disconcertingly is the fact that he compared the vulture circling its prey to his own song, his own poetic gift. As we stare back into the past and watch a twenty-four-year-old woman having her head severed from her body in a public square, we feel some of the ruthlessness not only of the Privy Councillor, but also of the poet. There were two souls struggling for mastery in Faust's breast, and the man who strove for a virtuous life, as well as for knowledge, at times seems as cynical as the devil with whom he has formed his partnership.

Goethe was a copious autobiographer. *Poetry and Truth* took the story from his birth to his arrival in Weimar in 1775. *Italian Journey* is a substantial volume, compiled in old age, but based on the letters and journals written when he was in Italy from 1786 to 1788. Of the first ten Weimar years, however, he was noticeably reticent. Though he continued to write letters, including hundreds to Frau von Stein, which constituted a kind of epistolary novel about his life, there was a great deal which went unsaid.

'The true history of my first decade in Weimar, I could only represent in the raiment of fable or fairy-story. If one wrote down the actual facts of the case they would never be believed.' Speaking to Chancellor von Müller, he said he was in a circle where he was working extremely hard, both at administrative duty and at his own studies; that he was enjoying recognition and benevolence, while being worked hard and playing hard. 'What I went through and what I accomplished, the world can eventually discover: but how it all happened, that will always be my secret.'[26]

Remarks such as this, made in old age, when he openly admitted he was glad he would not have to live through it all again, suggest that the emotional stresses outweighed the ecstasy. In 1797, he had a great auto-da-fé in which he destroyed hundreds of letters and diaries and began the laborious process, which went on for the next thirty years, of editing his previous existence. To date, the old sage has been proved right: the first decade in Weimar remains one of hyperactivity but of inner mystery, which any attempt to explain quickly comes to seem clumsy.

The hyperactivity of those years is a matter of record – the stream of productions at the Weimar theatre, the hundreds of letters written, the plays, the unfinished novel, the science. No *Faust*, and a distinct reduction in the amount of poetry. Fräulein von Göchhausen, wrote to Merck, 'Comedies, Balls, Processions, races, all follow one after another.' To the widow's mite which others lay out, Goethe has added his gold piece, and put on the most splendid *Comédie ballet* for Duchess Luise's birthday. It consisted of the following. A fairy and a magician have insulted a spirit, and he has in turn robbed them of the privilege of eternal youth. So they are made to grow old with all the fairies and magicians. They have to endure this punishment, until they discover a huge carbuncle in the mountain recesses, and in this all the magic is contained. They get back all the powers they had lost. The fairy and the magician, if they stay together and hold onto this stone, can regain their power. The mountain-spirits, fairies, gnomes and nymphs were implored to acquire the carbuncle, and when it has been found, Amor, the symbolic figure of love, leaps out of it. In that moment an extraordinary transformation takes place, and the entire theatre, which had appeared to be filled with old mothers and gnomes, suddenly is alive with beautiful girls and boys. The transformation was brilliant and so were the music and decorations. It was all accompanied by dancing and music and ended with a grand ballet.[27]

At the same time, from 1781 to 1782 he had delivered a series of lectures on anatomy to the Weimar Academy of Art, his subject being the structure of the human skeleton. After a further year's research into the subject, in 1784, he could write excitedly, both to Charlotte von Stein and to Herder, that he had made a significant discovery in the field of anatomy. Justus Christian Loder, the Professor of Anatomy at Jena, had been instructing him for a number of years. He had been focusing on the intermaxillary bone. The upper jaw of amphibians, reptiles and some mammals consists, normally, of two bones on each side, a maxilla and a premaxilla anterior to it. The Göttingen anatomist Johann Friedrich Blumenbach (1752–1840) had coined the word 'intermaxillary' to describe these often triangular wedge-line bones between the maxillae.

In primates there is a tendency for the premaxillae to fuse with the maxillae, reducing in size. Human beings do not have an intermaxillary bone. Goethe believed that the palatal suture is sometimes discernible in human skulls, particularly those of children, or in embryos. He read widely in the subject, both among the anatomists of previous ages and in those of his contemporaries Dutchman Peter Camper (1722–89) and German Blumenbach. He had not read a French anatomist of the time who was covering much the same area of research, namely Félix Vicq-d'Azyr, Georges-Louis Leclerc (1748–94), Comte de Buffon's successor at the Académie Française, who had demonstrated that in many mammals a fissure served to transmit nerves and blood from the nasal cavity to the incisive foramen on the palate.

In the midst of his political concerns, Goethe devoted every available minute of spare time to his anatomical obsession. In

Eisenach, where he had travelled for crucial financial discussions with the estates managers, he travelled with an enormous trunk, which he assured his landlady was a collection of porcelain. He had not wanted to scare her by revealing that it contained an elephant's skull.[28] He found the intermaxillary bone in the walrus, and, as he wrote to the great anatomist Samuel Thomas Sömmerring (1755–1830) in January 1784, he was confident that he would find it in the bone of the *Myrmecophaga tridactyla*, the giant anteater. Since in all these species the upper incisor is well developed, as it is in human beings, Goethe believed it was likely to be present in human jaws. And, since he was looking for them, he sure enough found them – 'in that the *canales incisivi* mark its boundary and the sutures running thence to the lateral margins indicate a division of the maxilla superior'. His paper, written in Jena in 1786, was entitled 'There is a connecting bone attributable to the upper jaw in human beings as well as in animals.'[29]

He did admit that in human skulls the intermaxillary which he had 'discovered' was invisible. 'We can only determine a part of the boundary of this bone in our species, as the rest is completely fused with the upper jaw.'

When Sömmerring read Goethe's preliminary paper on the subject, he was dismissive, denying the existence of the external suture even in human embryos. As Sömmerring wrote to Merck, the suture had not merely disappeared (Goethe's idea), it had never been present in human beings in the first place. Modern anatomists in fact side with Goethe against Sömmerring here. They believe that in the middle of the second month of gestation, the suture is present, and its disappearance 'appears to be due to the forward growth of the maxilla as a scale-like structure over the front of the pre-maxilla, such that the front wall of the sockets of the front teeth is now formed by maxilla instead of by pre-maxilla'.[30]

Goethe as scientist remains a figure of controversy to this day, in part because he himself regarded any rejection of his theories by the academy as a form of snooty trades unionism on behalf of the professionals: 'the narrow-mindedness of scientific guilds.'[31] Sömmerring was in fact quite generous to Goethe's paper, and said that it deserved to be published. In his old age, Goethe claimed that Sömmerring had endorsed his 'discovery', which he had not.

Part of the problem was methodological. A later evolutionist might be able to say that the 'vestiges' of the intermaxillary bone in human embryos point to a common ancestry from mammals in which the bones were developed and visible. Goethe and his contemporaries were aware of an evolutionary process at work, but they were decades away from either Jean-Baptiste Lamarck (1744–1829) or Charles Darwin (1809–82) who might explain to them how the mechanism of evolution might work, and how the horns and teeth of once-related species might diverge as their need, here for incisors, there for tusks, adapted to environment. Still less did Lamarck, Darwin or the eighteenth-century scientists know about genetics, which explained how the 'building blocks' of any species, and its characteristics, can be handed down.

Goethe, in common with many of his scientific contemporaries, classified Nature by archetypes to which the different species, to greater or smaller degrees, conformed. Richard Owen (1804–92), founder of the Natural History Museum in London, called these archetypes homologues. The basic building blocks of a mammal are the same. Evolution then moves forward, converting the two bones, and five-fingered hand or paw at the end of them, into human arms, fingers and thumbs, into moles' tiny digging limbs, and into the hoofs and long running legs of horses. The jury is out whether there is any evidence of these basic building blocks themselves having evolved or whether they were just 'given'. Cells. Feathers. They just appear in the evolutionary story, without, apparently, themselves having evolved. This in turn can feed the furious debates between 'Creationists' and those who believe that the 'homologues' of Owen are not 'given' but have themselves evolved. Whatever the truth of either viewpoint, it is clear that the science is in some part dictated by a metaphysical idea.

In Goethe's time, different distinctions divided the scientific community, but there was no less fervour in the preconceptions which animated the spirit of debate. Herder, for example, was convinced that the absence of an intermaxillary bone in human beings separated 'man and apes forever'.[32] Goethe, likewise, had a preconceived idea which animated the science.

Goethe was right to have discerned the vestiges of the intermaxillary bone, but it was not the single, narrow question which drove him on, the question of whether such a vestige could be discerned in a human embryo, as in a walrus. What animated him was a pair of beliefs which give life to a large part of his poetry and is absolutely central to *Faust*.

One is the essential unity of Nature. The fact that a tiny, scarcely observable vestige of a bone can be seen in its second month of life in a human foetus, just as it can be seen in the jaw and tusks of a walrus, should make us see the walrus as our sister or brother. This is one of the areas where Goethe is most modern-seeming. As our planet overheats, and species begin to become rapidly extinct, and rainforests and polar ice floes are destroyed before our eyes, the inhabitants of the planet have become sharply aware of the truths to which Goethe responded, and which of course are not unique to him – he would find them in the Hindu scriptures, for example.

When he was a very old man, his assistant Eckermann collected a nest of baby warblers. He was amazed to notice how the parent bird, who was capable of flying out of the window to freedom, would return over and again with food in its beak for the baby birds. Goethe laughingly said, 'You foolish man, if you believed in God, you would not be surprised.' And he quoted from his poem 'Prooemion':

It befits him to impart motion to the world from within,
To cherish Nature in himself and himself in Nature,
So that all that lives and is woven together and exists
Is never without his power or his spirit.

In the closing months of the year in which he made his pioneering researches into the intermaxillary bone, Goethe turned back to the work of Spinoza, whom he had first discovered ten years previously. Central to Spinoza's science, and theology, was that God is not something outside Nature, controlling it like a puppet master. As Goethe had said in the poem just quoted, what sort of a God would it be, who merely gave the *All* a push from outside and rotated it with his finger?[33]

For Spinoza, as for Goethe, Revelation occurred not in some scientific theory or scriptural text but within Nature itself, and central to Goethe's thinking was the attentive waiting upon 'the All'. Spinoza had seen the unity of mind with the Whole of Nature. Science was only possible when this immersion in the Whole had taken place. When he had first encountered Spinoza's thought, it chimed profoundly with Goethe's own developing experience of Nature.

Central to Goethe's philosophical outlook was the line in 'Prooemion' 'there is a Universe within us' – *Im Innerern ist ein Universum auch*. This is what the work on the intermaxillary bone revealed. We will encounter the same scientific outlook when Goethe turns to his colour theory, or his work on the metamorphosis of plants and animals. At every stage there is a consciousness of the Whole, the All, of which one area of scientific inquiry will give us a glimpse. The Whole is not composed of a multiplicity of parts, as Lucretius or Democritus would have taught. Rather, in each of the parts, as in our own capacity to perceive, the All is to be found. The philosophical inquiries, the poems, the ever-evolving *Faust* drama, the autobiographies and the science were all part of the same universalist exploration, a journey towards receptivity and true understanding.

There are those who try to belittle Goethe's scientific work, or to speak of it as if it were a fad, a sideline to his real work, which was literature. Any such distinction misses the point of Goethe entirely. He thought that his scientific work was the most important thing he did. When he died, his house contained over 18,000 geological, botanical and zoological specimens, many scientific instruments, with which to conduct experiments in electricity and optics.[34] He was not an 'amateur' scientist. He was a scientist whose approach to the subject was entirely different from – for example – British empiricist philosophers of the seventeenth century, or post-Victorian Darwinians. Indeed, his entirely scientific outlook challenged the atomist or materialist approach either to science or to our imaginative perceptions of life and the universe.

Jacobi had enlisted Goethe as a fellow-traveller in his Spinozist bombshell. Without asking permission, Jacobi published a poem which Goethe had written in his twenties at Strasbourg. It is a brilliant poem, although it is questionable whether, when he wrote it, it bore quite the materialist slant which Jacobi gave it by quoting it in his controversial Spinoza pamphlet.

Moreover, it overlooked the fact that, as Goethe said to him in that famous letter, Goethe considered himself a part-time pantheist, part-time polytheist, part-time theist, depending on which branch of writing he was pursuing. As a poet, he maintained, he was a polytheist; as a scientist, a pantheist.

In Goethe's poem of the same name, Prometheus, having been punished by Zeus for stealing fire and giving it to the human race, refuses to be cowed by the bullying Lord of Olympus.

Oh Gods! I know nothing poorer, under the sun, than you.
You miserably feed on sacrificial offerings, and the breath of prayers.
Fools full of hope, children and beggars invest you with Majesty.

He rails against Zeus. Why should I respect you? What have you ever done for me? Can you ever dry my terrified tears? He says, moreover, that he will create humanity in his image. A race – *ein Geschlecht* –

A race that will be like me
A race that will suffer and weep
Enjoy life, be happy and –
Just as I do –
Take no notice of you!

Goethe ruefully wrote to Jacobi, 'Herder finds it amusing that on this occasion, I'm to sit on the same funeral pyre as Lessing.' He objected, however, to being bracketed with Jacobi in his materialism. As he wrote:

Forgive me if I prefer to remain silent when there is talk of a divine being, which I recognize only in rebus singularibus ... Forgive me for not writing more to you about your little book! I don't mean to sound either lofty or indifferent. You know that in this matter, I am not of your opinion ... Nor can I approve of how you use the word 'faith'. I cannot allow you to get away with this manner; it is only suited to sophists of faith, whose greatest interests must be to obscure and wrap in the clouds of their wobbly, breezy realm all certainty of knowledge, since they are unable to shake the foundations of truth.[35]

A simple-minded match of Goethe's life as a court poet and that of the Italian poet Torquato Tasso (1544–95) would be crass. Nevertheless, there is a teasing sense in which the play could not have been written were it not for the author's relationship with Charlotte von Stein, and with the Duke. This would explain why he waited for decades – until 1807 – before staging the play at the Weimar theatre. It was this play, and not *Faust*, which was performed in that same theatre, on 27 March 1832 – the whole audience in mourning – as a farewell by company, court and audience to Weimar's poet-prince.[36]

Wilhelm Meister[37] read Tasso's *Jerusalem Delivered* (1581), not in the Italian, but in the translation by Koppen. The passages of the poem which touch him personally are those where Tancred, in the dark, plunges his sword into an unknown 'knight' who is actually Clorinda. As he loosens the helmet of the 'knight' he recognizes the heathen Amazonian warrior whom he loves, and he baptizes her. (Those who have not read the poem will still perhaps remember Poussin's depiction of this scene.) For Wilhelm Meister as a young, aspirant actor, it becomes the archetype of his capacity to wound those he loves – as, for Goethe, the thought of the tears of Frederika as he takes his leave of her, the embarrassment and justifiable anger of Lotte Kestner when she read *Werther*, and other examples came to mind.

Interestingly, though, he did not make this the centre point of his drama when he came to write about the poet of *Jerusalem Delivered*. Goethe read the biography of Tasso by Pierantonio Serassi which was published in Rome in 1785. Those of a suspicious nature might have wondered quite why, on top of his innumerable other duties and interests, he was brushing up his Italian.

The Tasso of history would be deemed by modern medical opinion to have suffered from a bipolar disorder. He died, aged fifty-one, having for the previous twenty years – since the completion of *Gerusalemme Liberata* – been tormented by persecution mania. For a time he was confined in a madhouse. Having journeyed to Rome to receive the Laureate's crown from the Pope, he was too ill to attend the ceremony on the Capitol, and he died in Rome. There would have been a drama to be made out of Tasso's madness, either at the court of Ferrara, or at the court of the Duke of Ferrara's elder brother, Cardinal Luigi d'Este. He was painfully in love with one of the ladies-in-waiting to Lucrezia Bendidio.

But Goethe's play is not, centrally, concerned either with madness or with love, so much as with the relationship between an artist and his patron, about the conflicting demands of intellectual and artistic freedom and personal and financial security. It is concerned with the discrepancy between art as the vehicle of courtly prestige and a more romantic, or even demonic perception of art as an autonomous activity.[38]

Another strand to the play, however, is Torquato Tasso's delayed adolescence. The poet carries the Whole, the All, in himself, and is caught up with the distraction, the burden, of older women being in love with him. If this is one of the themes, Charlotte von Stein must have read it, when it was eventually finished and published, with some pain.

One of the bones of contention between Tasso and the Duke of Ferrara, in the play, is that the Duke, his patron, believes himself to be the owner of the poem, *Jerusalem Delivered*. In Goethe's case, the great work – *Faust* – had not yet been written. Far from owning his great poetry, the Duke of Weimar, his Maecenas, as Goethe had described him when in happier mood, had filled Goethe's days with activities which made it all but impossible to do sustained literary work.

Goethe was not insane, like Tasso, but he was subject to mood swings, and, as he once remarked to Charlotte von Stein, there was no element of 'Lightness' in his character. Those who called on him might find a genial, boozy companion who was in the mood for talk; but, equally, they might find someone who was taciturn, preoccupied with the thoughts inside his head, and scarcely fit for company. Alfonso, Tasso's Duke and patron, tells him that he is confiscating his masterpiece and, whether or not it contains imperfections, he is taking a copy to Rome to present it to the Pope. Tasso should take things easy for a while.

Tasso responds in words which are spoken from Goethe's heart:

To me, the least peace and quiet
Is found in peace and quiet. As for me,
My Nature is not meant – alas, I feel it! –
On the broad waves to loll and swim.[39]

He goes on to tell the Duke that not being allowed to write is a form of death. Even though continual spinning will be the death of the silkworm, it is only in such hyperactivity that the silkworm finds life. We remember Rodin's advice to Rilke, 'Travaillez! Travaillez! Toujours travaillez!'

In July 1786 Goethe had written to Charlotte von Stein, 'whoever wastes his time on administration – unless, of course, he is a ruler – must be either a philistine, a rogue or a fool'.[40] What did this say about the previous decade of Goethe's own life? As if he needed an alarm bell to summon him back to heeding his muse, Goethe had signed an agreement with a Leipzig publisher – Georg Joachim Göschen (1752–1828) – for an eight-volume edition of his Works. He was to be paid 2,000 talers – a little less than double his annual salary as Privy Councillor. *Torquato Tasso* and *Iphigenia*, intended as verse dramas, were still only in their rudimentary prose versions. *Faust* was still only a fragment. He simply had to escape the routines of court life and the burdens of administrative office, if these works were to be brought to completion.

Moreover, he still nursed the dream that he might create a body of theatrical work which would enable German drama to stand beside the English and the French.

The inner demands of his poetic calling were symbolized by his feeling for an imagined Italy. Since childhood, there had been a symbolic contrast between the prosaic routines of his father's legal practice in Frankfurt, his respectable middle-class friends, his clockwork devotion to earning money and maintaining a distance between present comforts and the humbler beginnings of his innkeeper grandmother. There was another world, symbolized by the prints which adorned the drawing-room walls, the *Vedute di Roma*. They were more than simple decorations in a rich man's house. They were signals from another world, where the Imagination ruled. The crumbling pillars of the Forum Romanum, the temples, the triumphal arches, spoke of the world, less of the Caesars, than of the poets. These copperplate engravings were messages from Ovid, Horace, Virgil and Statius.

Herder used to mock Goethe by saying that he had learned all his Latin by reading Spinoza, since this was the only Latin that Privy Councillor Goethe of Weimar was seen by his colleagues and friends to be reading.

He did not realize how carefully I had to guard myself against the classics and that it was sheer anxiety which drove me to take refuge in the abstractions of Spinoza. Even relatively recently Wieland's translations of Horace's *Satires* made me really miserable; after reading only a couple, I felt beside myself. My passionate desire to see these objects with my own eyes had grown to such a crisis-point that if I had not taken the decision [to go to Italy], I should have gone totally to pieces.[41]

Wilhelm Meister's love for the androgynous Italian Mignon, a teenage boy-girl, was surely the most touching thing Goethe ever invented. Book II of the novel ends with Mignon's fear that Wilhelm is going to desert her and the old blind harpist. She clings to him in the public streets, strokes him, holds his arm. He is flattered, but he also tries to make her desist because he is afraid of the scandal this will produce. The harpist sings two of his most beautiful lyrics – 'Wer nie sein Brot mit Tränen ass' ('Who never ate his bread with tears') and 'Wer sich der Einsamkeit ergibt' ('Who longs to live in solitude, ah! Soon his wish will gain,' as Carlyle's version has it). There follows the extraordinary chapter in which Wilhelm feels trapped in 'indefinite wandering'. He feels he must escape and put down roots. At this point, Mignon bursts into his room and dresses his hair, unties his topknot and starts to weep. When he tries to comfort her, she falls into his lap. Her tears fall fast, as her own long, black hair is unwound and they hug one another in the tightest embrace.

'My child, my child, you are mine!' he exclaims. Just outside his door, the crazy old harpist strikes up another lyric, and Wilhelm's heart feels it is bursting with an indescribable happiness.

In this quite amazing fictitious scene, we feel the thirty-seven-year-old author has reached a crisis. Unlike Wilhelm, who feels he must stop wandering, Goethe feels he must stop being wedged in the 'same old, same old' routines of court life in a tiny, landlocked pumpernickel court. Mignon and Wilhelm do not have a fully sexual relationship – unlike Wilhelm and the androgynous actress at the very beginning of the story; but their relationship is intense, fed by kissing and weeping. She is, above all, young. Her creator has had enough of the peculiar *amitié amoreuse* with an older woman which has been the emotional backdrop of his life for ten years. Mignon calls him her father. But Goethe is ready for proper sex, a proper grown-up relationship with a woman. After a lifetime in the landlocked German world, he wants sunlight, the warm south. And Mignon's song is its symbolic expression:

Kennst du das Land, wo die Zitronen blühn –
D'you know the land where the lemons flower,
The oranges glow in the deep undergrowth,
A gentle wind flutters from the blue sky,
The myrtle is quiet, there stands the laurel tree –
D'you know it well?
O father, I want to go with you, beloved –
Thence! Thence!

Long before he actually achieved it, the fantasy of an escape to Italy, to a new life of erotic and artistic freedom, had been fashioned into unforgettable art.

8

ITALY

Suddenly he stopped and stood, musing, in front of a picture of Rome. It depicted the Milvian Bridge, which one crosses when entering the eternal city from the North. 'You probably have no conception,' he said, 'since crossing over that bridge on my way home, I have not really had a single day of pure happiness'.

Conversation with F. von Müller, 30 May 1814, twenty-six years after Goethe's return to Weimar from his Italian journey

The landlord of the Locanda dell' Orso – a Roman inn which had been known to Dante and to Montaigne – was well accustomed to German visitors. This one, in his mid-thirties, a Signor Jean Philippe Müller, with his dark brown eyes and brown, sunburned face, could almost have passed for an Italian; until, that is, in his deeply mellifluous voice, he spoke. His poor grasp of the language made the German unmistakable and, sure enough, within hours of his arrival, he had written letters to a German artist who lived nearby in the parish of Santa Maria del Popolo, just nearby – one Johann Heinrich Tischbein.

Signor Müller, it seemed, was also an artist, who had set out from the inn almost at once with his sketchbook, in the direction of the Roman Forum. He had returned, hours later, full of enthusiasm for the monuments and artworks of the Old World.

While Müller was absent, the innkeeper would have had the chance to make a rudimentary search of his belongings. The travelling trunks were new. One had been bought in the last few weeks from a store in Ratisbon; another even more recently, in Venice. In one of them, there were piles of papers, notebooks, manuscripts, written in the scarcely comprehensible German script. The landlord could just make out the names in large letters on the title page of the notebooks: TORQUATO TASSO; IPHIGENIA IN TAURIS. The clothes were new – a hat, two pairs of shoes, stockings, all purchased in Venice, as could be determined from a squint at the little bundle of bills on the dressing table, which also included the receipt for tolls paid on his journey, for entering the cities of Venice, Vicenza, Florence, and at length, via the customs officer at the Piazza del Popolo, the Eternal City itself.

Some of the sketchbooks already contained drawings of Italian cityscapes and landscapes. Some of them contained lyrics – these incomprehensible, and illegible. Beneath them were two enormous folios, Italian these – the works of Vitruvius and of Palladio.

So – an architect on holiday? Yet another German painter? It was impossible to guess from the sight of Signor Filippo's belongings. (That was how he had asked the maid, a little roguishly, to address him – 'Signor Filippo'.) There were no smart clothes, so he presumably knew no one in society. He had told the landlord that he would not be staying long.

Indeed, the very next day, when Signor Tischbein called for Signor Filippo, the German visitor came to his landlord and settled his bill. Tischbein had sublet two modest rooms in the nearby Casa Moscatelli to his friend. The Casa was a stately corner building opposite the Palazzo Rondanini, just near the Piazza del Popolo on the Corso.

Tischbein had been in Rome for a number of years[1] and was the centre of a small group of German-speaking artists and writers. In a letter which is famous in the annals of German literature (written thirty-five years later) he remembered his first meeting with that visitor.

Never have I experienced greater joy than the first time I set eyes on you in that inn on the way down from St Peter's. You were sitting in a green frock coat beside the stove. You came up to me and said, 'I am Goethe'.

Tischbein, known as well for his portraits as for his reconstruction of historical scenes, was a prolific artist. (He once said he could paint three portraits in a day.)[2] Goethe had corresponded with the painter for a number of years, and was responsible for persuading Duke Ernst of Saxe-Gotha, the grandfather of Prince Albert, to give him a pension while he was in Rome. The moment in the Roman *locanda*, however, was their first meeting and they immediately took to one another. Goethe, at thirty-seven, believed – as he would tell his own employer, Duke Carl August of Saxe-Weimar – that he had scarcely ever seen such a pure-hearted, good, clever, cultivated person as Tischbein. It was a mutual admiration society, since Tischbein told Lavater, 'Goethe is a really great guy' – 'ein Werckliger [i.e. *wirkliger*] Mensch'. He saw him as a fellow voluptuary.[3]

And it was Tischbein who created that image of the great poet which was to become the most famous – *Goethe in the Roman Campagna*. The Italian landscape, dotted with the ruins of antiquity, is the background. Goethe, in a large-brimmed hat, sits in modern dress, with breeches and silk stockings, but with most of his person draped in a billowing expanse of stuff, part Imperial toga, part hieratic chasuble, part artist's smock. The eighteenth-century rationalist is in vatic vestment. This is a man with a message to the planet even if, in his haste to create this icon, Tischbein gave the modern magus two left feet and painted the legs one and a half times the length they could have been in real life.

Both Goethe's long autobiographical works, *Poetry and Truth* and *Italian Journey*, were written in maturity. The first book, begun between the ages of sixty-two and sixty-five, was completed when he was eighty; the second, begun when he was sixty-seven, was also finished when he was eighty, though making use of materials, letters and diaries, written while he was in Italy in his thirties. In both books, travelling to Italy is seen as the great turning point in his life-experience. It was something much more than a cultural jaunt. *Poetry and Truth* ends with a superbly crafted cliffhanger. His lawyer father, having watched Goethe enter his own profession in Frankfurt, had been scornful of his son's willingness to turn himself into a court flunkey in a backwater like Weimar. Nevertheless, undeterred by this scorn – indeed, egged on to disobey it by his irritation with his father – Goethe had his bags packed and was awaiting the ducal landau. It failed to arrive. He took this as a sign that perhaps his father had, after all, been right, and he decided to set out instead in the direction of Italy, and to follow in the footsteps of that father who had collected the prints of Roman views which decorated the walls of the family house in Frankfurt.

Goethe made the first part of the journey to Heidelberg. On the last page but one of the memoirs, however, at one in the morning, a postilion arrived from Frankfurt. The landau had been delayed. Far from being forgotten, Goethe was eagerly awaited in Weimar. He saw this as the hand of destiny, and he quoted from his own drama, *Egmont*, upon which, at the time, he was engaged:

> Child, no more of this! As if whipped on by unseen spirits, the sun-steeds of Time draw on our Destiny's flimsy chariot; and there remains nothing to do, but hold tight to the reins, and steer the wheels to right and left, here avoiding a stone, and there a falling crash. Who knows where it's heading? He scarcely remembers whence it came.[4]

The second autobiography, *Italian Journey*, begins with another escape, this time, his setting forth from Carlsbad in 1786. The ten Weimar years are not covered. His silence about that decade is total, so we can only speculate about what triggered the departure for Italy at that particular moment. What we do know is that the Italian journey had been long planned and the testimony of both the autobiographies, and of the manuscripts in his trunk as he travelled, tell the same story. His life as a poet and dramatist had been interrupted, indeed swamped, by his life as a Privy Councillor. The Weimar life had been a ten-year interruption to his creative life. *Egmont* was still unfinished, a decade after he had started it. *Iphigenia*, though a hurried (written in six weeks) version existed, was still in prose and he was yet to turn it into the verse version which Thomas Mann would consider to be the finest work of German literature. *Torquato Tasso* was unfinished. *Faust* was still a fragment.

Goethe was to be in Rome from November 1786 to 24 April 1788. During 1787, he made trips to Naples, Sicily and, later that year, to the hill-town of Castel Gandolfo, which the popes made their summer residence. If we stick to our plan of reading Goethe's life through the prism of *Faust*, we shall note that this was the period when he wrote the scene of Faust's visit to the Witch's Kitchen. The biographers find an aptness here. The scene, one of the many departures from, and elaborations on, the original Faust myth, is the one in which Mephistopheles acquired a magic potion for his client which will make the scholar-recluse into a stud thirty years young.[5] In his enhanced sexual potency, Faust sees, as the devil tells him teasingly will be inevitable, Helen of Troy in every woman he meets.[6]

Austrian-born, later American, Freudian analyst Kurt R. Eissler, in a two-volume work of 1,000 pages, developed the theory that Goethe had been sexually obsessed by his sister Cornelia, a year younger than himself, who had died in 1777. Eissler's book is worth reading, as it is full of insights about Goethe's work. Not every reader will be convinced, however, that the poet remained celibate, unable to perform sexually, until he reached Italy. Some readers will believe that the whole of Eissler's 1,000-page edifice was demolished by one crude wrecking ball, released by Roberto Zapperi who, in a sprightly but scholarly account of Goethe in Italy, remarks that it is 'beyond doubt' that 'like all men of his age and time in Europe, Goethe sought out prostitutes'.[7]

This is not just journalistic speculation. A beady-eyed perusal of Goethe's cash books enabled Zapperi to tell that he spent 1 lira on a woman in Padua on 26 September, and on 14 October in Venice, 2 lira. There are other payments noted, both in Venice and in Vicenza. While not wholly conclusive, these notebook entries are distinguished from payments made to women for laundry. Moreover, Goethe wrote with extreme candour about his erotic adventures in the Venetian Epigrams, and these witty pieces of smut do not have the tone of a man experiencing such pleasures for the first time in his life.

> Boys loved I too, while much preferring girls.
> When I've had my way with her as a girl, I can always turn her round and treat her as a boy.[8]

Possibly, Goethe supposed, incorrectly, that anal intercourse was a way of avoiding infection. As the memoirs of Casanova make clear, doctors then were not able to distinguish between gonorrhoea, which was curable, and syphilis, which was not. 'The two were manifestations of a single disease' – the Pox, as the modern history of medicine reminds us.[9]

Carl August himself contracted venereal disease after a rash encounter in Amsterdam, as he told Goethe in a letter written from Mainz in January 1788 (the letter does not survive, but Goethe's reply makes it clear what had happened). In one of his epigrams, Goethe addressed a young friend, Adrian Gilles Camper, who had come to Rome as a tourist. In Goethe's little poem he playfully imagines Camper being guided by his zoologist father to an interest in four-footed animals. On his visit to Rome, having studied the four-footed, he turned his attention to the two-footed:

Poor Camper, now you have to atone for your mistake!
Eight days later, you are laid up, swallowing mercury.[10]

(The usual 'cure' for the Pox.)

After apparent incaution in the Italian towns where he spent only brief amounts of time, on his way south, Goethe's patterns of behaviour underwent a change in Rome. Although Eissler does not persuade us that the poet's first sexual experiences happened in the Celestial City, there can be little doubt that it was here that he had his first proper love affair. It was a transformative experience, enriching not only the pattern of his life, but also of his poetry.

Goethe was the rising literary star, the playwright whose *Götz von Berlichingen* had been hailed as the arrival of the German Shakespeare on its publication in 1773. It had been while he awaited its publication that he had spent his time in Wetzlar, mopping up the experiences which would turn into *The Sorrows of Young Werther*, holding his companions spellbound with his conversations, while worshipping Lotte Buff in a safely sexless kind of a way.

Goethe admitted he felt safe – *sorglos* – in Lotte's company, knowing that the relationship could never develop sexually since she was already committed to marrying Kestner. He was in the callow phase of believing that the greatest happiness was to be found in yearning – *Sehnsucht* – a very Goethean word which is repeated throughout his life and which in his *Faust* coloured his attitude not merely to Nature but to Life itself.

The best-selling ingredient in *Werther* had been the introduction, into the soppy theme of yearning, the starker phenomenon of suicide.

Thomas Mann, with wit, warmth and no doubt plenty of self-knowledge about the sliver of ice in every writer's heart, had made a novel out of the aged Lotte's reaction (and our own) to the ruthless creator of *Werther*. He had used her real name! He had ruthlessly exploited the tragedy of Jerusalem's suicide. But *Werther* had been more than a novel. It had been an event in European consciousness. Not only did it lay aside, with an insouciance which was positively insolent, the traditional Christian condemnation of suicide; it also made central to consciousness, as to art, the exploration of *self*. Thereby, the novel was not merely a prime example of what the Germans were calling Storm and Stress literature, a model of Romanticism. Goethe also made himself, as Freud and Jung readily acknowledged, the John the Baptist of the psychoanalytical movement.

It was to *Faust*, more than to *Werther*, that they both obsessively looked. Nevertheless, without Werther's insight – 'I look back into myself and find a world' – Freud would never have developed his concept of the Unconscious.

Goethe, in his Romantic phase, found a whole world in himself. Likewise, the Germans themselves, split into so many political entities, found their identity less in nationhood than in shared language and culture. In spite of its full name, the Holy Roman Empire and German Nation, there was no German Nation. Jacob and Wilhelm Grimm, best known to anglophone readers as the collectors of fairy stories, were primarily grammarians, the instigators of Germany through its language. Jacob Grimm wrote that the task of being a grammarian was 'durch und durch politisch', 'through and through political'.[11]

It was not exactly possible, while being the inhabitant of a German-speaking land, to escape the political questions – the future of Germany, the possibility of it uniting, and so on. Freud's gradual development of psychoanalysis, towards the end of the nineteenth century, was both political in itself and an attempt to withdraw from the political – finding the world in self.

Goethe's detachment from immediate political involvement is of a piece with all this. His arrival in Rome in the late autumn of 1786 was an escape from Weimar, an escape from his life as a politician and administrator, a holiday from being Goethe the public man and famous author. The incognito under which he travelled was an inner necessity. The variety of pseudonyms, misspelt in police stations, parish registers and the like, tells the story of a temporary detachment from the carapace of being Goethe.

The escape from the ducal party in Carlsbad had something about it of cloak and dagger. Travel in the Europe of 1786 attracted notice. To the huge majority of the European population, travel was simply an impossibility, forbidden either by their poverty or by the actual regulations of wherever they happened to reside. The Holy Roman Empire and the Papal States were heavily, if inefficiently, policed. Even on the first leg of the journey, in the magnificent, Danube-girt city of Ratisbon, the local newspaper, the *Regensburger Diarium*, noted the arrival of 'Herr Müller, Passagier von Leipzig logiert in weissem Lamm' (Mr Müller, traveller from Leipzig, staying at the White Lamb). He took the risk of looking in the local bookshop, was recognized, but shamelessly denied being Goethe. He was Herr Müller, a travelling merchant.

The very clothes in his modest luggage spoke of his desire to be anonymous, to lay aside his role as the Privy Councillor. Had he travelled under his true identity he would have been obliged to make courtesy calls on behalf of his Duke, and, when he reached Rome, to present himself at levees for cardinals and principessas. More vivid than Tischbein's icon of a German Genius in the Roman Campagna in his wideawake hat, is his watercolour of Goethe, back view, gazing out of his small attic window at the Roman rooftops. His stocking feet are clad in slippers. His baggy shirt is half tucked into his breeches. His hair is tied back in one loose band. Shoulders, elbows, haunches are all relaxed. This is the man who, in his late thirties, had found the freedom which had eluded him all his life. He had travelled alone, something he had never done before. It was the first time in thirty-seven years that he had not been accompanied by a servant. He ate all his meals at a nearby inn. Laundry and household cleaning was done for the whole household by Roman women who came in and were paid piece rates.

Italy represented release, as any reader of his celebrated anthology piece knows – 'D'you know the land where the lemons flower?' The mythic status of Rome, inside his head, had begun as a child, when his father had shown him his Roman *vedute*. By the time he himself was an old man, Goethe was editing versions of his own life and writing the *Italian Journey*. He had spoken to Charlotte von Stein of the very thought of Italy having made him ill with yearning. It had reached the point where even to open a page of Latin literature or to see a picture of an Italian scene would renew the mania.

The departure from Carlsbad was not an impulsive flit. It had been carefully planned for months. Back in January, he had written in a letter to Charlotte that he regretted not having studied Italian more deeply. In March and May, he dropped hints in letters to the composer Christoph Kayser that he wanted to travel to Italy, 'if only I had as good a command of Italian as I do of poor old German, I'd invite you on a journey beyond the Alps and we'd be very happy'.[12]

Moreover, being a practical man of affairs, Goethe had made arrangements for money to be sent to Italy. He had primed his secretary in Weimar, Philipp Seidel. He was detailed to look after Fritz, Charlotte von Stein's son. (Neither the boy nor his mother were to be told of Goethe's departure until it had happened.) Some 200 talers were 'laundered' secretly via a Jena merchant, Jacob Heinrich Paulsen. The Leipzig publisher Georg Joachim Göschen to whom Goethe had promised a new eight-volume edition of his 'works', which would contain the as yet unfinished plays mentioned above, was also primed to release cash which in a roundabout, carefully planned route would reach Herr Müller in Rome.

Once established in Rome, the pattern of his days made it clear that his surface explanations for the sojourn in Italy were the truthful ones. He devoted himself to a wholehearted embrace of art and antiquities; he explored the limits of his talents as a visual artist; he polished, revised and immeasurably improved the unfinished dramatic works in his portfolio; and he enriched his sexual experiences.

The old sage Goethe told young Eckermann that he had discovered 'in his fortieth year in Italy, that I had no talent for the visual arts and that my talents in that direction were misplaced'.[13] Since this is obviously true, and since there are so many other reasons for remembering Goethe, other than his paintings and drawings, it is easy to neglect the fact that he was not simply posing when he gave Herr Müller's profession as that of an artist. Apart from the paintings, 638 of his drawings survive from the escape to Italy.

The circle of women and men in which he moved were all, with the exception of the travel writer Karl Philipp Moritz, painters. Tischbein was his entrée into the bohemian, easy-going, German-speaking set of whom the most accomplished artist was Angelica Kauffman. She playfully called the household in Casa Moscatelli, which comprised Tischbein, Goethe, the landscape painter Johann Georg Schütz and the portraitist Johann Friedrich Burg, 'the German Academy of Rondadini'.[14]

Goethe was understandably quick to establish a routine whereby he spent every Sunday with Kauffman and her second husband, the protective Antonio Zucchi.

> I ate chez Angelika; it is now an established routine that I am her Sunday guest. Before dinner, we drove to the Palazzo Barberini, to see the superb Leonardo da Vinci [Vanity and Modesty, now attributed to Luini] and Raphael's mistress [probably by Giulio Romano] painted by himself. It is very pleasant, looking at pictures with Angelika, her eye is so very well educated, her knowledge of art is so great. What is more, she has an enormous feeling, for everything that is true, beautiful and tender.[15]

Angelica Kauffman, seven years older than Goethe, had literally sat at the feet of Winckelmann when she first came to Rome. When he had arrived in the city in 1755, the immensely learned, impoverished son of a cobbler, it could not have been better timing. His obsession with the Antique, his profound knowledge of Latin and Greek literature and culture, were recognized by Cardinal Albani, who saw the young German as the ideal curator of his burgeoning collection of caryatids, vases, statues and bas-reliefs, with which he filled gallery after gallery in his Roman villa. It was the time when Pompeii and Herculaneum were being rediscovered, and, among the ruins of Paestum, Winckelmann could find proof of his belief that the pure ideal of Art was to be found in the Hellenic. Goethe, when a student at Leipzig, had fallen under the spell of Winckelmann's illustrator and disciple, Adam Friedrich Oeser, but it was in the salon of Angelica Kauffman, with the prospect of actually seeing antiquities, not in copper engravings but in reality, at first hand, that imaginative engagement with the classical world caught fire.

It was through Angelica that he met the Swiss art historian and painter Johann Heinrich Meyer (1759–1832) whom he would later install as part of his own 'set' in Weimar, where his nickname, because of his strong Swiss accent, was Kunscht-Meyer. They later collaborated on *Winckelmann und sein Jahrhundert* (1800) and the *Entwurf einer Kunstgeschichte des 18 ten Jahrhunderts*, which, given how much both men owed to the hospitality of Kauffman's and her husband's hospitality, contains a breezy acceptance of the 'inferiority' of female to male artists which is scarcely sufferable. They acknowledged that women, being excluded from life-drawing classes, were at a distinct disadvantage, but they did not recommend any change to this state of things, accepting as a given that women could not *decently* expose their eyes to human nudity. (Neither Goethe nor Meyer seemed to consider 'their daily familiarity with nudity as midwives, nurses and mothers', and when Meyer established a school of drawing at Weimar, the women who attended were obliged to restrict themselves to seemly subjects such as flower-painting.[16])

It would seem that Goethe had only intended to spend a month in Rome before returning to Germany. In November, however, he changed his plans radically, having heard that Vesuvius had erupted. It was not a momentous eruption. Sir William Hamilton, British Envoy Extraordinary to the court of the King of Two Sicilies, felt the newspapers had grossly exaggerated the size of the eruption and was concerned it would attract yet more tourists to the Bay of Naples. Hamilton had been in the post since 1764. With his passion for science, and for collecting the artefacts of antiquity, he had earned himself the title of 'The Modern Pliny'[17] and his villa was a magnet for Grand Tourists.[18]

Hamilton told the naturalist Sir Joseph Banks that he dreaded the 'plague' of visitors following the minor eruption. The arrival of Goethe, however, so much a man after his own heart, was an altogether different matter.

It was a sign of how relatively free and easy the atmosphere of Naples was, compared with Rome, that Goethe could discard his pseudonyms. He was welcomed by Hamilton, not as Signor Filippo Müller, but as Goethe. Hamilton, now in his late fifties, had, as Goethe observed, found the 'acme' of his delight, in both Nature and in the arts, in the person of a twenty-year-old woman named Emma Hart, destined to be the second Lady Hamilton and, even more famously, the mistress of Horatio, Lord Nelson.

From Naples, Goethe made a trip to Sicily. It was while walking in the Botanic Gardens in Palermo that Goethe's mind reverted to one of his central scientific ideas, namely the evolution of all plant life from a single original, the *Urpflanze*. The abundance of different botanical species were, to Goethe's mind, manifestly all related to one another, all conveying individual clues to an overall Unity. 'Nature is the only Book every single page of which offers a single great united content.'[19]

In the sphere of botany, there flowed the attempt to advance further towards an understanding of *all* natural phenomena. Here was the chance to get to grips with what Spinoza had called the one and the all of Nature: the *En Kai Pan*. This was the point where science and religion shared the same goal, to be expressed in the language of poetry. For Goethe, the Desire and Pursuit of the Whole consumed his entire imaginative and cognitive being.

> Nature! We are surrounded and embraced by her – powerless to leave her and powerless to enter her more deeply. Unasked and without warning, she sweeps us away in the round of her dance and dances on until we fall exhausted from her arms. She brings forth ever new forms: what is there, never was; what was, never will return. All is new, and yet forever old. We live within her, and are strangers to her. She speaks perpetually with us, and does not betray her secret.[20]

It was while hearing these words read aloud at a lecture that the young Sigmund Freud (1856–1939) made the decision to abandon the study of law and to switch to science. A fact worth laying down here, for the curious expanded fibreglass figure to be seen in Frankfurt airport is not simply a peculiar polychrome emblem of German intellectual superiority to the rest of Europe. He is like a nineteenth-century deity and his works were a foundation course in two of the most fundamental and life-changing ideas of the 1800s: the story of evolution, and the discovery, or invention, of the Unconscious. When Goethe first expounded his theory of the *Urpflanze* to Schiller, the dramatist replied, 'That's not something found out by experience, it is just an idea' (*Das ist keine Erfahrung, das ist eine Idee*). But ideas (compare the strength of Marxism in the political story) are often stronger than epistemologically verifiable data.

Whereas it could be argued that Freud imposed ideas on the Greek mythology, rather than bringing out what was inherent in the stories of Oedipus or Electra, the relationship between Freud and Goethe, and more specifically Freud and *Faust*, is of a different order. Freud overtly derived many of his ideas from Goethe and it would not be entirely fanciful to see Goethe, in his quest for the secret of everything, as the forerunner of psychoanalysis – what he called *Nature* being, among other things, but primarily among other things, sexuality. It is not an exaggeration to name Goethe as Freud's 'master and mentor'.[21]

The drama, that of the Idea, not verifiable, the overpowering strength and mystery of Nature, the compulsion, on the part of any inquiring mind, to master the secret – this is what lies at the very heart of *Faust*. The time in Italy saw Goethe bring to completion three of his greatest dramas – *Torquato Tasso*, *Egmont* and *Iphigenia*. *Faust* lay apparently neglected in the portmanteau which he had purchased in Venice. It was, however, very much in his mind, and we know that, while he was in Rome, Goethe conceived and probably wrote the scene of the Witch's Kitchen in *Part One*. It is a scene which is totally extraneous to the original Faust legend, but very relevant to the place Goethe had reached in his own personal journey during the Roman interlude.

It is a scene about sexual awakening. Faust, in his dusty Gothic, northern study, disillusioned with the academic life, but ever more desirous to *master* knowledge, especially scientific knowledge, has summoned up the terrifying Earth Spirit. Nature, however, retains its mystery. It was after this experience that Faust encountered the irritating black poodle which had come into his study and eventually manifested himself as Mephistopheles, the jokey, cynical companion, whose conversation, as Goethe acknowledged, owed much to the friendships formed in Strasbourg, and especially the companionship of Merck. Goethe's friends and companions, in the years before he went to Weimar, had known a young man who was a curious mixture of conviviality and reserve, dissipation and inwardness, friendliness and pure ice.

> Goethe is life and soul of the parties now, going to balls and dancing like crazy. But he still has his old whimsicality. In the middle of the liveliest conversation, he may suddenly take it into his head to get up and leave, and not come back. He is wholly a law unto himself, conforms to no usages, and at times and places at which everyone appears very formally dressed, he arrives in the most casual attire – and vice versa.[22]

The ability to live life entirely on his own terms was something he had carried with him to Weimar. Although the duties of the courtier, civil servant and politician had eaten into his life as a writer, and he had been unable to settle and finish the Complete Works in eight volumes for which the Leipzig publisher was waiting, there had been a sense in which the life had suited him perfectly. Courtly Love for Charlotte von Stein supplemented, if Zapperi is right, by surreptitious paid sex, had been in every way more suitable to his professional needs than a bourgeois marriage in Frankfurt would have been. It was partly to escape the fate of bourgeois marriage that he had left Frankfurt in the first place. Marriage was only possible with someone of his own class and the stultifying conventions of bourgeois marriage were the last thing which he or his poetry required. Nor could his proud spirit ever have been happy had he married a woman of a higher social standing. Even Lili's banker family had felt that the Goethes did not quite cut the mustard, and Goethe would surely, in maturity, have been able to find someone more socially elevated than them, had he wanted to.

Yet – given the advance of time, his sensual disposition, his love of children – there was something missing, and Italy was going to reveal what that something was. Goethe and Faust would discover it together: Goethe, in the arms of his first proper girlfriend, Faust in the Witch's Kitchen. This is another way in which Goethe seems strikingly modern. He lived and wrote entirely as if the bourgeois Lutheran conventions had never existed.

Mephistopheles appears to be lowering the intellectual Faust into a purely sensualist way of life, making him a failed academic who is neglecting his scientific and philosophical researches in favour of the simple pursuit of pleasure. It could even be the case that, in an early stage of the play's development in Goethe's brain, this was how things appeared to the poet himself. *Faust*, however, undermines a great many of our preoccupations and presuppositions, and if the Witch's Kitchen seems like a place where a man has taken a decisive step on the road to damnation, it will turn out to be a place where a personal transformation had begun and a new vision of sex, and the sexes, has been opened up. Freud would refer to the 'Witch metapsychology'.[23]

The witch's knowledge, different from the brilliant but sterile knowledge of Doctor Faust, seems plainly to be the 'unknown' of Faust's knowledge, founded precisely on a misapprehension of what the Witch knows. For the Witch's enchanting knowledge puts the scientist Faust in touch with that dark, chaotic part of himself he repudiates as alien, failing to recognize it when it is right before his eyes.[24]

At the very outset of his Roman sojourn on 29 October 1786, Goethe could exclaim, 'Now I begin to live for the first time, and I pay homage to my genius!' Such was his capacity for turning feelings of love into poems and stories, and to make his own life into a work of art, that we cannot know his Roman love life for certain. There does, though, seem to be a pattern, a progression, in the three women he has immortalized. There is Costanza, the beautiful daughter of the Roman innkeeper Roesler. Roberto Zapperi has dated Goethe's flirtation with Costanza to the weeks when he was working on the completion of *Iphigenia*. One of the things which makes it difficult to disentangle fact from fiction is that in the Roman Elegy which he wrote about this flirtation, he used a common trope, that of the young woman writing the hour of their assignation with her finger in some spilt wine on the marble tabletop. The difficulty here is this. We can tell that *something* is going on. Tischbein did a jokey sketch entitled 'The Accursed Second Pillow' in which a frantic Goethe is removing the second pillow, which lies beside his own, to avoid the liaison being detected by the 'bedder'. Or – because he wanted his friends not to witness his humiliation – her failure to show? 'The *zitelle*' – the unmarried girls – 'are more chaste than in other places,' Goethe told his Duke. 'For either you should marry them, or marry them off, and when they have a husband, that's the end of the story.' (Incidentally, the tone of this letter suggests that he and the Duke had been used to frank exchanges about sex, perhaps even gone wenching together, and this is another piece of the jigsaw puzzle which makes me doubt the theory that Goethe was a virgin until he reached Rome.)

So, that is Costanza. Another love obsession, no less characteristic of Goethe's emotional story throughout life, was the idealized crush, this one formed in the summer months of 1787 at Castel Gandolfo. The object of the crush was a young woman from Milan with whom he had a flirtation.

The third love obsession, the subject of his most memorable Roman Elegy, is of a different order. Whereas the *zitelle* were off limits, and the Milanese beauty had been, like Frederika in 'Wilkommen und Abschied', like Lotte Buff, and like so many of the women in Goethe's life, a pretty face floating across his dreams, the third woman was something very different. Clearly, if you wanted to take a lover in the heavily supervised, and indeed policed, atmosphere of Rome in the 1780s, and if you wanted to avoid infection, your best bet was an association with a young widow.

This is what the Roman Elegy tells us that Goethe found. He named her … Faustina. There is no obvious connection between his lover and his work-in-agonizingly-slow-progress; but of all the Roman names he could have chosen it is striking that he chose a feminized version of Faust. There were two celebrated Faustinas in Roman history. One was the wife of Antoninus Pius who, after her death, was deified. She was the aunt of Marcus Aurelius, whose wife was also called Faustina.

So, it is towards Marcus Aurelius that our thoughts are led. Any Roman, whether or not they were familiar with the *Meditations* of Marcus Aurelius, would immediately think of the equestrian statue of the Stoic Emperor who sits astride his horse on the Capitol. Goethe chose to end his *Italian Journey* with a glimpse of this statue, as it was seen from the outside of his apartment on the Corso. No reader of that book can have failed to have registered a shock at the conjunction of associations which Goethe has so surprisingly summoned up.

> The statue of Marcus Aurelius reminds one of the Commendatore
> in Don Giovanni, and gave to the wanderer the impression that he
> was about to venture upon something unusual.[25]

How many people, looking at a statue of Marcus Aurelius, immediately think of *Don Giovanni*? In the words of Machiavelli, Marcus Aurelius had been one of the 'five good Emperors'. Those who look at his statue see a Stoic philosopher, known for his quiet wisdom. Students of church history might see one who approved of persecuting the fledgling Christian sect. Admirers of the Roman Empire will see one of the few examples of a dictator who was also a philosopher-king. But to Goethe, the statue is suggestive of the vengeful statue at the end of Mozart's opera, a statue which comes to life and drags the roué off to punishment in hell.

There are many reasons why Goethe's mind, on departing from Italy, might have reverted to *Don Giovanni*. The collection of dockets, noting payments to women in the early weeks in Italy, were not thrown away. He retained them, presumably aware that one day a biographer would see them as evidence of a catalogue of easily purchased *heterosexual* 'conquests'. Perhaps – one can only speculate – but perhaps his sexual habits before he left Germany had been for casual encounters with his own sex, and he was rather proud to have been trying out women – as the obscene, bottom-preoccupied Venetian epigram suggests. The hopeless passion for the young woman of Milan followed the pattern of so many of the early 'loves' of his life:

> And yet, what joy to find oneself beloved,
> And, oh ye Gods, to love – what joy!

In all the lyrics in which he dressed up farewells as laments, there is really a strong element of relief – once again, he has escaped an entanglement. What, after all, had the whole Italian journey been, on one level, except the most elaborate way of escaping the oppressive and repetitive drama of loving von Stein?

This is surely why the Commendatore of Mozart comes to mind? Don Giovanni's sin is not sensuality. It is the ease with which he leaves the women stranded. This is what Goethe had done in Rome to 'Faustina', his actual mistress, just as he had abandoned his platonic mistress, Charlotte, in Weimar, and just as he had abandoned Lili in Frankfurt. From the perspective of old age, when he was writing the final page of *Italian Journey*, he knew that, unlike Don Giovanni, he had, shortly after leaving Italy, in fact been able to forswear the everlasting chase and settle down. But he was only able to do so because, in Rome, he had abandoned a woman he loved and who had loved him.

On an imaginative level, the affair with Faustina had released his awareness of the *daemonic* element in life. Goethe came to believe that, as well as there being laws, laws of Nature, moral laws, which govern the universe, there is also the element of spiritual power, which, borrowing the word from Plato's Socrates, he calls the *daimon*. The majority of human beings are untouched by it and lead humdrum lives – they are sad guests on the dark earth. Others, adventurers, butterflies burning their wings in candle flames, surrender to the daimonic. Some people, such as Lord Byron or Napoleon, are possessed by the daimonic; thereby they live as if the moral code did not exist and their daimonic hyperenergy makes them figures of hypnotic attraction.[26]

How far does this *daimon* relate to sex, or sexual energy? Writing in old age to the composer Carl Friedrich Zelter (1758–1832) in December 1827, Goethe mockingly spoke of the response of learned readers to the *Xenien* (satirical jibes at the literary scene that he began to write with Schiller):

> Just as they torment themselves – and me – with 'The Prophecies of Baki' earlier, with the Witch's 'Time Table', and some other nonsense which they imagine they are making intelligible. They are seeking psychological – epistemological – aesthetic puzzles which are scattered throughout my work with generous hands and thereby hope to solve the puzzles of Life itself.[27]

Some readers will think this is one of those uncanny moments in the letters or conversations where Goethe is able to see into the future, since the description of clever readers looking for meaning in the apparent mumbo jumbo of the Witch's Kitchen must draw us inexorably to the most celebrated twentieth-century reading of this scene, that of Sigmund Freud. The difference between Goethe's contemporaries, seeking clues which could 'explain' the gibbering of the Witch's monkeys or the imprecations of the hag herself, is that Freud's interpretations would not necessarily be invalidated by Goethe claiming to have scattered secrets, images, etc. throughout his work, without specific regard for their meaning. Freud, after all, discovered the subconscious meaning of the Witch's Kitchen and hailed Goethe as his precursor in discovering the Unconscious itself.

The Witch's Kitchen is the place to which Mephistopheles takes Faust to renew his youth, perhaps to give him a youth he'd never had. Faust will be given a potion which takes thirty years off his age and makes him irresistible to women. The nonsense words, the mumbo jumbo, are a 'language soup'[28] and it would be a mistake to 'explain' their surface meaning.

What is being unlocked by Faust is his Unconscious; Freud would say his infant sexuality: '"we must call the witch to our help after all" – the Witch metapsychology'.[29]

Even if we do not accept Freudianism, even if we reject it vigorously, we can never deny that Freud was one of the great prophets or harbingers of the modern, one of those who changed the way Western humanity regarded itself. Goethe was not simply a poet whom a late nineteenth-century Viennese doctor used to illustrate his ideas. He was, for Freud, the acknowledged precursor, as he was for Jung, who even for brief periods of his youth fantasized that he was Goethe's great-grandson. What Freud and Jung derived from Goethe was the concept of recovering the inner truth about ourselves through myth. (This was what religion had always been doing, of course.) Like the founding fathers of psychoanalysis, Goethe returned, often, to the Greek myths for this purpose, retelling the stories of Prometheus, of Iphigenia, of Helen of Troy, for his own purposes.

It was in Rome, Paestum, Naples, following in the footsteps of Winckelmann and conversing with the likes of Angelica Kauffman and William Hamilton, that Goethe filled up his tank with deep reserves of classical fuel, memories of statues, temples and paintings. As well as being an interpreter of Greek myth, Goethe was also a mythopoeic Maker. In *Faust* he would create a myth of modern humanity, the intellect who has broken loose from religion, who will pursue truth through self-analysis on the one hand, and on the other, through scientific observation of Nature and the universe. *Faust* in all its depth and exuberance had its origin in the German legend of a sixteenth-century mage who had made a pact with the devil: his soul in exchange for deep knowledge.

The arbiter of truth and morality would be, from now on, not the Bible, or the Church, or the State, but the individual human brain. It is one of the paradoxes of intellectual history that the world view which would claim to be the most modern – namely the scientific world view – had its origins in the area which modern science would consider least rational – namely magic.

Goethe, when he came to revise *Faust* and make it into a finished drama, rather than scattered pages in a travelling portmanteau, would see his drama of a man who had wandered 'from Heaven, through the world, to hell'.[30]

By casting himself, leaving Rome, as Don Giovanni, pursued by the avenging statue, some of the old Lutheran spectres rise up to haunt Goethe. He had abandoned the first stable, happy, 'normal' sexual relationship of his life. He had done so in order to return to Weimar and its in many ways stultifying routines. Yet Faustina's legacy would have an almost instantaneous effect on Goethe. He returned to Germany not to find the punishment of a Lutheran God or the condemnation of Mozart's Commendatore. Like the modern serial monogamist he had by now become, he was just going to move on to another woman.

9

Vulpius

Schon wieder Krieg! Der Kluge hörts nicht gern.
[Not war again?
That news won't please you, if you've got a brain.][1]

Goethe penned those lines years after he had followed Carl August to the disastrous Battle of Valmy, but they reflect the depth with which he must have meditated on his Duke's desire to fight wars, and the sheer folly of it all.

Seismic change had shaken the world. By June 1789, the Third Estate, which renamed itself the National Assembly, had occupied the Jeu de Paumes in Paris, demanding a constitution. On 14 July 1789, the Paris mob seized the Bastille. All through the previous summer there had been hunger riots, in Paris, Grenoble, Dijon, Toulouse, Pau, Rennes. All those Europeans who belonged to the Old Regime, who worked to shore it up, could only look on at France and wonder how soon the spirit of change and rebellion would spread to the territories of the Holy Roman Empire.

It was during that hot summer of '88, when crops were failing in France and the mob were expressing their anger, and Jacques Necker, too late to save the situation, had been reappointed as the French Finance Minister, that the itinerant Goethe returned from Italy to Weimar. Always ambiguous in the extreme about the Revolution, he was about to encounter a revolution in his own life which was, in its private and personal way, as vivid an expression of rebellion against the norms and the class system as the uprising of the Third Estate.

One Sunday, 12 July 1788, less than a month after he returned from Italy, Goethe went for a walk in the park beside the Ilm. He was approached by a twenty-three-year-old woman called Christiane Vulpius with a letter from her brother, Christian August, at present engaged as a secretary to a nobleman in Nuremberg, but in danger of losing his job and wanting to get his work published.

Goethe knew – or knew of – the Vulpius family. The father had been the State Archivist in Weimar, earning 75 talers per year. The income could not support his wife and six children. Some of the children had died, then his wife; then he had married again and had four more children. His inefficiency had led to his dismissal. He had then died. By the time Goethe met Christiane, there were three Vulpiuses: she, the brother and a sister, living in a tiny house in Luthergasse. To make ends meet, Christiane had taken a job in a little manufactory, making artificial flowers, which she sold on street corners.

Christiane was chubby, sexy, funny, with curly hair falling over her shoulders. She presented her brother's begging letter to the great writer and somehow the conversation drifted into other areas. The next morning they woke in the same bed. They would remain together until her death on 6 June 1816.

> First of all, I must tell you, that my wife has not read a single line I have written. The Empire of the Spirit doesn't exist for her. She is just a housewife. In domestic matters, she takes all cares from my shoulders. The domestic is her kingdom.

These words were attributed to Goethe by the wife of Napoleon's ambassador in Kessel, writing to her mother in Hamburg. It is hard to know whether Goethe really said this, or whether it is what the world in general wanted to believe about his life-partnership with Christiane. In Weimar itself, when it became common knowledge that he and Christiane were living together – which they did from the moment of meeting in the park – the stereotypical dismissal of her was, understandably enough, even cruder. She was caricatured in the mind of the snobs as a kind of peasant, and his association with her was incomprehensible, even to (eventually) close friends such as Schiller.

Although she was not well educated, and her spelling was extraordinary – in her letters a 'bon mot' is a 'bommo', she thought his

'Iphigenia' was 'Efijenige' – 'mannichmal' for 'manchmal', 'Biebeldeck' for 'Bibliothek' – she did read his work, and, even more often, sit or lie while he read his work to her.[2] She was also a very keen playgoer – twice a week at the Weimar theatre. She thought his best work was *Egmont*.[3]

Because Goethe spent much of his time away from home, either on business for the Duke, or at the university town of Jena, or taking cures in spa towns, there is a considerable body of letters between the pair: 601 letters survive – 354 from Goethe and 247 from Christiane. Unfortunately, in the auto-da-fé of 1797 he destroyed all the letters pre-1792. For some reason, all her letters between 1804 and 1809 are also missing. Nevertheless, a strong impression is given by the body of correspondence which survives, and it is evidence of her wretched loneliness when he went away, of his great selfishness in not bothering to tell her when he was going, and for how long, of their continuing warm sexual relationship, of their shared grief for lost children, and of their evident and abiding fondness for one another. In some ways, the disapproval of Weimar society only seems to have deepened the bond between them.

She was his companion, lover and friend for nearly thirty years. She bore him five children, of whom only one survived. She eventually became his wife.

Since Christiane was kept in the background – and since, as his unmarried partner, there was no question of her going out into society, or being received by his friends, let alone at court – there has been a tendency among the biographers to keep her in the background, too. It is always difficult to assess the imaginative role which a life-partner played in a writer's work. Clearly, in some cases, such as the second Mrs Dostoyevsky, we can observe her actually suggesting improvements and changes to the work – she was both editor and agent for him in the latter part of his career. Of other spouses – we can say as little as we could say of Mrs Shakespeare. That Christiane did have a role in his imaginative, as well as of his domestic life is, however, beyond question, even if we do not know quite how to articulate this phenomenon.

As well as considering the nebulous question of how the partner enters into, or influences, the work, there is also the question of how far they actually make it difficult or impossible (the first Mrs Milton, Mrs D. H. Lawrence ...). Cyril Connolly's legendary pram in the hall and Larkin's fear (see 'Dockery and Son') that having kids would somehow blight or eat into not just his time but his poetry is a consideration even in the very different times and mores in which Goethe had his existence.

He was intensely, preternaturally, aware of the class barriers. Schiller, though the son of a poor army medic, married into the aristocracy. Goethe, given the 'position' he chose to adopt in his mid-twenties, as a Privy Councillor and court flunkey, could not really have done this. The only possible aristocrat for him, at this period, was Charlotte von Stein, and she was married with seven children. Both convention and his own character would have made it difficult for him to have married 'above' himself.

The easiest conventional wife he could have chosen was a bourgeois of his own class and it was precisely such a fate which, we have suggested, made him leap with eagerness to the strange world of Carl August's tiny Weimar court, to being the *cavaliere servente* of Frau von Stein and pursuing, with such time-consuming ardour, his life as the Privy Councillor of a pumpernickel state.

The truth must be that Goethe chose not to settle into a conventional marriage, either as a very young man, when his family were expecting him to choose a Frankfurt bride, or later, as a Privy Councillor in Weimar. Although his Venetian Epigrams contain casual references to prostitutes of both sexes, this does not constitute hard and fast evidence of Goethe's practice. Given the prevalence of venereal disease in the eighteenth century, it is perfectly possible that the poet did not have full sexual experience until he was in his late thirties.

But in Rome, with Faustina, he had learned the joy of having a lover. On his return to Weimar, this was what he was ready for, this was what he most wanted. Such was his directness of attack, his confidence that anyone – his ducal patron, his lover, when he met her, society – would allow him to live life entirely on his own terms, he was only too happy to find in Christiane the perfect domestic companion.

> While looking for women, I found only whores for most of my life.
> At last, little whore, I found you, and you turned out the perfect wife.[4]

And if the gossips and the prudes, egged on by a furious and jealous Frau von Stein, expressed their disdain – so what? Such was

An etching by Rembrandt known as 'Faust', c.1652.
© Penta Springs Limited / Alamy Stock Photo.

Clockwise from top: The philosopher Friedrich Heinrich Jacobi, Goethe's lover (© GL Archive / Alamy Stock Photo); Friedrich Schiller, poet and playwright (© Iberfoto / Bridgeman Images); folk-lorist, preacher and thinker Johann Gottfried Herder (© Lebrecht Authors / Bridgeman Images).

Opposite page: A soirée hosted by Anna Amalia, Duchess of Saxe-Weimar, with Goethe and Herder (© The Trustees of the British Museum). Below, Major Brown, the US Commandant of Weimar, attends the reburial of Goethe and Schiller in May 1945 (Photo Günther Beyer © Constantin Beyer, Weimar).

H. Meyer   Fr. v. Fritsch   Herzogin Amalie   Ch. Gore   Frl. v. Goechhausen
Goethe   Einsiedel   Frl. El. Gore   Frl. Em. Gore   Herder

Abendkreis der Herzogin Amalie

Verlag v. Baumgärtners Buchhdlg.

3

Clockwise from top: An illustration from Goethe's *Theory of Colours*, 1810 (© Science History Images / Alamy Stock Photo); Thomas Mann visits Goethe's Garden House in 1949 (© Klassik Stiftung Weimar); a drawing of Goethe in Rome by Tischbein, 1787 (© imageBROKER.com GmbH & Co. KG / Alamy Stock Photo).

Goethe in the Roman Campagna by Tischbein, 1787.
© Heritage Image Partnership Ltd / Alamy Stock Photo.

Goethe's sketch of Christiane Vulpius sleeping, 1788.
© Goethezeit portal / Wikimedia Commons.

Peter Cornelius' illustration for *Faust Part One*, Faust and Mephistopheles race to
Gretchen's cell, after Walpurgis Night on Brocken Mountain.
© Web Gallery of Art / Wikimedia Commons.

Goethe's drawing of the Earth Spirit, doodled sometime after his sixtieth birthday.
© Jörg Zägel / Wikimedia Commons.

Christiane's generosity to him, she never appears to have nagged him, either to make 'an honest woman of her', nor to have complained when, for very long periods, he went on journeys, either working for his Duke, or having fun.

Apart from the sex – of which more in a moment, and it was clearly fantastic – there was one other thing which they had very firmly in common. Malicious descriptions of Christiane, especially in middle age, describe an overweight red-faced woman who was far gone in drink. To what extent this was a pattern of life before she met Goethe in the park, there is no evidence one way or another. Clearly, his own high income allowed plentiful supplies of wine to come up from the cellars, wherever he happened to be living.

Goethe himself was a functioning alcoholic, or an alcoholic in control. Christiane, who was to die aged fifty-one, was perhaps less able to absorb the quantities of booze which to her partner were normal, and their only surviving child, August, was a non-functioning alcoholic who would die aged forty-one. ('The poor chump is in a club with the class of his mother, who has drunk seventeen glasses of champagne in one go,' exaggerated Charlotte von Stein.[5])

It has been well remarked[6] that although E. T. A. Hoffmann is the figure in German literary history most renowned for alcoholism, he in fact drank far less than Goethe.

Goethe's own intake was prodigious, and it was something which struck everybody even in those hard-drinking days when it was not always safe to drink the water. An ordinary domestic day for Goethe would start with coffee and mineral water at 6 a.m., but by 10 a.m. with his Second Breakfast, he would drink half a bottle of Madeira. At lunch, around 1 or 2 p.m., he would drink a whole bottle of wine. If he went to the theatre, he would have a bowl of punch taken to his box, and he would have another bottle of wine waiting for him when he returned home in the evening. His average consumption was around three bottles per day, minimum. You don't begin to get the feel of the way Goethe lived unless you are aware of this. It almost certainly explains why so many of his literary and scientific and theatrical projects were left half finished, why he worked in fits and starts. It probably also explains the phenomenon, observed by a cloud of witnesses, that one never knew what mood he would be in. Sometimes, a visitor, friend or colleague would find him taciturn, grumpy, remote; sometimes, the talk flowed unstoppably. Christiane was his joyful companion as the bottles came up from the cellar. When he went away, many of her letters are about drink – often complaints that she is not getting enough: she would lament that the cellar was not always filled with her favourite tipples. On 13 August 1797, when he was in Frankfurt:

> If only some wine could arrive – otherwise, I am going to be a bit miserable! The trouble is, I don't really like the Wertheimer, and we haven't got much of that: and for your birthday, we really have to get in quite a lot of bottles if I am going to invite my friends, old and young: If only I had a few bottles of Malaga! What really cheesed me off was that there wasn't a single bottle of champagne drunk for me in Frankfurt.

Five days later, she wrote, 'If only you would order some wine from Frankfurt from the house of Herr Zapff! [the wine merchant in Suhl] I've really got nothing to drink.' And, even more insistent on 24 August, 'Please don't forget to write to Herr Zapff. For the first time – when we've run out of wine – I see how really necessary it is for me.'

———

As well as a shared fondness for booze, there was the sex. Goethe wrote most of the so-called Roman Elegies after his return to Weimar. Opinion divides between those who think some of these (highly) erotic poems all refer to the women of Rome. There seems little question, however – given the fact that they were written after he had met Christiane – that the experiences they recall with such loving sensuality owe much to his new-found discovery of full-blown, regular sex, as opposed to the emotionally unsatisfactory life of cruising and one-night stands.

> Darling, don't feel regret that you gave yourself to me so quickly.
> Believe me, I don't think you cheap, you've lost none of my respect.
> The arrows of Amor fly off in different ways: some simply graze us,
> And as the poison slowly works, the Heart is sick for years.
> But there are other arrows – well-feathered, freshly pointed and
> sharp,

Who shoot right through to the core, and quickly set the blood on
   fire.
In the Heroic Age, the Gods and the Goddesses fell in love,
Desire followed the merest glance, and satisfaction followed desire.[7]

There can scarcely ever have been a more joyful celebration of the
simple act of sexual intercourse than the third elegy. It refers to a
Roman mistress, but there is no reason to suppose Goethe was not
describing experiences he had with Christiane –

The little woollen dress is undone in no time,
So, as the friend unfastens, it slips down to the floor.
Hastily, he carries the child, in her light linen dress
As befits a good nursemaid, he jokingly takes her to bed,
No silken bed-curtains here, no embroidered mattress,
It stands in the wide bedroom, wide enough for two,
Jupiter himself did not have more pleasure from Juno,
Nor is there a mortal man alive, happier than your lover.

And then, the last two lines:

The joys of pure, naked Love delight us
And the rocking bed-springs rattle in tune with our joy.[8]

Of course, these elegies are works of art, and as such, even as he is
describing the experiences of love he is making these experiences into
artefacts. The seventh elegy describes the lovers' post-coital moments
of talk; and then, even as she falls asleep,

Often, even as I hold her in my arms, I've started
A composition, counting out the hexameter's measure with my
   fingers
On her naked back.[9]

There was no doubt an ambivalence about erotica, and about overt
sexual candour, in Germany at this time. The distinguished Göttingen
theologian Johann David Michaelis attracted large and appreciative
audiences when he read aloud from erotic books. The family of

Novalis's beloved Sophie von Kühn loved erotica quite openly. Georg Christoph Lichtenberg, Professor of Physics at Göttingen, had an affair which was no secret with an underage girl and was known by his students as 'Strong/Stiff August'. The Duke Carl August was known to have fathered many illegitimate children and in later years lived openly with the actress Caroline Jagemann rather than with his wife. And yet,[10] there would have been cities in the Holy Roman Empire and German Nation where the censors would not have allowed Goethe to go into print.

Goethe had by now begun his friendship with Schiller – which will be the subject of a later chapter – who had founded a magazine called 'The Hours' – *Die Horen (The Horae)* – published in the university town of Jena. It was simply a question of who would make the joke first – that if it published filth like this, the mag ('The Hours') should have been called 'The Whores'. It was the headmaster of the Weimar Gymnasium, Karl August Böttiger, who excitedly quoted Herder, who was spluttering with indignation that the offending poems had been published in a university magazine which bore the Imperial insignia. 'The HOREN must now be printed with a "u".' [HUREN – Whores.] They had no doubt who was to blame for Goethe writing all this filth 'in the first flush of his entanglement with Dame Vulpius'.[11] Charlotte von Stein wrote as if she had not read the poems, but spoke of Wieland having given her such a full account of them; clearly, they did not merely depart from morality, they were also ridiculous.

Vulpius had provided something which Goethe could not find with von Stein. As he had written to Charlotte, 'I am not an individual, not an independent being. All my weakness I have leaned on you, protected my soft sides with you, filled my gaps with you. Now, when I am removed from you, my condition becomes most strange. On one side I am armed and steeled, on the other like a raw egg, because I have failed to snuggle up where you are my shield and umbrella.'[12]

Such a strong, superior woman had to frighten the narcissist Goethe, afraid of self-loss, of being devoured. However, the fear was alleviated by the distance that resulted from Frau von Stein's status as a married woman.

In the relationship with Christiane Vulpius, this distance was not necessary. She was so much younger than Goethe, socially and educationally so far below him, that an intimate relationship was possible for him here.

The pretty, medium-sized twenty-three year-old with the undressed curly head became Goethe's 'bed treasure' (the indulgent word used by Goethe's mother to describe her). Throughout her life, she remained a subject to Goethe. Until her end, Christiane Goethe never called him anything other than 'Herr Geheimrat' (Mr Privy Councillor).[13]

In January 1790, Goethe confronted the phenomenon of colour, which had begun to interest him with particular force when in Italy, and he had devoted himself both to painting and to admiring the great works of visual art which had been opened up to him. In Italy, he had begun to realize that colour must be a natural phenomenon if it could be used in art. He assumed, as did everyone since, that Isaac Newton's study of the matter was definitive.[14] He decided, on his return from Italy, that he wanted to investigate the matter from the point of view, not of the art critic, but of the physicist.[15] Privy Councillor Büttner, who had moved from Göttingen to Jena, arranged for Goethe to get hold of a prism and the necessary equipment to set up the experiments in his house in Weimar.

Büttner had no sooner lent the equipment than he asked to have the prism back. Before he returned it, however, Goethe decided to do one of Newton's simple experiments. He had looked through a prism in his youth, and seen the spectrum of colours which Newton described. Now, he was in a small office, with window shades and white walls. As he looked through the prism, expecting to see colours, he saw only whiteness – a blank.

But I was quite amazed that the white wall showing through the prism remained as white as before. Only where there was something dark did a more or less distinct colour show. The cross frames of the window appeared most actively coloured, while the light-grey sky outside did not have the slightest trace of colour. It required little thought to recognize that an edge was necessary to bring about colours. I immediately spoke out loud to myself, through instinct, that Newtonian theory was erroneous.[16]

The surprise was so great that he decided he could not possibly, at this crucial moment, send the prism back to its owner in Jena.

Goethe was compelled by this, as by literally hundreds of experiments, to reject Newton's differential refrangibility. But he did not, as is often wrongly suggested, reject Newton altogether. He affirmed Newton's mechanics. It was experiments which led him to his alternative colour theory. Goethe came to realize that in order to explain colour one needed to investigate not merely light, as Newton had suggested, but also *the relative differences of light across the visual field*.[17]

Goethe would come to consider his work on colour to be the most important of his writings. The very fact that, in pious legend, if not in fact, his last words were supposed to have been 'More light!' is indicative of how central it is to his self-perception, and to his reputation in his lifetime. For many years it was fashionable to sneer at Goethe's attempts to dislodge Newton from his throne, but there is lately a recognition that, in many important respects, Goethe was right and Newton was wrong. (See pp. 271–2. Olaf L. Müller's researches, based on repeated experiments, have found that Goethe does indeed prove Newton in need of modification.)

What marks Goethe out among the scientists is the fact that he saw, as Newton and the mechanistic physicists of the Enlightenment did not, that you cannot separate phenomena from our means of perceiving them. Therefore he refused to make distinctions between 'art' and 'science', since the artist and the scientist are both looking for the truth. When Sir Charles Eastlake came to translate Goethe's *Theory of Colours* into English he saw that 'by an extraordinary combination of circumstances, the theory of colours has been drawn into the province and before the tribunal of the mathematicians, a tribunal to which it cannot be said to be amenable'.[18] This, as Eastlake said, was because it was a great mathematician, Newton, who had first proposed his theory of colours. To a practical man, a dyer say, or painter, Newton might have had little to say, but Goethe had much to say.[19]

Consider these words of Goethe's about the eye:

The Eye sees no forms. It only sees that which differentiates itself through light and dark or through colour.

In the infinitely delicate sensibility for shade-gradation of light and dark as well as colour lies the possibility of painting.

Painting is truer to the eye than reality itself. It creates what man should see and not what he usually does see.

The sensibility of forms, particularly beautiful forms, rests much deeper.

The enjoyment of colours, individually or in harmony, is experienced by the eye as an organ, and it communicates its pleasure to the rest of the man. The enjoyment of form rests in man's higher nature, and is communicated by the inner man to the eye.

The eye is the last, the highest result of light upon the organic body. The eye as a creation of light is capable of all that light itself is not capable of.

Light transmits the visible to the eye; the eye transmits it to the entire man.

The ear is deaf, the mouth is dumb, but the eye perceives and speaks. From the outside, the world mirrors itself in one eye; from within, the man. The totality of the inner and the outer is completed by the eye.[20]

Without wishing to impose myself too much on the reader, I'd urge you to read this passage two or three times, because it is a vivid example of Goethe's profoundly original methods, as scientist, poet, philosopher. In many respects, by the time he grew old and was finishing *Faust*, he would come to reject the anthropocentrism of the Enlightenment and of Western philosophy and move to a much more 'oriental' view of science, Nature and humanity's place in Nature. Nevertheless, the very fact that you are reading this sentence, that your eye is falling on the page, that your eyes and senses are perceiving the environment in which you happen to find yourself – knowing that the sky is grey or blue, that the book and our clothes, are particular colours, and so on – all these come about solely because you are able to perceive them. *Cogito ergo sum*, but the phenomena you perceive do not exist solely because you have thought about them. Goethe sees the organs of perception, and the eye above all, as the mysterious link which enables us to know we are part of the universe. The mystery of Being Itself is disclosed to us, and not to our companions in Nature. The badgers, the leaves, the drops of dew on grass, the beetles might, for all we know, possess their own types of consciousness, but they are unaware, as far as it is possible to conceive, of their own awareness. This is what distinguishes the human observer. It is what both torments and thrills Faust as he moves from his cobwebby northern study to the bright sunshine of the classical, Grecian south. These were the phenomena engaging Goethe's mind as he settled into his new Weimar life with Christiane Vulpius. No wonder he retained a certain distance from the convulsive political earthquakes in Europe, and the petty malice of Weimar's wagging tongues.

Nevertheless, it is difficult for the modern reader to appreciate how utterly scandalous the little world of Weimar found Goethe's association with Vulpius. For months, he kept it a complete secret, even though she was by then occupying the house on the Frauenplan. We have a vivid picture of how the news of it all leaked out, from the correspondence between Herder and his wife Karoline. Herder had been invited to go to Rome, as the travelling companion of a young aesthete, Baron von Dalberg, discovering, only at the last minute, that they were to be accompanied by a widow von Seckendorff – an addition to the party which caused Herder irritation. But the chance to visit Rome was not to be turned down. He, naturally, asked Goethe for advice about whom, and what, to see, and was increasingly dismayed to discover that Goethe really had lived like an art student while in the Celestial City, and had not even brought with him a formal dress suit. ('Er hat wie ein Künsterbursche hier gelebet.'[21])

While Herder's letters told his wife about a Monsignor Borgia in scarlet stockings climbing the marble stairs to his apartments, of the social climbing of Frau von Seckendorff, as well as of his culture-vulture explorations of the classical sites, Karoline unfolded the strange story. Goethe, she said in one letter, is like a chameleon.[22] He asked her to drink tea with him, and she said, yes if she were to be accompanied by 'the Stein'. Ah, Goethe had replied, this might be difficult. 'She is upset and it does not appear she will want to visit me.' The Stein for her part complained to Frau Herder that the poet had changed. He had become a sensualist, a voluptuary. By the end of November, Karoline was repeating to her husband the *on dit* – that Goethe was no longer 'suitable' for Weimar society. It was not until March of 1789, however, seven months after she had remarked upon his 'chameleon' character, that Karoline could explain the situation to her husband:

I've now got the secret from the Stein herself – why things are not so good between her and Goethe. He's got the young Vulpius as a *Klärchen* [a floozy] … Stein blames him greatly. When a man is as great as he is, and especially when he is forty years of age, he should do nothing which so degrades him in the eyes of others. What do you think about it? It's all totally sub rosa![23]

What Herder thought was somewhat predictable, and to his pompous letter ('What you tell me of Goethe's Klärchen is highly displeasing'), Karoline wrote a rather splendid rebuke: 'Goethe is our best friend, and we need a good friend right now, believe me. Goethe loves you, and deserves to be loved in return … It hurts him that you have gone silent on him. I've made excuses for you. When we all meet up in Karlsbad again this summer you must patch things up.'[24]

There was a reconciliation when Herder returned to Weimar in July. By then, the *Klärchen* was pregnant, and she gave birth to their first son – the only child, of five, to survive infancy – on Christmas Day 1789. By then, the Revolution in France was far advanced and it was already clear to Goethe that the optimists – who had hoped for it to progress in gentle stages from superstition to Reason, from Absolutist Monarchy to a Constitution – were going to be disappointed.

The great ones of the world can muse on the sad fate of France:
Yet more should the smallfry reflect thereupon:
The great ones perished: but who could protect the mob
From the mob itself? Then the mob tyrannized the mob.[25]

On the anniversary of the storming of the Bastille, a crowd of 350,000 assembled in the Champs de Mars for a renewal of the oaths of the National Guard. King Louis XVI was there. Talleyrand, Bishop of Autun and president of the Assembly, celebrated Mass; General Lafayette, inventor of the tricolour cockade, was present, the hero of this hour, as he had been, in many European eyes, of the American War of Independence.

This attempt at a constitutional revolution was not going to be peaceful. Already the National Constituent Assembly had abolished all hereditary nobility, all titles and coats of arms. Aristocratic landowners could not escape France fast enough, and poured over the border into Lichtenstein and the Rhineland. Inevitably, these were dubbed traitors by the friends of the Revolution, and the prisons were soon filling up with traitors. The guillotine, invented as a humane method of dealing with criminals, was of great use in disposing of political dissidents.

Mirabeau, constitutional optimist and friend of the King, who had tried to save the Old Regime from its own worse follies, died in April 1791. The republicans already suspected that the King was in touch with his in-laws, the Austrian Emperor's family, and it was rumoured – rumours Louis vociferously denied – that he was planning to flee the country with his aristocratic supporters and raise a counter-revolutionary army. The denials were proved false when the King and Queen, with their children, attempted to escape, and were apprehended at Varennes-en-Argonne. He was arrested and taken back to Paris. Any pretence that the Revolution wanted to maintain a monarchy was now discredited. Europe could see that the monarchy was finished in France, and the Reign of Terror began.

Moreover, the revolutionaries were not content to limit their activities to French soil. They rightly saw the German-speaking lands as their enemy.

IO

WAR

Ach! darum treibt ihn, Erde! vom Herzen dir
Sein Übermut, und deine Geschenke sind
Umsonst und deine zarten Bande;
Sucht er ein Besseres doch, der Wilde!
[O, that is the reason, Earth, why his arrogance drives you away
From your Heart, and your gifts, your tender bonds
Are in vain! For he's looking for something
Better yet – the wild one!]

Hölderlin, 'Der Mensch'

One effect of the French Revolution on the German-speaking lands was that it brought about a rapprochement between Prussia and Austria. Goethe remarked, in October 1789, that Emperor Joseph II had so 'ruined Austria', that it would take them a hundred years to recover. Joseph died on 20 February 1790 and was succeeded by his nephew, Leopold II, who quickly set about confirming the rapprochement. Herder captured the immense change which had happened in the atmosphere. 'When he ascended the throne,' he wrote of Joseph, 'he was worshipped as a demigod. Now, he is carried to his grave as a sin-offering to our times.'[1]

Leopold broke the alliance with France, which had existed since 1756, and signed the Defence League with Prussia. Three weeks later, he was dead. He was succeeded by his son, Francis, destined to be the last Holy Roman Emperor. His coronation was provocatively fixed for the third anniversary of the storming of the Bastille – 14 July 1792.

Just days after the new French Republic declared war on Austria, a captain of engineers, stationed in Strasbourg – Claude Joseph Rouget de Lisle – wrote a war song. He dashed it off in a single night – 'Chant de guerre de l'armée du Rhin' ('Battle Hymn of the Army of the Rhine'), which saw their enemy as a horde of traitors, slaves and king-conspirators.

The horde of slaves, or, depending on one's viewpoint, the counter-revolutionary army, was made up of Austrians, Prussians and French émigrés.

The war had actually been declared by France – not by the Assemblée Nationale or the revolutionaries themselves, but by France. They had forced Louis XVI to sign the declaration of war against the King of Bohemia and Hungary: that is, it was not, therefore, a war against the Holy Roman Empire itself. Territories of the Empire, such as Weimar, were therefore not involved in the conflict. Austria, however, was part of the tripartite alliance – with Prussia and the French emigrants, resolved on the conflict.

Weimar as a duchy was out of the war, but its Duke Carl August had become a colonel in the Prussian army. It was in a personal capacity, commanding a regiment of Prussian cuirassiers, that he was on the march, loyal to the formidable King Friedrich Wilhelm II, nephew of Frederick the Great. This was a family obligation for Carl August. Blood will out, no blood more warlike than Goethe's boyhood hero, and Carl August's great-uncle, Frederick the Great.

His heir and nephew, Friedrich Wilhelm II, who forbade his subject Kant to write on religious subjects, was physically much bigger than his famous uncle, but no less warlike. He had given refuge in Berlin to large numbers of French emigrants, and he was a determined, huge, loud-voiced man, as he rode at the head of his army, to fulfil his rallying cry – 'On to Paris!'

The Duke of Brunswick, Carl August's cousin, was the commander-in-chief of the combined army – Austrians, Prussians and Emigrants. The Prussian army was legendary in Europe, and it was difficult to see how the ragamuffin French sans-culottes could stand a chance against them. As someone who, as a young man, had served as a cavalry officer in the Seven Years War under Frederick the Great, the Duke of

Brunswick planned the campaign to go down as a piece of textbook strategy and tactics. Such was his Europe-wide reputation as the military star, he had even been offered, before they boldly declared war, command of the *French* army by the revolutionary government. At first, the campaign worked exactly as Brunswick had intended. The fortresses of Longwy and Verdun fell very quickly.

The Prussian army, however, had failed to reckon on a number of factors. One was the dreadful weather. Had the Prussian army been fighting alone, they could probably have slogged on through rain and mud – On to Paris! But, as Goethe so vividly described, the tripartite army was a bedraggled, ill-disciplined progression. Very few of the French emigrants were professional soldiers. Many in the Austrian army were mercenaries who did not care much, one way or another, which side of this war emerged victorious. As well as the military, there were cartloads of hangers-on, camp followers (none more distinguished than Goethe, in his own hired carriage with a servant noting down the scientific theories dictated by his master as the coachman negotiated the puddles, potholes and bedraggled, hungry crowd in the road). There were women, some of them whores, some wives.

The muster had occurred in the city of Mainz, and, before they left that beautiful town, Goethe had enjoyed a couple of pleasant evenings of precisely the kind he most enjoyed, with Sömmerring, the great anatomist (over from Kessel), with Georg Forster, famed throughout Europe as the boy who had sailed on the second voyage of the *Resolution* with Captain Cook, and Forster's wife, Therese Heyne, herself an intellectual, the daughter of a distinguished classical philologist, and their lodger, a rather boring young writer named Huber – with whom she was having an affair. They were all passionately engaged with the current political situation, most of them on the side of the Revolution.

Very many young German intellectuals were – perhaps the majority. This was the period when Hölderlin, still a theological student at Tübingen, wrote his 'Hymn to Freedom'. His room-mate Hegel was considered by his coevals to be a 'Jacobin'. Even older figures like Klopstock had seen the summoning of the States General as 'the greatest act of this century'. 'France free – and you hesitate?' asked Klopstock of his fellow Germans. The new classicism went hand in hand with revolution as it did in France itself – witness the canvases of Jacques-Louis David, who saw the figures of the Revolution as embodiments of the old heroes of Greek and Roman republicanism. Lafayette, a 'cannibal' in Goethe's reported remark, was hailed, in Germany as well as in France, as the new Timoleon, Mirabeau as the Demosthenes of the Epoch.

Duke Carl August was not entirely unsympathetic to the more enlightened ideals of Mirabeau, though the Jacobins terrified him. As far as he and Goethe were concerned, the prospect of the mob, or the anarchic rule of the masses, was repellent ('Sudden, impulsive action is for the masses, and for that they deserve some respect; but their judgement is pitiful'). Hence the campaign.

For Goethe, as for his master, it was in essence a campaign against anarchy, rather than necessarily a defence of the Old Regime. In Weimar, there were no masses. There was no press freedom, because there were in effect no presses, no newspapers such as the revolutionary papers which poured out of Paris, or which were printed in Mainz and devoured by, and written by, the likes of the Forsters.

The allied army set out in bright summer weather, and by the time they had quickly secured the surrender of Lon, all the French emigrants were assuring the Germans that, wherever they went in France, they would be received as liberators. Hatred of the Revolution, spelled out in the Duke of Brunswick's Manifesto and Justification for the Invasion, so possessed the Emigrants, and the German war leaders, that they had miscalculated the effect, even upon French monarchists, of having their country invaded. Brunswick saw it as a Campaign against Revolution. Patriots on the other side of the Rhine saw it as a rape of La France.

The invasion in fact hardened even the will of republicans, and, even, of moderate monarchists, to unite against the invaders. What is more, they were not, as was supposed, a ragamuffin army. A highly trained military force was assembled by Dumouriez, Minister of War, who had been the chief architect of going to war and who had overall command of the operation.

Once the allied army had reached Verdun, Brunswick had only one major geographical obstacle between himself and Paris: the forest of Argonnes. Dumouriez was joined by a considerable army, led by the Alsatian commander Kellermann. Brunswick was determined to meet both armies as they conjoined, defeat them, and so bring the campaign to a triumphant, swift conclusion.

Goethe left his carriage, his secretary and his notes on colour theory, and in driving rain and mud set out to join the Prussian Life Guards to witness their victory at first hand. They had reached Valmy. By then, however, Brunswick saw that he had been outmanoeuvred. Dumouriez's army had united with that of Kellermann and they had occupied the heights, a sort of wide amphitheatre as it seemed to Goethe, above Valmy. Below, on a plateau, the Prussian army squelched through the mud. Goethe was by now beside the Duke and in the vanguard of the action. The highest point of the plateau was a farm called La Lune. It was wet, misty, muddy, as the Prussian hussars trotted onwards, unaware that Kellermann had already established an advanced battery in the farm. As the German army advanced, the French opened fire, the horses turned tail and retreated. As the day wore on, Goethe noted that none of the fighting men around him had had anything to eat. He heard the whizzing of cannonballs, the frightened screech of the songbirds as the earth literally trembled. To the Duke of Brunswick's astonishment, it became clear the French position was immovable, and the German armies simply withdrew rather than suffer unnecessary casualties. The total loss among the German cavalry during the Battle of Valmy was one horse.

The Prussian army, one of the most highly trained military machines in Europe, had been defeated by a fighting force which, until that morning, Goethe and his patron the Duke had imagined to be a gang of amateurs. The only option was to retreat. That evening, German and Austrian soldiers walked about silently, and without catching one another's glances. Goethe found himself in a circle who had been accustomed to ask him to give his opinion on the state of things. With thirty years of hindsight, he was able to hone the sentence: 'From this place and from this day forth, a new era in world history begins, and you can all say you were present when it happened.' In a more immediate description of the implications of the Prussian defeat at Valmy, Goethe had written to Knebel that he was pleased to have had the chance to see it with his own eyes, 'et quorum pars minima fui' ('and that I was a small part of it').[2]

Whether he really said this at the time, or whether thirty years had given him time to polish the insight, it was certainly true. A few days later, news reached them from Paris of the 'horrors' which were taking place. Murder and robbery were rife. The King was in prison, as was his family, a Republic was on the verge of being declared. Goethe returned to his carriage, which trotted as fast as it could through the mud and the potholes, beside German cavalry. As so far as daylight, and the potholes, allowed, Goethe sank himself into a reading of Gehler's *Dictionary of Physics*.

A third French force, led by Adam-Philippe de Custine – veteran of both the Seven Years War and the American War of Independence, when he had fought against the British – now joined the armies of Dumouriez and Kellermann. Flushed with their success, the revolutionary army advanced into Germany. Sporting thick black moustaches as a token of his republican credentials, General Custine moved into the Rhineland, occupied Mainz on 21 October, and Frankfurt the following day.

On the outward journey, Goethe had visited his mother in Frankfurt: it was the first time they had set eyes upon one another in thirteen years, and he had planned to remain with her longer on his return. She had told him that his uncle, old Textor the senator, had died. Goethe was thereby entitled to inherit his role as a *Ratsherr*, a Councillor. He could come, covered in honours, and resume the sort of life which both her father and uncle had lived, distinguished old burghers.

As things then stood, during that autumn of 1792, there was no possibility of returning to discuss the offer with his mother. *Le général moustache*, leading the 14,300-strong Armée des Vosges, pressed on into Germany, and by 31 October Frankfurt had surrendered. The city was forced to pay a levy of 2 million francs. The General Moustache stood in the marketplace and declaimed: 'Some years ago, you witnessed the coronation of the Emperor Franz. Have you seen him since? You will never see him again!' The blood-curdling National Anthem was heard for the first time – the Marseillaise.

Against us, tyranny's
Bloody banner is raised.
Do you hear in the countryside
Those ferocious soldiers roaring?
They come right into your arms
To slit the throats of your sons, your wives!

Goethe's mother was forced to flee her house, which had been filled in happier days with curios, treasures and artworks by her long-dead husband. Goethe begged her to come to live in Weimar, but she refused.

She had no fear for her own safety, and strengthened herself in her Old Testament belief; turning up pages in the Bible at random, and especially in the Psalms and the Prophets, that she might appropriate their contents as special messages of guidance for herself, with the result that she decided to remain in Frankfurt and did not even pay me a visit.[3]

Brunswick's army, in pursuit of the invading revolutionaries, forced Custine to abandon Frankfurt before Christmas, but the general's occupation of Mainz in October had forced the French emigrants who had found refuge there to stream out of the city into surrounding villages to avoid rape and plunder.

Goethe, after the retreat from Valmy, had neither visited his mother in Frankfurt nor returned to his partner and son in Weimar. One reason was illness. Like so many on that campaign, he suffered from a bad bout of dysentery. When he recovered, his natural tendency to cosset himself was encouraged by two friends – first of all Jacobi, who had him to stay in his beautiful country estate near Düsseldorf – Pempelfort – and then on to Munster, where he was lionized by the daughter of one of the Prussian generals, now married to a Russian diplomat. Adelheid Amalia Gallitzin reminded him of Fräulein Klettenberg, who had nursed him so devotedly as a young man after he left Leipzig, and who had read aloud to him from occult books. Whereas Fräulein Klettenberg was a Protestant Pietist, the Princess Gallitzin's spirituality was Catholic, as was her circle. She collected antique cameos, finely cut with the mythological figures of paganism. It inspired him to write his lyric 'The New Amor'. In the poem, Cupid, who has seduced Psyche, looks round the Olympian heights for a new conquest, and lights upon Venus Urania.

Oh! The saint herself, she put up no resistance,
And the daring Cupid held her tight.
 Then, from their lovemaking,
 A new Love-God arose,
To his father, he owed the meaning, to his mother the custom;

And you will always find him in the lovely Muse's company –
His charming arrow shoots with/or establishes [double meaning]
  the love of Art.[4]

The Princess, with her pieties and her bibelots, had awoken in courtier-Goethe that quality which wallowed in the theatre of the grande dame. The poem shimmers, however, with the awareness, more appropriate to the bedroom in Weimar, that Goethe was more at home with his version of the sensual, pagan immortals than with the plaster saints of the Church. (It would be decades before his imagination, in concluding *Faust*, could find a fusion between Venus Urania and the Virgin Mother.)

———

A Polish aristocrat named Trenzinsky had been in Paris when the Revolution broke out, and remained, until it became clear that, between the two dangers – remaining and flight – it was more dangerous to remain in a place where 'people who were completely crazy, with dishevelled hair and greasy tunics, displayed themselves in the Paris salons'.[5] Trenzinsky and his sixteen-year-old son followed the line of refugees out of the French capital to meet up with the army, mobilized by the King of Hanover and the Duke of Brunswick, and some of the French refugee aristocrats, who were marching on Paris with the aim of rescuing the royalists and subduing the crazy people with dishevelled hair and greasy tunics.

When they reached the line, they were shocked to find 'an army perishing from hunger and dirt'. They met up with 'a reigning prince', however, who invited them to spend the evening in the house of the local priest. Upon entering the room, they found a number of German colonels, with grey moustaches, all smoking cigars. They appeared to have no doubt that they would soon be 'feasting' in the Palais Royal.

Rather later than the other guests, another German entered the room, a man in a tailcoat, quite tall, solidly built and with a 'proud, important-looking face'. The Prince offered this visitor – whom the Poles took to be a diplomat – an armchair beside himself. His manner was a little stiff, and he told an anecdote – that morning, he had been driving in the Duke's carriage when a soldier, heavily muffled against the weather, had ridden up. Seeing the coat of arms on the carriage door, the soldier assumed, when he looked inside, that he would find the Duke, Carl August. Instead, he found the diplomat, who was also surprised – since he recognized in the well-muffled soldier the face of none other than the King of Prussia himself.

The Prince then led Trenzinsky up, saying to the diplomat that the Pole, lately come from Paris, would be able to give the latest news.

'What are General Lafayette and all the other cannibals doing?' asked the diplomat.

'Lafayette,' said Trenzinsky, 'is intrepidly defending the King and is openly at odds with the Jacobins.'

The words did not convince the sardonic German who shook his head and said, 'It is only a mask. I am almost certain that Lafayette is in concert with the Jacobins. I had intended to go to Paris two years ago, but I wished to see the Paris of Louis the Grand and of the great Arouet, not a horde of Huns raving among the fragments of its glory. Could one have expected that an insolent gang of demagogues would be so successful? ... If Louis XVI had listened not to his own such as Necker, whose forebears had flourished for centuries under the lilies, we should not now have had to rise in a crusade. But our Gottfried will soon disabuse them. I have no doubt, and then the French themselves will help him!' The German was comparing the Duke of Brunswick with Godfrey de Bouillon (1058–1100), the leader of the First Crusade.

The Pole could not agree. 'You still believe the French will receive us with open arms, when every day gives us proof of what a savage national war this is becoming?' The diplomat smiled sardonically.

One of the colonels came up and began to bluster. 'Of course, we can't advance now, and it would be hard to retreat. However, this isn't the first autumn there's ever been in France: the mud might have been foreseen. I pray to God to send us a general engagement. Better to die at the head of one's regiment, with one's weapon in one's hand, of a bullet, than to go on sitting in this mud.'

With a scornful smile, the diplomat turned to the Prince and said, 'This thirst of Teutonic soldiers for victory, one cannot regard it without emotion. Of course our present situation is not of the most brilliant, but let us remember Joinville when he was a prisoner with Saint Louis, "Nous en parlerons devant les dames".'

The colonel said he would not dream of speaking a single word about the campaign to his wife or sister, were they with him. The diplomat turned aside and said, 'The world of politics is utterly foreign to me: it is tedious to me to hear of marches and revolutions, of debates and state measures. I can never read a newspaper without boredom: all this to us is something so transitory, so temporary, and also so utterly, essentially alien. There are other fields in which I understand myself to be the king; so why should I set out unsummoned, like a ten-penny moralist, to interfere in affairs with which providence has charged those administrations which are chosen to bear such heavy burdens?'

The poor old colonel exuded a cloud of cigar smoke.

'Now I, a simple man, nowhere find myself either a king or a genius; but everywhere I remain a man, and I remember how, when I was still a boy, I learned by heart the saying, Homo sum et nihil humani a me alienum puto. The two bullets which have passed through my body have confirmed my right to interfere in affairs for which I pay with my blood.'

The lofty diplomat appeared not to have heard, and the Prince asked him what he was working on at present. He replied that it was on the theory of colours.

The teenage son of Trenzinsky asked the identity of the lofty diplomat in the tailcoat.

'Ah, bah! C'est un célèbre poète allemand, M. Koethe, qui a écrit … qui a écrit … ah, bah! La Messiade.' (The famous poem by Klopstock.)

When the young Pole had grown to maturity, he could reflect, 'So this is the author of the novel I was mad about, *Werthers Leiden*, I thought, smiling to myself at the emigrant's knowledge of literature.'

They would not meet again for another ten years. Then, it was in Weimar. Trenzinsky junior, by then a young man, was taken to the theatre in Weimar to see a rather indifferent play by Goethe called *Der Bürgergeneral*, supposedly a comedy mocking the Revolution. In the stalls with the Pole was none other than the old colonel who had been so mocked, and who was still remembering the incident. 'I don't understand people who laugh when countries are shedding their blood and who don't see what's happening in front of them … But perhaps genius is entitled to do that,' he was spluttering.

Goethe, that evening, was in the ducal box with Carl August. He looked depressed, as the audience failed to laugh at this supposed comedy. (Though it seems feeble stuff when read today, the strange fact is that it was the most popular of all Goethe's plays in his lifetime: but this was not saying much – it had just fifteen performances in the first few years after he had written it, far more than the great *Iphigenie* or *Torquato Tasso* which audiences found boring.)

After the performance of *The Citizen General*, attended by the young Pole and the old colonel, Goethe came out of the Court Theatre and tried to get into his carriage, when three drunken students started hissing. When Alexander Herzen (1812–70) decided to include these reminiscences in his voluminous memoirs, published 1860–62, he knew that Trenzinsky's rather mocking scepticism about Goethe would be seen by some as almost blasphemous, since by then Goethe had been deified, not only in Germany, but among intellectuals throughout Europe.

Goethe's own recollections of the campaign in France are part of that large body of work – the autobiography from childhood to arrival in Weimar, the Italian journey, the carefully edited versions of his correspondence with Schiller and others – which occupied his old age, when he was honing the image of himself as the Sage of Weimar. The first published edition, in 1822, thirty years after the events it described,[6] bore the title *Aus meinem Leben* and was intended as an appendage to *Poetry and Truth*. An indication that it is a decidedly post-dated and well-crafted account comes in the very first page, where Goethe meets, among the French exiles, the mistress of Louis Egalité (who would be guillotined in November 1793), the Princess Monaco, intimate friend of the Prince Condé. 'Nothing could be more charming than this slender, fair young woman; young, sparkling and humorous, no man whose attention she wished to attract could resist her. I watched her unmoved, and was surprised at thus meeting Philina again, whom I did not expect to find here, fluttering about so bright and gay.'

The 'again' is the giveaway. Philina is a character in Book Two of *Wilhelm Meister*, which Goethe did not in fact write until 1794, two years after the campaign in France. In spite of its subsequent title, the *Campaign* was not intended as a military book. The two hundred pages or so are taken up with his observations of the countryside and the people he met, and with his interrupted work on colour theory. He used the diary of the Duke of Weimar's chamberlain for reference, but most of the book was written fluently, from memory, rather in the manner of an autobiographical novel. One thinks of the beautifully painted scene when he comes across a group of soldiers, encircling a hole in the ground which turns out to be a funnel-shaped pool, full of fish. The men have brought fishing tackle on the campaign, and are busy hooking the fish. Goethe notes the remarkable play of colours on the fish, and then realizes that it is not their colour, but the reflection of a piece of earthenware which has been thrown into the pool. It is a perfectly made little prose-poem. It is also grist to his theoretical mill, an example of the way that our perception of colour actually operates in life. Part of his objection to Newton's optics was that they could be understood by one who was colour blind. For Goethe, science was what fiction was for Henry James, a part of 'felt life'.

The blues, violets, reds and yellows, playing on the gleaming scales of the fish.

Goethe remarked upon these moments of scientific insight as opportunities to see 'into the life of things'. 'It was the same with my investigations of natural phenomena as with my poems; I did not make them, but they made me.'[7] It was his preoccupation with the colour phenomenon, as he tells us,[8] which kept him sane during the tedium and danger of the campaign.

The colour phenomenon at the spring has never for a moment left me during the last few days; I thought of it over and over again, in order that I might succeed in making some experiments with it. So I dictated a short account of it to Vogel, who in this case also proved himself a good secretary. I then sketched the figures beside it myself. These papers I possess still [1828], my thoughts, with all the marks of the rainy weather, which are witnesses to my faithful study in the dubious path I had entered. The road to truth has this advantage, that we are always looking to the uncertain steps we took, the circuitous paths we pursued, nay, even to our false steps.

The soldiers came to realize that they had an everlastingly curious scientist in their midst. This prompted them one day to bring to

Goethe, during a brief cessation of hostilities near Sedan, what they thought was a cannonball, covered with tiny crystallized pyramids. He could not make out what it was.[9] Later, when he inquired about it, the men told him that the ball had exploded. He asked for the fragments and discovered crystallization at the centre, radiating towards the surface. It was pyrites, and when they searched about, they found other examples of it, formed into strange shapes, of balls and kidneys and other irregular shapes.

The devisers of this campaign, on the German side, which was designed to defeat the Revolution itself and to reclaim France for the royalists, had profoundly misread the mood of the times.

Goethe reached Christiane and August by Christmas 1792. 'Sweet Friend, just one, just one kiss grant to these lips/Why are you being so withholding today?' is a poem written at this date. Those are *his* words. *She* in turn replies that she has happy memories of a wonderful Yesterday.

> Words tumbled into one another, kiss followed kiss
> To part at evening was pain.

Goethe tells us that all his poems were occasional poems, they were *all* snatches of autobiography. His return to Weimar was, alas for Christiane, not merely to see her and their child, but to report for duty at court, and, not long into the New Year of 1793, to prepare for more military service.

January brought news that King Louis had been executed in Paris. The Terror was about to begin in earnest. Unaware that his bungling campaigns in Germany and his benign, Mirabeau-esque form of republicanism would not be smiled upon by Robespierre, and that he himself would be guillotined at the end of August, General Moustache (Custine) was still occupying Mainz. During the era of the German Democratic Republic of 1949 to 1990, it was fashionable in East Germany to speak of the Mainz Revolution, and to believe that this city ruled over by a Bishop-Elector of the Church had enthusiastically embraced the values of the Left.

This was not really the case, and the occupation of Mainz by the French was very much resented by the population at large. The enthusiasts for the Revolution tended to be, not those whose shops and market stalls were looted, or whose houses were requisitioned by the champions of Liberty and Fraternity, but the intellectuals. Goethe's friend Georg Forster, the boy who had sailed with Captain Cook, was one of the most notable enthusiasts, requesting affiliation with France. He and another man called Adam Lux were, through the offices of the Marquis de Custine, made members of the Assemblée Nationale, and would go to Paris to represent the 'Republic of Mainz' in the assembly. It would not have happy consequences for any of them, in that bloody and bloodcurdling year. Both the young Germans were appalled when they actually saw the blood flowing over the cobblestones and the tumbrils trundling towards the guillotines.

Charlotte Corday – the fifth-generation descendant of Corneille – stabbed the Jacobin Marat in his bath as a protest against the appalling violence of the Terror. Adam Lux, believing he was in the land of the free, or at least of the free press, wrote in praise of L'Ange d'Assassination as she would come to be known, and so, inevitably, found himself being trundled off to the guillotine – as was General Custine, when he returned to France, having failed to retain the Republic of Mainz. As for Forster, there seem to be signs that his glancing and ambivalent mind, on sight of the Terror, had changed sides. He was of English origin, after all, he had sailed with the great English cartographer, and there are some indications that, when Robespierre used him as a go-between to negotiate the return of French prisoners of war in exchange for the British at Arras, he was involved in counter-espionage. Whatever the truth, he was a broken man; his health and his marriage collapsed and he died of pneumonia in Paris, far from home.[10]

The Prussian army easily retook Mainz, and Goethe was there to witness it. He would say afterwards that a single day at the military headquarters in Champagne and a single day in the ravaged city of Mainz were for him symbols of contemporary history, and of the collapse of all contemporary institutions.[11]

On 16 October, the Revolution performed its bloodiest coup de grâce, the execution of Marie Antoinette. Goethe had watched her arrival, the Austrian princess, at Strasbourg when he was a student. He was bitterly upset.[12]

Carl August had, like his *Heimatrat* (Privy Councillor), had enough of war, though the French Revolutionary conflict and its Napoleonic aftermath would dominate the next two decades of European history and see the bloodiest of conflicts in Weimar and Jena themselves. This, however, lay in the future. Revolutionary Mainz, and blood-soaked Champagne, and Goethe's failure to reach Paris, which had always been an ambition of his, were translated, as so much of experience was, into symbols. He would bank these symbols and they would come to birth when he was in the autumn of life, and the *Faust* dramatic poem had matured.

Some of Goethe's apparent indifference to the war can be put down to egotism. He was certainly *not* indifferent to the possibility of revolutionary ideas on the French model spreading to the Holy Roman Empire.

It was also, however, his contribution to the growing discussion – perhaps the central discussion in all European politics from his day until the late twentieth century – about the nature and place of Germany. The young men who hissed him as he came out of the theatre in the early years of the nineteenth century were liberal patriots who wanted a united Germany, independent not only of the Austro-Hungarian Empire but, more fundamentally, independent of the old hierarchies of throne and altar. Goethe's studied loftiness about such aspirations stemmed from a distrust of where such ideas might lead. He would have agreed with Johnson that patriotism is the last refuge of the scoundrel, and some readers of history, seeing the direction which German patriotism would later take, might rather agree with him.

The experience of war had quickened his longing for a republic of art and science, heedless of national boundaries and free of political ideology. He did not want, as so many Germans of a younger generation did, a German republic, or even, as such, a German nation. Before he went home to Weimar, he turned off to Mannheim where he fell in with his brother-in-law, Cornelia's widower, and shared with him his dream of an international academy of art and science, but Schlosser was scornful. Goethe left him in fury, never to speak to him again.

He wanted to set down his ideas about science, more than he wanted to draft manifestoes or set out political dreams. As his correspondence with Jacobi shows, he had been planning for some time to set down his ideas on evolution. When he accompanied the Duke, in July 1790, to the Schlesian encampment, he occupied himself primarily there (in Breslau) with his studies on animal development. He also began really to write down his thoughts on this subject. On 31 August 1790, he wrote to Friedrich von Stein: 'In all this bustle, I have begun to write my treatise on the development of the animals.'

By the time he reached Weimar, he found that Carl August had resigned his commission in the Prussian army and was now intent on governing his small domains – with any luck, with Goethe's help. Poor Christiane: if she had hoped that her man was coming back to her, she did not see Goethe for long. He took lodgings in Jena and it was there, towards the close of 1793, that he intended to stay and write. Goethe's involvement with great public, still less international, affairs was at an end. He did not know it, but he was on the verge of the decade-long friendship which, during an apparent period of creative doldrums, would be the greatest imaginative stimulus of his life: the friendship with Schiller.

I I

The Friendship with Schiller

A total iconoclast, Goethe inherits everything that is wildest and most idiosyncratic in Western aesthetic culture.

Harold Bloom, *The Western Canon:*
The Books and School of the Ages

The double statue of Goethe and Schiller by Ernst Rietschel, erected outside the Court Theatre in Weimar in 1857, is a monument not merely to two giants of literature, but also to a fructiferous friendship. It is doubtful whether Goethe would ever have got going on the expansion and revision of his early *Faust* had it not been for Schiller urging him to complete the fragment. Equally, a case could be made for saying that Schiller's later masterpieces – above all the *Wallenstein* trilogy, *Mary Stuart* and *The Maiden of Orleans* – owed much to Goethe, who read each of the plays scene by scene and act by act as they were being so laboriously composed.

Likewise, their shared love of Homer, and, almost equal to this love, their admiration for his German translator, Voss, undoubtedly inspired Goethe to write the 'epic' which, in his lifetime and for much of the nineteenth century, was easily his most popular work in his own country – *Hermann and Dorothea*.

Yet this was no bromance. Before they actually met, Goethe nursed a strong aversion to Schiller's early play *The Robbers*. Schiller, ten years younger than Goethe, revered the 'great man' but also took the cult of him with a pinch of salt. The friendship, moreover, remained very largely an intellectual passion, not least because Schiller took a rigidly conservative view of Goethe's domestic arrangements and scarcely acknowledged the existence of the older man's life-partner, Christiane Vulpius.

The very first meeting between the pair had occurred when Schiller was a twenty-year-old medical student at Ludwigsburg – the Schwabian Versailles – at what would become the Hohe Karlsschule, the Military Academy founded by the tyrannical Duke Karl of Württemberg. Attendance there was compulsory. Had Schiller pursued his original intention of studying for the Lutheran ministry, Duke Karl's press-gang would have rounded him up and forced him into military service. (Schiller's father was a soldier.) Similarly, there was no nonsense about students choosing which subjects they wished to pursue. Schiller had been assigned the study of medicine and a medic he was therefore to become. Already, however, he had mastered Latin and English and read the plays of Shakespeare and *The Vicar of Wakefield*. The early plays of Goethe – deemed so Shakespearean by his contemporaries – were Schiller's favourite reading. He would perform the title role in Goethe's *Clavigo* in a school production (the audience thought his rendition 'too passionate') and he carried *Götz von Berlichingen* in his pocket. Literature held more allure for him than medicine and his fellow students claimed that, while he was sitting at the bedside of patients, he would compose poetry rather than listen to them reciting their symptoms.

In 1779, Duke Carl August visited the Academy, accompanied by Privy Councillor Goethe. Schiller at the time was clothed in the uniform of the place – a blue coat with silver buttons and black collar, white waistcoat and trousers, a small black hat with plumes, and at his side a sword. His long hair was tied in a pigtail. There is no evidence that Schiller made much impression upon his visitors at the time, though, clearly, Schiller glowed at the visitation of a giant of literature. His own 'Shakespearean' drama *The Robbers* would not have been written had not Goethe stormed and stressed the way with *Götz*, and, obviously, Goethe's later dislike of *The Robbers* sprang largely from the fact that he had outgrown his own Storm and Stress phase, and, post-Italy, was striving towards his own version of classicism.

The two men had much in common. Both were interested not merely in being poets, but in the advances of contemporary philosophy and science. Schiller, as perhaps befitted a medical student, was more systematic in his mastery of these disciplines. From an early age, he had interested himself in the scientific bases for character and motive, the essence of what would be his dramatic enterprise. Side by side with his writing for the theatre – and there would be very long gaps in his life as a playwright – he was wrestling with the philosophical problems of knowledge and perception.

Like Goethe, Schiller became famous overnight as a very young writer. After seven years of the Academy, and twenty-one years of living with his father, a tyrannical army captain, Schiller made a run for it. His escape was not successful; he was arrested, and taken back to Ludwigsburg and imprisoned. It was in his cell that he composed *The Robbers*, a play which embodied the Storm and Stress. The second attempt to escape was successful. The mother of one of his school friends offered him refuge at her country house at Bauersbach, later at her house in Mannheim. Here he borrowed the money – it was years before he had enough to pay off the debt – to have *The Robbers* printed. Like *Götz*, eight years before, it was a sensational *succès d'estime* as a book, although, because it was regarded as politically subversive, it was not performed. (It waited until 1783 before it was staged in Berlin.)

Poverty dogged him. This was one of the great differences between him and Goethe, who had been born into financial security. True, Goethe ran up debts, but he did so as one who had never needed to worry about money. Schiller, by contrast, was compelled to worry about money all his adult life. He doodled with the idea of a play about Mary Queen of Scots – which did not come to completion until years later. And he began the play of Don Carlos.

By this stage, he had attracted the patronage of a Frau von Kalb, and it was she who arranged for him to read the first act of *Don Carlos* at court in Mannheim. It was heard by the Duke of Saxe-Weimar, who had visited his school not long before. Full of admiration, the Duke conferred on young Schiller the title of Councillor. Schiller did not, however, go to Weimar immediately. Christian Gottfried Körner (1756–1831), the lawyer son of a Leipzig theologian (three years older than Schiller), took him up, paid him a modest allowance and found him accommodation in a village outside Leipzig, which gave him time to finish *Don Carlos*.

The friendship between Körner and Schiller led to one of the most formidable correspondences in literature, their letters giving us portraits of many of the illustrious names of German literary life over twenty years, in addition to their multifarious intellectual interests. It was during his first happy summer in the company of Körner – who had just married Minna Stock (daughter of the man who had taught Goethe engraving at Leipzig) – and Minna's sister Dora, engaged to the aspirant young writer Huber – that Schiller wrote 'Ode to Joy'. It was Körner who urged Schiller to read Voltaire's *Charles XII* and himself to become a professional historian. Together they read Laclos's *Les Liaisons dangereuses*.

Schiller did not want to become a sponge or an appendage to Körner, so, in order to strike out on his own, he moved to Weimar, seeking out the company of Wieland and his old friend and patroness Frau von Kalb. He also came to know Herder in that summer of 1787, and was able to visit Knebel who was living in Goethe's Garden House.

Goethe himself was still in Italy. Such was the reverence felt in Weimar for the great man, that, on 18 August, a birthday party was held for him, *in absentia*, in that very house. 'Little would Goethe dream – away in Italy – that I was one of his guests! After supper we found the garden illuminated and had some very fair fireworks.'[1]

That same year Schiller also made the 30-kilometre trip to Jena where he could hear the lectures of Wieland's son-in-law Karl Leonhard Reinhold (1757–1823). It was through Reinhold that he heard of the forthcoming publication of Kant's *Critique of Pure Reason*, and listened with rapture to Reinhold's lectures. Reinhold was a Catholic. It was his wish to marry which had prevented him from becoming a priest. Nevertheless, though the Church would condemn Kant – for his assertion that it was impossible to prove the existence of God – Schiller reported of Reinhold, 'He actually asserts that in a hundred years' time, Kant will have won a reputation equal to that of Jesus Christ.' For anglophone readers, especially for British readers, this sentence needs to be borne in mind if we are to understand the differences between the English-speaking and the German scene in nineteenth-century life. Think of the observation made by his contemporary Mark Pattison, that the whole history of the English would have been different if John Henry Newman had been able to read German; or think of poor Mr Casaubon in *Middlemarch* who wrote his catastrophically bad 'Key to all the Mythologies' without having read German.

Kant was responsible for a revolution in thought which he deemed comparable to the Copernican revolution in astronomy. The British empirical philosophers, above all David Hume, had reached an impasse of epistemology – i.e. the deep question of how we can know *anything* at all. Hume's scepticism did not merely apply to religion. By denying the possibility of induction as a path to knowledge, Hume had in effect stopped scientific inquiry in its tracks. Was it possible for the philosopher to reclaim the possibility of saying that some propositions could be verified, some things could be known?

Kant's way out of the difficulties created by Hume was to posit the concept of Categories. The human mind is so programmed – this was Kant's 'revolution' – as to bring to our perception of the world a unifying perception which is not simply the sense-impressions playing upon the empirical self. Kant, in other words – to quote T. S. Eliot's succinct summary – distinguishes between 'an external reality from which we receive material, and the formative activity of consciousness'.[2] Goethe's world view, as we shall see, was actually radically different from Kant's, but he would nonetheless see Kant as 'der köstlicher Mann', the invaluable man, and he would never forget the important part played by the last decade of the eighteenth century on his own mental development. This would feed into *Faust*. For the time being, suffice it to say that the point of divergence, which would eventually open up widely, between Kant and Goethe stemmed from Kant's view of the universe itself. Kant believed the Categories to be an innate part of the structure of the Newtonian universe. He did not question Newton's mechanical, Deist picture of the universe itself. Indeed, it was essential to his entire philosophy, since Kant thought empirical knowledge, stuff which could definitely be known, was confined to the universe of Newtonian physics. This is what enables us to speak of physical objects, this is what enables us (to use Popper's judgement of scientific truth) to determine that some statements about the universe are verifiable or falsifiable. There is nothing to be known outside this universe, which is why it would be impossible for the human mind to prove the existence of God. Famously, Kant believed that our moral sense, dictated by the Categorical Imperative, was something contained within this universe. But central to his epistemology was the distinction between what could be demonstrated by what he called Experience (*Erfahrung*) and what he called merely an Idea (*Idee*).

Schiller absorbed, and accepted, Kant's arguments as they were set forth in the three great Critiques. Goethe would eventually part company with them in important imaginative respects. Intimations of this change are to be found in the letters he wrote from Italy to Weimar friends, at about the time that Schiller had arrived in that city. While Schiller, desperate to earn some money, was spending twelve hours a day writing his historical work, *The Dutch Rebellion*, Goethe was in Sicily. In March, he wrote to Charlotte von Stein that he had removed *Faust* from its fifteen-year-old paper wrappings and was beginning to draw up a plan for the entire work: 'It is the original one in which I wrote the principal scenes straight off, without following any definite plan, and time has made it so yellow and ragged! The sheets were never fastened together – all so old and frayed that it looks like the fragments of some old Codex.'[3] But this was not the only thing on his mind. A couple of months later, he wrote to Herder from Taormina that he was planning a 'dramatic concentration of the Odyssey' – his tragedy of *Nausikaa*. And he had also had one of the moments of vision which led to his theory of the metamorphosis of plants.

'I must confide in you,' he wrote to Charlotte von Stein – with injunctions to pass on the information to Herder – 'that I am quite near to the discovery of the secret of reproduction and organization of plants; and that it is the most simple thing imaginable. Under these [Sicilian] skies one can carry on the most beautiful observation. Tell Herder that I have reached the point, quite clearly, of finding where the germ is concealed: I have got it quite clearly and without a doubt. All the rest I already have before my mind's eye. There remain only a few points to be decided. The original type [*Urpflanze*] will be the most wonderful thing in the world: Nature itself will be envious of it.'[4]

It would not be possible to distinguish, as Goethe spelled out his theory of the evolution or metamorphosis of plant life, between his *scientific* and his *poetic* interests. One here sees his close kinship with Erasmus Darwin (grandfather of the more famous Charles; 1731–1802) who wrote *The Botanic Garden*, an epic poem in two parts – *The Economy of Vegetation* and *The Loves of the Plants* – and who expressed his evolutionary theory through poetry.[5] Goethe came to regard his own poetic output as a form of botanical or plant life. In *Faust* it is the plant which holds within it all the possibilities of the vegetative kingdom. 'In Goethe's plant morphology, the play between male and female leads along a spiral path and through a number of transformational stages to a fusion in the pigmented flower.'[6]

It was, specifically, in his botanical theory that Goethe first, and most specifically, spelled out his own difference from Kant. His *Metamorphosis of Plants* would appear in the same year, 1790, as Kant's *Critique of the Power of Judgement*. Kant asserted, in that book, that the fundamental difference between machines and organisms was that machines are composed of parts which also exist independently of the whole, and are then assembled for a predetermined process; whereas the parts, or organs, of organisms have no existence independent of the whole. A whole is made up of parts – that we can grasp. But how should a whole produce its parts, in a sense, precede them? The *idea* of the whole was inconceivable to the human mind; only God, or a godly being, could move from a discernment of the synthetically universal (the intuition of the whole as such) to a perception of the parts – the parts which we have not, specifically, seen or experienced.

Goethe could not agree with this since he believed he had quite directly and specifically realized precisely this kind of intuitive understanding in *The Metamorphosis of Plants*. The young Goethe, through his *Urfaust*, had expressed this as an ambition:

That I recognise what holds the world
Together in its innermost depth.[7]

The scientist Goethe of mature years believed he had achieved the ambition.

He had seen into the life of things. If one does not know the essence or the fundamental idea of a thing, one has to start from the synthetic whole in order to find it.[8]

When Goethe first returned to Weimar from Italy, the time had not been ripe for the friendship with Schiller to develop. There were too many other things happening – in Goethe's life, the domestic preoccupations with Christiane and her succession of children, all of whom died except August; the world scene; the campaigns in France and Mainz.

Schiller had moved to Jena. Goethe had been responsible for his appointment as Professor of History at Jena University, a move which friend Körner had opposed unless they paid Schiller a proper salary.[9] He was paid 200 talers per year.[10]

In 1790, when he wanted to get married, Schiller calculated that he needed to earn at least 800 per year. In 1804 he would calculate that in order to lead a comfortable bourgeois life in Weimar it cost 1,900 talers per year. (Goethe was on 1,200, and in addition was given, gratis, his Garden House and his large house on the Frauenplan.) Even when they became good friends, this discrepancy in their circumstances was always something which caused tension between them.

In those days university lecturers in Germany were paid a per capita rate. Each attendant at the lecture paid a fee. The per capita rate determined whether the lecturer would be rich or poor. Schiller's inaugural lecture at Jena was a triumph. He filled Reinhold's lecture hall; the audience was easily 400 people, with students sitting on the tops of desks and on window ledges. When the lecture was finished they cried aloud, 'VIVAT! VIVAT!'[11] He modestly averred, 'I am treated with a veneration which is quite startling!'[12]

Still, the two great men of German literature were keeping their distance from one another. In July 1790, as he was preparing the eighth volume of his Collected Works, Goethe told Duke Carl August he had decided to publish *Faust* as a fragment.[13] Körner and Schiller mulled it over when the volume appeared, Körner writing:

Certainly I find inequalities in it and of course, some of the scenes were written at such great distances apart, as regards time, but much of it delights me, especially the main idea that Faust, through his character, always remains a brighter kind of being than Mephistopheles, even though the latter may be his superior as regards his stock of ideas, in experience and versatility. This might, it is true, have been given a greater prominence in many instances, and the low class of the rhyme [Bänkel-sängerton] which Goethe has chosen, often decoys him into platitudes which disfigure the work.[14]

Not long after writing this letter, Körner received Goethe in Dresden and spent a week with him; 'he was more communicative than I expected him to be'. The two discussed Kant obsessively but 'we did not confine ourselves to philosophy'.[15]

This was a fallow period for Schiller's poetry – he wrote none between 1790 and 1794, busily engaged as he was in lecturing and on translating to keep the wolf from the door – he translated Virgil and Plutarch. He was overworking, and – like so many of his generation – doomed to die of tuberculosis, or, as they called it, consumption – he was suffering from sharp pains in his chest whenever he breathed deeply. His work on the Thirty Years War was leading his mind in the direction of his great masterpiece – *Wallenstein*.

Goethe, meanwhile, who had temporarily vacated the Frauenplan at the Duke's request, to accommodate a distinguished guest to Weimar, had set up a dark room in his Garden House, and was busy with experiments with the theory of colours.

Duke Carl August had greatly lightened Goethe's workload, as far as administration and political duties were concerned. He had, however, asked him to take over the directorship of the Court Theatre. He would retain this position until 1808.[16] In those times there were not long theatrical 'runs'. There was a fast turnover of productions, and, since Goethe often undertook the direction of productions himself, it was a considerable enterprise. Probably the most spectacular dramatic success of his early years as director was a production of Shakespeare's *King John*, with great actress Christiana Neumann playing Prince Arthur. She, however, was an exception. For the most part, few of the really good actors from Berlin were tempted to come and perform to a small audience, on a tiny stage, for very little money.

Goethe wrote over forty plays to be performed in the Court Theatre, and you might think that this would have been an incentive to finish *Faust*, and to craft it in such a way that it would appeal to wide audiences. The truth, highly paradoxical for a man who was so in love with the theatre and – see *Wilhelm Meister* – in love with the idea of himself as a man of the theatre, was that Goethe despised popular audiences. The more he saw of such figures, such as students from Jena crowding into the stalls of the Court Theatre, or the middling classes of Weimar having the impertinence to expect to be entertained, rather than elevated, the more he despised them. In the Dedication to the expanded *Faust Part One*, composed after 1797, he would loftily write:

> My tragic song will now impress the many,
> Applause from them, it fills my heart with dread.[17]

'No one can serve two masters, and of all masters the last I would select is the public which sits in a German theatre,' he said to Schiller.[18] They in turn found even his more famous plays, such as *Torquato Tasso* or *Iphigenia*, boring, and made no secret of the fact – one of the reasons these pieces were so seldom performed in Weimar.

Moreover, especially when drink had been taken, he found it impossible to disguise his contempt for his public. In his preface to *Faust*, the theatrical impresario consults a poet and a comedian about what to stage, and the comic recommends him to ask the question – Who can be amusing? *Wer machte denn der Mitwelt Spass?* It was not always a question to which Goethe himself paid much attention when staging plays. When he put on Friedrich Schlegel's tragedy *Alarcos* in 1802 it was greeted with unwanted guffaws from the audience. Goethe stood up in a fury and called out in his deep voice, 'Let NO ONE LAUGH!' As a Privy Councillor, War Minister and Home Secretary of the little place, he was entitled to enforce what he had shouted. He placed uniformed hussars in the lobby and any rowdies – often Jena students – were in danger of finding themselves marched off to the guardhouse and imprisoned. Uniformed hussars were placed at the dressing-room doors of the actresses to prevent them entertaining their amorous fans, as the androgynous actress Marianne does in the charming opening chapters of *Wilhelm Meister*.

Goethe's prejudice against the public enjoying itself was all the more ironic, since, as it happened, there was one extremely popular dramatist who had been born and bred in Weimar. When a more fun-loving Goethe had first arrived in Weimar, he had enjoyed acting, and writing plays for the Court Theatre. One of his fellow actors was Amalia Kotzebue who performed with him in his play (dashed off in three evenings) *The Siblings* (*Die Geschwister*).[19] Amalia's little brother, August Friedrich Ferdinand Kotzebue (1761–1810), was one of the most popular playwrights of the late eighteenth century and certainly in all senses a prolific figure – author of more than 200 plays and the father of eighteen children. In England, he was the most famous German playwright of his day, though it is probably fair to say that today, in the English-speaking world, he is probably only remembered as the author of *Lovers' Vows*, the play being rehearsed in Jane Austen's *Mansfield Park* in the absence of Sir Thomas Bertram.[20] (The baronet's unexpected return from the West Indies brings the production to a halt.)

Kotzebue was destined to die at the hands of an assassin – a German liberal – because Kotzebue was on the side of reaction. In 1806, to escape a Germany dominated by Napoleon, he went to work at the court theatre in St Petersburg and was as popular in Russia as he had been at home. Married to the daughter of a Russian general, he had estates in Estonia, then, as for most of its history, part of the Russian Empire. He was a serving consul in St Petersburg, and many believed (wrongly) that he was a Russian spy. Whether he was writing comedies or melodramas, he had the one quality which Goethe never mastered as a dramatist – the ability to construct a gripping plot which kept audiences watching and listening. He could also be very funny.

Whatever his personal feelings, Goethe could not overlook – in his capacity as director of the Weimar Court Theatre – the obvious fact that Kotzebue was 'box office'. Of his 116 plays, there were 1,728 performances in Weimar, compared with just fifteen performances of *The Robbers*; *Don Carlos* had a mere three performances.[21]

Kotzebue was not a philistine exactly. (Beethoven begged him to write a libretto for an opera about Attila the Hun.) Relations with Goethe, however, after the fun of acting and working with the young Goethe in the 1780s, were never easy. He returned to Weimar after the assassination of Tsar Paul, but Goethe and his circle cold-shouldered him, and he went off to Berlin.[22]

Certainly, the theatrical scene in the Prussian capital was considerably more impressive, and professional, than the Court Theatre at Weimar under the directorship of Goethe, which was run on the cheap, and the terms offered to the actors were unfavourable. Even Caroline Jagemann, the Duke's mistress, who was the prima donna of the Weimar theatre, was on a salary of just 600 talers a year.

Contracts were strict and those who signed up for a season at the Weimar theatre were not allowed to work elsewhere.

Goethe was anxious to introduce the audiences to higher thought, and persuaded Schiller, when they eventually became friends, to translate some plays of Shakespeare.

Audiences, however, were most easily wooed by operas and musical theatre. There would be many productions of *Don Giovanni* and *The Magic Flute*, though they could not always afford singers of the highest quality. The Queen of the Night was so heavily pregnant by the time Goethe's production of *The Magic Flute* came off, she had to devise a truly ridiculous arrangement, with the Queen singing her part hidden behind some scenery, while another actor mimed her on stage.[23]

Though they are now famous for writing plays, it was not the theatre which brought Goethe and Schiller together. A Natural History Society had been founded at Jena, and Goethe and Schiller happened to attend it together. As they emerged from a lecture, they discussed what the speaker had had to say, and Schiller remarked that such a piecemeal, fragmentary method of dealing with Nature could not fire the imagination of amateur inquiries. He had touched what was the core of Goethe's own holistic science. Certainly – whether he was discussing geology, anatomy, botany or any other branch of science – Goethe was interested, as all scientists are, in the truth or falsehood of what was being said; but he was even more concerned with the way in which any scientific fact or discovery illuminated the Whole.

Erasmus Darwin's *The Loves of the Plants* had appeared in 1789 (anonymously). Darwin was a man-giant medical doctor, friends with the so-called Lunar Men (Joseph Priestley, Josiah Wedgwood et al.) and a free-thinker. Although today, readers of the English language might guess that the most famous poets in England in the 1790s were Wordsworth and Coleridge, at the time, Erasmus Darwin was infinitely the best-known and most widely read poet in English and – rather as Goethe would do in German – he put his scientific knowledge into his verse.

These books of Darwin's were the first in English to expound a theory of evolution, and to posit that the species which we recognize at present had developed from simpler, and fewer, originals. 'People forgot that science developed out of poetry,' Goethe would write later. 'They failed to grasp the truth that with the swing of the pendulum the two might again meet, and for their mutual advantage, upon a higher plane. Lady friends, who had quite approved of my wandering upon the lonely mountains and gazing at bare rocks, were in no way satisfied with my abstract gardening. Plants should, of course, be distinguished according to their form, colour and scent, but now they were being distributed among uncanny classifications ... Then I made an attempt to win back the approval of my fair friends by presenting them with a poem in the form of an elegy.'[24]

This 'elegy' bears an unmistakable resemblance to Erasmus Darwin's *The Love of the Plants*. It was this theme, the evolution of plants, which sparked the first deep conversation between Schiller and Goethe.

He went on:

Schiller, who was far more of a man of the world than I, and who was far more anxious to attract than to repulse me – on account of his forthcoming publication, the Horen, for which he was anxious to secure me as a contributor – answered me in the manner of a fully fledged disciple of Kant. As my stubborn realism afforded many openings for a lively discussion, we fought valiantly, and then proclaimed an armistice.

Neither of us could claim he was the victor: both of us felt ourselves invincible. Such sentences as the following made me quite unhappy: 'How can it ever happen that experience can be adjusted to an idea? For therein lies the peculiarity of the latter, that it can never coincide with an experience.'

Schiller was quoting directly from *Critique of Pure Reason*.

For a moment, Goethe was stung. But he pulled himself together and replied, 'I am very glad to find I have ideas without knowing it, and that I can even see them with my bodily eyes.'

It was a long conversation, and by the time it had concluded, the two men had embarked on their deep friendship.

Goethe left Jena, and was travelling for the next month. Schiller descended into one of his periodic bouts of chest illness, bedbound for three weeks. On 23 August, less than a week before Goethe's forty-fifth birthday, Schiller wrote:

Our recent conversations have set the whole mass of my ideas in movement, for they centred on a subject which has occupied my thoughts for several years past. In the case of many points where I have been unable to get a clear idea in my own mind your mental intuition – for so I must designate the sum total of your ideas as they have affected me – has brought me unexpected light. Hitherto, I had lacked the object, the body, on which to hang my various speculative ideas, and you put me on the right track.

Your observant eye, your glance so tranquil and unbiased, which takes in facts so comprehensibly and fairly, is never in danger of leading you to the wrong path, as speculation and an arbitrary imagination so often lead people who are too much under their sway.

All that analysis seeks so industriously to attain is attained in your case by intuition, and in a form that is much more complete. It is only because it is to be found in you as a single whole that you are unconscious of your wealth in the realm of ideas, for, unfortunately, we are only conscious of what we separate. Minds like yours know how far they have penetrated and how little cause they have to borrow from philosophy, which, indeed, can only borrow from them.[25]

Later in the letter, he gave a description of Goethe's inward journey which could serve as a summary, almost as a manifesto, of *Faust*.

By reconstructing man according to Nature's laws you hope to penetrate into her concealed technique – a great, and truly heroic idea, which bears enough testimony to the beautiful unity within which you have marshalled your ideas. It is impossible that you should ever have hoped to see this goal attained within the short span of your own life. But the very fact of your starting out on such a path means you have made more progress than would have been possible by any other road. Like Achilles, in the Iliad, you have chosen immortality rather than a long life in Phthia.[26]

Schiller's letter exactly parallels the soliloquy spoken in the 'Forest and Cave' scene, in which Faust refers back to his debt to the Earth Spirit. Not in vain did the Spirit turn his terrifying fiery countenance towards Faust and

> Gave me glorious Nature as my domain
> The power to feel and to enjoy you:
> You did not permit me merely a cold visit of curiosity. No, rather,
> You let me look, as into the very bosom of a friend.

This is Faust speaking, but it is of course the manifesto of Goethe the scientist-poet; Goethe the inspiration of the great English-speaking Romantic poets Shelley and Byron.

> You led me to a cave of security.
> Show me your very self, and to my very own bosom.
> The secret deep miracles open up ...

Critics have drawn our attention to Faust's isolation in this scene, almost, it could be said, his solipsism. There is the world of difference between his complete imaginative and intellectual immersion in 'Nature', in this speech, and the desolation of poor Gretchen in the following scene in which she sings at her spinning wheel that all her serenity and tranquillity is gone (the lyrics made unforgettable by Schubert).

But Gretchen is not the only one who is cut out of the picture by Faust's 'egotistical sublime'. Faust certainly shows no knowledge of the Prologue in Heaven, where Mephistopheles and the Lord have their amusing little bet about the fate of his soul. In this scene at least, Faust claims mastery of his own destiny, his own journey into the heart of scientific understanding, his own grasp, *pace* Kant, of the Thing Itself, *pace* Newton, of the very essence of colour itself.

It is one of the high points of the whole drama, and indeed of German literature. There is nothing quite like it anywhere else, though so many poets have tried to imitate it. Faust himself has these moments from time to time throughout both parts of the drama in which he seems grandly, agonizingly, greater than the drama in which he is taking part. It was Schiller who drew this from him, and the emotional temperature, the engagement with the other Jena 'set', all this made for the perfect moment and contributed to the all-but-finished *Faust*. But, *Faust* was not going to be finished in Schiller's lifetime. At many points it looked as if it would not be finished in Goethe's lifetime either. The perceptions which Faust here both embodies and articulates are in context in part an explanation of his insufferable, arrogant neglect of Gretchen's suffering – parallel no doubt to Goethe's own willingness to put on one side, or neglect, or actually escape, all the deeper relationships of his life. It is much, much later, when both Goethe and Faust have become old men, that the shape and context of his Nature-worship/science take on their sublime glory.

Goethe, who had known Schiller's wife since her childhood, was enchanted with them both, and Frau Schiller was friends with Charlotte von Stein. Such were the stiff conventions of the time, and of Schiller's obedience to them, that he scarcely acknowledged Christiane Vulpius's existence.

There would be one occasion when, in Weimar, Schiller found her alone in a public park, and in danger of being molested by some drunks. He escorted her back to Goethe's house and she expressed gratitude. Otherwise, however often Schiller stayed under Christiane and Goethe's roof, when he wrote to thank for the hospitality he only ever wrote to Goethe, never to her. In May 1800, when Christiane was going to Leipzig he wrote to Goethe, 'I have this moment heard that someone [*jemand*] is going to Leipzig from your home and I take this opportunity of sending you a few words of greeting. I have felt your absence greatly and I feel it doubly because I cannot lose myself in my work. The rehearsals for *Macbeth* cut into my time too much.'[27]

This refers to Schiller's own translation of *Macbeth* which was performed at the Court Theatre in Weimar. This is the *only reference* to Goethe's life-partner in all Schiller's many letters to his friend. 'Someone is going to Leipzig.'

Schiller and Körner freely corresponded about Goethe's domestic set-up. 'That Goethe's domestic situation must depress him I can well understand; hence I clearly see he must find life more enjoyable away from Weimar than at home. We cannot infringe upon the laws of morality without suffering for it.' ... 'The other sex has a higher mission than that of being lowered to the condition of a tool for sensuality.'[28]

Presumably, it was the sense that people were saying such things about him which prompted Goethe, in 1797, to undertake his ruthless auto-da-fé in which he burned nearly all his personal correspondence. He was approaching his fiftieth birthday. He was in every sense a changed person since his return from Italy, the establishment of his irregular liaison with Vulpius and his rejection by Charlotte von Stein.

Some alcoholics survive on drink alone and become skeletal. With others, the need for drink fuels greed for food and both Christiane and Goethe became fat. 'He eats dreadfully,'[29] the German Romantic writer Jean Paul (1763–1825) had recorded in 1796. And Charlotte von Stein in the same year also noted the uncontrolled eating and the change in appearance: 'He was dreadfully fat, with short arms which he thrust deep into his trousers-pockets and kept them there. I long to know whether he could be aware of how utterly, physiognomically, he has changed in my eyes.'[30] The great French writer Madame de Staël (1766–1817), visiting Weimar, gasped in amazement that so great a spirit could be housed in such a dreadful encasing ('puis être si mal logé').[31] In 1799, Charlotte's son Karl von Stein was even less merciful when he wrote:

His gait is extremely slow, his belly hangs beneath him like that of a heavily pregnant woman, and his chin is practically sunk into the folds of his throat, swallowed up in double chins and jowls; his cheeks fat, his mouth a half-moon; his eyes alone still pointed in the direction of Heaven ... his whole expression a sort of self-satisfied indifference, without really looking especially happy. I feel sorry for him.[32]

As one of his best twentieth-century English biographers put it, 'The world was beginning to think that it had nothing more to expect from him in the way of first class literature. Goethe recognized the caricature and was stung to the quick.'[33]

The world was wrong. The friendship with Schiller, leading to a close absorption into the clever set of Jena intellectuals, stimulated Goethe to resume work on *Faust*. The earlier versions of the play had drawn on his conversations, and sometimes scratchy Strasbourg friendships with Herder, Merck, Jacobi, Lavater. These younger Jena intellectuals confronted Goethe's imagination with the phenomenon of German Idealism, the philosophical revolutions and counter-revolutions which were coming to terms with Kant – in the works of the Schlegels, Schelling, Hegel and Fichte.

We see this process at work in Goethe's reworking of an earlier scene in Faust's study, shortly after Mephistopheles and the mage have sealed their pact. We recall C. S. Lewis's verdict on Marlowe's play quoted in my first chapter: 'You will read in some critics that Faustus has a thirst for knowledge. In reality, he hardly mentions it. It is not truth that he wants from the devils, but gold and guns and girls.'[34] This was very much not the case for Goethe's Faust, who despises the devil's lures, of food, girls and gold,[35] and imagines that Mephistopheles is too mired in sensuality and magic to recognize the high striving of the human mind.[36] In one of the first adjustments he made to the play after the long interval of silence – probably writing in 1797 – Goethe added a soliloquy by the devil, the only such speech in the play. It occurs after Faust has left his study and before the devil, who has put on the professor's academic robes, interviews the student and gives his advice about which faculty to follow.

In his soliloquy, Mephistopheles tells the audience that he is immediately going back on his pact with Faust. Far from offering him the capacity to 'strive' to higher realms of intellectual capacity, he is going to fuddle him with sensual longings. He will descend (but only temporarily) into the version of the story outlined by Lewis/Marlowe. Mephistopheles, however, is no longer the demon of popular puppet shows, nor the sixteenth-century 'foul fiend' of popular Lutheranism. He is thoroughly a figure of the post-Kantian Enlightenment, and it is this speech which was singled out both by Schelling, in his discussion of *Faust* in *The Philosophy of Art* (c.1804), and by Hegel in *The Phenomenology of Spirit* (1807). In this speech, Faust is seen by his devilish new friend to be trying to aspire after Reason and Science. It will be Mephistopheles's task, during the second, highly dramatic half of *Faust Part One*, to distract the Enlightenment intellectual with alcohol and the lure of sex.

Mephistopheles, in Faust's long robe, says:

Go, and despise Reason and Science now,
The highest strength of humankind.
May the Spirit of Lies only strengthen you
In blindness and magic mumbo jumbo.
I have already got you unconditionally.
Fate has endowed him with a spirit
Of untamed impetuousness spurring him onwards.
This precipitate striving would lead him to leap over earthly
    delights:
But I am going to lug him through the wildest experiences,
Through the shallows of utter frivolity.
He'll struggle for me, he'll go numb, he'll get stuck
And his total insatiability
Will beg for food and drink for his greedy lips.
Quite in vain, he'll yearn for refreshment.
Even if he'd not given himself to the Devil,
He'd still have had to perish in this way.[37]

The dogged austere life of Professor Kant in Königsberg, celibate and utterly committed to the life of the mind, might have been possible to the Patron Saint of German Philosophy. It was simply impossible, for most human beings, to lead lives governed by Reason, without the constant interruptions produced by emotional chaos and carnality. A glance at his circle of new acquaintances in Jena would have confirmed the fact, with the Schlegels in a state of marital chaos, Fichte a bruiser, Goethe himself leading the double life of the Sage-Councillor in a frock coat, front of house and backstage, the drunken, pot-bellied companion of Christiane and August.

It was during the period 1797–9 that Goethe composed most of the very strange scene entitled 'Walpurgis Night'. Mephistopheles takes

Faust up into the Harz Mountains for the May Day Witches' Revels. Goethe borrowed books from the ducal library to acquaint himself with the nature of these orgiastic customs, when witches and warlocks would allegedly process to the summit of the Brocken, the highest of the Harz Mountains, including sexual intercourse, kissing the anus of a goat and making obeisance to Satan. Goethe even planned making Satan himself appear on his mountain throne – in which case it would have been the only such appearance in the poem. (Mephistopheles is a minor devil compared with the Prince of Darkness.) The orgiastic scene is scattered with satirical references which are lost on the modern reader. For instance, there is a whole sequence in which Goethe gets his own back at Nicolai, who had lampooned *The Sorrows of Young Werther*. Out of the chaos, however, there comes one powerful and unforgettable incident, when Faust is confronted by a naked young woman and recognizes Gretchen. As this fantasy Gretchen performs her lewd dance, he is jolted back into recognizing, what Mephistopheles had made him forget, that the real Gretchen languishes in her prison cell, condemned to death. Needless to say, Mephistopheles tells Faust that the wraith-like Gretchen is an illusion, and Faust rails in fury at Mephistopheles for having lured him into the sordid chaos in which he finds himself. Those who skip the Walpurgis Night scenes and the not entirely successful Shakespearean parody of a Walpurgis Night Dream would be missing an essential ingredient in the poem, and an essential feature of Goethe's character, both as a writer and as a man. In his one personality, beside the exquisite lyricist, the passionate scientist, the soulful lover, the conservative statesman, there was also a wild man, obscene and out of control, foul-mouthed, coarse and alcohol-fuelled.

12

THE PARADES OF DEATH

That Faustian 'desire' to penetrate and enjoy – even if in
forbidden directions – the huge mystery of the Cosmos.
                    John Cowper Powys, *Maiden Castle*

It was at some point before 1800 that Goethe conceived of a
Prologue to his *Faust* play – the Prologue in Heaven. Once this had
been conceived, the entire focus and direction of the material he had
written hitherto – the *Urfaust*, written as a young man in Strasbourg,
the scene in the Witch's Kitchen, composed in Italy, and so on – were
shifted. We are a long way from the finished poetic drama, but,
both in style and content, *Faust Part Two*, the crowning glory of his
achievement, was beginning.

Goethe boldly set the Prologue as an echo, or parody, of the
beginning of the Book of Job, when the 'sons of God came to present
themselves before the Lord'. Satan is among them. He has been 'going
to and fro on the earth and from walking up and down in it'. The
Lord asks Satan to consider God's servant Job, and Satan suggests
that the only reason Job is so faithful to God has been his very great
prosperity, his many children, cattle and possessions. Take these away,
Satan suggests, and Job will start to curse God.

A grotesque wager is then suggested, and the Lord says to Satan,
'All that he hath is in thy power.' There follows the death of all Job's
children, and the ruin of his crops and farms. Job is dispossessed.

In a similar way, Goethe's Prologue depicts the Archangels of God, assembled before the Lord. He has also invited his Fallen Archangel, called here, not Satan, but Mephistopheles, the name of the Tempter in the old *Faust* puppet plays. (The derivation of the word has never been explained.)

After the Archangels have sung a hymn to the wonders of Nature, it is left to the cynical Mephistopheles to remind them all that he cannot make elevated speeches about the awesome night or the foaming seas or the rocks or the glorious sunlight, gleaming as on the first day of Creation, as his confrères have done. Mephistopheles is concerned with that less than satisfactory natural phenomenon, humanity. The Lord has given to this confused Daddy-Longlegs a glimmering of light, which he calls Reason. As far as Mephistopheles can see, it only enables the 'little god of this world' – i.e. humanity – to behave more bestially than the beasts.[1]

The Lord casually inquires, 'Do you know Faust?' Mephistopheles replies, 'The Doctor?' He goes on, mockingly, to allude to the unworldliness of the mage, who abstains from good living for the sake of his scholarship. Mephistopheles says to the Lord that he is sure that Faust can be lured from the straight and narrow, and the Lord, having extracted Mephistopheles's promise that he will not actually kill Faust, allows him to tempt him.

There follows the declaration which, for many of the nineteenth-century readers of the poem, was the core of the Goethean Credo.

A good man in his darkest stress
Is yet aware of righteousness.[2]

However deep the misfortune or despondency which the good man suffers, he will hold onto his awareness of 'the right way'. Wilhelm Wagner, Professor at the Johanneum in Hamburg in the late nineteenth century, described the famous couplet as 'now used as one of the "winged words" of the German nation'.

The Lord trusts that Faust, however far Mephistopheles lures him into dissipation or wild courses, and however much his own strivings and seekings cause him despair, will cling to righteousness. Different readers will draw contrary conclusions, by the end, about the appropriateness of the Lord's prediction. As far as the readership of the poem has been concerned, however, and certainly as far as the nineteenth-century *German* readership was concerned, it is fundamental to believe that Faust is not damned, nor is he amoral; he holds onto consciousness of the Right Way. He believes in Kant's Categorical Imperative. There is a puzzle here, certainly, in what the Lord is saying about a 'good man', since on the one hand he tells Mephistopheles that 'Humanity makes a mistake by striving' or humanity should not try so hard,[3] and on the other, there is this holding onto righteousness. In his final speech on the matter, the Lord says he has never disliked Mephistopheles, and the cynical jester – of all those who deny – is the least troublesome to him.[4]

The Lord and Mephistopheles, then, unlike Milton's God and Milton's Satan, are not at war. As Mephistopheles himself remarks, when the Lord and the Heavenly Host have departed the stage, he enjoys dropping in on the old boy from time to time:

It's handsome of him, great Lord as he is,
To speak in such a human way to the Devil.[5]

The Prologue, then, has greatly altered the traditional perspective of the *Faust* puppet dramas. The Lord and Mephistopheles are not exactly adversaries.

Rather, Mephistopheles represents the set of perceptions which are likely to be found in comic or satirical literature, in banter, in cynical jokes. He is aware of the fallibility, and the absurdity, of human nature. (He is very far from having a sense of tragedy.) On the other hand, the Lord and his servants the Archangels are possessed of awestruck awareness of Nature itself, as an everlasting process of evolution and Becoming.

May Evolution, working and living forever,
Embrace you in the lovely bonds of Love:
And may you fix, with thoughts which never waver,
The hovering, changeful face of Appearances.[6]

This is not Dante's belief in love moving the sun and other stars, so much as Teilhard de Chardin's (1881–1955) sense of all evolution moving in some inexplicable way towards the flowering of human perception; since without the human capacity to perceive Nature, to master it in all senses of the word, we would not – fairly obviously – be able to consider the matter. Humanity would heedlessly continue its existence as – we imagine – lobsters, giraffes, moles, beetles, geraniums do, each in their distinctive way, but without awareness of their place in the whole, and without – we guess from lack of evidence – self-consciousness.

Our sense of personhood is not detached from Nature – this is what makes Goethe so uncannily similar to Teilhard's *Le Phénomène humain*. Whether there is a Personal God is not (in either thinker) altogether clear, though Teilhard seemed, in *Le Phénomène* and in *Le Milieu divin* to believe in a sort of personalizing element to the evolutionary process. Already, in Goethe's *Urfaust* fragmentary conversation between Gretchen and Faust, this question has been 'parked', but here we see the irrelevance of it for our purposes (our purposes as the human race):

> Does not the All-enfolding,
> All-upholding,
> Fold and hold up
> You, me, Himself?[7]

More than a hint of pantheism here, since the Lord who upholds and sustains Nature is also a part of Nature, and is far from either the Newtonian Deist machine-maker or from the Creator of the first chapters of Genesis. We see here how deftly Goethe, as *Faust* evolves, is going to sidestep the Kantian assumption that knowledge and perception are only possible within the framework of the Newtonian clockwork universe. As Carlyle put it, 'Goethe alone seemed altogether to retain his wonted composure; he was clear for allowing the Kantean scheme to have its day, as all things have. Goethe had already lived to see the wisdom of this sentiment, so characteristic of his genius and turn of thought.'[8] This would have its effects within the thinking of the post-Kantian German philosophers, above all upon Hegel. Hegel would champion Goethe against Newton. His understanding of the fact that God is 'spirit' would assert that God is distinct from and above the physical world, but, for Hegel – this is the especially Goethean perception – the universe itself is conceived as possessing a mind.[9]

––––––––––

The friendship between Schiller and Goethe happened, chiefly, in the two towns – Goethe went to Jena for extended periods, and, when Goethe was forced to return to Weimar, Schiller, when his health permitted, accompanied him. Jena, however, offered more intellectual stimulus. Reinhold retired as Professor of Philosophy in 1794 and, on Goethe's recommendation, was replaced by Fichte, a controversial choice. Fichte only lasted four years before the 'conservators' of the university, of whom the most senior was Duke Carl August, felt they had no choice but to dismiss him for religious reasons. (He had endorsed Friedrich Karl Forberg's essay 'Development of the Concept of Religion', which explicitly rejected the Revealed God of the Bible, and declared that God only exists in our absolute moral decisions. Christianity was thereby dismissed.)

As well as Fichte, at this time, a galaxy of intellectuals was shining. Wilhelm von Humboldt had taken up residence there. He occasionally brought his brilliant younger brother Alexander – traveller, scientist and perhaps the last European polymath; a man who lacked Goethe's poetic gift but rivalled his ability to know almost all that there was to be known. To Jena also were drawn the Schlegel brothers and their brilliant wives, Caroline Schlegel (who had affairs with, among others, Georg Forster and Schelling) and Dorothea Veit. Attracted by the Schlegels came, occasionally, younger poets such as Hölderlin (who had shared digs at Tübingen with Hegel) and Novalis – though neither Goethe nor Schiller were generous enough, really, to see merit in these two young Romantics of such high genius. Any one of these figures would have seemed outstanding, but taken together, at a time when we remember Beethoven was in Vienna on the verge of composing his greatest works, and our eyes dazzle at the German glory age.[10]

Faust was not much advanced during this decade, but, as already described, it lifted from the shoals and began its journey out into open sea. The three great Goethean works of the decade demonstrate the range: he finished his long novel *Wilhelm Meister* (in 1796); he finished an outline of his *Theory of Colours* in 1797; and at the same time – while delving deeply into research on insects – he completed and published his most accessible work, *Hermann and Dorothea*.

Early in 1798, Goethe wrote to Schiller, 'For once I gave the German public what it wants and it is satisfied.' The story is very simple. In a village near Mainz in 1796, three years after the fluctuating fortunes of the Revolutionary war, the French emigrants are beginning to arrive in huge numbers. Goethe chose to tell the story, not in prose, not in any of the rhymed verse forms at which he was adept, but in an unrhymed version of Homeric hexameters. For a modern reader, especially a modern anglophone reader, a word of explanation is required.

As well as science, and as well as reviving the drama as a great German art form, and as well as all the other things they did together, Schiller and Goethe steeped themselves in Homer.

It would be a mistake to think that the classicism of Goethe, and of his German contemporaries, and their scientific interests and philosophical ideas all belonged in separate compartments. When Zeus summoned an assembly of the gods, before the final battles of the *Iliad* (Book XX), we are told that almost all attended – there was no river who failed to attend, save Oceanus; every nymph of all that feed the fair copses, the springs that feed the rivers and the grassy meadows, all came, as did Poseidon, the god of the sea. The full collection of the Homeric theogony, and the world view which developed out of it, spoke of the immanence. The divine was found in Nature, the groves and streams and oceans were permeated with these presences.

Two generations before Charles Darwin removed the necessity of believing in 'the watchmaker', science and poetry were discovering the indwelling, mysterious organic life of Nature itself, what Spinoza had called God-or-Nature. Not a God Outside the Universe who congratulated himself and said bravo on the sixth day (as Mephistopheles pertly says) but a divinity in life itself, in rocks and stones and trees, in which the Hindu mystics, and many of the Greek poets, had always believed.

The Deist viewpoint – that a watchmaker had made the universe, this elaborately constructed machine which now worked independently of the divine essence, but according to the watchmaker's immutable laws – derived from one, rather unimaginative reading of the Creation stories in Genesis. The science which interested Goethe – evolutionary biology both of plants and animals – the interconnectedness of human and other mammalian anatomy, the vividness of colour and light – these were all, for him, part of a Whole, appreciated through poetry which was a form of scientific expression, and science which was a form of poetic expression.

It is not a surprise that the century of the revival of classical learning in Germany – Winckelmann, Heyne (at Göttingen), Moses Mendelsohnn, Nicolai, Oeser – should also have been the century of Sömmerring, the anatomist, and so many other scientific innovators. And, of course, that they should be the contemporaries of Kant who awoke from his dogmatic slumbers after reading Hume and devoted the rest of his life to making sense of the new world. Or trying to. Embellishing the exterior of your public buildings with Ionic friezes or caryatids; reviving the notion of Greek tragedy on the stage; developing the modern art/science of archaeology in the Mediterranean lands; laying the groundwork of classical philology; returning to the classical disciplines of astronomy, physics and biology – these cultural developments were interconnected and contemporaneous.

Goethe was a part of all this. If he was unique, it was not in the range of his interests or in the subjects which attracted his study and notice. It was merely in the intensity and imaginative intelligence of his responses. *Faust Part Two* grew out of the years of scientific research, and out of his decades-long self-marinade in Greek literature, architecture and aesthetics.

They owed their reading of Homer, however, to Johann Heinrich Voss, whose translation of the *Odyssey* came out in Hamburg in 1781, followed in 1793 by his *Iliad*. When Schiller wrote to his friend Körner that he was reading almost nothing except Homer, he went on to explain that he meant Homer in the translation of Voss.[11] When Goethe delighted friends by his recitations of Homer, it was Voss's Homer that he read.

Voss would eventually come to live in Jena – in 1802. By then, it had become the custom among the Jena 'set' to find fault with his translation. Wilhelm Schlegel said that Voss's hexameters did not satisfactorily reflect or imitate Homeric metre. Schiller, who had at one stage been completely addicted to reading Voss's translation, confessed to Körner that 'they become less and less pleasing to me'.[12] But Voss had been a key ingredient in shaping their knowledge of Greek literature. Not only did Goethe befriend him, but he had his son – who became the classics teacher at the Weimar Gymnasium – to live in his house in the Frauenplan for a few years from 1804 onwards.[13]

On New Year's Day 1799, Schiller wrote from Jena to Goethe:

> My OPUS is now in your hands ... and in the meantime, I have already turned my mind to the third play [of the *Wallenstein* trilogy] so that I may be able to go on with it during my stay in Weimar. There is still a great deal to be done, but it will go more quickly than the other because the action is determined and full of life.[14]

Goethe worked in spurts. He left huge schemes unfinished for months, years, and then with a great surge of energy he moved them forward. Schiller, probably haunted by the knowledge which habitual pulmonary illness brought, that his time on earth was to be short, laboured with agonizing intensity. To Körner: '*Wallenstein* should be finished. As it is, sleepless nights rob me of every third day.'[15]

There was a sense, however, that the three *Wallenstein* plays were a joint effort. This is not to say, as was believed at the time, that Goethe wrote any of them, but that Goethe was the most patient friend and midwife to his friend's masterpiece which, when complete, can be seen as the supreme masterpiece of German theatre. 'It is not true, as was currently supposed in Germany, that Goethe wrote any portions of that work ... But his counsel aided Schiller through every scene, and the bringing it on the stage was to him like a triumph of his own.'[16]

The help given to Schiller by his older friend was fully reciprocated. Without Schiller, Goethe would have remained, in the theatre, a Wilhelm Meister, a brilliant, hit-and-miss amateur. Schiller, both by his own work, and by the translations which he wrote for the Weimar theatre, taught Goethe about stagecraft, the management of a scene, so many of the things which he, Corneille, Shakespeare knew by instinct, but which were mysteriously absent in Goethe's understanding of the drama. Moreover – and that is why we dwell on it here, in a book which is primarily the story of how Goethe came to write his most enduring work – without *Wallenstein* there would be no *Faust*. This is true in two ways. On the one hand, the actual character of Wallenstein will eventually influence and subtly change Goethe's hero-mage. Less palpably, but no less crucially, *Wallenstein* is a (three-part) play which absorbs and dramatizes ideas. It has been said that history played the role in Schiller which Nature and science played in Goethe.[17] The challenge, when he came to work fully on the second part of *Faust*, would be to alter, eventually to break, the conventional forms of dramatic art in order to reflect the concepts of the age engendered in Goethe himself, through the medium of science. Among the many things which the second part of *Faust* is 'about' is modern science. *Wallenstein* is not only 'about' modern history. It is about the destiny, fate, of human beings caught up in events. Thus, although it is based on the complex figure of the Thirty Years War general who changed sides – from the Emperor's right-hand man to his most stalwart enemy – it is also the supreme play of French Revolutionary times, when it was written. It reflects the limitations of human power in the face of historical destiny: to this extent anticipating, and certainly placing itself beside, Hegel's *Philosophy of History* (lectures given between 1822 and 1830) and Tolstoy's *War and Peace* (finished 1869). *Wallenstein* is a historical tragedy in the true sense, a tragedy of history, not merely of a person in history. Schiller restored the movement of history itself to a prominence it had not known in tragedy since ancient times, and which Shakespeare himself only hints at in the Roman plays – *Antony and Cleopatra* and above all *Coriolanus* which is one of the great works of art haunting and influencing *Wallenstein*. It also anticipates a movement in German literature towards epic drama, which has immense influence, not just in his own times upon *Faust Part Two*, but also, in the twentieth century, in the theatre of Brecht.[18]

At the beginning, then, of 1799, Schiller and his family moved to Weimar. Goethe found them accommodation in the castle, and thereafter the two friends were more or less inseparable.

It was Goethe who first staged *Wallenstein's Camp*; the first part of the play was performed on 12 October 1798, the second part, *The Piccolomini*, on 30 January 1799.

Audiences responded with immediate enthusiasm, first in Weimar, then in Berlin. The advance, since *Don Carlos* and *The Robbers*, was not just in the quality of the writing but in the breadth of the ambition. In the first part of the trilogy, *Wallenstein's Camp*, the flawed hero does not even appear. We see instead the whole cross-section of his soldiers, discussing which way he will jump – for or against the Emperor – and the progress of the war. It is mysteriously dramatic, mysterious because nothing much happens, yet the attention is gripped, not as by a staged melodrama but as by a novel. *Wallenstein's Camp* is in fact the first great historical novel. The second part, *The Piccolomini*, prepares us for all the great personal dilemmas of the final part, *Wallenstein's Death*: namely that the Catholic Austrian Empire to which Wallenstein had devoted his ruthless military skill is going to let him down. Wallenstein, like Faust, is a deeply conflicted soul, an egomaniac, a megalomaniac, cruel, dishonest. His tricking Buttler into supporting him is the case in point which finishes him. He had pretended to help Buttler, an Irish soldier of fortune, become ennobled. In fact, he had badmouthed Buttler to the Habsburgs. His sole motive in ruining Buttler's career by sleight was to make Buttler hate the Habsburgs and support his own rebellion against them. When Piccolomini senior reveals the truth to Buttler, it seals Wallenstein's fate, since Buttler decides to kill him.

But these are all just the details of a complicated and always exciting plot. What Schiller's enormous canvas reveals, grippingly, eleven years after the French Revolution, is the sheer chaos of European history. Twenty years before Hegel lectured on the subject, the play reveals an Hegelian vision of historical inevitability. This magisterial historical achievement is brought about by a great poet. The play contains the most superb speeches, from Wallenstein's great soliloquy in Act I Scene 4, 'Wärs möglich? Könnst ich nicht mehr wie ich wollte' ('Is it really possible? Can I no longer act as I would choose?'), which Goethe thought the core of the whole drama – a very revealing judgement, since he is going to store this up and make it the central feature of *Faust* – to moments of intensely moving tenderness, such as the recollection of Wallenstein of being a substitute father to the boy Max Piccolomini – a figure invented by Schiller, and without whom the play would be dry: 'Max bleibe bei mir, geh nicht von mir, Max ...' ('Max, stay with me, don't leave me').[19] To such sublime moments as Wallenstein at the window looking out at the night sky when his sister, the countess, says, 'Am

Himmel ist geschäftigt Bewegung' ('There is such movement in the sky!').[20] His obsession with astronomy/astrology is of course very Faustian. Faustian, too, is Wallenstein's exclamation 'Mir ists allein ums Ganze' ('I am completely alone').[21]

There is no doubt about it, Wallenstein the trilogy is a before-and-after book. You will never be the same person once you have read or seen it. European literature, and in a way, Europe, was not to be the same, and nor was Goethe. The great historical question which it posed was – if Europe and its people cannot decide how to be governed, and if all is chaos, to whom or to what do we look forward? What rough beast, its hour come round at last ...? Schiller would not live to see what Goethe came to believe to be the cruel answer to this: Napoleon Bonaparte.

In a relationship as close as Goethe and Schiller's friendship, there were bound to be tensions. Even before both became ill – one fatally – Goethe had developed what in Schiller's view was a different 'illness':[22] his friendship with the Schlegel brothers and their circle. August Wilhelm Schlegel became, at just less than thirty years old, Professor of Philology at Jena University in July 1796. He was already known, and would become a household name in Germany, as the best translator of Shakespeare: he would translate, in all, seventeen of the plays into German verse. In the same year he moved to Jena he married Caroline Michaelis (1763–1809), a superb conversationalist, powerfully intellectual, thickly chestnut-tressed, and if one adds big trouble, it was the sort of trouble which men eagerly sought out. She was the daughter of a distinguished Hebraist from Göttingen University; had married a doctor and been widowed at twenty-five, having moved to Mainz, where she was the centre of the group surrounding Georg Forster (with whom she probably had an affair) and his wife Therese – daughter of another Göttingen professor, and an entertaining novelist.

At Jena, the Schlegels inevitably befriended the Schillers and equally inevitably quarrelled with them. In 1798, together with his younger brother Friedrich, August started a periodical called the Athenaeum, which set up in rivalry to Schiller's Die Horen. Naturally, they swooped down upon Goethe, who found their company stimulating. 'Not a moment was idly spent,' Goethe said of their company.[23] Schiller was deeply resentful when he discovered that Goethe was acting as an adviser to the Schlegel brothers as they set up their periodical.

Around the Schlegels clustered their satellites – Ludwig Tieck, Novalis, Schelling, Fichte. Jena was still reeling from the implications of Fichte's enforced resignation as Professor of Philosophy on the grounds of his presumed atheism. In 1799, the *Athenaeum* was faced with the possibility of being accused of a fault in the opposite direction – religious obscurantism. This was not a vice noticeable in either of the Schlegel brothers, still less in the openly unbelieving Caroline. But mystical, God-haunted, love-obsessed Baron Friedrich von Hardenberg – of whom Goethe had never seen the point – was different. He wrote an essay called 'Christianity or Europe', which appeared to advocate a return to the Catholicism of the Middle Ages. Novalis – his pen-name – was a Protestant Mystic, not a potential Catholic. Nevertheless, like so many contemporaries, such as the equally Protestant Walter Scott, he had a rosy-tinted picture of the Middle Ages, and not merely because he loved Gothic arches, stained-glass windows and women dressed as nuns.

The *Athenaeum* had published his beautiful 'Hymns to Night', full of that yearning for, and love affair with, death which was to be so richly and cruelly satisfied, first when he fell in love with, and became betrothed to, the tubercular twelve-year-old Sophie von Kühn – his 'Blue Flower' – who died before she was fifteen – and he, too, would die of that most Romantic of diseases, aged less than thirty. To publish his achingly morbid, hauntingly melodic Night-verses was one thing. To publish his prose, advocating a recovery of the Catholic roots of medieval Europe, as a remedy for the divisions, wars and confusions of the modern political scene, was quite another. After some considerable debate, the Schlegels decided not to run 'Christianity or Europe' – 'They were beautiful, shining times, when a single Europe was a Christian land and when a united Christendom held and inhabited this part of the world.'

(Faust, listening to the sound of Christians singing the Easter hymns, exclaims, 'How well I hear the message, but I lack the faith.'[24] But these questions do not entirely evaporate and we shall see surprisingly Novalis-like developments before the second part of *Faust* was complete.)

It was to Goethe that the Schlegels turned, uncertain whether to publish Novalis's beautiful, if a little crazy, essay. He firmly advised against.

Schiller, whose *Die Horen* was losing money hand over fist, resented Goethe taking such an interest in a rival publication, and was also quizzical, not to say jealous, of Goethe's friendship, amounting to an infatuation with the Schlegels' young friend Friedrich Wilhelm Joseph von Schelling, with whom Caroline Schlegel had begun an affair. She was twelve years older than Schelling. They went to the spa town of Bad Bocklet, near Kissingen, with her sick daughter Auguste who died there. Rumours – false – flew about that Schelling had killed the child by practising quack homeopathic cures on her. He was so distressed that he came close to suicide, and Caroline was also plunged into nervous collapse. But she rallied, reminding him that she – so much older – would be a good mother to him, and that in Goethe he had found a new father figure. 'He loves you like a father – I like a mother – what marvellous parents you have!'[25] Caroline and Schlegel were divorced in 1801 and she married Schelling in 1803.

When one considers Schelling's philosophy, it is difficult to assess how much he drew from Goethe, and how much Goethe found in the young man's work and developed on his own. Central to it all, which appears to be expressed so vividly in the figure of the Earth Spirit in *Urfaust* onwards, is both an identification of Spirit and Nature, and combined with this rather mystic sense of natural phenomena there was a central awareness of Nature's utter indifference to us.

Goethe would recommend Schelling for an (unpaid) professorship to Voigt with the words, 'He has a very lucid and energetic mind, organized according to the newest fashion; nor have I been able to discern the slightest hint of a sans-culottes turn of mind in him. On the contrary. He seems moderate and educated in every sense. I am convinced he would do us honour and be of use to the academy.'[26]

13

DEMONS

One of the most interesting features of Goethe's theory [of colours] ... is that it contains, undoubtedly with very great improvements, the general doctrine of the ancients and of the Italians at the revival of letters.

Charles Eastlake's translator's Preface to Goethe's
Theory of Colours[1]

Around this time, Goethe passed through a shift of perspective on the world. A couple of months after Schiller's death, Goethe spent a few weeks in Lauchstädt, interrupted by a short journey to Helmstadt. During this break, he sketched out a Critique of Plotinus. This has been described by the twentieth-century philosopher Herman Schmitz as perhaps the most important document of his mature years. For the first time he developed the concept of the daimonic.[2] I render the term in this slightly strange spelling to link it to Plato's concept of the *daimon*, the divine spark which Socrates saw in human beings. Goethe had been reminded of the term in his reading of the third-century non-Christian, Neoplatonist philosopher Plotinus.

Goethe had first dipped into Plotinus when he was a boy, in July 1764,[3] but it was in August 1805 that we find him reading the Italian humanist Marsilius of Padua's Latin translation of Plotinus's *Enneads* Book V – and the life of Plotinus by his friend Porphyry. He had been recommended to read Plotinus by the philologist Friedrich August Wolf – 'I am deeply indebted to you who would lead me into so many areas of interest, by alleys, bridges and mountain paths.'[4] To Zelter, he would write (in September 1805) that he was translating Marsilius's translation into German.[5]

The passage Goethe had chosen to translate was where Plotinus took issue with his master Plato, in his desire to banish art, poets and artists from his *Republic*. The great sculptor Phidias (490–c.416 BCE) could create a god out of stone – 'though he imitated, really, nothing perceptible to his senses, but he grasped such a divinity in his mind'.[6] Plotinus reminded Goethe that the artist's task – whether sculptor or poet – is essentially religious. It is a perception of reality. Goethe is moving towards the mindset which would be proclaimed at the very end of *Faust*, that all the passing shows of art and of Nature are themselves only foreshadowings, only parables or metaphors for a reality which is at the moment hidden. The inspiration for all this was the 'old mystic',[7] Plotinus.

Goethe was revivified in mind and soul by Plotinus, a Greek who had in third-century Rome neatly sidestepped the agonies which would surface in Kant's epistemology in eighteenth-century Königsberg. Nature itself is only a foreshadowing or a suggestion, so there is no need to worry about the fact that our perceptions of it can only be spoken about as representations. With the capacity to harness our inner *daimon*, we grasp the reality to which the unimaginative or imperceptive are, in any case, always going to remain blind. The *dämonisch* is the quality which unlocks reality to us.

It is a term that he will flesh out, and that will colour the whole of his later work – scientific as well as poetic – and which is especially noticeable in his revisions and reworkings of *Faust*.

Dämonisch in Goethe does not mean devilish, but it is morally ambivalent – witness the two individuals whom he saw as most *dämonisch* in his lifetime: Napoleon and Byron.[8] We get a sense of what the term means to Goethe in his first poetic use of it in a sonnet of 1807 entitled 'Mighty Surprise':

A stream cascades from rocks, enshrouded in cloud.
So eager is it to connect to
the ocean.
Whatever shimmers up from space to spaces,
It rushes

Unstoppably into the valley.
But, daimonic, quite suddenly, there are crashing sounds.
The woods follow her; the mountain stares,
Down Oreas to find a kingdom of graces,
Hems in the basin. The storm crashes.
Astonished, the billowing foam bends away
And swells up the mountainside, drinking its very self.
It is dammed up and is striving towards the everlasting Father.
It sways, it calms down, it flows into the lake;
And the night stars are reflected in the surface of the water,
And see the blinking of the waves on the rocks.
New life is coming.[9]

A real catastrophe in the Swiss Alps, the Goldau Rockslide (or Landslide) in 1806, inspired Goethe. The *Zürcher Zeitung* described it thus: 'Noises, crashing, cracking fill the air with deep roaring thunder: Whole stretches of soil torn away – pieces of rock, large and even larger than houses – whole rows of fir trees, standing upright and floating, are being flung through the thickened air at the speed of an arrow. Our paradise is transformed into hundreds and hundreds of wild death hills.' A 10-metre-high (33-foot) tsunami followed and the village of Goldau ceased to exist.

The neatly organized Newtonian machine which was the universe conceived by the early Enlightenment scientists was in fact a frightening and unpredictable place. When we 'commune with Nature', or feel ourselves 'at one' with Nature, the phrase is sometimes used to suggest something peaceful, relaxing, well-ordered. So often, in Goethe – we think of Faust himself at the beginning of *Part Two* with the pulse of Nature thundering like a heart attack, and the sunrise blinding his eyes and the bellowing cataract behind him making a deafening din – being 'at one' with Nature is to be reminded of our own *dämonisch* temperament. Two of the great achievers in Goethe's generation, Napoleon and Byron, were 'possessed'.

In August 1805, Goethe, accompanied by Henke and Wolf, paid a visit to a Herr von Hagen in Nienburg. The conversation turned to Kant, and the concept of the Categorical Imperative, Kant's phrase to describe our inner awareness of the moral code. Herr von Hagen maintained that if one were sufficiently attentive to the Categorical

Imperative, one could turn into a morally perfect human being. Goethe would have been aware – though this is not mentioned in the write-up of the conversation by one F. Weitze – that the Neoplatonist Plotinus thought something very similar.

But no, Goethe said. The perfectly moral 'great man' could only be imagined. 'Such a human portrayal as you imagine consists of nothing but light without shadows and leaves us cold. There is such a thing as the *dämonisch*. It is wrong to envisage greatness as an objective characteristic, rather than a seizing of the impression which an individual can make upon us.'[10]

The Kantian 'Imperative' presupposes an autonomous, autocratic human being – perhaps not unlike Professor Kant himself – in which passions scarcely exist, still less have mastery over the 'reasonable' self. But, said Goethe, we watch human beings in the grip of an unseen Force, which they are unable to resist, which drives them in the direction they will follow. Even the supposedly immoral can, in such cases, possess something like greatness.

When we think of this conversation, happening a year before the invasion by Napoleon of Weimar and Jena, it is almost like hearing the opening chords of Beethoven's Fifth Symphony, foreboding, threatening. Later in the day, Goethe tried to put Weitze at his ease. Weitze was a teacher of religion, and Goethe told him that his son August had recently been confirmed – by Herder, in Weimar. Goethe himself had attended the confirmation classes and he had found them impressive. Herder had taken the young confirmation candidates through a course on ethics and religion. He had told them that we all possess free will. A moral life is something not merely to strive towards but to pray for. We all need redemption, benediction. 'These were apparently proven to be found in Jesus,' said Goethe, in a manner which almost implied he had never before heard the doctrine. The Christian concepts of Grace, or of redemption through Christ, were not dwelt upon. What Goethe drew out of his son's experience as a confirmation candidate was that we are all, as human beings, to ask ourselves whether we want to belong to the light or to the darkness.[11]

It is a good example, in miniature, of why many readers of *Faust* will find Goethe a puzzle. In the evening, the late-middle-aged Privy Councillor was assuring the young clergyman that he supported the status quo, that he was pleased for his son to be an observant Lutheran, and that in the eternal struggle between light and darkness he wanted to walk in the light. But in his deeper self – the self of the morning, which questioned the adequacy of Kant's Categorical Imperative, 'light, good', 'dark, bad' idea – Goethe realized that human life is very much more complicated. There are forces at work in Nature, in the human soul, which defy the neat analysis of 'good', 'bad', 'light', 'dark'. We live in a world where landslides can utterly destroy a village, where human lives can be swept away by earthquakes and floods – and by the passions. We live in a world where, as Napoleon observed, Politics is Fate. Probably at about this date Goethe gave Mephistopheles the unforgettable, but terrible speech when he tries to numb Faust's scruples about the seduction and deception of Gretchen. Mephistopheles himself, however, is devoid of what Goethe called the daemonic. Mephistopheles is all negative. The daemonic – Napoleon, Byron – were positive figures of vast energy, but Goethe saw no point in trying to impose pietistic, moralistic limits on daemonic energy.

> *Mephisto:* Oh, aren't we being holy! Just listen to him!
> Is it really the first time in your life
> That you have, ahem, committed a perjury?
> Have you not with the greatest force and glibness
> Formed judgements of God, of the world, of humankind
> *In all the stirrings of its head and heart?*[12]

The demonic was on the march.

A year after Schiller died, a twenty-six-year-old colleague of his at Jena University, a Professor of History called Heinrich Luden, with a wife and a daughter of one and a half years old, had gone on a round of family visits, over the Harz Mountains to Celle. On the entire journey, they had not seen a newspaper, nor felt inclined to read one, having, as Luden said, no interest in politics.

Having no interest in politics, of course, means holding views which you prefer to keep from other people. Luden was a liberal German patriot. His lectures at Jena, extremely popular, would often end with the audience bursting into patriotic songs, and indeed it would be one of these liberal enthusiasts – an eager fan of young Professor Luden – who, far in the future, 1819 – would take it upon himself to murder Kotzebue for his reactionary views.

Luden was a patriot, and the autumn of 1806 was a painful time to be a German patriot. The unthinkable had happened. The Ludens had set out in peaceful summer weather, and, by the end of the summer, Thuringia had become a theatre of war. Leaving his wife and child with her parents, he was anxious to get back to Jena before the invading French forces looted their modest flat near the parish church. It was quite a journey. In the little town of Naumburg, Luden had his first, shocking glimpse of the wounded, being brought back from battlefields. On 18 October, he encountered a Prussian and a French officer travelling together in a coach – the Prussian army had accepted defeat at the hands of Napoleon. Luden fell into conversation with the French soldier. Where was Luden from? Hanover? The Frenchman loved Hanover. But, said Luden, all his life was now bound up in Jena, with his wife, his child, his job. 'Then,' said the Frenchman, 'I can do nothing but offer you my sympathy.'

Four days before, the Duke of Brunswick's army had been utterly routed. The Germans had no idea that Napoleon had two-thirds of the *Grande Armée* on the enormous field of battle.[13] Some 20,000 Prussians of General Julius von Grawert's Division held the line for hours, most of them eventually being mown down by superior French artillery, and by the relentless cavalry. The noise of heavy fire was so thunderous that it could be heard 30 kilometres away in Weimar. Thousands of Germans were taken prisoner.[14]

Luden travelled a further 15 kilometres as far as Merseberg, where a thousand wounded men were being carried into the town, and thousands more prisoners of war. It was a heartrending sight. In Berlin, his patriotic pride had swollen to see the prancing soldiers and the splendid uniforms of the hussars, the 'Gensd'armes' of the royal army. Now he saw these cavalry officers hobbling along, their bright uniforms in tatters, spattered with mud and blood.

After a seven-hour journey, he reached Jena. The scene was something he could not have envisaged, even with all the forewarnings of wounded and defeated men encountered on the road. Meeting a French officer, Luden exploded with rage. The officer prodded Luden's chest with his finger, and told him to moderate his language. 'Yes, war is a monstrous thing, but maybe it's worse for the soldiers in battle than it is for the civilians. Maybe wars should not happen, but you and I have no say in the matter. We simply have to submit to fate.'

Luden yelled about the vandalism, the wreckage of buildings. The arson, the thefts.

'Yes, my dear sir, but more than 100,000 men under arms have been marched through your little town, without bread, without wine, without anywhere to sleep.'

The scene of desolation in Jena was horrific, with many houses burned out or ruined. When he got to the house containing his flat, he was pleased to see it was still standing, and the landlady and her daughter had somehow managed to survive. He climbed the stairs and let himself in through the door, from which the locks had been wrenched. There was straw all over the floorboards. Mess and filth predominated and anything of any value had been stolen. In all the wreckage, however, a stray book had somehow survived. Lying among the dust and straw and filth was a volume of Goethe.

How different everything had been when they were last living in this flat in May! Luden, who had invested in the eight-volume set of Goethe's Complete Works, had been reading *Faust A Fragment* in Volume 8. Goethe happened to be in town, and the two encountered one another. On the first occasion, on 10 August, Luden was asked to dinner with the Knebels, and turned up rather late, having been out for a walk and, miscalculating time and distance, been distracted by the beauties of the scenery. Goethe was silent with impatience when the young man arrived, but calmed down over their meal, and when wine had been taken.

On the second occasion, nine days later, Luden bearded Goethe with the question which must have confronted all readers of *Faust* – long before *Part Two* made an appearance: namely, the coherence or unity of the work. At this stage, Goethe had, as it happened, sent *Part One* to the publisher, but the only version known to the public was the *Fragment* in the Collected Works. Luden asked the poet whether the different parts of the *Fragment* had ever been conceived as an organic whole, a larger idea. He asked whether the poet would ever be able to fashion them, or rework them, so that they began to look like a dramatic unity.

It was a bold thing for a young nobody to ask the great man, but it is, of course, central to our entire understanding, not only of *Faust*, in its changing forms, but of Goethe, and the way he went to work. Goethe seems to have replied defensively and testily at first:

> How do you suppose that I first had the idea of writing *Faust*? If I have understood you aright, you thought – still think – that the poet does not have the slightest idea what he was doing when he began the work, but wrote entirely randomly, just as it came to him, and was just using the name 'Faust' as a thread on which he could thread his individual pearls to keep them from being dispersed?

The true interest in *Faust*, Goethe assured the young historian, was to be found in the central idea which had been animating the poet, which links all the elements together in a coherent whole, governing them as a single law, and conferring significance upon them.[15]

Goethe had a tendency to conceal, obfuscate his true intentions, and, when challenged, to contradict. In the long course of *Faust*'s composition, we find him taking different views of the coherence or otherwise of the piece. But here we have a good witness to one of his states of mind in a crucial year of German life – 1806 – and of his own life – the year he got married, the year he was compelled to witness and confront the dissolution of the old political order, and to see the effects of his hero Napoleon on his fellow Germans, fellow human beings. Luden was in many ways a tactless conversationalist, and we can perhaps sense more than he could – in writing it down – how clumsy a twenty-six-year-old pedant had been in challenging the fifty-seven-year-old writer who had been wrestling with questions about *Faust* for a very long time, and who had, presumably, reached a point of some confidence in the work – since he had sent *Part One* to press, after a gestation period of thirty years. Stawell and Dickinson, whose translation of *Faust* and commentary on it is still worth reading, suspect that poor Luden 'unconsciously sat for certain traits in the finished portrait of Wagner' – i.e. Faust's junior colleague, the dull-witted unimaginative academic.[16]

The conversation with Luden was not simply about *Faust*. It was, among other things, about the possibility of a historian arriving at the truth. The historian is bound to be subjective in Goethe's view. He cannot arrive at truth as a mathematician would hope to do in his subject. But that does not make him a liar. He is more like a 'fence', or receiver of stolen goods. The poet, however, should not be judged by these criteria. The poet does not need to explain his own work, or to translate it into everyday prose. The aesthete, the critic, can tease out the meaning of the poet, but the creator's job is simply to be the 'maker', to create a world out of his own imagination.

The conversation about *Faust*, both among its general, intelligent readers, and among the close scholars, has always been, for the last 200 years and more, between those who believe they have found a coherent unity or message, and those who have found it to be – precisely – those pearls on a string which has been randomly named *Faust*. The rest of Goethe's creative journey, and of ours as we accompany him, from his late fifties to early eighties, composing this mysterious work, is actually a journey which demonstrates the truth of both, apparently contradictory viewpoints. *Faust* the 'incommensurable', as he would call it in old age, cannot be forced into the narrow textbook explanation of one big coherent work which explains everything, or sums up Goethe's view of the world. On the other hand, it is a single book, which we can hold in one hand and read as a whole, and to this extent it has a unity. And there is more to it than that, which is why it is helpful to read it in the context of Goethe's biography, even though the biography is by no means the only legitimate key to the poem's meaning. At one point in the conversation, Goethe said to the young professor that maybe he should have stayed with his first discipline, mathematics, rather than venturing into the more nuanced and inchoate discipline of history. Goethe, in a way which finds its parallels in the writings of Hegel, goes further than this, however, and sees history, and individual human lives, as mirrors by which a greater reality may be perceived; science itself as a parable or a metaphor.

In the fourth act of *Faust Part Two*, in which the Emperor and the Anti-Emperor fight it out for mastery, Goethe allows the battle to be decided by the surprise seizure of a rocky mountain pass. Goethe could not publish this part of his dramatic poem during Carl August's lifetime, since it was quite clear, to anyone with memories of the Battle of Jena, that the Privy Councillor, outwardly loyal to Carl August for over half a century, regarded the catastrophe as the fault of his

'Maecenas'. Jena was lost by the Prussian army not having sufficiently considered the lie of the land. The officers who came from Prussia could be forgiven for this oversight, but Carl August could legitimately be held responsible for knowing what could, or could not, be achieved in his own territory. He regarded this particular rocky pass in the hills as impregnable, and too steep to allow the passage of heavy artillery. Napoleon, who had surveyed the land surrounding Jena and Weimar, thought otherwise. With a torch in his hand, he personally drove on the gunners to haul the heavy field guns into position above the town. It could be said that Jena was a battle lost before it even started.[17]

In consequence of Carl August's strategic failure, the town of Jena went up in flames, and Weimar came close to being utterly destroyed.

Napoleon had considered a Putinesque elimination of Weimar from the map. His reasons for sparing the town were not sentimental ones, still less because he sympathized either with *The Sorrows of Young Werther*, nor with the Sorrows of the Middle-Aged Goethe. The French Emperor needed a billet for his troops, not least for his senior officers. Marshal Murat (later King of Naples from 1808 to 1815), Napoleon's brother-in-law, was housed in the Schloss. Marshal Ney took Goethe's house as his billet, which is probably why the Goethe archive survived. Herder's widow, as well as having her house wrecked, suffered the loss of her husband's entire literary remains, papers, books, notes, the lot. Professor Meyer, painter and art historian who ran the drawing school, had nearly all his work looted and wilfully destroyed. Goethe would come upon Meyer's father-in-law, sitting, still as a stone, in an empty room, surrounded by wrecked statues, and *objets d'arts* and torn-up drawings and paintings. The poet said he had never seen a picture of more abject human misery than this silent, still old boy. He said the thought of King Lear flickered in his head, and then he realized – Lear was mad, whereas this was a sane man in a world gone mad; by comparison, Lear would have seemed happier.

Joanna, mother to the philosopher Arthur Schopenhauer, was there throughout. She heard the French officer cry out, '*Mangeons, buvons, pillons, brûlons – toutes les maisons!*' (Let's eat, let's drink, let's pillage, let's burn!).

She took in two women – Madame Jagemann, widow of the Duchess Amalia's librarian, and her actress daughter Caroline, Duke

Carl August's mistress. The French hussar who was enforcing the curfew called out to them to keep the house in total darkness, to block all windows with curtains and blankets and to light no lights. Outside in the street she heard them shouting, '*Du pain, du vin, nous montons!*' (Bread! Wine! We're coming up!)

Over the next few days, having huddled at home with her daughter and the Jagemanns, she realized that the French hussar had given good advice. Those who left their houses came home to find them utterly looted, sometimes demolished. The Duke himself had fled. He did not return to Weimar until January 1807. His wife, however, remained, earning enormous respect for her bravery, and his mother came back at the end of the month.

Although the house in the Frauenplan had been assigned to Marshal Ney, Goethe and Christiane were not safe from the oafish invaders. One night, Christiane apprehended some soldiers from Alsace who had burst in looking for something with which to toast their Emperor's health. Goethe came out of his bedroom, wearing the nightshirt he nicknamed the prophet's mantel, and was impressed by the courage with which Christiane was standing her ground. She screamed loudly to protect herself, and thereby she protected the poet and his treasures from the drunkards. Heinrich Voss would recall, 'In those days, Goethe was the object of my deepest sympathy. I saw him weeping, and crying out, "Who will take my house and home so I can just get far, far away?"'[18]

The invasion had forced on Goethe and Christiane the conviction that they should formalize their long union. On 17 October, Goethe wrote to the *Konsistorialrat* (Registrar) Wilhelm Christian Gunther:

An old intention of mine has, during the last nights and days, come to ripeness: I want to make a formal, civic recognition of my little friend as My Own One. She has done so much for me, especially during these hours of trial. Worthy Reverend Sir and Father, tell me how we can set this in motion as soon as possible, to plight our troth, on Sunday or sooner if that is possible. What has to be done to set it all in motion? If for some reason, you cannot do all this yourself, I want, if possible, for it to be done in the sacristy of the town church. Let me have an answer when it suits you, if you please!

On Sunday 19 October, in a quiet corner of the sacristy of St James's church, they were married at last.[19] Joanna Schopenhauer was the first person in Weimar officially to receive Frau von Goethe as a respectable married woman, five days later, at one of her soirées, which resumed, a trifle relentlessly, the minute the French bombardments had ceased. She wrote to her philosopher son Arthur in Hamburg, 'I think if Goethe is prepared to give her his name, the least we could do was to give her a cup of tea.'[20]

Goethe and Christiane would be married for a little less than ten years. As already suggested, he was not unfaithful to her – or so one would infer, from his rather touching erotic poem 'A Diary', written in the first year of marriage, in which the protagonist is tempted by a chambermaid in an inn where he spends the night and finds himself to be impotent, only able to perform with his wife at home, however apparently tempting the young chambermaid's offer of herself.

This is not to say, however, that the relationship with Christiane absorbed all his emotional or imaginative energy; nor did he ever pretend that it did. He spoke in the Annals of his longing for Schiller,[21] his deep sense of loss requiring some compensation. It came, after a fashion, in one of Goethe's endless crushes, this one on Minna Herzlieb, the eighteen-year-old ward of a Jena publisher – Friedrich Johannes Frommann. It had no dangerous effect, he said, because he was able to direct all his feelings for her into sonnets. What Christiane thought about it is not recorded.

The obsession with Minna – pretty, but a bit dim, by the accounts of others[22] – fed into his remarkable novel *Elective Affinities*. Conceived originally as one of the tales within the tale of *Wilhelm Meister's Journeyman Years* and eventually expanded into a full-length novel, which grew from its original short-story status during 1808, it would be published in October 1809. It is certainly one of the most disturbing novels of the nineteenth century and it is easy to see, on the strength of this one book alone, why in the English-speaking world, where novelists were called upon to shore up the mythology of middle-class marriage, its bliss and its innocence, this devastating critique of marriage and its emotional falsehoods should have been seen as so wicked. 'Marriage is the beginning, and the peak, of all culture,'[23] as one of the characters lays down at the beginning of the story – giving this as his reason for not wishing to spend a night under the same roof as a count and a baroness who are conducting an adulterous affair. The conversation of the baroness and the count, when they arrive, still, in the twenty-first century, has the power to disturb, even though we now live in a post-Christian world in which a high proportion of couples in Western society do not contract formal marriages. Their casual suggestion that marriages should only be regarded as contracts lasting for a maximum period of five years is inwardly, and secretly, pleasing to Edward and Charlotte, the couple who hear it – a couple, who at the beginning of the book, had appeared to be in a rock-solid, satisfactory relationship.

The title of the story is, highly characteristically of the author, a scientific one. The happily married couple have a captain to stay with them, with whom Charlotte, the wife, will fall in love. The Captain is a know-all, among other things about science, and tells them about 'elective affinities'. Take a piece of limestone which is more or less pure oxide of calcium. It is tightly combined with a weak acid known to us in gaseous form. If you put a piece of that rock in dilute sulphuric acid, this combines with the calcium to form gypsum.

Edward and Charlotte immediately cotton on to the idea that elective affinities are found not just in chalk and sulphuric acid but in human relations. Already, only a few dozen pages into the story, what appears to be the happy marriage has fundamentally altered, thanks to the catalyst of the Captain's arrival.

'In your opinion,' Edward says to Charlotte, 'I am the lime – reacted upon by sulphuric acid in the person of the Captain, torn from your pleasant company and transformed into an uncooperative gypsum.'[24]

In the metaphorical science of the Captain, the chemical reaction which has come about is an inevitability. The separation of different elements in a chemical reaction is something beyond their control, just as the separation of human beings is beyond their control when a different combination of the sexual partners is put on offer. The dissolution of relationships, the re-forming of new ones, is thus seen as something more or less impersonal. Edward, the loyal husband at the beginning of the story, becomes obsessed by the beautiful, innocent, child-like Ottilie; Charlotte is in love with the Captain; and although the married couple make love, as these things are happening, and produce a baby, the child 'inherits' the characteristics not of the biological parents, but of the two with whom the parents have been in love.

Goethe conceived of the title, and the scientific conceit, of the work relatively early on, before much of the story had actually been written down (11 April 1808 in a notebook written in Jena). He had evidently composed most of the story mentally before he dictated a single word to his secretary Riemer. According to his diary, the first two chapters were taken down by Riemer in four and a half hours on 11 June 1808, and Chapters Three and Four a day or two later. Goethe's later secretary, Johann Christian Schuchardt, recalled that the concentration was total. Even if Goethe had to break off to receive a visitor, he would return and take up the text exactly where he had left off without needing the secretary to read back the text to him.[25] Having completed the dictation, he expanded and revised the work the following year, but not before committing himself to publication in 1809 – so the final chapters were written to a deadline.

The revisions were not, fundamentally, changes to the original conception so much as deepenings and stirrings of further complexity. In the early version, the married pair, Edward and Charlotte, make love with one another, while each thinking of the person with whom they are actually in love – in Charlotte's case the Captain, their visitor, and in Edward's the beautiful anorexic teenager Ottilie. However you understand the scene, Professor Nicholas Boyle is right to remind us that 'it must be the first direct representation of sexual relations in the history of novel writing that is wholly serious and neither comic nor pornographic'.[26]

To call the story strange would be an understatement. Nicholas Boyle, the author of the gigantic biography of Goethe which (at the time of my writing this) has only reached 1805, argues[27] that this is not a novel about private passions at all; nor is it the story of four emotionally selfish aristocrats living quite isolated from the social and political story of their times. On the contrary, it is a novel about the dissolution of the Holy Roman Empire, and about the crushing defeat of the German armies at Jena in October 1806. Professor Boyle is not saying that the story is an allegory, or that the idyllic country estate and its well-ordered gardens and walks and parks into which we step at the beginning of the story is a metaphor for the Old Regime. Rather, that the plight of Edward and Charlotte reflects, embodies, shows forth what was happening in these years – the cracking-up of the old order, the chemical reaction which leads to something new. The story is much too subtle either to be an allegory or a 'moral' tale. Or an immoral or amoral tale either. It remains deeply shocking, for any sensitive reader, to see that there is a kind of 'inevitability' about the sequence of events once the elements have been put into the laboratory – the exact moment when the Captain arrives somehow makes it inevitable that Charlotte will fall in love with him. Selfish, middle-aged Edward could have married Charlotte in an earlier phase – they delayed it all and now they are finding happiness in this second-chance marriage. (Both of them have had unsatisfactory first marriages.) But because of the timing, and the set of circumstances in which they all find themselves, Edward 'can't help' but fall in love with vulnerable, anorexic Ottilie. And the girl, though clearly the victim in the novel, in the sense that she is the youngest member of the fatal quartet, is not without the capacity to be manipulative herself, not least in her using her unhappiness, her eating disorder, as a way of tormenting the elders. How 'accidental' – spoiler alert, readers! – is her irresponsible behaviour which leads to the death of little Otto – Charlotte's child – by drowning? And then Ottilie is able to play the ultimate power card (shades of *Werther*) by destroying the happiness of the other three with her suicide.

So, it is certainly on one level a highly disturbing psychological, personal drama. But Professor Boyle was right to remind us that the dates and the setting are highly significant. It is all set in 1806. Carl August haunts the pages. Goethe's awareness of the truly horrendous state of his marriage, Goethe's professional catastrophe, trying to deal with Carl August's mistress in the Weimar theatre, Goethe's own marriage, and his capacity to fall in love with young girls being on full display to himself, and to others, at the same time as the great political and military crisis, all play their part in this – candidly – unbearably overwhelming novel. And, of course, Napoleon is hovering over it, too.

One of the things which makes Professor Boyle's essay a useful one for us, as we continue with our chronicle of how *Faust* evolved, is that it shows the strange way in which Goethe's imagination/mind/ creative process set to work. Everything which passes through Nature is only a parable, as we will be reminded when, as a very old man, he reached the end of his creative journey.

Parables speak and speak. They stand just as stories. But they resonate, and their implications come back to haunt us as we read other stories. History – for Goethe, as for Hegel – was a parable. You can't escape the fact that on one level the overwhelming story of the quartet, doomed to make one another unhappy, is more than just a domestic drama. And if that's the case, Ottilie's capacity to utilize vulnerability to the ultimate, to make suicide a weapon of power, would resonate many years after Weimar had buried the sane generation of Goethe and Schiller.

We have come full circle from the moment, when discussing *The Sorrows of Young Werther*, we remembered Goethe's encounter with Napoleon at Erfurt in 1808. The ambiguities and complexities of *Elective Affinities* revisit the theme of the depressive young person committing suicide. Whereas in the youthful novella the author himself is, in part, the would-be self-slayer in a first-person epistolary narration, in *Elective Affinities* the narrator is the god-like third person, and the young suicide is one who finds herself, as did Goethe's son (drinking himself to death at an early age), the objects of his various crushes, and, perhaps, his long-suffering wife, victims of the middle-aged, predatory 'love' of the other three characters.

It is also, as we have observed, a novel which, beneath its disturbing emotional surfaces, is concerned with much more than private passion. It is a novel about the dissolution of the old order, and the vulnerability of that order in the face of advancing power. All these things feed into the whole-life masterpiece – whole life in the sense of it being the work of over sixty years of Goethe's life, and in the sense of all-embracing and all-encompassing – which is *Faust*. It is possible for the modern scholars to observe Goethe at work in *Elective Affinities*, partly from manuscript evidence in notes and diary entries, partly from the testimony of his secretary Riemer. He was able to carry around in his head finished versions of his work which remained unfinished on the page – for hours, weeks and even decades. The fact that the writing of *Faust* was often on pause does not mean that its composition was on pause. The life-experiences, both of the author and of his Germany, his Europe, all feed into the poem which an old man would one day write down or dictate: this includes the career and aftermath of Napoleon, the revolutions – as convulsive and world-changing as those in politics – in the scientific sphere, as well as the everlasting fascination of sexuality and romantic love which remained at the forefront of Goethe's life.

––––––

Back in 1800, Goethe had turned to the legend of Helen with a drama provisionally entitled *Helena in the Middle Ages*. This only survives as a fragment, and is incorporated into the finished *Faust Part Two* – lines 8489–802 – that is, from the arrival of Helen in Sparta, at the palace of her father King Menelaus, to her dawning recognition, fed to her by her 'maid' Phorkyas (Mephistopheles in disguise, as we'll learn in *Faust*), that, far from wishing to welcome her home, her husband will punish her adultery with death.[28]

Goethe had been aware, even as he conceived it, that the notion of casting Helen of Troy as a character in the Middle Ages was a piece of eclecticism bizarre even by his own inventive standards. He was not planning to write a pastiche piece of ancient Greek literature, as he had unsuccessfully done in an unfinished epic about Achilles, the *Achilleid*. Rather, he would transport Helen, the image/symbol not only of feminine beauty but of classical order, and Greek culture, into the barbaric heart of a medieval German court of the Hohenstaufen Emperor Frederick II – whose court in Sicily had been such a curious eclectic blend of Arab, pagan and Catholic culture – and of whom Goethe had been made fascinatingly aware during his sojourn in Sicily in 1787.

In the finished version in *Faust Part Two*, Frederick II is laid aside, and the German castle in which Helena finds herself is that of Faust himself. (There really are many 'crusader' castles in the Peloponnese, built by Teutonic warriors in the Middle Ages, so the conjunction is not entirely fanciful.)

What Goethe would retain in *Faust* from the *Helena in the Middle Ages* sketch is his truly masterly transposition of Greek iambic trimeter into modern German.

> *Bewundert viel und viel gescholten, Helena,*
> *Vom Strande komm' ich, wo wir erst gelandet sind,*
> Helena, much admired, and scolded much
> Up from the beach come I, where we first landed,
> Still drunk and reeling from the waves' impetuous
> Swaying, which from the Phrygian plains have borne us here
> On high backs reared up, through Poseidon's grace
> And Euro's power, drawn to ancestral coves.[29]

Schiller was so beguiled by Goethe's conception that he conceived the idea of writing a whole battle scene in trimeters in his *Maiden of Orleans* – hoping to render his version of the Joan of Arc story into a Sophoclean, classical dimension.[30]

When Carl August read *Helena*, after its publication in 1826, he was unimpressed. By this stage of his life, the Grand Duke had totally adopted the literary tastes of his great-uncle, Frederick the Great, and he considered the mishmash of different styles in *Helena* to be an affront to good taste. The classical theme demanded, he thought, a classical form: it should have been written in Alexandrines, like a tragedy by Racine. When Goethe heard of this scornful judgement, he spoke furiously to Councillor von Müller: 'It's a shame that this giant intellectual prince remains, as far as poetry is concerned, stuck in the narrow limits of a French education.'[31] Carl August's slight was not forgotten. The old man laid it down, and, once the Grand Duke was dead, he could launch the oblique attack on his memory in *Faust Part Two*.

Germany was the birthplace of Greek Revival architecture, just as its universities were the cradle of Greek learning in post-Renaissance times, with such giants of classical scholarship as Christian Gottlob Heyne (1729–1812) in Göttingen, who pioneered classical archaeology, Greek and Latin philology and the scientific and philological roots of Greek mythology. His work, and that of other classical philologists throughout German-speaking lands, complemented the aesthetic endeavours of Goethe's old mentor Adam Friedrich Oeser and his hero Winckelmann. Greek Revival, perhaps in part because it was so enthusiastically adopted in German-speaking lands, was never popular in France. Carl Gotthard Langhans (1732–1808), by designing the Brandenburg Gate in Berlin (it was erected between 1788 and 1791), made the Prussian capital seem a new Athens. Karl Friedrich Schinkel (1781–1841), after the catastrophe of Napoleonic invasion and the destruction of the city, rebuilt Berlin in the Greek Revival manner. The love affair with Greece which Goethe's *Helena* represents can be imagined against this architectural background. The Athenian failure in the Peloponnesian wars against Sparta in no way diminished the legacy of Socrates, Plato, Aeschylus, Sophocles and Euripides. Likewise, when Napoleon was consigned to imprisonment on St Helena, and to military history, Europeans would be reading Kant, Hegel, Schiller and Goethe. This is the idea of *Helena*, though it would take other catalysts to bring it to its final shape in *Faust*. In a scornful remark to Eckermann, Goethe would say that his generation could now see how wretchedly bad the neo-Christian German painters were, because their generation were able to see – thanks to Lord Elgin plundering the Parthenon Marbles – the supreme genius of the fifth-century BCE Athenian sculptor Phidias.[32] But this lay in the future.

Neither the *Helena Fragment* as first conceived, nor the Helen drama as incorporated into *Faust* would stand alone as a piece of mere 'Greek Revival'. Neither would come to life until, in old age, he had seen the classical world through the Romantic eyes of Lord Byron. Perhaps Homer himself had seen Helen as the embodiment of Greek beauty, snatched unlawfully by their oriental enemies in Troy, and hence the cause of the war. Certainly in later interpretations of the myth she may be seen as the aesthetic and philosophical embodiment of the Hellenic. But before this, fairly obviously, she was a woman. Mephistopheles would mockingly tell Faust that he would see Helen of Troy in every woman. It was the theme, and the experience, of love which possessed his imagination during the problematic years of Napoleon's removal from the European scene. Moreover, Greece, and Hellenism, and Napoleon, were far from being at the forefront of his mind at this point. The years 1814–16, while Napoleon's destiny was being decided by others, coincided with Goethe's rediscovery, and revisiting, of his native Rhineland; explorations of Islamic literature, of the Quran, and of Sufi poets; and an *amitié amoreuse* which helped to fuel one of the most productive two years of his life as a lyric poet.

One of the most perfect lyrics Goethe ever wrote is called 'Phenomenon'.

When Phoebus, God of Sun
Mates with the curtain of rain,
There appears at once an arching rim
Shaded with colours.
In the mist, a circle just like it –
It is a white bow
Yet it is a bow of Heaven.
So, old grey-beard man,
Do not be gloomy!
Though your hair may be white,
Yet you will love.[33]

Like so many of his lyrics, it holds back all that it suggests. In a mere forty or so words, he is an ageing man looking at the sky. He is a scientist whose eyes have been opened to the phenomena of sky formation. He is a throbbing heart, longing for the excitement of love. None of this needs to be expressed, since, in the densest economy of words, he is simply looking, first at a rainbow and then at a cloud formation.

It was Duke Carl August who drew Goethe's attention to the work of an English Quaker, Luke Howard, *On the Modification of Clouds, and on the Principles of their Production, Suspension and Destruction*, which had first appeared in Alexander Tilloch's *Philosophical Magazine* in 1803. It was Howard who devised our method of classifying cloud formations – cirrus, cumulus and so forth. Goethe wanted to add a further form, paries, or 'wall cloud', but this has never been adopted by the meteorological establishment. This is in spite of the fact that twentieth-century research into thunderstorms and tornadoes in the United States identified 'wall cloud' as a phenomenon produced when an area of rotating cloud lowers, to form a swirling funnel extending to the ground. This phenomenon enables those who observe it to predict the coming of a 'twister'.[34]

Goethe became so interested in meteorology that he was active in establishing weather stations throughout the Duchy of Weimar, where volunteers took recordings of rainfall, wind direction, cloud cover and formation, and temperature. The Duchess Luise nicknamed him 'The Guardian of the Barometer'. Interestingly enough, however, he put no faith at all in any theory of weather forecasting, seeing it as a pseudo-science analogous to astrology.

His debt to Howard was acknowledged by reviewing the Englishman's book *The Climate of London* when it appeared in 1823. And he wrote a trilogy of poems to Howard.

When Godhead Kamarupa, high, sublime
Wanders through the atmosphere, swaying, lightly, heavily,
Gathers the folds of his veil, and disperses them again,
Delighting in their changing shapes,
Now holds them fast, then dwindles, as in a dream
We marvel, and can scarce believe our eyes.[35]

Kamarupa is a Hindu god who changes shape at will. The poem and his reading of Howard as a whole are confirmation of his vision of science – which begins with childish or superstitious 'explanations' for natural phenomena, develops through empirical experiment, is fixed in scientific classification and then – crucially for Goethe, though not perhaps for Howard – into Mystic Idealism.[36]

The evocation of an Indian deity is a token of the fact that it was during this spectacularly fecund period of his poetic life that Goethe was looking east for inspiration. It was Herder who had pointed out to Goethe, when he was a very young man, the beauty of the Hebrew poets in the Bible, especially in the Psalms and the Song of Songs. In January 1814, when the Bashkir Host, serving with the Russian army, were billeted in the School Hall in Weimar, he saw Muslims at prayer, and was deeply impressed. It sent him back to his early fascination with the Prophet, and with the translation of the Quran which he had read in Strasbourg. In June 1814, he read Joseph von Hammer-Purgstall's translation of the *Divan-i-Hafiz*, and immediately began to read all he could get his hands on, relating to the Sufi poets of the Persian tradition. It inspired him to write over thirty 'Poems to Hafez'.

> The North, the West and the South are splitting apart
> Thrones are bursting, Empires are trembling:
> Make your escape! And in the pure East
> Savour the air of the Patriarchs![37]

Hafez's wellspring would refresh the war-torn cynical European, tired of revolution, tired of war, tired, if the sad truth were known, with marriage.

Goethe was so inspired by Hafez that at one point he was writing two or three lyrics per day. In late summer 1814, he visited Frankfurt, partly with the aim of meeting a newish young friend, Sulpiz Boisserée (1783–1854), who wanted to show him his collection of medieval German art which Goethe had agreed to write about. He also called on his friend Johann Jakob von Willemer (1760–1838) – banker, playwright, man of letters, who lived at the Gerbermühle, an old mill upstream on the Main a few kilometres out of town. Willemer lived there with Marianne Jung (1784–1860), raven-haired, pale as porcelain, now aged thirty. The relationship between the pair had evolved. She was initially his foster-daughter, and, by the time Goethe became obsessed by her, she and Willemer were married. Yet again, as with the relationship with Kestner and Lotte Buff, or with the von Steins, Goethe became the third party in a marriage.

Marianne was herself a poet, who accompanied herself on the guitar as she sang her lyrics.[38]

> Among the many I'm but one,
> And you call me your little one.
> I'd be happy, you must know,
> Would you always call me so ...
> You're a great man; people know you.
> No pantheon would dare forego you.
> Your absence makes us feel bereft,
> We wish you had never left.

In the intervening months, after Goethe went back to Weimar, the two of them exchanged dozens of lyrics. The following year, Goethe repeated his journeys. He went to Heidelberg to talk about art with Boisserée, and then to the spa town of Wiesbaden to spend time with the Willemers. A stream of erotic poems, purportedly an amorous dialogue called 'The Book of Suleika', passed between Goethe and Marianne. It was a kind of game. The two were not having an affair. Willemer was all but complicit, certainly tolerant of it.

The most celebrated of their joint efforts was the lyric 'Ginkgo Biloba'. It is a tree which has become divided within itself. Like Faust, who had two souls in one breast, the Ginkgo Biloba is an emblem both of Goethe himself, and of what it is which attracts them to one another, he and Marianne. The poem deftly incorporates the bisexual theme of Plato's *Symposium*: the myth that human beings were once quadrupeds who have been cut in half, and who now spend their lives everlastingly searching for the other half.

> Are these two who have chosen one another,
> So that one knows them as one being?
> To these questions, I have found the right answer.
> Don't my lyrics make you feel
> I am both one, and my double?

'Suleika', that is Marianne, wrote back to Goethe that the wind from the East is cooling, refreshing with its true message from the heart, *Herzenkunde*.

She gave this poem to him in person at Heidelberg, where she and Willemer went to meet him, between 23 and 26 September 1815. It was on one level a bit of nonsense. In another, as in the case of Plato's *Symposium* itself, it was the expression of perhaps the deepest mysticism which is possible between two people, the mysterious 'it' which attracts us to one another, not simply sexually, but spiritually.

When they parted, there was merry talk of their all meeting again in the following summer of 1816. But it never happened. Marianne, who would live until 1860, never saw Goethe again. He published her contributions to the *Diwan* as if they were his own work: quite a compliment, in its way.

Even as he was coming away from the Willemers with Sulpiz Boisserée, the younger man noted that Goethe seemed deeply disturbed, as if he was on the verge of some emotional crisis.[39] It was partly that he was worried by his breach with the Duke over Napoleon; partly that he had been quarrelling with the Duke's mistress Caroline Jagemann – now Frau von Heygendorff – about the Court Theatre.

Goethe did what he had done before – what he had done when he needed to escape the engagement with Lili in Frankfurt in 1776; what he had done when life with Charlotte von Stein became too intense in 1786. He did a runner. The flirty correspondence with Marianne continued through the winter. Would he have met up with her again had things turned out differently? Or had he already made the break in his mind? She had served her creative purpose. He was ready to move on. In July 1816, he was actually in a coach, planning a visit to the Willemers on the way to Baden Baden, when the coach broke an axle and was overturned. The almost sixty-seven-year-old was badly shaken. He took it as some kind of omen, and he cancelled the trip to the Willemers. He would never see Marianne again.

But something much more decisive than the coach accident had happened a month previously. On 6 June 1816, Goethe became a widower.

Although *Elective Affinities*, both as a novel and as a quasi-scientific idea, is about the chemical reactions and changes caused by new partners displacing old, there is surely implicit in the book the idea that we are all (sort of) programmed to love, and to mate with, those that suit us, simply as animal beings. Although there were those who would always be completely baffled by Goethe's relationship with Christiane, and who would imagine that his life with such a fat, drunken, coarse person must be a torment for him, the evidence largely points the other way. True, he spent long periods apart from her, especially when he took himself off to Jena for writing space and intellectual companionship, or when he went to spa towns for health cures and occasional bouts of sentimental crushes. But the language between them in their letters cannot all have been a fiction. Moreover, though the malice of the court, and especially of the everlastingly bitter Charlotte von Stein, saw in Christiane only a fat drunkard with no conversation, they overlooked the possibility that Goethe might actually enjoy the company of a fat drunkard. 'The idiotic woman has more and more power over him, and cuts him off from society and draws him into her *Komödiantwirtschaft*'[40] – farcical household or actress circle? Or both? So Caroline von Wohlzogen in 1811. And a year later, Wilhelm von Humboldt: 'To the comforts of Weimar, which he once enumerated for me, he also adds "the little wife". This is one of the most ghastly things about the marriage, that the man or the woman bring one another down through habit or mutual attraction, that they find the mediocrity and commonness utterly indispensable.'[41] Charlotte von Schiller shuddered at the sight of Goethe, presiding over a table on which china and silver had been laid out, in a fully lit box in the court theatre, pouring out hot tea for Christiane because she felt the cold. Others would have found this charming, but they could not bear the evidence that he actually – at least some of the time – loved his wife. 'Wieland compares the Vulpius with an Otaheitin,' said Chancellor von Müller in December 1808. (The reference is to the 'discovery' of Tahiti by European travellers at the end of the eighteenth century, and clearly Wieland and Müller meant that Christiane was what they would doubtless have called a 'savage'; but, as the memoirs of Georg Forster and Captain Cook both make clear, the inhabitants of Tahiti had a powerful attraction for the European voyagers who encountered them, rowing out, or swimming naked towards HMS *Resolution*.)

> Won't you lie by me, naked, you sweet beloved one,
> Bashful, you stay covered with your clothing.
> Say to me do you want your clothing? Do you desire the appealing
>   body?
> *Now, now shyness is a clothing – let's get rid of it between lovers.*[42]

The 'Urfreund', Knebel, who had introduced Goethe to Duke Carl August all those years ago, wrote to the poet in 1810:

> I've just recently spent a few days in Weimar and had the chance to visit your house where your wife received me with her customary love and friendship. I spent some of the happiest mornings in your

beautiful garden and ... and I loved its ordering and situation and arrangement. It is the most charming corner of all Weimar. Everything is so well chosen and better considered than anything we have here in Jena. I have nothing but praise for the calm and orderliness of your garden.

As Knebel recognized, this achievement was as much Christiane's as it was Goethe's. Knebel's wife Luise praised Christiane's 'clear mind'.[43]

Yes, there was something bizarre, to a modern sensibility, about the extent to which Christiane accepted the hierarchy of things within the marriage. Visitors were puzzled, even then, or at least took note of the fact, that she addressed him – in company at least – as 'Herr Geheimrat'. She spoke to him with the formal second person plural – *Sie*; whereas he called her *Du* – thou, the form you would use when addressing a child. All the time that young Voss, son of the Homeric translator, lived in their house, he noted no variation in this pattern, and other witnesses – Wilhelm von Humboldt, historian Franz Bernhard von Bucholz, the Danish poet Adam Oehelenschläger – all said the same.[44]

Yet one would see them going for walks together, hand in hand. The English diarist Henry Crabb Robinson, on his visit, said, she had 'an agreeable countenance and a hearty, cordial tone, her manners were unceremonious and free'.[45] Their many letters to one another are filled with endearments.

She had a drinker's end, aged fifty-one. In the early summer of 1815, she had begun to have fainting spells, stomach cramps and was coughing up blood. A year later, Goethe was writing in his diary, 'My wife in extreme danger. My son, a helper, adviser, the only thing I can cling to in this darkness.' The next day – 6 June 1816 – 'She died towards mid-day. Emptiness and deathly silence within and around me.' He became 'as one distracted'.[46] Three weeks later, he would write to Sulpiz Boisserée, 'I am on the edge of total despair.'[47]

By then, Goethe's hero Napoleon was in exile on St Helena. The carving-up of Europe at the Congress of Vienna gave him little reason for optimism, and he despised the nationalist aspirations of the Germans.

Sixteen more years of life remained for the sixty-seven-year-old widower. Goethe the political factotum had transmogrified into

Goethe the Sage of Weimar, the Grand Old Man whose very nightshirt was a prophet's mantel.

He took to heart Plotinus's instruction to his adepts – 'Never cease working at thy statue.'[48] His past he had edited and rewritten, as the first parts of his autobiography *Poetry and Truth* were published, his *Italian Journey* in preparation. He was putting the finishing touches to the self-portrait of a genius, and for the next sixteen years he would live up to the image, with every visitor who made the pilgrimage to the Frauenplan to see the great man.

These, too, were the years, not only when he would pursue his scientific researches – which for many months of each year seemed to be the largest of his concerns. In the December after his wife died, he showed that he had not yet abandoned the great work. He sketched out the plan for *Faust Part Two*.

In *Elective Affinities*, Goethe the scientist turned an acute eye onto the ineluctable consequences of sexual and emotional attachment. In his work on colour theory, he turned a poet's eye on a scientific problem, which, he believed, the narrowness of Isaac Newton's *Optics* had got fundamentally wrong. For the first few months of 1810, he worked daily, repeating the very experiments which Newton himself had performed to write his *Optics*. As we observed, when Goethe had begun to address himself to the physics of colour theory twenty years earlier, he did not set out to rival or to demolish Newton; there was much in Newton's theory which he accepted. In the end, however, the difference between Newtonian and Goethean physics is seen in two manifestations. First, whereas Newton believed that colour is contained within light itself, Goethe maintained that this was inaccurate. Colour could not be examined without resource to optics. 'When the eye sees a colour, it is immediately excited and it is its nature, spontaneously and of necessity, at once to produce another, which with the original colour, comprehends the whole chromatic scale.'[49]

This is a specific difference between the two. But it is the consequence of a vast difference in their whole approach to perception, and, in general, to the human perception of Nature: what is called in German

Vorstellungsart, or mode of perception. This is essential to our whole understanding of Goethe, and his originality as a poet, not just as a scientist. Newton regarded light as corpuscular, as streams of corpuscles. It could be divided up, and categorized, and described, in the way that material beings could also be categorized. The ultimate origin, in the history of human ideas, of this Enlightenment viewpoint, is found in the atomism of the ancients, Democritus and Lucretius. Nature, Being, is divided up into a series of detached and minute units – atoms – and existence can be explained, or understood, by our scientific acquaintance with each of these detached units.

Galileo, in his physics, openly introduced ancient atomism.[50] He therefore divided the primary and secondary qualities of any of the units in Nature. A thing's primary qualities were physical. Such things as tastes, odours, colours were secondary qualities which only had reality in so far as they derived from the primary thing.

> Hence I think that tastes, odours, colours, and so on are no more than mere names so far as the object to which we place them is concerned, and that they reside only in the consciousness.[51]

This is one strand of viewing the world which Newton inherited from his profound study of Galileo. Behind this is the whole history of science, stretching back to Aristotle, in which the science of quantity is measurement science. Nature is seen as that which can be categorized or measured by reason, or more narrowly by mathematics. Locke and Hume purported to be following through the genesis of our knowledge of the world; they were actually introducing the quantitative, measuring techniques applicable to the solid world into their description of mind. Everything could therefore be categorized or explained. The universe could be explained in terms of mathematics. When the mathematical laws of Nature are understood, it would be theoretically possible to understand everything. The late twentieth-century expression of this mindset was in Stephen Hawking's view that we 'would know the mind of God'.[52]

Goethe made a mistake in his analysis of what Newton had actually said, since he relied not so much on reading Newton directly, as on the existence of German physics textbooks representing the Newtonian viewpoint. He therefore believed that Newton had maintained that the colours contained in light meant that the entire white surface would appear coloured, not just at the edges.[53]

Newton himself, however, made mistakes. He claimed the light which comes from the blue half of the paper through the prism to the eye 'does in like Circumstances suffer a greater Refraction than the Light which comes from the red half, and by consequence is more refrangible'. In fact,[54] had Newton observed blue and red rectangles on a white background, he would have found in this case that the red appears to be more refrangible – owing to the way that the prismatic colours at the edges merge with the colours of the background.[55]

Two questions – whether Newton or Goethe were closer to the truth in the specific matter of the colour spectrum, refrangibility, etc. Secondly, which of them had a more useful methodology as scientists. As Dennis Sepper has said, 'It is not an *a priori* poetic prejudice against mathematical analysis but rather performing the experiments that led [Goethe] to reject the [Newtonian] theory.'[56]

And, as Bortoft has written, 'What is particularly important is that there is no *separation* between the primal phenomenon and its instances. Goethe's science does not subscribe to the two-world theory.[57] There is no underlying reality *behind* the appearances, but only the intensive depth of the phenomenon itself.'[58]

Goethe always approached the phenomenon itself, and focused on this. A favourable comment was made on his scientific work by a Leipzig professor, namely that Goethe's thinking works objectively: 'Here he means that my thinking is not separate from objects: that the elements of the object, the perceptions of the object, flow into my thinking and are fully permeated by it; that my perception itself is a thinking, and my thinking is a perception.'[59] Newtonian and Galilean physics had *imposed* thinking and theorems *on* Nature. Goethean science is received *from* Nature.

Carolyn Merchant, in a groundbreaking book *The Death of Nature*, pointed out that Francis Bacon, who had been Lord Chancellor of England, and who was a progenitor of the modern or Enlightenment approach to Nature, derived much of his imagery from the courtroom. 'Because it treats nature as a female to be tortured through mechanical interventions, strongly suggests the interrogations of the witch trials and the mechanical devices used to torture witches.'[60]

Nature, female, is compelled to answer 'interrogation' by male theorists. Faust, even in his earliest version, is overwhelmed by the spirit of Nature. He, too – as in Carolyn Merchant's highly pertinent image of Bacon the Lord Chancellor thumbscrewing and racking the female body – sees empirical scientific methodology as a form of torture.

> I never used your ancient gear
> To extract from her by torture with screw or lever
> Nature's mystery.[61]

From the beginning, Faust has been wanting to understand Nature, not to impose theories upon it.[62]

> That I can recognize what
> In the innermost core of innermost being
> Holds the world together.

In this approach, the human scientist is not imposing mathematical theories on the universe, or attempting to control it, but *paying attention* to natural phenomena. Faust, who admitted he was a divided nature with two souls in his breast, was frequently tempted to dominate and control Nature. But, from the first encounter with the Earth Spirit, through his powerful soliloquy at the beginning of *Part Two* – 'with renewed freshness, the very pulse of Life is beating',[63] he gives himself up to involvement in Nature, recognizing that he himself is a part of Nature, while observing it. Humanity alone, among all the phenomena which fill the multiplicity and variety of the natural world, has the capacity to contemplate it, to attend to it. And of nothing is this truer than colour, as Faust sees, in his almost mystic adoration of the rainbow.

As a fairly recent convert to Goethean science wittily pointed out in his book *Goethe and Newton at Odds over Colour*, Goethe did not do himself any favours by writing about the subject at such length.[64] Olaf L. Müller's close analysis of both the Newtonian and the Goethean position is undertaken over 400 pages. As Professor of the Philosophy of Nature and of Scientific Theory at the Humboldt University in Berlin, he knows whereof he speaks, and his book is of special interest because, having believed fervently in the rightness of Newton, he now believes Goethe to have been fundamentally right and Newton fundamentally wrong. Moreover, Professor Müller corrects the view that Goethe's contemporary scientists all pooh-poohed his colour theory. Müller itemizes eighteen favourable responses in learned journals or academic papers between 1810 and 1832, eleven ambivalent responses and twenty-five negative responses from contemporary physicists.[65]

By saying that Schelling's mind was organized according to the newest fashion, Goethe conveyed that he was a follower of Fichte.

Ever since I tore myself away free of the traditional kind of nature study and, like a monad thrown back on myself, had to float around in the cerebral regions of science, I have seldom felt a pull in one direction or another; the pull towards your teaching is decisive. I wish for a complete confluence, which I hope to effect by studying your writing, or even better, by personal contact with you.[66]

He took Schelling to stay with him in Weimar at Christmastime 1800, and they spent a lively New Year's Eve in conversation with Schiller. When Goethe then developed shingles, he was so ill that his life was despaired of, and Schiller, the squabbles over the Schlegels and the *Athenaeum* laid aside, sat beside his friend night and day.

Nevertheless, when Goethe recovered his strength, the tensions in the friendship revived. In these, the last years of Schiller's life, the younger poet enjoyed a flowering. After the magnificent *Wallenstein* trilogy, came *Mary Stuart*, his most perfect play, rippling with scenes and poetic lines which were better than anything he had ever written, and by *The Maiden of Orleans*. There would follow *The Bride of Messina* and *William Tell*. Goethe's poetic well, by contrast, had run dry, and he was unable to make progress with *Faust*. It was hard for him not to resent this. When he returned to running the Weimar theatre, he was faced with the fact that it was badly in debt. In an outburst which seems outrageously unfair, he snarled at Schiller that things would have been improved had Schiller been able to supply 'more – and if I may say so, more theatrically effective – productions'.[67] So the author of plays which, most of them, were so boring that audiences would only endure two or three performances at most, to the author of the most magnificent plays, written before or since, in the history of German theatre.

In February 1805, as four years before, Goethe was again afflicted by shingles. This time it was not life-threatening, although it affected his eyes. Schiller wept at their separation, but he himself was by now a sick man, confined indoors and habitually coughing. Tuberculosis, the scourge of the age which killed Keats and Novalis, killed Schiller on 9 May 1805.

Goethe was himself ill again when this tragic event occurred. He had taken to his bed with the liver complaint which was bound, sooner or later, to catch up on so heavy a drinker. For some days, those caring for him could not bring themselves to tell him the news. They allowed Goethe to lie in darkness, groaning with discomfort. When eventually they came to him to say that Schiller was dead, he turned his face away and wept.

Pleading illness, he did not attend Schiller's funeral on 11 May. In one of his best and most celebrated lyrics, he wrote that the path to wisdom lay in the capacity to grasp the truth of death: 'Die in order to become!' But he could not stand death in reality. He avoided funerals whenever possible. Of the loss of his friend, he wrote, 'Unannounced and without fanfare he came to Weimar, and without fanfare he departed from here. I have no love for the parades of death.'[68]

14

OTTILIE

'Now you know Ossian's type of woman? ... the kind of woman
you see in your dreams ... Well, these women exist in reality. And
these women are terrible. The subject of women, you see, will
always be completely new, however much you study it.'
'Oh, no. Some mathematician or another said that pleasure
comes from the search for truth, not in finding it.'
  Tolstoy, *Anna Karenina*, Part Two, Chapter 14, translated by
                                              Rosamund Bartlett

Goethe sketched out *Faust Part Two*, but it was not clear to him that he would ever finish the work. Indeed, when he was cobbling together an unfinished version of his autobiography, he considered adding this outline of *Faust Part Two* as an appendix. The sketch was not even *written* by Goethe. As happened more and more often, he dictated it – on 16 December 1816. In a comparable manner, he would dictate snatches of fiction. These would be assembled haphazardly, during this period, to become the utterly incoherent *Wilhelm Meisters Wanderjahre* – his *Journeyman Years*, a book which is full of good apothegms, episodic stories and strange characters, but which could in no sense be seen as a unity. It's a hotch-potch.

In the period that we are considering in this chapter – roughly from the ending of the Napoleonic Wars to the time when Eckermann arrived in Weimar to become his sycophant and tape-recorder, his editor, his secretary, his representative on earth – Goethe was concerned with different modes of seeing. To finish his autobiographical works would be to finish his earthly pilgrimage, to write *FINIS* on his life, and he was not ready for that, so we find him tinkering and refashioning the two great studies, *Poetry and Truth* (galleys were revised in February 1814, but he was still not ready to publish them) and *Italian Journey*, which first seems to have become a project in 1813. These were written simultaneously with the *Wanderjahre*, and with the science. He was, in particular, concerned with his theory of entoptic colours.

The modern way of reading this is to see all these phenomena as coming together. The autobiographies, and the colour theory, the poetry and the conversations; 'the way self-knowledge in Goethe was no longer predicated as an act of seeing yourself as an other, but instead as an act of seeing yourself *through* others. "Self-reflection" emerges in Goethe's late work as the aggregate of medial refractions of one's self in the world – as an egology.'[1]

Goethe himself refused to categorize. Fiction, poetry, science, autobiography philosophy – they were all ways of seeing, all ways of perceiving the truth. One of his many epigrams is: 'It is as necessary to have a Categorical Imperative in scientific research as in ethics: only one considers it in that regard, not at the end, but at the beginning.'[2]

The second decade of the nineteenth century is the great era of *seeing*. Hegel's *Phenomenology* appears at the same time as great strides in optics. Philosophical and scientific ways of describing how we see the world, see experience, what it is we are seeing, how we see. Goethe was absolutely at the centre of all this.

His seventieth birthday approached, and none of the great work that he had attempted was quite complete. He was still capable of being possessed, for a day or two, by the Muses, and to write a short lyric or a scintillating epigram. *Faust*, *Poetry and Truth*, *Italian Journey* and *Wilhelm Meister* were all, however, incomplete.

The defeat of his hero Napoleon, the carve-up of Europe at the Congress of Vienna in 1815, and the death of his wife, combined to make Goethe feel his age. As always when cares beset him, he reached for the bottle.

When he met Beethoven in the summer of 1812, Goethe had confided in his friend Zelter, 'he is, unfortunately, a completely untamed personality, who would not be wrong if it found the world detestable, but admittedly, for that very reason, he makes it a more enjoyable place, both for himself and for others'.[3] There was always the side to Goethe which was the everlasting denier, which found the human race detestable, contemptible and which had to strive to transform his world-vision – a blaze of bright glory shot through with the deepest thunderclouds of pessimism – into a coherent poetic whole. One of the finest poems he ever wrote was the speech he put into the mouth of the dying Faust. It is his anthem for old age, though it was probably penned 1800–01 when Goethe was a vigorous fifty.

> The only person who can say he's earned
> Freedom; or that to Life Itself he's fitted –
> Is one who every single day has learned
> To strive for them! Yes! Yes!
> To this law I'm utterly committed.[4]

Many a day went past in the rambling house in the Frauenplan, with its room after poky room, connected by the enfilade of his own designs, in which freedom did not feel like freedom and life was not much fun. Home was a prison, and so was his own personality, the personality he had so elaborately shaped: the personality of the Privy Councillor/World Genius that the fictionalized Lotte Buff (in Mann's version) found so unappealing when she visited him in October 1816, and complained that his house was a museum.

Goethe was one of those strange beings who was an accumulator, a collector. Naturally, he accumulated books, but for a man who lived so long and read so much, his library is patchy. The 8,000 or so volumes do not contain a single work by E. T. A. Hoffmann, for example, nor one by Clemens Brentano. As he said in his *Italian Journey*, 'Nature is the only book which in all its leaves offers a great content/meaning [*Gehalt*].'[5]

While the library grew up higgledy-piggledy, this was not the story when it came to other aspects of collecting. Cameos and plaster casts of classical sculptures – 8,770 examples; 1,926 medallions, mostly Renaissance; 2,059 Roman coins; 2,512 drawings; nearly 10,000 engravings or prints of Italian paintings; 50 paintings, mostly copies of Italian masters; 348 maquettes and small statues. Then there were the mineralogical collections – nearly 18,000 stones, together with bones, skeletons and other specimens of natural history.

Goethe's lifetime spanned the era when museums began. The brothers Humboldt established the first great German museum in Berlin. In London, the British Museum, which had begun in 1759, was hugely expanded in the early nineteenth century, with Robert Smirke's gigantic Greek Revival palace erected in Bloomsbury not merely to house the newly acquired Parthenon Marbles, but also to establish London as a would-be Athens *rediviva*. The collection in the Louvre, which opened as a public art gallery in 1793, was enormously enlarged by Napoleon with treasures looted during his campaigns. Nowadays, understandably enough, the ethics of museums are under close scrutiny: not merely the means by which all the artefacts were acquired, but the idea of different people's cultures being objects of display for an often heedless drift of tourists – objects which began life, perhaps, as sacred in a distant land. For generations, it has seemed 'natural' that the great cities of the world should contain great museums, even though 'natural' is precisely what it isn't.

The desire for nations – emergent, modern nations, with their own set of values or non-values, often totally alien to the nations they have plundered – to display such objects is part of the story of the early nineteenth century, of imperialism, of commercial expansion, of capitalism. The desire for private collectors, such as Goethe, to accumulate stuff – bones, feathers, majolica, coins, copperplate engravings – clearly mirrors the greater picture of the large museums, but it is also an area of inner psychology. The desire not merely to acquire, but to categorize, as Linnaeus created the taxonomy of Nature itself, is perhaps suggestive of a need to impose order on some inner chaos; or a need to dominate and conquer immaterial things, when the emotional life has failed. Nearly all the private collectors, when you read their lives, turn out to have some kind of screw loose, whether they are kleptomaniacs like Andrew Mellon or near psychopaths like Sir John Soane. To own one or two majolica plates or vases is a natural response to the beautiful object: to place them on your chimneypiece or table to enhance the visual pleasure of life. To own a hundred or two hundred takes you into a psychotic dimension. And that is the other strange thing about 'collectors': the consequence of their mania is to produce (almost invariably) ugliness. Whereas a few vases look beautiful, a multitude makes you feel that you are in either a salesroom, or the interior of a madman's head.

On another level, however, you could see the collection as the outward and visible sign of the profuseness of Goethe's imagination, the plenitude of his knowledge and curiosity about the world. So many visitors to the Frauenplan could have echoed the French philosopher Victor Cousin, who came at this time:

Goethe received me in a gallery full of busts in which we walked to and fro. His gait is as calm and unhurried as his speech; but certain rare emphatic gestures betray an inner excitement beneath this placid exterior. His conversation, rather chilly at first, became gradually animated. As he walked he would stop to gaze or to meditate, to trace his thoughts in increasing depth, and to find a more precise expression or to give an example and details ... He put forward not one paradox, and yet there is a novelty in everything he said to me. A flash of imagination from time to time; much wit in the details and the development of his ideas, and a veritable genius in their actual substance. I think what is most characteristic of his mind is its wide range.[6]

That Goethe, when widowed, felt his life to be an emotional disaster area could not be doubted. He had enjoyed the drama and emotional pain of 'crushes' over and over again, usually crushes on unattainable young women – clearly the more unattainable the better. He also had, now far behind him, the experience of worshipping Charlotte von Stein. This was something rather different. It had begun as a kind of emotional religion. It ended in bitterness. And then, eventually, when the bisexuality of youth had more or less evaporated, there had been the middle-aged discovery of women as sexual partners – the time in Rome, followed almost immediately by the sensually satisfying relationship with Christiane Vulpius. And now she was gone, and the one thing they could have had together – a family circle – was absent. Nearly all their children were dead, and only August Goethe, the somehow embarrassing son, was all that remained.

Two of the best chapters in Mann's *Lotte in Weimar* are those (Chapters Five and Six), first, in which Demoiselle Schopenhauer expresses her grave reservations about August – his womanizing, his drunkenness, his attempts to ape his father, both in his collecting mania and in his political conservatism; and the next, Chapter Six, in which August himself appears at the Hotel Elephant and Lotte sees in the dark brown eyes such a close resemblance to Goethe, and yet in his pompous, old-fashioned language and his intellectual limitations, so unlike.

Goethe's wish was that they could somehow start again, and create a family by finding the son a wife. August was twenty-seven, and by no means to be relied upon to find a suitable candidate. Adele Schopenhauer, in Mann's novel, was accurate when she made allusion to August's affair with the wife of a hussar, which caused mockery and scandal in Weimar; as well as his association with 'women one can only call creatures'.[7] Goethe himself lighted upon a pretty and highly intelligent person, Ottilie von Pogwisch – twenty years old, the child of divorced aristocrats – her father from the Holstein, her mother from the Silesian nobility. Father had long since fled the nest, so that Ottilie, a highly flirtatious, socially voracious person, was a flirt in need of a daddy. She was oval-faced, sharp-chinned, dark-eyed. She loved reading Byron. Her thick, beautiful *dunkelblond* hair was plaited and wound in a circlet around her head. Her lips were both satirical and sensual.

One of the many charming, but extremely odd, episodic narratives in the *Journeyman Years*, which has nothing to do with Wilhelm

Meister nor his destiny, is *The Man of Fifty*. It was largely composed in 1807, long before Ottilie came upon the scene, so it is in no sense a *roman à clef* about her and Goethe. There were moments, however, when those who read it must have recognized the familiar phenomenon of life, if not imitating, then, echoing life. The Man of Fifty is a retired major who discovers that his prospective daughter-in-law, Hilarie, is in love, not – as expected – with his son (Flavio), but with himself. Flavio is in love with a young widow, who is herself in love with the Major. It is a love tangle as complicated as *Elective Affinities* – but, unlike that novel, *The Man of Fifty* resolves itself reasonably happily. (The young people eventually get together and the Major marries the widow.)

There was never an affair between Ottilie and her father-in-law, but there could be no doubt that she had far more in common with the old Privy Councillor than she ever did with his son. She never pretended to be in love with August, who continued to drink to excess and to have other lovers. Ottilie herself had a *mouvemente* emotional life, punctuated by adultery. Her best friend was Adele Schopenhauer, the philosopher's brother. It seemed apt, in 1829, that when Ottilie started a literary magazine it bore the title *Chaos*.

She and August had three children: Walther Wolfgang von Goethe (1818–85), Wolfgang Maximilian von Goethe (1820–83) and Alma Sedina Henriette Cornelia von Goethe (1827–44). Visitors attest to the children running in and out of the room as the great poet conversed, and to his playing with them, fondling them and delighting in their prattle.

Goethe was a doting grandfather, and it distressed and annoyed him that Ottilie and August could not make a better fist of their marriage. They occupied the top floor of the Frauenplan and the old man was frequently disturbed by their domestic rows. Nevertheless, the marriage had brought Goethe some of what he had wanted: a household, and a woman at the centre of it. Unlike his wife, his poised young daughter-in-law was a practised diner out, and could be a hostess in the Frauenplan, both at the rather stiff little dinners regularly given for Weimar courtiers, or for the stream of visitors come to glimpse the sage. She could hold her own at table, whether conversing with politicians or philosophers, poets or scientists, English, German, Italian or Frenchmen. She would, in time, be more than a domestic help: she would urge on her father-in-law, whom she always called 'Father', to finish *Faust*, and she had a real understanding of the work. The outline, hastily dictated that December day in 1816, both did and did not bear a relation to the work as it would eventually be completed. That is to say, it tells the bare outline of the story – Faust and Mephistopheles's engagement by the Emperor; Faust's deep sleep; Faust and Helena having a child. There is no Homunculus, the strange test-tube baby created by Faust's old colleague Wagner; Faust's son bears no relation to Lord Byron, as in the finished version, and his death occurs not through his daimonic rashness, but because he is killed by neighbours. Above all, the outline lacks the essential phantasmagoric quality which makes *Faust Part Two* both such a baffling and a stimulating reading experience.

The Congress of Vienna, at the end of the Napoleonic Wars, tried to bring a new order to Europe. France reverted to monarchism. It was never united in this reversion and in 1830, 1848, 1851 and 1870, would replay its old and irreconcilable divisions. Great Britain was poised to become not merely a commercial and technological powerhouse without historical parallel, but a world power, an Empire.

Goethe was highly critical of the Congress. How could he not be, when he was an enthusiast for the Napoleonic vision of Europe, which, while embracing the principles of the Enlightenment, resisted the anarchic excesses of the Revolution? Act IV of *Faust Part Two*, which he would write after the Grand Duke's death, is, as has already been stated, a biting satire on Carl August and the resolutions of the Congress.

The destiny of so many European peoples was determined by the Congress that few outside Weimar would perhaps see much significance in the fact that Duke Carl August was now a Grand Duke. Goethe was now a *Staatsminister*, and the sentries keeping guard outside the castle in Weimar were therefore required to salute him and present arms when he appeared. This piece of ceremonial, however, did not disguise the fact that, in contrast with the old days of their brotherly friendship, Goethe had in effect been demoted by Carl August. His political responsibilities were more or less suspended and he became Superintendent of Arts and Sciences. Given the way German politics were going, this suited Goethe perfectly well.

For what was to become of the old Holy Roman Empire – now dissolved? What of the powers of reaction, embodied in Metternich and his Emperor in Vienna? What of Prussia, conqueror of Waterloo? The old Prussian general Blücher had been, with Wellington, the co-victor over the Corsican monster, so it was not surprising that in the beer cellars of Jena the students drank 'To Blücher and Weimar!' – seeing Blücher as the man who saw off Bonaparte, and the Duke of Weimar as the defender of their liberties. 'The old student radical', Carl August was scornfully known as in Berlin, in the court of King Friedrich Wilhelm. 'Der Altbursche.'

Goethe's rift with Carl August, played down by the early German biographers, has already been mentioned. The fundamental thing was not merely that Goethe admired the Napoleon who had told the Duchess Luise that he would 'crush' Carl August. It was the difference between the German patriotism which flowered after the war, and the larger vision of Europe which Goethe considered not merely less petty, more noble – but also, more realistic. For, how – from a perspective of 1815 – could the many little kingdoms, city-states, bishoprics and the like possibly agree on a political system which could enable them to cohere?

In the *Xenien* he quipped:

Oh German, you hope to become a nation, but it's unrealistic; you would develop into a free-er being if you simply thought of yourself as a human being.[8]

That was not how the student associations of Jena, or the liberals anywhere, saw it in those heady post-Napoleonic times. They exchanged their civilian clothes for military uniform, dressing themselves as volunteers in the Prussian army. The colours – black cloth, trimmed with scarlet facing and gold buttons – became the colours of the student banners – red, black and gold. After 1948, these colours would be adopted by West Germany as emblems of its democratic credentials.

The students sang hymns to Carl August:

Be true to your word
Which you gave us in pledge

Protector of the People, as of the Throne,
In a word to the Constitution.

Newspapers and periodicals sprang up like spring crocuses throughout the Grand Duchy – Friedrich Johann Bertuch's *Oppositionblatt*, Lorenz Oken's *Isis*, old Wieland's son Ludwig's *Volksfreund*, Professor Heinrich Luden's *Nemesis – a newspaper for History and Politics –* and these were only a few of them. The students clamoured for their own press freedoms, but they were none too tolerant of the freedoms of others. French literature they regarded as 'foreign trash'. Poor old Father Wieland, rococo Francophile of a vanished age, found his book *Zeinide* being burned in a public bonfire. Wieland himself was denounced as a 'low-down bastard' – a 'Hundsfott', a rogue, a destroyer of the good old German past. As the student unrest increased, the decision was taken to ban political journalism in the Grand Duchy altogether. Goethe approved. He satirically noted – a phenomenon which persists to this day – the extreme intolerance of the revolutionary young:

O glorious freedom of the Press!
At last we have our joy.
We thump out our message from place to place:
Oh glory be on high.
Come, let us print whatever we like!
For now the power is ours:
But don't let's hear so much as a squeak
From those who don't think as we do![9]

Along with book burning, they decided, many of these student radicals, that the Jews merely wanted to mock and abuse Germany. Hans Ferdinand Massmann's words, but they were believed by thousands. The student associations, the *Burschenschafte*, were now only open to Christians and Germans. 1817, the tri-centenary of Luther's declaration in Wittenberg, was seen as a great German festival. Heinrich von Kleist's 1808 play *The Battle of Hermann* became hugely popular, a celebration of the defeat of the Roman general Publius Quintilius Varus (i.e. Napoleon) by the German superhero Hermann in 9 CE. In commemoration of this great Battle of the Teutoberg Forest, the men, long-haired and bearded, would dress up for the celebration in unbleached linen; women – good German women, 'Housewife, Mother, Spouse' – would be comparably arrayed in 'folk' costume, with no French lace or finery.

At first, when he heard of the student mob's distaste for Kotzebue, Goethe could not help being frivolously delighted. Kotzebue had, after all, become openly scornful of Goethe, peppering his works with satirical references, as in his Cleopatra:

> My Caesar is now dead! And with him all my joyful tomorrows.
> So I sit and drink green tea and read of Werther's Sorrows.
> Oh, writer sublime!! Oh oracle of all good taste –
> I sit and read thee, but somehow get nothing out of it.[10]

Goethe would have had to be a Christian saint (which he never was) not to be amused when he first heard of the radicals' Bonfire of the Kotzebue Vanities.

> The Youth have given you your deserts
> All ends come here together
> While they condemn your books and fame
> St Peter delights in the crackling flame.[11]

While Goethe would find it hard to fill the Weimar court theatre for one of the rare appearances of his own plays, he always knew that a play by Kotzebue would guarantee a full, raucous house. No wonder he loathed the Weimar-born playwright.

But a feud, albeit a semi-jokey feud, between two famous authors is one thing, and the deadly consequences of political fanaticism are another. One of Professor Luden's pupils at Jena, a theological student, and a keen reader of Luden's periodical *Nemesis*, decided upon his own version of patriotic duty.

Karl Ludwig Sand had begun his student life with the aim of becoming a missionary. He grew up in a fiercely patriotic home and his mother, a member of the Bavarian *Bund*, the local patriotic group, always spoke of the Napoleonic Code as a 'wicked system'. He studied theology first, at Tübingen, then at Erlangen and Würtzberg, eventually fetching up at Jena, enlisting in the 'religious, German Students Union'.

Sand became a fervent believer in a civilian republic, German, racially pure, anti-foreign. By his friends Sand was destined to become known as 'a saint of the new religion' (*Heiliger neuen Religion*) of German nationalism, a hundred years before the politically motivated murders perpetrated in the early days of the Weimar Republic in 1919, the so-called *Femedmorden*. (*Feme* comes from Middle Low German *Veime*, meaning punishment.)

Hearing that fifty-seven-year-old Kotzebue was resident at the time in Mannheim, Sand was paid by political activists to take a coach. In his knapsack he carried the poems of Theodor Körner and the Gospel of St John, together with a large dagger. Pretending to be the deliverer of a letter from a friend of the playwright, he was granted admittance. The two stood opposite one another – Kotzebue in a grey frock coat, and the guardian of Germanic purity, with his hair parted in the middle, in a coat with a pointed collar.

Sand produced his knife and stabbed Kotzebue, first in the face, then in the left breast, to punish the traitor's heart, and then in the lungs. As the playwright fell to the floor, Sand knelt beside him, continuing to stab the body, while praying, and thanking God for this victory over anti-German corruption. His attempt to then kill himself was unsuccessful, and he was taken back to Mannheim where he was beheaded with a sword.

Goethe's opposition to freedom of the press is a source of embarrassment to readers in the twenty-first century, but the same arguments apply today between those who would protect the freedom of the individual to read and write whatever comes into their head, and the dangerous effect of 'radicalization' from reading inflammatory material. And there can be no doubt that Sand killed Kotzebue because of what he had read in the radical press.[12]

It was clear that in a world where crazed theological students with the Gospel in their luggage could stab playwrights for the sake of the Fatherland, the sedate world of Classical Weimar was now a thing of the past. Equally obvious – that the themes which Goethe had cogitated since his young manhood, of the ease with which scholars and theologians and philosophers could be lured into devilish clutches

– was on open display. The Enlightenment was not enlightened.
More light! Better light? The inability of Reason alone to lead the
human mind to a knowledge of the Truth, the human dependency on
searching through the veil of Ego – of *Ich* – to grasp the Truth – these
were to be the matters which concerned him for the remaining years
left to him on the planet. But the great poem, or poetic drama, was
still not written, and in these years, two of the other (and perhaps
not unrelated) themes obsessed him: the Colour Theory and the
Experience of Falling in Love.

Nicholas Boyle concluded the second volume of his biography
with a masterly analysis of the difference in attitude to the French
Revolution in Goethe, and in the younger generation of Romantic
poets. For Hölderlin, the Revolution had been the decisive public
event of his lifetime; 'the disappointment of the hopes put in it by
him and his generation for a recovery of human wholeness was one
of the well-springs of his mature poetry. For Goethe the Revolution
had almost the opposite significance, as the destruction of the hopes
he had entertained before it and of the foundations on which he
intended to build wholeness in his life and his art.'[13] Eugenia, the
'Natural Daughter' of Goethe's wonderful play of that title, is
an embodiment of poetry itself. 'She embodies,' says Boyle, 'the
belief of a whole generation, Goethe included, that poetry might
transform life, that, at least in some few select circles an aesthetic
education might in modern Germany bring human potential to the
perfection it had once known in ancient Athens and again, almost
in Renaissance Italy.'[14]

Goethe's fear was that the Revolution and its aftermath might
somehow have destroyed poetry itself. *Faust*, as he came to write and
rewrite and complete it, over the final fifteen years of his life, reflected
these concerns.

———

As director of the Court Theatre, Goethe's relations with Caroline
Jagemann, the theatre's prima donna and the Duke's mistress, were
never easy. After she was ennobled, and was renamed Frau von
Heygendorff, and especially after she formed an alliance with Johann
Heinrich Stromeyer – a double bass player who was honoured as a

'court minstrel' (*Kammersänger*) – Goethe felt himself increasingly marginalized, the Court Theatre increasingly vulgarized. 'Why should we not be absolutely candid and spell out, what is by now notorious, that he [Stromeyer] is definitely not to be regarded as our superior?'[15] A breaking point came in April 1817 when they asked an actor from Vienna – Karsten – to come and perform a melodrama called *Aubry de Montdidier's Dog*, or *The Forest of Bondy*. The star of the show was to be Karsten's poodle, dressed up in a Pierrot costume, with a ruff round its woolly neck. Faust's fateful first encounter with Mephistopheles was when the devil was disguised as a poodle. No one mentioned this. Where Goethe himself had played Orestes, and where the first performance of *Wallenstein* had held a rapt audience in thrall, a poodle was going to teeter on its hind legs. Goethe felt that the high standards of world drama which he and Schiller had tried to bring to the German stage were being made a mockery; that Weimar classicism had turned into a circus.[16]

Looking back on it all years later, Goethe would reflect that the amount of time he had spent, during those twenty-six years as director, putting on productions had left him very little time to finish any of his own plays. While year after year he was staging plays by Schiller, Kotzebue, Beaumarchais and others, *Faust* was left unfinished. In one of those throwaway lines which gave his conversation in old age a vatic air, he said that he had no regrets for the plays which might have been written. 'I have always regarded my works and achievements as only symbolic, and basically, I'm indifferent about whether I am making a pot or dishes.'[17]

The quarrel over the performing dog would have its effect on the development of *Faust*. Goethe's release from the grind of running the theatre now gave him time to finish the great work – though he would not do so finally until fifteen years had passed. The Court Theatre was now in the hands of the Jagemeier and Strohmann Company. Goethe had no more to do with it, and the theatre where he and Schiller had worked eventually burned down in March 1825.

Had Schiller lived, had Goethe enjoyed the constant friendship and companionship of a playwright while he was contemplating the completion of *Faust*, the piece would likely have been very different. Schiller would have constantly drawn attention to the need to make the play playable. Now that Goethe had lost interest in the theatre, however, and indeed felt positive hostility towards it, he would feel no such constraints. *Faust Part Two* is an extended poem, but it is only a play in so far as it continues to be a printed text, its scenes and dialogues divided into Acts. These disparate and vividly imagined scenes, in which Faust is transported through the skies to the Peloponnese, in which a tiny homunculus is formed by science in a test tube, in which gods, goddesses, centaurs, spirits appear in the company of lemurs, angels and saints might be possible to make into a surreal piece of modern cinema but, as every attempt to do so has proved, it is not really stageable. The author does not care whether it is a pot or a key. The reader who is about to finish reading *Faust* will have an exciting time – one of the most exciting reading experiences which it is possible to have – but they will be taken on a mind-journey, rather than a piece of stagecraft.

Although his literary work, during the phase we are considering, came in fits and starts, and although he was for much of the time gloomy, both in his personal life and in his understanding of the political direction of his fellow countrymen, Goethe's scientific interests were continuous. In April 1813, Goethe received a small booklet from his friend Thomas Seebeck (1770–1831), now residing in Nuremberg, entitled 'Einige neue Versuche und Beobachtungen über Spiegelung und Brechung des Lichtes' ('A few new experiments and observations on the reflection and refraction of light'). It prompted Goethe to begin work afresh on his theory of entoptic colours, and to place this work in the context of his other interests and researches.[18]

It concerned the question of the polarity of light, which was observable through the combined effects of double refraction and multiple reflection and which had been treated two years earlier in a prize-winning article by the French researcher Etienne-Louis Malus (1775–1812), 'Théorie de la double réfraction' (1811). Malus's work would go on to become the single most important influence for optical research for the next two decades until the wider acceptance of Augustin-Jean Fresnel's wave theory of light over the course of the 1820s.[19]

Malus argued that light must consist of properties independent of its directionality with respect to the reflecting surface. This he ultimately chose to call the polarity of light.

In taking up Malus's work, Seebeck's primary aim was to argue against the French theory of the internal polar structure of light and argue instead for the Goethean theory of the unity of light. 'Das Licht ist einfach,' writes Seebeck in a passage underlined by Goethe in his copy of the article – 'Light is simple and only through an interaction with that which is not-light in and on the bodies will a polarity of light appear.'[20] It was a reminder to Goethe that, in many quarters, his scientific research was taken very seriously indeed: a consolation for the unsatisfactoriness of his domestic life at this period, and for the feeling that he could not with ease make progress with his literary projects, especially the autobiographies. He felt, like Wilhelm Meister, that he was adrift. Though he was living in Weimar, where he had been resident for well over forty years, he felt like a wanderer. When Wilhelm Grimm wrote to him regarding a project for a cultural union of all German territories, Goethe replied that he had 'always been a restless, homeless wanderer, never settling anywhere'.[21]

It was in November 1821 that Zelter made one of his fourteen visits to Weimar, this time accompanied by his star musical pupil, a twelve-year-old boy called Felix Mendelssohn-Bartholdy. The child wrote to his parents in Berlin that 'one would not take him for a man of seventy-three,[22] but for a man of fifty'. 'Every morning I get a kiss from the author of *Faust* and *Werther*, and every afternoon from my father and friend Goethe. Just fancy that!'[23]

The music which seemed to delight Goethe the most, when the boy played on the excellent grand piano, was that of Bach. He played fugues. Mendelssohn, together with his teacher Zelter, was largely responsible for the revival of Bach's reputation, which – to our minds so incomprehensibly – had faded into oblivion. Mendelssohn also played some Beethoven to Goethe – a piano setting of the C Minor Symphony. Goethe's response: 'It is tremendous. Quite mad; one could fear the whole house might collapse. Imagine the whole lot of them playing it together!'[24]

The apocryphal story is told that when Goethe and Beethoven met, they strolled along the promenade of Teplitz. The Imperial family came in their direction, the Emperor Franz and his children. Hofrat von Goethe, naturally, bowed in reverence. Beethoven stormed through the royal party, refusing to leave the pavement. Genius was the equal, or the senior, of the royal.[25]

But it would be to misread Goethe's deferential behaviour as the mere pomposity of the courtier. When she met the Hofrat in 1816, Lotte Buff had been disappointed by his stiffness and formality. But the formality of his manners was a manifestation of his belief in what a later genius, Jakob Burckhardt, would call merely Civilization.

Humphrey Trevelyan, in his *Goethe and the Greeks*, makes a very similar point: 'For Goethe in his old age, the only valid distinction between man and man, or nation and nation, lay in the degree of civilisation which they had attained, or of barbarism in which they still dwelt. In so far as modern man was civilised, he owed this merit to the Greeks. This, in prosaic terms, is the meaning of the *Helena* episode in *Faust*.'[26]

The published version of *Faust Part One* had, understandably enough, been seized upon with rapture by the younger generation, by precisely those liberal firebrands whom Goethe found so deplorable. This fact was well captured by Goethe's 1963 biographer Richard Friedenthal:

Here is no gentle, strict classicism, as taught by the W. K. F. [Weimarer Kunstfreunde; Weimar Friends of the Arts], and the master himself, no well-balanced compositions on archaeological themes, but wild, detached scraps of genius savagely thrown down on paper. Here is the Brocken of the Walpurgisnacht, not portrayed in carefully executed foliage, but with desolate, cleft giants of trees. Here is the very desire to 'embrace everything' that Goethe criticized in Ruge and Beethoven: mysticism, medievalism, the old Germanic world, God and the devil, insanity, all that the Olympian tells the younger generation to avoid. Here is irony, satire and deep significance, not in classic hexameters but in the liveliest Hans Sachs verse and rhyme, with short couplets that get wafted all over Germany, like dandelion seeds, to become household words.[27]

Philipp Otto Runge's paintings of the various hours of day almost alarmed him. 'Enough to drive one crazy, beautiful and mad at the same time.'[28]

Ever since Goethe died, and the completed *Faust* was published, its readers have divided between those who found it a poem with a unified theme, and those who saw it as a series of brilliant parts, which had little to do with one another; between those who saw *Part One* as a melodrama which had its own cohesion, but which had all but nothing in common with *Part Two*; between those who see the 'classicism' of the Helena play completely at odds with the Mephistophelian pact; between those who find an utter lack of cohesion between the 'old German' witchiness and the cool sunlight of Greece. The inevitability of this divided response is found in Goethe's response to Beethoven.

He wanted to belong to the clean, ordered, pre-revolutionary world of his youth, the world against which, as a Storm and Stress man, he had a different attitude. He had, as a young man, been instrumental in helping to blow that world to bits. But, knowing how delicate a thing is civilization, he was moved by it, cherished it. The music of the Easter choir comes to Faust's ears and saves him from the ultimate act of rebellion, suicide. Yet, 'I hear the message loud and clear; only I lack belief.'[29]

Haydn had been asked how it was that his Masses were so joyful, almost jovial. Papa Haydn replied, unselfconsciously: 'Because whenever I think of the dear God [*den lieben Gott*] I always feel so indescribably happy.'[30] When Goethe was told this anecdote by Chancellor von Müller, tears poured down the poet's cheeks.

Goethe was acutely conscious that the century of revolutions had made such certainties problematic, if not impossible. He, like Faust himself, was not going gently into a peaceful old age. He was tormented by the existential angst of the modern condition. The impulse which led Faust to fall in love with the innocent young Gretchen ends in murder, mayhem, confusion. The controlling, managerial old Faust, who wants, literally, to reshape the world, to control Nature, ends up authorizing a pointless murder by arson. Theology, which to Haydn was the Queen of Sciences expounding received truths which naturally sprang into joyful music, was to be something more challenging.

The reactionary Sage of Weimar is therefore a difficult person to read, and his masterpiece is something which ultimately defies simplistic analysis. It is, as he admitted, 'incommensurable'. This is not, however, because he was incoherent or did not know what he was saying. It is because in a post-revolutionary world, in a world where science was advancing human knowledge of that world, in a world where the young theologians of Tübingen were dismantling the Gospel itself, it was not possible to put the clock back. The urgent tasks, however, were to avoid what he saw as the fatal mistakes of the young Romantics. Their zeal for political revolution was going to end in anarchy, passing into despotism. German unity, seen as a liberal ideal by the likes of Novalis, Hölderlin or Fichte, would come about by Prussian militarism. The Germans, who could have emulated the Athenians of the fourth century in devoting their lives to philosophy, drama, poetry and music – to the civilizing of the world through sculpture, architecture, philosophy, science, mathematics – were going to ignore all the catastrophic lessons of the Napoleonic era and build themselves new militaristic nationalisms, more dangerous even than those of the demonic Napoleon. *Faust* therefore, in a prophetic manner which is sometimes uncanny, prefigures the political story of the century which passed after the author's death.

Its 'incommensurability', however, does not allow itself to be imprisoned in the existentialism of Mephistopheles, the spirit who always negates. And here it prefigures not merely the nightmarish history of revolutions and world wars and dictatorships which shadowed the lives of our grandparents. Its sublime, passionate sense that the human race is a part of the mysterious natural order, an order which it requires scientific imagination, poetic knowledge to plumb, speaks to the twenty-first-century awareness of Nature, twenty-first-century holistic science. The cold negativism of Baron d'Holbach, the Spinozan materialism of Jacobi, are never embraced by Faust, however deep his temptations to despair. Here, he is closer to Papa Haydn in his profound joy. And, as Goethe once said to Jacobi in a letter already quoted, he was polytheist, pantheist and monotheist depending on which part of his brain and which aspect of his imagination he was exercising. God, however understood, or not understood, had not been discarded as an unnecessary hypothesis. Far from it. As well as fearing that the post-revolutionary world might have shattered the fragile shell of civilization which made poetry impossible, he was also, the Sage of Weimar and the poet of *Faust*, deeply afraid that religion itself was going to be transformed or destroyed, on the one hand by the pseudo-medieval pieties of Novalis and friends and on the other by the stubborn materialism of the atheists.

He was more and more at home in the Orphic world of the Greek mysteries. His Orphic 'First and Last Words' was a salute, at first to the *Daimon*:

No time nor power can quite suppress
The moulded form, developing in the living being.

Of the Orphic 'last words' – *Daimon*, Chance, Love, Necessity and Hope – the last word goes to Hope:

There is a Being, light and unbound
Which lifts us, with herself, out of the fog and rain,
And lets us fly! From place to place, she floats her rapturous way
We are one wing-beat behind her – behind us – what ages![31]

Such hopes were difficult to sustain. Writing to Boisserée, he admitted, 'I will not deny, that I am in a state bordering on despair, as a result of which, in seeking a diversion, I have adopted the most utterly wrong means, and for the simple reason that for the time being I could see no prospect of producing anything.'[32]

Such was his perpetual capacity for personal renewal, and his intellectual curiosity, that despondency could never be his only mood. He felt agitated by the fact that his papers remained in chaos. Johann Friedrich Cotta, the publisher, now ennobled as Freiherr von Cottendorf, persisted in printing Collected Editions of Goethe's work. He could sell them, and paid the author handsomely – 10,000 talers for the first, 16,000 for the second Collected Edition.[33] But the editions were incomplete and riddled with mistakes, and Goethe needed a harmless drudge who could edit them. He had no idea, as the year turned into 1823, that such a helper was at hand.

To a young admirer, Schubarth, who was planning upon writing a book about Goethe, the Sage of Weimar could write, 'Persevere in the study of my legacy.' The legacy, for those in the middle and late years of the nineteenth century was very much a scientific one. Goethe was among the first prophets of evolution. He pioneered the idea that Nature is not static but everlastingly moving, changing, becoming.

His research into optics, his attempt to understand entoptic colours, was an investigation into what he called 'das Grundphänomen von allen übrigen'[34] ('the foundational phenomenon of all others'). The experiments depended on equipment. Malus had named the particular device which he had invented to test these theories the polarimeter. Andrew Piper sees a metaphorical significance in the advanced technology of early nineteenth-century optical instruments; that much 'would depend in crucial ways on the specific apparatus upon which its observation was indebted. In this, the entoptic apparatus, which Malus had named a polarimeter, was an integral part of the history of technologically assisted viewing, although it has seldom if ever been read this way.'[35]

Unlike other, more canonical instruments such as the microscope or telescope that emerged out of an early modern milieu of natural inquiry aimed at allowing the human viewer to see more deeply into Nature, the entoptic apparatus had a crucially generative function. Where the microscope allowed researchers during the contentious eighteenth-century debates on epigenesis to observe generation (most notably in the figure of the hen's egg), the entoptic apparatus was itself generative, a generativity that depended upon a torsional aspect of turning and returning light. In this, it was remarkably similar to another early nineteenth-century instrument, the kaleidoscope, invented by David Brewster. As Brewster described his invention, 'The fundamental principle of the Kaleidoscope is that it produces symmetrical and beautiful pictures, by converting simple into compound or beautiful forms, and arranging them, by successive reflections, into one perfect whole.'[36]

Like the kaleidoscope, the entoptic apparatus did not reveal something hidden in Nature, but brought it forth through a compound process of successive turns. Only in conjunction with one another in a serial process of revolutions would such transparent bodies reveal the relational chromatic forms that resided within them.

Only through such turning and returning could we see within, what Goethe notably called the 'lines of restraint' or 'Hemmungslinien' that resided within tempered pieces of glass.[37]

In his translation of Byron's *Manfred*, Goethe would write, 'im Leben ist nichts Gegenwart' – 'in life there is no present'.

Goethe's imagination was not a microscope or a stethoscope, but a kaleidoscope.

Before we reach the end, I want to say a word about the puzzling ending of *Faust* itself, because, for the last few decades of his life, long before he finished the poem, we find Goethe meditating, changing, mulling over, not only the poem, but the great themes which colour it. The sage was always on the move, and the old man encountered in the Frauenplan was not the same as the Storm and Stress novelist of Strasbourg days, nor the Privy Councillor of the earlier Weimar days, nor the incognito tourist of Italy, nor even the man first hitched to Christiane. These earlier selves all morphed into the mistier, more benign figure of his maturity.

When we have recovered from the mind-blast of Mahler's Eighth Symphony and its high Catholic interpretation of the ending of *Faust Part Two*, are we any closer to understanding what it means, or, slightly different question, what Goethe wanted us to think it means?

It is probably true to say that every person reading *Faust* for the first time, if they do not know how it ends, will be surprised by Goethe's ending. The angels snatch Faust's soul from the grasp of Mephistopheles. A chorus of Blessed Boys welcome Faust as a fitting teacher.[38] One commentator donnishly, but pertinently noted, 'It is with some concern for the celestial peace of the blessed children that one contemplates the possible substance and manner of his instruction.'[39]

Many readers would echo the opinion of Thomas Davidson, an American 'Transcendentalist' follower of Emerson, who, having devoted a lifetime to the study of Goethe and knowing *Faust* almost by heart, concluded that '*Faust* is a distinct failure. Its conclusion is utterly lame, and in no sense the logical or even the aesthetic outcome of the action of the play.'[40] This high-minded American of the very earliest years of the twentieth century was dismayed by Goethe's use of Catholic imagery, which appears to endorse a 'medieval' and 'institutional' vision of Christianity, which Protestantism had firmly put aside. Of Goethe he wrote contemptuously, 'He saw no way of bringing man to redemption except by falling back upon the Catholic doctrine of grace, thus finally reducing his work, viewed as a whole, to an absurdity.'[41]

A century and more later, a professor of German at Illinois State University, J. M. van der Laan, argues, '*Faust* makes sense for us, if on the one hand the protagonist is punished for his evil deeds. Likewise, the play makes sense to us, if, on the other hand, the hero is rewarded for his accomplishments. It does not make sense, however, if Faust is not damned but saved, albeit not by anything he has done or accomplished, but by an all-transcending grace.'[42] Van der Laan continues, 'Goethe offers a finale strongly reminiscent of Pauline, Augustinian and Lutheran, in short, Reformation theology, but stripped of its Christian content.'[43]

At the end, Gretchen appears, to tell us that Faust is not yet able to understand the bright morning which awaits him beyond the grave. We are more or less in the world of Dante's *Paradiso*. And the Blessed Virgin Mary tells Gretchen, 'Come, raise yourself up to a higher sphere!/As he begins to guess your meaning, he will follow after.'[44]

You can see why many of Goethe's most devoted admirers will, at this point, be squeezing their way through the crowds of disappointed punters to the box office in the foyer, and demanding their money back. Among them, we see the Nazis, who wanted Faust to be an *Übermensch* who had overcome everything by striving, and being dismayed to discover that Faust can only be redeemed by love. We see the materialist atheists – of Goethe's day down to our own times – disappointed to find that Faust, who, when he heard the Easter hymn in his dusty study, pronounced his ability to hear the messenger but his inability to believe, was now being carried away on clouds of sentimental Catholic piety. More or less anyone who had hoped for a single, unambiguous 'message' from *Faust* was going to be disappointed, and that perhaps includes most of the readers of this book.

I am not of their number. The plot of *Faust* makes no sense if you cannot conceive, *even for dramatic purposes only*, that there is a life beyond the grave. There are moments, especially when Faust makes his bargain with Mephistopheles, where it would appear that he is so cynical, and so despondent, that he does not really believe that he has a soul to sell, or to betray, or to offer as a bargaining chip. But, equally, there are many moments in the drama, especially in his monologues, where this gloomy, pessimistic, suicidal Faust is replaced by another, transported by the mystery and beauty of Nature, of light, of colour, or shaken by the profundities of love to which he is ever unfaithful. The older Goethe, in particular, shared with Plotinus, with Plato, the sense that human beings are immortal souls. It is entirely fitting that Faust should be wafted into a kind of emblematic Heaven at the end.

Anyone who wants to pin Goethe down, when it comes to finding out his religious opinions, is going to have a frustrating time. Remember (in Chapter 13) his conversation in 1805 with F. Weitze, about his son's confirmation by Herder:

> Light and Darkness, Good and Evil, in mixture and in conflict, in humankind, these were the foundations. Then followed the teaching about human freedom and morality, both how to define it, and its helpfulness to us. From here sprang, and was demonstrated, the necessity of redemption, of blessing. And these as demonstrated in the person of Jesus. What really pleased me was everything was so well explained to the confirmation candidates.[45]

Goethe made no secret of his own inability to accept the orthodox Christian faith, though in old age he moved very close to it, with his discovery of the little-known eclectic sect living in fourth-century Cappadocia, the Hypsistarians, who followed a blend of Christianity, Neoplatonism, Judaism and bits of wisdom culled from elsewhere. Steeped as he was, by this stage of his life, in Persian poetry, and what Chinese and Indian philosophy as was available to Western readers, Goethe would have had no difficulty at all in saying that our apprehension of the divine was not something which we needed to project into an imagined afterlife. It was discernible now, through our experience of Nature, of Love, of contemplation.

The final gnomic verse is something which is surely meant, by Goethe, to be a key to the whole:

> All that is transitory
> Is just a Parable;
> The unattainable

Is realized HERE:
The Indescribable
Is accomplished HERE:
The Eternal Feminine
Leads us upwards.[46]

Our professor of Illinois State University, J. M. van der Laan, says that this is the 'first and only time' that the Eternal Feminine has been mentioned.[47] True, it is the first time that Goethe introduces the coinage *das Ewigweibliche*. But surely it has been present as an idea from the very beginning. It is the golden thread running through the entire tapestry, not only of *Faust* but of Goethe's collected life work. For a start, it means the 'feminine' as opposed to the dry materialism of the Enlightenment: it means an intuitive response to natural science, as to life itself. It means Yin as well as Yang. It means both hemispheres of the brain activity. It means creative, organic Nature, not a Leibniz- or Newton-manufactured toy train set of a universe.

It also means absorbing and making central to our life-experience the fact of love, which includes sexual feeling, but also the mysterious fact of love, as recorded in more or less every human life. David Hume and the other ultra-sceptics of the Enlightenment wanted to make sense-impression the only truly reliable guide to verifiable epistemology. Unless you had felt with your hands or seen with your eyes you could not find any criterion by which you could say a phenomenon was true or false. But, *precisely on a level of experienced phenomenon*, this is too limited a definition. When we fall in love, we are carried into a palpably new area of experience. Hume and friends might say that this is an area where nothing can be defined, nothing can be proved, so that it is an area of life which must be discounted when we are saying that something is or is not the case. But the experience of love belongs to the world which is the case. So, incidentally, does the language of music which, again, is not satisfactorily described or 'explained' in purely materialist terms. All this, surely, is contained in the phrase *das Ewigweibliche*.

We come across the word when we have read, in *Part One*, the clumsy, inexperienced intellectual, blundering into a sexual relationship and getting it all hopelessly, criminally wrong. But, Gretchen insists at the end of *Part Two*, what led him to love her, and to fancy her, in the initial stages was an impulse which connected in some mysterious way with the love which moves the sun and other stars. The central action of *Part Two*, after the pageant of the Classical Walpurgis Night, has been the summoning up of Helen of Troy, the emblematic, distilled figure not only of Hellenic civilization, but also of the Feminine. Faust, the north European theorist, mates with Helen, the embodiment of all that the Greeks gave the world, including their mythology and their erotic dance and poetry, and produces Euphorion, Poetry. It seems paradoxical to believe that we have not been introduced to the concept of an Eternal Feminine until the last page.

As for whether we are meant to suppose that Faust goes to Heaven at the end ... This, again, misses the entire point of Goethe's way of looking at experience. Everything before death is, potentially, something which a human being could experience, and hence describe. By definition, this is not true of death. We can use language to describe the death of others, but not our own death, or our own experience of death. This means that any language we use about death and beyond-death is mythological; is 'only a parable' – *nür ein Gleichnis*. That is just as true of statements expressing scepticism about a future life as it is of Plato's *Phaedo* or the Gospel of St John.

The only way in which life after death could be spoken about is in a different order of language from that which describes life before death. Hence Goethe's *Gleichnis*, parable, metaphor. When he told the clergyman that he had found help and meaning in Herder's confirmation classes, I do not think Goethe was being hypocritical or unnecessarily 'polite'. I think that, as a conservative member of the government in Weimar, who had heard of the guillotines erected in Paris by the same people who converted Notre Dame cathedral into a Temple of Reason, he would have urged anyone to think twice before discarding Christianity altogether. He was dismayed by the Tübingen theologians who wanted to 'demythologize' the New Testament. Strictly orthodox Christians might dislike his reasoning – namely that the Gospels, and the entire New Testament, are a sort of mythology or poem by which Europe had been living, or mapping its understanding of the universe for two thousand years. His rejection of the *Herrnhuter*, the Holy Rollers, did not mean that at any stage of his life, and particularly not towards its close, did he want to reject Christianity in its entirety. What Goethe saw, and what the

Catholic faithful saw, when a crowd assembled beside a statue of the Virgin to recite the rosary, might have been very different things. Or not? The Eternal Feminine leads us upwards. The salvation of Faust is achieved not, as he had supposed throughout the poem, by his striving, but by love. 'The Lord', in the Prologue in Heaven, had already warned the devil that 'So long as he devotes himself to striving, the human being is making a mistake' – *Es irrt der Mensch, solang' er strebt*.[48] The devil, of course, does not hear or understand, but, by the end of the poem the reader does. The salvation of Faust comes about as a result of, not in spite of, his divided self, his carnality, his catastrophic moral failings. Though he does not believe in the Easter embassy, or message, he hears it, and understands it. The template of Christianity is still useable even for the person who does not identify as a fundamentalist.

15

ECKERMANN

If one leaves aside Goethe's own writing, and especially Goethe's
Conversations with Eckermann, *the best German book in*
existence, what really remains of German prose literature that is
actually worth reading and rereading?
                    Friedrich Nietzsche, *Human, All Too Human,* II

At the end of the summer of 1823, Goethe's was an unfinished life
and his masterpieces – the autobiography, *Poetry and Truth,* his
imperfect, but great, novel *Wilhelm Meister,* and above all, his *Faust*
– remained unfinished masterpieces. He could finish short lyrics and
short works of fiction, but the great things he had to say, in expansive
forms – whether they were scientific texts, or ... how do we continue
to define *Faust*? By now, as a philosophical Oratorio? – were almost
by definition unfinishable, and his life, like any human life, was a
tangled skein of loose ends.

This was all about to change. He was going to be edited, so that his
life would be seen, not as any human life, but as something finished and
exemplary. During the very years that Eckermann would set to work,
writing down 'the best book in German' (according to Nietzsche),
the German biblical exegetes were demolishing the Historical Christ.
David Friedrich Strauss's *Life of Jesus* was published in 1835–6 (to
be translated into English by George Eliot with tears streaming down
her cheeks as the demythologized Jesus emerged from its pages and
she realized that her faith was gone). Human beings require their

saving illusions, and Goethe, the incarnation of Enlightened European Culture, Scientist, Poet, Napoleonist, Good German, could, with very little distortion, become what the educated nineteenth century required. Carlyle's cry of 'Close thy Byron, open thy Goethe!' was the watchword for many nineteenth-century readers, and not just the intellectuals.

His autobiography would be crafted, polished, written, published; so, too, would his alternative autobiography, the road untravelled which was *Wilhelm Meister*, his deepest, most loveable prose work. As for *Faust*, how could it be finished? It was not even clear to its author, let alone any possible reader, how its various strands would add up. Only an editor with a clearer sense than Goethe had himself of who he was and what his literary intentions might have been at the various stages of the poem's composition could have forced him, cajoled him, flattered him, into continuing with the project; moreover, such an editor had to be the perfect combination, or cocktail, of comprehension and stupidity. He (or she) must understand and not understand: he must be the Wagner to Faust. Wagner, that is, the harmless drudge, the famulus, the factotum who thinks, when his master is crying out in existential despair, that he is entertaining himself by quoting from the Greek tragedies.

But there was also, as there had always been, the fact that Goethe's greatest work of art was Goethe himself. The perfect midwife for the works – with the qualities of diligence, boundless sycophancy, obedience but also the courage to nag, to cajole – must also have a sense of how Goethe would be if he could become that impossible thing, a finished, or fully edited human life, *ein vollendeter Mensch*. This would be a formidable undertaking when trying to 'edit' any human life. Had not the whole eschatological world-picture been, since post-classical Europe began to see life through the prism of the Christian Bible, of a book which would be opened on the Last Day, and those virtuous or praiseworthy elements in a human character be weighed against the false turns, the lapses, the basenesses, the failures to live up to what could have been attained? The Christian Bible saw the eternal destiny of all human souls as something which would be found written in a book.

'The Lord', in the Prologue in Heaven, in what would become a mantra for the nineteenth-century liberal Protestant hunger for the virtuous life, had implied that the *vollendete Mensch* was not a possibility this side of Judgement Day; but that

A good man, though he has dark urges
Is fully aware of the right course he should follow.[1]

Finished, or fragmentary, the message of *Faust* to the planet would surely be that our strivings after virtue will always be handicapped by our selfishness, carnality, hunger for power, enjoyment of power games; our wild lust for wickedness always shocked into the memory of that serene, serious spirit-world, the *Geisterreich*, where behaviour is not tortured by conscience.

Since his teens, Goethe had impressed those who met him by his fluency, his capacity to feel at home with any subject, his brilliance as a conversationalist, and there were many who had recorded his conversations in snatches, just as his dozens of correspondents had caught the flavour of his utterances on paper.

But now, in that summer of 1823, a thirty-one-year-old poet, largely self-taught, poverty-stricken, dusty and sweaty, completed his journey to the centre of Weimar, and looked up at the object of his journey, the rambly old house in the Frauenplan. This was Johann Peter Eckermann (1792–1854).

It had been a broiling week's walk, 150 kilometres in the sweltering June sunshine, along the dusty roads from Göttingen, where he had briefly studied at the university and subsequently earned a living as a hack teacher. He had been born into poverty at Winsen an der Luhe and until he was fourteen had had little education, being compelled to accompany an elderly father on local expeditions peddling woollen stockings.[2] A talent for drawing manifested itself but his parents had resisted him going to study art in Hamburg. He worked hard at school after he was fourteen and became a local government clerk in Bevensen, Westphalia, until the French invasions. He was still nursing the ambition to become a painter in the manner of the great seventeenth-century Dutch interiors. In a sense, this was what he was to achieve in literature, since his *Conversations with Goethe*, the huge proportion of which happen indoors, in Goethe's house, have much of the cool light of Vermeer; the after-dinner reflections of the widest of subjects – science, Greek drama, politics, the future of the planet, both economic and environmental, religion, as well as anecdotes and recollections of the old man's life and times – take place in the calm atmosphere of an interior by Pieter de Hooch. Such scenes as the one with which this book began – a petulant, silly old Goethe, self-importantly furious that they should go behind his back to stage a production of *Faust* – this 'human, all too human' side of Goethe – has been rigorously edited out of the *Conversations*, comparable to the way, it might be safe to conclude, Xenophon and Plato 'edited' their memories of Socrates. Eckermann alludes to the mood swings, but not to the alcoholism which was their origin. The often embarrassing behaviour with young women – 'crushes' rather than groping or worse – are represented as decorative outbursts of romanticism.

The war interrupted Eckermann's hopes of becoming a painter or – an ambition which was growing in him as a teenager – a poet. (He was chiefly inspired by the ballads of Schiller and the poetry of Körner. And, of course, Klopstock.) To do his bit against Napoleon, he joined the Kielmannseggeschen Jaegerkorps, the so-called Hunting Corps named after its leader Friedrich von Kielmannsegg, and trekked through Hamburg and eventually to Brabant. Military duty notwithstanding, he took the opportunity to see the Dutch Masters he had hitherto only enjoyed in copperplate engravings.

When the war ended, he returned to literature, and to teaching, in order to eke out a very modest living. By the time he was twenty-three he had decided to become a poet, and that was when he discovered that a lyric which had begun to haunt his mind and ear, 'Da droben auf jenem Berge', was written not by one of his existent heroes but by Goethe. In fact, the lyric, based on a folk song, is:

> Up there on that mountain
> I have stood a thousand times,
> Leaned on my staff
> And looked down into the valley.[3]

Simple stuff, and hardly, among his early lyrics, the best thing Goethe ever wrote. But Eckermann went on to devour Goethe's published lyrics. He read *Faust A Fragment*. He read the published volumes of *Wilhelm Meister*. 'Amazement and love increased by the day.'[4]

The poem he wrote in appreciation of his new-found hero is in the manner of a Lutheran hymn-lyric (Eckermann had been confirmed in the Protestant Church at sixteen) and even among the least cynical of readers must occasion a smile.

> So, too, I had the strong desire
> To brag of you, Master, as My One,
> And I searched in my mind how to bring this about
> Without actually naming you 'High One'.[5]

Disraeli, in attempting to shed light upon the close bond he formed with Queen Victoria, explained that when flattering royalty one should lay it on with a trowel. The advice would not have come amiss, half a century earlier, when approaching the shrine at Weimar. On this first attempt – in 1821 – however, Goethe put Eckermann off and thanked him – in a letter dictated to a secretary and sent from Jena.

Two years later, however, and the time was right. Not only had Eckermann by then put together a collection of his own, fairly pedestrian lyrics (not all of them paeans of praise to Goethe), he had also written a defence, in prose this time, of Goethe against his more hostile critics: *Beiträge zur Poesie mit besonderer Hinweisung auf Goethe* – 'Essays on poetry with particular reference to Goethe'. When Goethe read this, he was moved to send both the poems and the essay to Cotta, his publisher, and suggest that the works of this promising young individual be made available to the public.

When the manuscript of Eckermann's *Beiträge* arrived on Goethe's desk, the poet was engaged in the tedious task of sifting his abundant Juvenilia, deciding which poems were suitable for inclusion in his Collected Works. Cotta, who was eagerly waiting to publish the final volume, wanted to get these poems into print as soon as possible. Goethe was reluctant, and the more he read of his early work, the more he discovered that he had grown away from his youthful Storm and Stress self. The task would be better left to someone else. Goethe needed a 'harmless drudge', but he also needed one with literary discernment, and as anyone reading *Beiträge* would recognize at once, Eckermann had steeped himself in Goethe's style. The prose manner is almost parodic.

For some time Goethe had been considering employing one of two pioneers of Goethe criticism, Zauper, a Pilsen teacher, and Schubarth, a Berlin private tutor, but something made him hold back. When

Eckermann actually arrived at the house in the Frauenplan, it was the perfect opportunity to harness his talents.

He did not engage Eckermann as a secretary, but he arranged for the young man to be paid a modest fee by Cotta to get the Juvenilia into a publishable state. Whether by lucky accident or by Goethe's intuition, Eckermann was therefore, from the first, not engaged as an underling, as, for example Professor Riemer so humiliatingly had been. He came, at first, as one who was not in Goethe's employ at all, and for his initial visit to Weimar he did not stay long. He saw Goethe between 10 and 19 June 1823, and then travelled to Jena, where Goethe gave him letters of introduction to various friends. When Goethe returned from taking the waters at Marienbad, he repaired to Jena, where he met Eckermann again (15 September 1823) and the great man uttered the stirring words, 'I'll undertake to find you lodgings near me. You'll have a whole winter with not an insignificant moment.'

Their great collaboration had begun.

You would think – and, indeed, Eckermann probably did think – that, by attaching himself like a limpet to the Sage of Weimar in 1823, when Goethe was seventy-four, he was merely going to arrange a grand Retrospective Exhibition. In fact – almost the most remarkable single fact about Goethe – Eckermann had found a phenomenon who, in his eighth decade, was coming to the very height of his powers. Goethe was one of those rare beings, such as Titian or Verdi, whose genius blazed in a red-golden sunset at the end of a long life. Behind him was the whole rich existence of creativity and scholarship, and of life-experience. But he was now, by a supreme effort of will and a recovery of youthful energy within his creaking, elderly frame, on the verge of finishing *Faust*: and, by finishing it, changing the perspectives and meanings of what had already been written. For, *Faust* was, strange as it all is, to be seen as a whole, and by completing *Part Two*, he entirely altered the perspectives by which we read *Part One*. Mephistopheles's scornful, randy suggestion, in the Witch's Kitchen, that from henceforth Faust would see Helen of Troy in every woman is to be transformed into something beautiful and strange. 'Eckermann, the companion of his old age, was to be the witness of a huge, powerful cycle.'[6]

'One must be young to do great things!' Goethe exclaimed one day when he had known Eckermann five years – 2 March 1828. Napoleon was at his most brilliant in youth. 'It should mean something when someone of obscure origins, and in a time which put all capacities into confusion, had so forced himself forward, in his twenty-seventh year, as to become a demigod for a nation of thirty million people!'

In this conversation, Goethe appeared to be all on the side of youth. Were he a prince, he declared, he would never promote to positions of authority old duffers who had been born into a position of privilege. He would, rather, choose men of high capability, young men of the best will and noblest character. He went on to say that it was a mistake to think that an early death necessarily cuts young genius short. Every exceptional man has a particular mission to fulfil. When he has accomplished what he came to earth to do, then it is time for him to go.[7] Mozart died in his thirty-sixth year, Raphael at the same age, Byron – more of him in a moment – only a little older.

It might seem from this particular utterance as if Goethe was writing off his old-age self, and asking to be judged solely on his achievements in youth, when his Duke did indeed hire him, and when he had already written *Götz* and *Werther*, two books which had taken Germany – then Europe – by storm. But we read the passage again and find that what he is saying is rather different. A man does not leave the stage until he has accomplished his destiny. Mozart, Raphael et al. could die young because their best work was done.[8] And it was clear that, although he was approaching the age of eighty when he said the words, the destiny of the author of *Faust* had not yet been fulfilled.

Goethe had created himself, over and over. Behind the wild Storm and Stress poet and the morally anarchic author of *Werther* there had always lurked the competent administrator, the well-trained constitutional lawyer who was ideally placed to become the Privy Councillor of Weimar. Behind the Privy Councillor, there was the scientist. Behind the besotted platonic lover of Charlotte von Stein there was the libidinous bisexual longing for adventures. Behind the free wanderer among the ruins and painters of Rome, there was a man longing for domesticity in Weimar. And all these images fed into his multitudinous works.

He was careful, always, to destroy or edit versions of the self that displeased him – witness the great auto-da-fé of 1797 when so much of his childhood and young manhood was consigned to the bonfire.

Images of self had been frozen, changed, sculpted in *Poetry and Truth*, in the fiction, in the lyrics and poems, and in a different way in *Faust*. He had also kept up a stream of alternative selves created in his letters. But in the conversations with Eckermann a new man would be born. And although we must assume that Nietzsche was joking – or sort of joking – when he said that Eckermann's *Conversations* were the best book in the German language, he was – sort of – right. If you belong to this school of thought, the accuracy of Eckermann – whether Goethe did or did not actually say the words attributed to him in the *Conversations* – becomes only partially relevant.

Of course, those who recognized what Eckermann was 'up to' have never been slow to diminish his achievement. Heine, for example:

> In Weimar, the widowers of the Muses are found
> And I hear there the voice of much grieving:
> There's weeping and wailing, for Goethe is dead –
> And Eckermann's carried on living.[9]

Eighteen twenty-three had been a dramatic year: so dramatic, that, in a way, the arrival of Eckermann in Goethe's life was not recognized as especially momentous. In February, he had suffered a serious infection of the pericardium and nearly died. He lost consciousness several times, and was suffering from sharp abdominal pains. 'Death lurks around me in every corner. Oh, you Christian God, how much suffering you heap on your poor people, and yet we are supposed to extol you and praise you for it in your temples!'[10]

When he recovered, in defiance of the Christian God, and of his doctors' expectations, there was a special celebratory performance of *Torquato Tasso* at the Court Theatre. He was determined to live, but the near-death experience had sharpened the sense of what he was to live for.

Goethe had, for a long time, even while his wife was alive, been away from home a great deal. Especially during the Schiller friendship, he had spent weeks, months, at a stretch at Jena. And the summer was given over to restorative visits to spas. Life at the house in the Frauenplan was not happy. The marital rows of the young couple upstairs, August and

Ottilie, were so loud that he could hear their voices coming through the ceiling. August was unable to control his drinking.

The summer routine of leaving Weimar and taking the waters in spa towns had, of late, been varied. Rather than Carlsbad and Teplitz, he had begun to visit the new spa of Marienbad, in Bohemia, present-day Czech Republic. He first saw it in 1820 when it was still being built. 'I felt as if I was in the forests of North America, where they build a whole city in three years.'[11]

The estate on which the spa was being built belonged to Friedrich Leberecht von Brösigke. He had built it with funds from a silent partner, Count Klebelsberg, who was hoping to marry Brösigke's daughter Amalie von Levetzow. She had already been married twice; first, aged fifteen, to the man by whose name she was known. By him, she bore two daughters. Then, when he had deserted her, to his cousin, who had gambled away her money and then been killed at the Battle of Waterloo. Goethe had met her when she was a teenager and his private name for her was Pandora, a figure for opening a box of trouble. The years had passed, and now, in Marienbad, her eldest daughter, Ulrike, was about the age that Pandora had been when she first caught Goethe's fancy at Teplitz in 1810. He would tell Ulrike that her mother had been 'a bright star, so happily remembered, on my early horizon'.[12]

When he first met Ulrike, she had just returned from Strasbourg where she was a pupil at a girls' boarding school. It was observed, during their first summer together, that the old man was flirtatious and playful, and he would write to her at the beginning of '23 – as he anticipated their meeting again in the summer – praising her 'daughterly disposition' towards him.

But then came the illness of February, and life seemed almost to have been snatched from him before he was ready for death. Apart from the three great works – *Wilhelm Meister*, *Poetry and Truth* and *Faust* – being unfinished, there was surely space in his widower's existence for one last *grande passion*? An obvious recipient of such devotion was the Polish composer and pianist Madame Maria Szymanowska. He heard her play at Marienbad and was enchanted. The pair took walks together in the park. She was divorced, unattached, dazzlingly beautiful. Her own compositions, notably *Le Murmure*, were dreamily romantic. In a letter to Zelter, he said he had not listened to music for over two years. He felt that his fist had been clenched and that the palm was opening. He felt the power of her music – 'suddenly and at the hands of great talent this heavenly thing descends upon us and exercises over us its whole power'.[13] Typically, the consequence of this was that music awakened memories.

But although Maria Szymanowska and her piano playing transported him, he was not truly in love. Did he remember the blinding moment in the first part of *Faust* when the mage passes the innocent young girl in the street and reassures himself that it is proper to pursue her because she is, at least, over the age of fourteen?

Ulrike! She was the *tabula rasa* on which Goethe could write his last love story. But we would be mistaken were we to think that Goethe's passion for Ulrike was purely *voulu*, no more than affectation which allowed him to versify, even in old age, about love. To the most extreme degree, Goethe was what the Victorians called 'susceptible'. He had a tendency to fall passionately in love, and in the Last Attachment, Ulrike, we see the phenomenon working as strongly as it had done when he was a very young man in Strasbourg and his violent crushes, first on Frederika, then on Lotte Buff – had inspired some of his best early work: the lyric 'Willkommen und Abschied' and, of course, *The Sorrows of Young Werther*. Both, in turn, look forward to some of the most haunting passages of *Faust*, and to its culmination, its hymns to the Eternal Feminine.

This is surely the aspect of Goethe's work which is both most absurd and most accessible: easiest to mock and easiest to identify with our contemporary culture. Almost every successful lyric in contemporary popular music for the last fifty or a hundred years has, after all, taken as its subject this peculiar phenomenon – falling in love. It arose as a great theme in European literature with the Provençal troubadours, gradually coming to rival, and in many places and cultures to supplant, the epic themes of war and heroism, death and fate, as Western poetry's chief preoccupation. It is clearly related to our sexual appetites, but it is not something which evolutionary theory can satisfactorily explain: since we do not always fall in love with those we find physically most attractive, and it is possible to feel the most intense love for individuals who are not accessible, or not immediately accessible. That is to say, while sexual desire for the Beloved is part of the sensation, it is by no means all of it. Evolution, and the breeding of the species, would get along perfectly cheerfully without love. There are those, perhaps they are very many, who have never actually experienced what poets and songwriters mean when they sing of falling in love. One could even go so far as to wonder whether the majority of those who 'fall in love' would have done so had not pop music persistently suggested it to them.

'The Trilogy of Passion' is one of the most painful and most beautiful poems that Goethe ever wrote on this theme, and the trilogy draws on, meditates on, this most extraordinary phenomenon, which we must assume is one of the features which separates us from our fellow mammals. Cole Porter was surely wrong, and Pekineses at the Ritz might fall in lust, but they do *not* fall in love. Sentient beings who do not read, write, or listen to lyrics being sung, do not fall in love. How much *we* do so in imitation of art, and how much it is an in-born faculty, who knows?[14]

The first lyric in the trilogy was the last (1824) to be written and is about Werther. The third concerns his love for Madame Szymanowska – *Das Doppel-Glück der Töne wie der Liebe*, the double-joy of love and of music combined. But the great central lyric of the trilogy – entitled 'Elegy' – is about his feelings for Ulrike. By the end of the summer of 1823, his feelings for the girl were out of control. When she first met him, she was still a schoolgirl. She had never read a word he had written and as far as she was concerned he was the distinguished old Privy Councillor, a friend of her grandfather. He was seventy-three, she was seventeen.

One of the many things which gives the relationship its extreme poignancy is that Ulrike lived so long – until 1899 when she was ninety-five. In an age when there were telephones, motor cars, machine guns, iron-clad battleships, she looked back to a period just before photography, to a man who had been born in the era when witches were still being hanged and the Holy Roman Emperor was still crowned in Frankfurt in a crown allegedly belonging to Charlemagne. Her long pilgrimage straddled such utterly different worlds. The old lady – who had never married – insisted that she had never regarded Goethe as anything but a grandfather figure, and when she was told that he wanted to marry her, she had regarded it as a joke – as had all her family.

He was in such deadly earnest that he could not bring himself to put the matter into his own mouth or his own words. Grand Duke

Carl August was in Marienbad for the summer and Goethe persuaded him to approach 'Pandora' on his behalf, and ask for the girl's hand in marriage. It was a totally serious offer. In old age, Ulrike said that one reason for her turning down the proposal was that she did not want to disrupt Goethe's son and daughter-in-law, resident in the Frauenplan. Carl August, however, had promised to give Ulrike and Goethe a different house in Weimar, luxuriously appointed. Knowing that her aged husband could not long remain in this world, the Grand Duke offered her a pension, when widowed, of over 10,000 talers per year. There would be no necessity to separate from her family, who would all be welcome to come and live in Weimar. Given his common sense, Carl August must have found it difficult to make these suggestions without feeling that the situation was ridiculous; but it was a token of his deep fondness for Goethe – the differences over Napoleon notwithstanding – as well as his reliance on the wisdom of the Privy Councillor. Perhaps he also feared losing face, should Goethe's marriage proposal be accepted and he decided to go and live somewhere else with his young bride.

Of course, she turned him down. It was a bitter blow to Goethe, and he reacted, not with the haughty pride which he might have displayed when having a row with actors and impresarios about the staging of *Faust*, but with the broken, heart-torn despair of a young lover. All the way home to Weimar in the carriage, he wept and he scribbled. The poem says that he had believed he had lost his capacity for love and for falling in love. Ulrike had revived in him, after his near-deadly illness in the spring, a capacity to hope, to make plans for the future. He compared what she had brought to him with the peace of God which passeth all understanding.

In the purity of our bosom springs a striving (always that Goethean word, striving, which 'the Lord' in Heaven, before the play begins, says is so pointless! – a striving towards something higher, purer, unknown – to give ourselves to another without reserve and to unpick the riddle of the eternally Unknown).

With her refusal, life had lost its point.

Mir ist das All, ich bin mir selbst verloren.

It is one of his most despondent lines: 'I have lost myself, I have lost everything.' When he got home, he relapsed into the symptoms which seemed to be killing him back in February – coughing, fevers, inflammation around his heart. He could not work.

It was at this low point in his life that the young Eckermann, who had returned from his summer break, resurfaced. They met in Jena, and Goethe spoke those lines which were to lead to the great conversation book: 'I want you to spend the winter with me in Weimar.' There are moments, during the first November after Eckermann's return, where it seems as if he is going to lose his hero. By December, however, his spirits and strength had revived. There is more than a suggestion that, in the sadness and loneliness of his illness, Goethe had once again confronted the mystery of things. As the Pariah says to Great Brahma in one of his strangely haunting lyrics:

Wendet euch zu dieser Frauen
Die der Schmerz zur Göttin wandelt!
Turn your thoughts to this woman
Whom pain has transformed into a goddess.[15]

The Ulrike experience shows us that, although to the Levetzows, and certainly to the younger members of the family, Goethe was the distinguished old statesman in a frock coat, inside he was still the cauldron of conflicting emotions of Storm and Stress who had created *Werther*. He was the Aeolian harp through which the gusts of passion played their threnody. The fragile frame at eve was shaken with throbbings of noon-tide.[16]

––––––

Goethe was yet to complete his autobiography, and it was probably already clear to him that *Poetry and Truth* would end with his arrival as a young man at Weimar. On 27 January 1824, Eckermann spoke with Goethe about the continuation of the memoirs beyond this point. By now, the painful summer at Marienbad had become, like so much in his life, a metaphor.

When I look back on my earlier life and middle years, and now think of my old age, and realize how few people are left who were young with me, I think of a summer residence at a spa town. When

313

one arrives, one makes friends with those who have already been there for a while, and who are going to leave in a few weeks. The loss is painful. But then, now one attaches oneself to the next generation with which you live for quite a while, and you become really intimate with them. But then, this lot goes too, and leaves us alone with a third, which arrives just as we are leaving, and with whom we really have nothing to do.[17]

There was a sense in which, with the constant stream of visitors to his house in Weimar, Goethe was in the perpetual condition of a holidaymaker, who says farewell to friendships as soon as they have been forged.

We have already quoted the conversation in which he said that a young life, cut short, could still be seen as completely fulfilled – Byron, for example, dying at the same sort of age as Mozart and Raphael and achieving his artistic prowess at about the age when Napoleon won his greatest battles, could be seen as the archetypical example of this. The conversation took place four years after Byron's death, an event which had a profound effect on the old poet.

When he showed Eckermann his 'Elegy' on leaving Ulrike behind in Marienbad, the younger man said he thought he could see the influence of Byron. Goethe conceded that this was the case.[18] Goethe admired Byron's 'Cain': 'The English clergy will not thank him, but it would surprise me if he did not go on to write about similar biblical subjects.'[19]

On another occasion Goethe said that for Byron the world was 'transparent'.[20] It is not entirely clear what he meant by this, but he was moving towards the idea, which is probably true of all great poets, that Byron's life was more than a parable of his times; it had a symbolic significance. Byron, he would aver, was only great when he wrote poetry. When he reflects, he is a child.[21]

It is remarkable how many of the conversations related to Lord Byron – 'That which I call invention [*Erfindung*] is, for me, to be found in no one in the whole world in greater profusion than in Byron.'[22]

Goethe saw Byron's going to Greece, where he met his end at Missolonghi, as a sort of necessity. 'His lack of harmony with the world drove him to it.'[23] Goethe also meditated on Byron's capacity to be unlimited – 'Hang zum Unbegrenzten'[24] was both an essential part of his Romantic genius and his undoing.

Whether the reader agrees with Goethe's assessment of Byron is in some ways irrelevant. What the reader of *Faust Part Two* sees in these conversational reflections is the figure of Byron being gradually and imaginatively transformed into the figure of Euphorion, the love child of Faust and Helen of Troy.

'If it were still my job to preside over the theatre,' Goethe said, 'I'd bring Byron's Doge of Venice, Marino Faliero onto the stage.' As it happens, not long after he said these words, a devastating fire in the Court Theatre put paid to the possibility of staging any dramas there for some time. For Eckermann, it was an especial tragedy.

> You know how passionately I love the theatre. When I came here two years ago, apart from three or four plays which I'd seen in Hanover, I knew nothing at all. Everything was new to me – the actors, the plays; and since then, following your advice, I have given myself up entirely to the subject. Without thinking about it or meditating on it deeply, I have, during the last two winters, spent the most harmless and agreeable hours I have ever known in that theatre. I was so utterly stage-struck that, not only did I never miss a performance, I also managed to get into rehearsals. More than that, not content with going to rehearsals, if I ever passed the theatre in the daytime and found the doors open, I would go into the empty auditorium, and for half an hour I'd sit on a bench in the empty pit, envisaging the scenes which might be spent there.[25]

This made Goethe laughingly exclaim, 'You are a maniac – but that is what I like. Would to God that all the general public consisted of such children!'

So, it was a terrible evening, 22 March 1825, when they made the short walk to the theatre and found – from a blaze which had begun in the heating apparatus – an inferno, with sparks flickering high above the greedy flames against the blue-black of the night sky. Among those who watched the firefighters with their inadequate buckets and hosepipes was the disconsolate figure of Grand Duke Carl August himself, who – realizing there was no hope of saving the theatre – gave orders that they should let it burn, and be demolished. He could remember the same happening to the Schloss where he grew up, and he would pay for a new theatre to be erected immediately.

Goethe set to work designing the building. All the time, as he did so, his mind went back to the innumerable productions for which he had been responsible in the old building: his own plays, of course, and the masterpieces of Schiller, Shakespeare, Mozart operas and other contemporaries.

When he made his way back to his lodgings, which were very near the theatre, poor Eckermann could not resist wandering among the smouldering rubble, where he came across a few charred leaves of *Torquato Tasso*.

The theatre was rebuilt in remarkably short time – a matter of months – but the fire was a decisive moment for both Eckermann and Goethe. For, while it was being built, the performance of Goethe's set-piece conversations became ever more essential for the younger man to enjoy. Between them, they were composing dialogues to rival *Torquato Tasso* or *Iphigenia*: the drama of the *Conversations*.

An important ingredient in the composition of the book is that Eckermann had never been on a financial retainer with Goethe. He was always hard up during the last nine years of Goethe's life, and the *Conversations* were to be his pension, his bread ticket. Goethe inserted a clause in his will which assured Eckermann a percentage of the profits in the last volumes of *Ausgabe letzter Hand* (The Last Productions, the Final Edition), but having quarrelled with Privy Councillor von Müller, Eckermann was denied the honour of writing the Introduction to the work, even though the volume would never have appeared without his help and collaboration.

His nine years in Weimar passed through distinct phases. In the first, he was the simple drudge, discharging specific editorial functions and, whenever possible, hurrying home to his lodgings to transcribe the words of the master. Then, he developed into a much more collaborative figure, often discussing, as the *Conversations* make clear, the major works, especially *Faust Part Two*. During this phase, the *Conversations* came to be composed, in literary form. Having had time at the beginning to rush home and scribble down versions of the master's utterances, more and more he worked them up several days or even weeks after the words had been uttered, from scrappy diary entries, or from the letters which he wrote to his fiancée in Hanover. No one ever saw him taking notes while Goethe spoke, although, after the master had agreed that the *Conversations* should be made into a book, visitors would sometimes observe the absurdity of the great man turning to Eckermann and repeating some *obiter dictum* in a louder tone of voice, to make sure that it was preserved for posterity.[26] It was wisely said that 'It would seem that he intended Eckermann to bear witness for him beyond the grave – but certainly he did not intend to lay bare his soul to the public whilst he was still alive to experience any possible reaction.'[27]

The next stage of Eckermann's Weimar life was more difficult. He had quarrelled with Goethe's son, quarrelled with Müller, the most politically powerful man in the Goethe circle, and his love life was in a mess. He was having an affair with an actress at the theatre and it took up so much of his time and emotional energy that he somewhat lost touch with the house on the Frauenplan, even though it was only a matter of yards from his lodgings. (It is now an Italian restaurant, family-run, cheap and cheerful, and I wrote some of this chapter sitting at my table there.) One of the reasons why Eckermann's accounts of Goethe's death are so sketchy is that he was not around much during the last months and weeks of the great man's life. It was as though he had slipped out of the auditorium for some mundane reason and missed the sword fight with Laertes, the intentional poisoning of Gertrude and the last gasp of the Prince.

There would be a fourth phase, after the death of the poet. This was when Eckermann was working on *Ausgabe letzter Hand*, and on the first volume of the *Conversations*. He had made many enemies by the time the first volume of *Conversations* was published, so the vast *succès d'estime* which followed was not an uninterrupted joy. And he was dismayed to discover that, although all Germany devoured his book, the publisher, Brockhaus, diddled him, and he reaped no great reward financially from writing the best book in German. He fell into a series of psychosomatic illnesses and retreated to his native Hanover to escape the backbiters of Weimar. To some extent, he landed on his feet. Alexander von Humboldt intervened on his behalf and secured a generous pension from the King of Prussia. He took the third volume of *Conversations* away from the firm of Brockhaus, but published them in 1848, not a year when Europe was in a mood for the reflections of an old reactionary like Goethe.

It is sad for us – whatever view you take about the authenticity of the *Conversations* – that Eckermann never wrote the fourth, planned, volume, which was to contain his memories of Goethe's reflections on *Faust Part Two*. However inaccurate these might have been, one would value *any* light shed on the greatest, yet most baffling, of all Goethean texts. And Eckermann, whatever his faults, was not only the man who nagged Goethe to finish *Faust*, he was also very often the scribe who wrote it down. He was closer than anyone else to Goethe in this sunset phase of creativity.

Many of the conversations in the third volume were worked up from the diaries of Goethe's French translator, the Swiss amateur scientist Frédéric Jacob Soret (1795–1865) – who was an invaluable assistant to Goethe in editing his scientific treatises – and are not truly the work of Eckermann at all. Soret was of patrician birth. He had come to Weimar to be the tutor to the Crown Prince of Weimar (Carl August's grandson) and he was to become a firm friend of the poet, able to discuss science with him as an intellectual equal. It is a tribute to both Goethe and the Swiss that the friendship survived both Soret's republicanism and his total scepticism about the famous colour theory.

It is understandable, therefore, that Eckermann's three volumes were viewed by sneering scepticism, and, 101 years after his arrival in Weimar, he would receive the most severe of posthumous reviews. Julius Petersen's *Die Entstehung der Eckermannschen Gespräche ind ihre Glaubwürdigkeit* (The Composition of Eckermann's Conversations and their Believability), published in Berlin in 1924, was a thunderous indictment, doing for the text of Eckermann what Strauss, a hundred years before, had done for the Christian evangelists.

A well-balanced response to Petersen was put together thirty years later in English by Derek van Abbé,[28] and the interested should consult both texts, too long and detailed for a narrative of our kind. Van Abbé's generous-hearted and intelligent defence of Eckermann, while admitting that there are many passages which are, technically, inauthentic, usefully categorizes two types of invention. The first are those sayings which, while they might not have been said by Goethe in so many words, were the type of things he would have said. They correspond to other, authentic sayings, or to remarks made in his written work. In this class, one can include some of his remarks about the demonic, on Napoleon, on literary creativity.

The remarks which are palpable inventions, in the third volume, were written by Karl August Varnhagen von Ense (1785–1858) – conservative-minded biographer, man of letters, friend of the von Humboldts – who wanted Eckermann to underline Goethe's distaste for the young Romantics of the 1820s. The remarks which Eckermann places in his mouth denouncing their German nationalism need to be taken with a pinch of salt, though it seems perverse to doubt that Goethe probably *did* defend his pro-Napoleon stance during the war. Petersen, with many readers, doubted that Goethe made the remarks in defence of Christianity which Eckermann places into his mouth in Volume Three. (We'll return to this.) Petersen's scepticism deserves to be read, and to be borne in mind, just as the German biblical critics of the nineteenth century cannot, by any responsible student of the Scriptures, be ignored. But having been read, they need not be regarded as the last word. What remains, in the case of a scripture, whether it is the Bible or Eckermann, is the effect of the book as a whole. And the effect of reading Eckermann is joyous and elevating; and it would be crass, for all the book's probable inaccuracies and blemishes, not to see that it is a highly plausible, as well as profoundly delightful, book. Almost all biographical masterpieces, from Plato's Dialogues to Boswell's *Life of Johnson*, have had their gainsayers. We would be the poorer, nonetheless, if they did not exist. We do not meet here Goethe, the over-confident young literary lion who shocked staid little Weimar on his first arrival with his oafishness. We do not meet the lovelorn companion of Charlotte von Stein. We hear nothing of the libertine in Italy, with the mysterious little payments to women in inns.

Garrick, who had been a schoolboy literally looking through the keyhole as Samuel Johnson (his headmaster) made love to his wife in the bedroom, could share the comedy with Boswell. No such witness told Eckermann of the domestic life of Goethe with his bona-roba Christiane. And, although the enthusiast for Napoleon remains in these pages, the high-minded pan-European who, with so large a part of himself, was snooty about the German patriots, has been edited out of existence. But the old man who remembered these earlier selves is still there. So, too, is the man who, so recently visited by near-death experiences and the heartbreak of romantic love in Marienbad, found these peculiar visitations an occasion for an ever-cloudier sort of mysticism; the sense that we walk in mysteries and shadows was confirmed by his continuing scientific inquiries and his obsession with developments in contemporary science which, as other sources show, was very far from being Eckermann's invention.

Above all, the *Conversations* retain and record the general truth that Goethe's daily life was an intellectual exploration. They are faithful, for example, to the awestruck admiration Goethe felt for Alexander von Humboldt and his affection for both the Humboldt brothers. Alexander's desire to penetrate the heart of Nature's 'secret powers' was Faustian. His travels, both the vast extent of his geographical explorations in South America and Europe, and his intellectual journey, were a constant source of wonder to Goethe, and this is fed into both the *Conversations* and to *Faust*. When, on one of his trips to Weimar from Berlin, Alexander visited Goethe at the Frauenplan, Goethe's words to Eckermann are plainly a reflection of what the actual Goethe actually thought, and they reflect not only his deep admiration for the younger man, but also a sense of his own continuing intellectual quest:

> What a man he is! I've known him such a long time, and yet every time I meet him, I feel renewed astonishment. He has a knowledge, a living wisdom, which you could say was completely unequalled. I have never come across such many-sidedness! Whatever subject you touch upon, he is at home, and he generously lavishes upon his intellectual treasures. He is like a fountain with many pipes, under which you need only hold a vessel: refreshing and inexhaustible streams are forever flowing.[29]

No one reading Goethe, either in his own works, or in Eckermann, could fail to see that these words also apply to himself, but they reflect a true admiration, not only for the man Humboldt but also for the values he embodied – breadth, curiosity, devotion to research and to truth.

You get a sense of Goethe's intellectual penetration, as of Humboldt's geographical as well as personal breadth, when Eckermann found

Goethe reading Humboldt's accounts of his visits to Cuba and Colombia, and his reflections on Panama. It makes one think that both Humboldt and Goethe were not merely clever, but gifted with a prophetic sense, when one reflects that it was not until 1881 that the French began work on the Panama Canal, and that this work was then taken over in 1904 by the US and not finished until 1914.

> If they manage to cut such a canal, ships of any burden or size can be navigated through it from the Mexican Gulf to the Pacific Ocean. Innumerable benefits would result to the human race. But I'd be surprised if the United States allowed the chance of getting such work into their own hands to escape. One can foresee that this young state, with its marked predilection for the West, will, in thirty or forty years, have occupied the large tract of land beyond the Rockies. It can be seen, moreover, that along the whole Pacific coast, where nature has made the most capacious and secure harbours, important commercial towns will eventually arise for the furtherance of huge trade between the United States, China and the East Indies ... Would I might live to see it – but I shall not![30]

He foresaw the building of the canal as the establishment of the United States as a world power.

There was almost a consolation in the fact that when Carl August, now the Grand Duke, spent what were to be his last days in Berlin, he should have spent them in the company of Alexander von Humboldt. When the Grand Duke died in 1828, Humboldt wrote an account of his last conversations with Carl August, which he sent to Goethe. They had spoken of the granite brought from Sweden across the Baltic to German shores. They spoke of the recent comet, and whether it would affect the European ecosystem. They spoke of climate, and the cause of the extreme cold on the German east coast. When the Grand Duke had his heart attack in the palace at Potsdam, Humboldt sat for many hours beside his sofa discussing physics, astronomy, meteorology and thermodynamics. Towards the end of one such conversation, Carl August had murmured, on the edge of sleep, 'You see, Humboldt, it's all over with me.'

Eckermann noted, as Goethe conveyed all this, that there were tears in his eyes.[31] There are frequent moments in Eckermann where the poignancy of old age is conveyed. The sage is often vulnerable, gentle, nostalgic. There is a subtlety in Eckermann to which his detractors were wilfully blind, for, especially in the reminiscences about his closest friends, Goethe is providing him, and us, with a leisurely, conversational version of the autobiography which is so highly formalized in *Poetry and Truth*. Nowhere is this truer than in his memories of Schiller, which punctuate all three volumes. Whether they are walking in Weimar, or sitting on the stone bench in Jena where Schiller composed some of his greatest dramas, or rereading his letters, the golden decade of the friendship with Schiller is relit again and again.

It was twenty-one years after the former poet died that the most gruesome chapter in the history of Schiller and Goethe was enacted. Schiller had been buried in St James's Cemetery in Weimar. It was a hasty funeral. There was no money for anything fancy and, as Thomas Mann would put it, when describing the event in 1955, there was 'no mild sound of music, no word from the mouth either of priest or of friend'. The body was placed in what was in effect a mass grave. Charlotte Schiller intended to move her husband to a private grave at a later date, but never got round to doing so.

In 1826, Carl Leberecht Schwabe, Mayor of Weimar, decided that the playwright deserved a more hallowed final resting place. He obtained permission to open the grave. He found that the vault in which Schiller's body had been deposited had burst open, and the remains of other bodies had been mixed up with those of the playwright. Schwabe and the labourers who were engaged in this lugubrious task retched at the stench which was coming from the graves, and it was only by continually smoking, holding tobacco pipes between their teeth, that they could accomplish what they set out to do, grabbing what they took to be Schiller's skeleton from the 'chaos of rot and decay', together with the skulls and bones of between twenty-three and twenty-seven individuals and hastily refilling the grave with earth.

Schwabe laid out the skulls and decided that the man of genius must be the one with the largest cranium. Goethe, when he was taken to see the grisly collection, secretly purloined the skull of Schiller, and took it home, writing 'Lines on Seeing Schiller's Skull'. It was in 1827 that the skull, and the skeleton which Schwabe had placed alongside it, were removed to the ducal vaults, the Weimarer Fürstengruft: this was where Goethe himself was destined to lie.

It was in 1883 that the anatomist Hermann Welcker, comparing the supposed skull of Schiller with the death mask, pointed out that they could not possibly be the same man. The pious were furious, and insisted that the body in the Fürstengruft must be the author of 'Ode to Joy' and *Wallenstein*. A team of scientists in 1911 were enlisted to reopen the grave and to find a skull which matched. One was selected and, together with the old skull (whosoever that might have been), they were placed in a coffin in the ducal vault.

The remains were moved to Jena during the last stages of the Second World War to avoid them falling into the hands either of the Reds or of the Americans. They were then brought back and buried with full honours in the ducal vault once more, but they were not destined to rest in peace. They had, after all that, fallen into the hands of the Communists, and a decade later, a team of East German experts decided that neither the new skull nor the old one were Schiller's.

In 2006, the Klassik Stiftung Weimar (Foundation of Weimar Classics), pooling resources with the TV station MDR, organized a team of forensic scientists, led by Ursula Wittwer-Backofen, to examine the two skulls from the ducal vaults. They created forensic facial reconstructions of both skulls, and found that the abnormally large skull did in fact, *pace* Welcker in 1883, bear a marked resemblance to Schiller. Analysis of the cementum of the teeth showed that the owner of the skull had been between thirty-nine and fifty-two years old. Schiller had died aged forty-five. This was enough to suggest that, as a matter of reasonable certainty, the skull was that of Schiller. The skull which had been substituted in 1911 turned out to be that of Luise von Göchhausen, Duchess Anna Amalia's first Court Lady or lady-in-waiting. As it happened, she was a woman whom Schiller had especially disliked. The bones which had been hastily put together in 1826, and laid out in 1827, turned out to belong to as many as six different individuals, neither of them Luise von Göchhausen nor Schiller.

16

The Myth of Weimar

In one sense, there is nothing like it [Faust] and in another sense,
everything that has come after it is like it. Spengler called Western
man Faustian man, and he was right. If our world should need
a tombstone, we'll be able to put on it: HERE LIES DOCTOR
FAUST.

Randall Jarrell, words affixed to his translation of *Faust*, 1976

On 26 September 1827, in bright, warm weather, Eckermann
and Goethe set out, a few kilometres from the centre of Weimar,
to the wooded hillside of Ettersberg. The air trilled with the song
of yellowhammers, hedge sparrows and whitethroats. Goethe
thought they were larks, but Eckermann, a knowledgeable amateur
ornithologist, was bold enough to correct him.

Friedrich, the servant, spread out a picnic and to the south-west
they could enjoy the prospect of the Thuringian Forest. To the east,
they could see the big baroque-military castle of Gotha.

They ate a 'couple of roast partridges with fresh white bread, and
they drank a bottle of very good wine with it – indeed, drank out
of a very fine, flexible golden vessel which Goethe usually, on such
expeditions, carries with him in a yellow leather case'.

Goethe fell to reminiscence. Far to the north were the mountains,
where he had made a poem out of his winter ride in 1777. He recalled
riding out beyond Ettersberg towards the mines of Ilmenau. 'What
things I accomplished in the mountains of Ilmenau, in my youth! And

there below, in my beloved Erfurt, what adventures I experienced.'
(How could anyone forget that it was in Erfurt that he had conversed
with Napoleon about *The Sorrows of Young Werther*?)

All pain and sorrow is still.
Though pain may double,
So refreshment and healing is doubled.
The spirit of eternal life hovered in the blue sky.[1]

The old man led Eckermann into the beechwood. 'I'll show you the
beech,' he said, 'where we carved our names fifty years ago.'

Any human life, when viewed in retrospect, ultimately becomes a
parable. Goethe had long known himself to have become a symbol
and Goethe as a symbol would have a long afterlife. Luden, the Jena
historian we quoted at the time of the Battle of Jena, would record a
conversation with Goethe (in 1813) which appeared to make him out
to be a fervent nationalist, whereas nearly all his remarks to others –
especially after the defeat of Napoleon – and the aspirations among
young writers and intellectuals for a united Germany, were usually
objects of derision for him.

But there were exceptions. And he was prepared, when commissioned
to do so, to write *Epimenides Awakes*, for performance in Berlin to
celebrate the peace. (It was written when Napoleon was confined to
the island of Elba.) At first the authorities in Berlin hesitated about
performing the play – its symbolism seemed too obscure, and in so
far as its meaning was clear, they felt he was too ambivalent in his
feelings about the defeat of Napoleon. But in the following year, after
Waterloo, it was staged.

Epimenides was a semi-mythical Cretan shepherd who was said to
have fallen asleep in a cave for fifty-seven years, and emerged from
it a prophet. Goethe, in his version, was attempting to explain his
own apparent distance from current affairs. His Epimenides, in a final
chorus, expresses his shame at having remained aloof while Germany
suffered and there is a patriotic chorus at the end extolling the joys of
their liberation from the French threat.

This relatively minor work, very far from Goethe's finest, would
return to the collective consciousness 120 years later when German
nationalism had a very different flavour from the days when figures

such as Professor Luden or Hölderlin or Hegel dreamed of the fragments of what had been the Holy Roman Empire uniting to be a great, new European nation and voice.

The cloudier Goethe's self-image and his nature-mysticism became, the easier it was for the interpreters to make him into anything which suited them. Early in the twentieth century, Albert Schweitzer would, with a sad, satirical ruefulness, compare the liberal Protestant interpreters of Christ to men gazing into a well and seeing their own faces reflected in the dark waters. The same, only more so, could be said of the pantheists and atheists, the modernists and the supporters of the Old Regime, who found a Goethe of their own making each time they opened the pages of *Faust*. But the twists and turns of the Weimar myth will not always conform to our wishes. The dramatic poem began as a meditation on the *humanist* scholar who resorted, in Renaissance times, to magic. He had dabbled in law, tormented himself with philosophy, tried his hand at science, and even – with a groan – become a theologian. To fast-track his road to power and knowledge, he had thought he could embrace the Dark Side and not be tainted.

I am in Weimar now, and I have come to commune with Goethe and Eckermann on their Ettersberg picnic, and in order to do so, I have caught the Number 6 Bus in Goetheplatz. The direction of the bus, clearly labelled on the front, is BUCHENWALD. Beechwood. On this plateau, looking down at the scenes of his distant youth, old Goethe had said that he felt he was gazing at the Kingdoms of the World and the Glory Thereof. The author of *Faust* could scarcely forget who it was, in a Judaean wilderness, who spread out that tempting prospect to the young Galilean. In Goethe's favoured picnic spot, the Nazis built the notorious 'Beechwood' concentration camp.

One of the prisoners, Jorge Semprún, with the prison number 44904, in a bitter fiction entitled *Quel beau Dimanche* (1980), imagined Goethe – who had opposed allowing press freedom – accompanied by his useful idiot Eckermann, looking round the camp. They survey the gate, the work (incidentally) of Bauhaus designer Franz Erlich, with its gnomic motto *Jedem das Seine*, 'each to their own'. The fictionalized Goethe says (in Semprún's dream): 'Isn't that an excellent definition of a society which has been taught to defend Freedom and above all Freedom of the general mass of people, even if it must be the exaggerated and unhappy individual freedom?' That is why Goethe expressed the wish to limit press freedom – 'a restrictive law could only benefit especially as restriction affects nothing essential, but only affects individuals/personalities'.[2]

At which the worthy Eckermann studiously nods and in the notes for 18 January 1827 on the necessary restrictions of any freedom, Goethe opined:

> What use is a superfluity of freedom to us if we can't use it? Look at this and the neighbouring room, in which, through an open door, you can see my bed, neither are especially large and besides, you see they are hemmed in by all kinds of necessary objects – books, manuscripts, objets d'art, but they are enough for me. I have spent the whole winter in them, and I've hardly ventured into the rooms at the front of the house. What [use] have I had of my spacious house, and of the freedom of going from one room to the other, when I did not need to use such freedom? If we only had enough freedom to live and carry on our business we have enough, and so does everyone else – easily. And, then again, we are only free under certain conditions, which we have to fulfil. The ordinary citizen is as free as a nobleman, so long as he keeps within the limits which are appointed by God for him in the position in which he is born.

I have quoted more of the conversation in Eckermann than Semprún does in his anti-Goethean satire. Goethe ends his musings, in the Semprún version, 'I can't defend that motto, *Jedem das Seine*, whoever thought it up.'

Madame de Staël, when she visited Weimar, remarked, 'The love of freedom isn't highly developed in the Germans; neither through its enjoyment nor through its lack have they learned to value a quality in which humankind can find its highest good.'

Goethe, of course, was not trying to be funny when he made his analogy about freedom, but it will remind readers of Bertrand Russell's *A History of Western Philosophy* and the joke that for Hegel, freedom meant freedom to obey the law.[3]

This is not to suggest that Goethe's old-fashioned views about political freedoms were responsible for the existence of concentration camps just over a century after he died. But there always was a sense – even before he came to Weimar, and Anna Amalia had established the place as the Court of the Muses – that Weimar and its illustrious talents would symbolize something.

There was an element of Weimar deliberately representing an idea of what it meant to be German. This is why, in his old age, Goethe found himself unpopular with the Romantic firebrands who tried to dethrone him as the symbol of German intellectual excellence and enthrone Tieck instead.

Goethe and his house had been symbols from the beginning. Yet, as Richard Alewyn, the great critic and philologist, would remark, 'between us and Weimar, stands Buchenwald'.[4]

As we have said, the Goethe of Eckermann's *Conversations* is a joint creation, almost a fiction, but very much something which the Sage of the Frauenplan himself endorsed.

The three great works – *Wilhelm Meister's Journeyman Years*, *Poetry and Truth* and *Faust* – were all finished at the very end of his days. *Wilhelm Meister* as a complete novel, including the corrected version of the *Wanderjahre*, was published in the year that Goethe became eighty. The autobiography was completed in September 1831, when he was eighty-two. *Faust* had been finished at about the same time.

One of his wittiest sallies occurred a couple of weeks before his eighty-first birthday in August 1830. The French newspapers were beginning to reach Weimar with the exciting news of the overthrow of the conservative monarchy of King Charles X. After a last-ditch attempt to close down all the newspapers, abolish the National Assembly and declare himself an absolute ruler, Charles was driven into exile, arriving, bedraggled, on British shores in a packet sent by the Duke of Wellington. Louis Philippe, from the more liberal, *Orléaniste*, branch of the Bourbon family, had been declared the constitutional monarch and many old Bonapartists were coming back into positions of influence.

It was clearly something which caused tremendous excitement in the court, and among Goethe's friends. The old man teased Soret.

'What do you think of this great event? The volcano has really erupted this time!' he said. Both men were speaking of events in Paris, but Soret soon realized that Goethe was talking, not of the transitory detail of who was, or was not, King of France, but of the quarrel between the two great French life-scientists Georges-Frédéric, Baron de Cuvier and Etienne Geoffroy Saint-Hilaire. The debate between the two naturalists lasted two months and was conducted in front of their colleagues at the French Academy of Sciences. They were discussing how animals evolved into particular physical shapes and types. Some thought Cuvier was the victor – he certainly brought a plenitude of examples to substantiate his idea that animals adapted to their environment and this explained their physique. Saint-Hilaire felt they were governed by some set of, to science sometimes indiscernible, laws. Most modern evolutionists think that Saint-Hilaire was closer to the truth. Goethe, naturally, was interested in knowing the outcome, and the truth, of the debated topic. But he also delighted in astounding and shocking his young interlocutor. Systems of European government come and go, but science, and scientific truth, remain. Goethe himself, with his work on the metamorphosis of plants and of animals, had played an influential role in the gradual understanding of evolution, which was such a huge part of the nineteenth century's discovery of Nature itself, and where the human race stands within it.

These would all feed into *Faust Part Two*. Soret's record of how Goethe responded to the July Revolution were incorporated into Eckermann. Soret himself translated Goethe's *Metamorphose der Pflanzen* into French and the edition appeared in the old man's lifetime. He continued to gaze, with an informed eye, at the night sky, and he sent notes to the observatory in Jena, telling them to make preparations for the appearance of the comet which was due to be visible in 1834. He read the latest Balzac novel. He sorted through his collection of medallions. He continued to receive the stream of pilgrims, the last of whom was the son of his friend Frau von Arnim.

Eckermann wanted his last great conversation (Sunday 11 March 1832) to contain the poet's reflections on religion. Eckermann's harsher critics,[5] of course, believe this passage in the *Conversations* to be simple invention. We shall see in the final chapter of this book that *Faust Part Two* is not really comprehensible unless we believe that there was a softening of Goethe's anti-Christian bias in the latter years. And, given his self-confessed love of entertaining contradictory opinions, it is not necessary to believe that Eckermann fabricated the entire passage. As he approached the end, and fully aware that Eckermann was engaged on his elaborate work of art, Goethe for posterity might well have chosen to speak in this vein. Either way, and without wishing to seem blasphemous, one could liken the difficulty of the modern reader in determining the authenticity of the passage to that faced by New Testament scholars in Tübingen at more or less the date that Eckermann was engaged on making Goethe's remembered talk into a book. David Friedrich Strauss (1808–74) published *The Life of Jesus Critically Examined* in 1835–6. There is little in it which is not to be found in Goethe or in his talk. But the critical reader might wish to say that, at the very period when Strauss was demythologizing Christ, Eckermann was mythologizing Goethe. The point would not be an entirely cheap joke, since, as the German intelligentsia was deprived of the capacity to believe, the need for some other 'Perfect Man' or *vollendete Mensch* was palpable.

> One could doubt the genuineness of the Gospel, if by that we mean whether Mark or Luke based what they wrote on immediate witness or experience, rather than being compositions based on oral testimony and transcribed much later; and the last one, by the disciple John, was written when he was very old. Nevertheless, I can look upon the Gospels as entirely genuine, because there truly is in them a reflection of a greatness, which emanates from the person of Christ, and which was of as divine a kind as has ever appeared on earth. If I am asked, whether it is in my nature to give him reverent worship, I would reply – Certainly! I bow before him, as towards the highest Principle of Moral Greatness ... the mightiest that we children of earth have been permitted to behold ... I adore in him the light and the creative power of God through which we all live, and move and have our being.[6]

He went on to say that he had nothing but contempt for Catholic superstition, and rejoiced in being brought up as a Protestant. 'We scarcely know what we have to thank Luther for, and the whole Reformation in general.'

It is not inconceivable that Goethe said such things to Eckermann in the last year of his life, not least when he/Eckermann bring(s) the colloquy to a conclusion with a reflection of the Great Man story of Culture. God's finest creation is, in these sentences, seen to be the creative human being of whom, of course, Eckermann's subject is one of the most conspicuous and treasured examples.

> Just let any human being try, with merely human will and effort, to produce something which could be compared with the creations which carry the names of Mozart, or Raphael or Shakespeare. I know very well that these three are by no means the only ones, and that innumerable excellent geniuses have been at work in every area of art, and produced things as perfect as the ones I have named ... And after all what does it amount to? After the imagined six days of Creation, God did not retire to rest! Rather, he is as constantly active as he was on the first day of creation. It would not have been much fun for him to put together this lumpen world with simple elements, and to keep it rolling in the beams of the sun year after year, had he not the plan of founding a nursery of the Spirits on this material base. So in order to attract the lower orders of being, he is constantly at work in the higher Natures.

Eckermann adds: 'Goethe was silent, but I kept his great and good words in my heart.' This is almost a quotation from the Gospel of Luke (Luke 2.51) where Christ's mother, after she had found her twelve-year-old son among the teachers in the Temple at Jerusalem, treasures his sayings in her heart.

No wonder that T. S. Eliot, who described himself as combining 'a Catholic cast of mind, a Calvinistic intelligence, and a Puritanical temperament', had difficulties with Goethe.[7] He received the Hanseatic Goethe Prize in 1954 and clearly felt obliged to devote his acceptance speech to a consideration of Goethe – even though, in his Norton lectures of 1933, he had said, 'Of Goethe, perhaps it is truer to say that he dabbled in both philosophy and poetry and made no great success of either.'[8]

The twenty or so printed pages of Eliot's oration – 'Goethe as the Sage' – are remarkable for their abstention from quoting either from his poetry or from his 'philosophy'. And, although he begins his lecture by describing the drawing of Goethe made in old age, which was propped on his mantelpiece in his office in Russell Square, London – 'this is the Goethe of the days of the conversations with Eckermann' – he does not quote from the *Conversations* either. Rather – quite an achievement – he spends twenty pages reiterating that he has reconciled himself to Goethe, and that Goethe is a Great Poet and a Great European. How? Why? Because he is a sage. He possesses Wisdom. 'Whether the "philosophy" or the religious faith of Dante or Shakespeare or Goethe is acceptable to us or not ... there is the Wisdom that we can all accept.'[9] What is the Wisdom of Goethe? he asks in his final page. 'I feel a wiser man because of the time I have spent with him.'

In the first instance, Eliot declined the award, and it was only when the chairman of the judges pleaded with him that he accepted the honour, and donated the prize money – 10,000 Deutschmarks – to flood victims in Bavaria and Austria. The members of the audience at Hamburg University, when he went to address them, might have felt puzzled by their distinguished Anglo-American honorand. But these were the days when memories of the Second World War were green, and presumably, even though Eliot plainly still disliked Goethe and what he supposedly did or did not stand for, they might have felt some gratification that so distinguished a poet should have graced them at all with his presence.

Although Eliot's essay is woeful, it is not unique. Many – and perhaps especially those who have not always managed to find much in the poetry which is to their taste – have looked to Goethe as a sage, or as an embodiment of what they hope for in a wise and learned person, or as an incarnation of the German soul. Hence the need for some last words which would confirm his status as the Wise Man of Weimar, the Magus of the Modern World. 'Everyone knows' that Goethe's last words were 'More light!' South Hampstead High School in London, a stone's throw from Freud's last consulting room, has the words emblazoned as their motto, over the entrance, and there must be many academies and places of learning throughout the world which have done the same.

Lutz Saltner, in a satirical fiction, imagines the dying Goethe muttering, 'Not here!' – 'Hier nicht!' – perhaps indicating that he had hoped not to die in Weimar, having been stuck there for fifty years. Or maybe the Thuringians clustering around him would mishear his Hessian accent and when he said he was not comfortable, 'Mir liegt so schlecht', it was heard as 'Mehr Licht!' 'More light.' 'Where there is much light, there is bound to fall a shadow – a platitude from my *Götz*,' thinks Saltner's fictitious poet.[10]

Ottilie von Goethe said that on the last evening of his life he was still discussing optical phenomena. It is true that he maintained that his book on the theory of colours was his most important work, and, given the fact that he had become the Enlightenment Made Flesh long before that book was published in 1810, he might be considered, in his dying gasp, to have been crying out for ever more illumination.

In a letter to Sulpiz Boisserée, written on 22 March 1831, in explanation of his religious position, Goethe expressed his feeling of kinship for the Hypsistarians, a cult that appears to have flourished between 100 and 400 CE. Their name means worshippers of the Most High. They were not Christians. 'I have found no confession of faith to which I could ally myself without reservation,' Goethe admitted to Boisserée. 'Now in my old age, however, I have learned of a sect, the Hypsistarians, who, hemmed in between heathens, Jews and Christians, declared that they would treasure and honour the best, the most perfect, that might come to their knowledge, and inasmuch as it must have a close connection to the Godhead, pay it reverence. A joyous light thus beamed at me suddenly out of a dark age, for I had the feeling that all my life I had been aspiring to qualify as a Hypsistarian. That, however, is no small task, for how does one, in the limitations of one's individuality, come to know what is most excellent?'

Some have questioned whether the famous words *Mehr Licht!* were ever spoken. It is certainly surprising that the faithful Eckermann would not have made these two pregnant syllables the last words of his hagiographical tribute. Yet they are the testimony of a normally reliable witness, Chanceller von Müller, writing to Bettina von Arnim only two days after the poet's demise.

He was, Müller reported, fully conscious and cheerful, without apparent awareness of his coming death until his very last breath, and in no pain. It was a gradual, gentle sinking; the flame of life as extinguished without struggle. Light was his last demand. Half an hour before the end, he ordered, 'Open the window shutters – let in more light!'

What is beyond question is that, to facilitate his breathing, Goethe had been helped into the upright armchair beside his bed in the simple little chamber where he passed every night. He died in Ottilie's arms.

Perhaps Eckermann, having served him so faithfully on the page through three volumes, decided, when he prepared his second volume for the press in 1836, that he would like to give himself the last word, and the last teardrop, in his rather splendid set-piece finale:

The morning after Goethe's death, I was gripped by a profound yearning to look once more on his earthly frame. His faithful servant Friedrich opened for me the room where they had laid him. Stretched out on his back, he looked as if he was peacefully asleep. In the features of his sublimely noble face, deep peace and security reigned. The mighty brow seemed to be nursing great thoughts. I had a longing for a lock of his hair, but reverence prevented me from snipping a lock. The body lay naked, in a white sheet. Large lumps of ice had been placed near it to keep it fresh for as long as possible. Friedrich drew the sheet aside and I was astounded by the divine magnificence of those limbs. The breast was powerful, broad, vaulted; arms and thighs were full and gently muscular; the feet were elegant, the most perfect shape; on the whole body there was not the smallest trace of fat, or leanness or decay. A perfect man, in great beauty, lay before me, and the delight which the sight caused me made me forget for a moment that the immortal spirit had left its husk. I laid my hand on his heart. Over all, there was a deep silence. And I turned away to give free vent to the tears which I had been holding in.[11]

The ice was not melting as Eckermann wept. One reason for the rooms being so small in that enfiladed warren on the Frauenplan is the extreme cold of the Thuringian winter. When he died, it was rather as if they were going to dismantle a theatrical set. Throughout his occupancy, Goethe had been building and rebuilding, inhabiting the tiny rooms backstage, and emerging from time to time in the public rooms to receive the pilgrims.

After he died, Ottilie, moving from one unsatisfactory love affair to the next, went to live in Vienna. When the money ran out, she came back to live in the Frauenplan, letting out rooms to lodgers. She died in 1872, when Germany had changed out of all recognition. Neither of her sons (her daughter died young) had children. They did not welcome visitors to the old house in the Frauenplan, and they died far from home. Wolfgang Maximilian, who trained as a lawyer, worked for many years in Rome as a diplomatic representative of the Prussian court. Walter, Ottilie's eldest son, who had been taught to play the piano by Felix Mendelssohn-Bartholdy, had a musical talent, but very little outlet for it. He spent much of his life huddled in the attic of the Frauenplan, and died on a trip to Leipzig in 1885. By his will of 1883, he decreed that the house and its collections should become the property of the town of Weimar.

By then the disparate parts of German lands had been united into a Reich, an Empire, the creation of Otto von Bismarck. Goethe's Duke, Carl August, had been a proud general in the Prussian army. But this was as the nephew of Frederick the Great, upholder of the Enlightenment. His grandson, Carl Alexander (1818–1901), who had begun as a liberal, became a keen Bismarckian patriot, and in latter years always wore his splendid Prussian uniform. In his eyes, as for so many Germans, the victory at Sedan, and the humiliation of France, by declaring the creation of the German Empire in the Hall of Mirrors at Versailles, began the process of compensating for the massacres perpetrated by Napoleon at Jena, Weimar, Austerlitz. History, of course, sees these triumphs as stage one in the ineluctable progress of events, from the creation of the Reich, the arms race, the estrangement of the British royal family from their Imperial cousin in Berlin and the outbreak of the First World War.

Not only Goethe, but his *Faust*, had by then been enlisted in the nationalist cause. It was alleged by Rudolf Wustmann in his 1915 essay 'Weimar and the Germans' that those who fought for the Kaiser on the Western Front did so with more valour and resolution than the French or the English because they had read *Faust*. 'You don't have anything like that.' Goethe himself had spoken of *Faust* being a very serious joke, but perhaps even he, ironist as he was, and despiser of patriotic propaganda, might not have been prepared for this hideous development.

It was as if the house itself, in the Frauenplan, was caught up in the march of iron and blood. Even during Ottilie's lifetime, much of the collection had been muddled or dispersed in order to pay bills, even though there had been a movement afoot, since Goethe's death, to preserve it all as a national collection. Wolfgang Maximilian, her second son, continued to live in the house until his death in 1883. He was plagued by illness all his life, and had to abandon his place in the Prussian diplomatic service. His work on the Life and Times of the Renaissance humanist Cardinal Bessarion was never completed. His attempt to write his own *Italian Journey* only emphasized the abyss which lay between his own limitations and the legendary genius of his grandfather.[12]

Wolfgang Maximilian had never had the money to maintain the house as a museum, or to reclaim the items which had been scattered by his mother's need to sell. On his death, the house and its contents, which had, after all, been a gift from the Duchy, passed back to the Grand Duchy.

When, after the calamity of the First World War, a modern generation of art lovers, aesthetes and intellectuals wanted to make Weimar into the emblem of a new Germany, based on humane values, the restoration of Goethe's house was not necessarily something which came high on their agenda. There was a gulf between his Weimar classicism and the Bauhaus, just as with his studied distance from politics it was difficult to see Goethe as the godfather of the Weimar Republic. The post-war Republic was so-named (by Hitler, as a term of contempt) because Friedrich Ebert was declared the first President of a Democratic Germany in the Court Theatre at Weimar on 21 August 1919. It was in that theatre that the hopes for a new, democratic Germany were forged. In his speech, Ebert had said, 'Now must the spirit of Weimar, the spirit of the great philosophers and poets once more fill our lives.' Ebert claimed Goethe as his ally in addressing the problems which faced the new nation. The Democratic Germany would be animated, he claimed, by the spirit which had created the second part of *Faust* and the *Wanderjahre* of *Wilhelm Meister*.

The house in the Frauenplan, however, and the vast collection – over 50,000 separate objects – casts, medallions, majolica, books – continued to gather dust. As is notorious, the Weimar Republic, with its many ups and downs of fortune, was bled dry by the demands by France for reparations for Germany's war crimes, and by the fluctuations of the world markets, especially the Wall Street Crash of 1929. During the terrifying years of hyperinflation, when Germans were carrying surreal quantities of banknotes in wheelbarrows to pay for a kilo of potatoes or a packet of cigarettes, there was not much appetite for restoring an eighteenth-century house, however central it was to the cultural story.

Besides, to the brightest minds in the new Weimar, the house in the Frauenplan was not an object of great beauty. Harry Graf Kessler in 1903 was asked to become the director of the Museum of Art and Art-business (*Kunstgewerbe*) and made it an opportunity to exhibit the works of Gauguin, Munch, Toulouse-Lautrec and Kandinsky. The first time this attractive aesthete set eyes on Goethe's house, when he visited Weimar in August 1891, he saw only a 'joyless ugliness' in the poky room where the great genius had died.[13]

No state money had been found to restore the Goethe collection or his house as the twentieth century unfolded. It is melancholy to record that the money was only found in the century's third decade. The finance came not from the state but from a private donor who spent a substantial part of his best-seller royalties – from *Mein Kampf* – on the project.

The newly built National Goethe Museum was opened on 28 August 1935, on the Führer's behalf, by one of the keenest Nazis in Thuringia, Hans Severus Ziegler, editor of the party newspaper, and one who had been a Gauleiter and Hitler Youth leader since the early 1920s. He had boycotted the Goethe Festival of 1932 on the grounds that there were still Jews associated with Goethe studies. But three years later, he was able to proclaim, 'We know that the German and the Aryan man has attained large measure of self-knowledge, if, in the course of his life, he recognizes these spiritual and moral lessons which Goethe has provided.'[14]

Hitler visited Weimar every year. He said he loved Weimar, no – needed it, just as he needed Wagner's Bayreuth. He explained this to Hans Severus Ziegler.[15]

He shared the view of the liberals and social democrats, such as Harry Kessler, that Weimar had symbolic cultural significance, but he took an entirely contrary view of what that significance was. For Kessler, the true shrine of Weimar was not the Goethe house, but that other Weimar shrine the Villa Silberblick, where Elisabeth Förster-Nietzsche had kept her utterly insane brother Friedrich. For Kessler, as for so many moderns, Nietzsche's writings enshrined a totally new way of looking at the world, unshackled by the philosophical preoccupations which had weighed down the contemporaries of Fichte or Hegel; and which had liberated itself from religion, with the poetic reflection that God had died.

What Kessler did not realize was that Elisabeth Förster-Nietzsche was busy rewriting the stray notes of his unfinished work to make her brother into a proto-Nazi. Nietzsche who, in fact, had deplored anti-Semitism, militarism, all forms of xenophobia and patriotism, was made into the prophet of Fascism. His dangerous concept of the *Übermensch* was made into a glimpse of the Aryan, racially pure future and the dominance of the Third Reich over those deemed to be less than human – the Jews, the Slavs, the disabled and the sexually 'deviant'. While being fond of Kessler – as were most people who knew this charming, amusing man – Elisabeth Förster-Nietzsche far preferred the company of Hitler, and his visits to the Villa Silberblick were high points of her year, just as the townsfolk flocked to hear his speeches made through the window of the old Hotel Elephant in the central square.

If you have tried to watch *Faust* on a DVD or downloaded it on the computer, the likelihood is you will have seen Gustaf Gründgens's rendering, filmed by his adopted son Peter Gorski and produced in Hamburg in 1960. (Gründgens died of a drug overdose in Manila in 1963.) In the law of most countries, you cannot libel the dead, but Gorski managed to use the German courts to suppress any suggestion that his 'father' had been complicit in the darkness of 1933–45.

Gründgens is undoubtedly part of our story. From the early 1930s, he made Mephistopheles his own. And his highly stylized, and on all levels repellent, version of the role has had an enormous impact.

'Gründgens's influence is to be felt in much subsequent work that was done for the German stage, where new milestones were set by a series of outstanding directors among whom were Claus Peymann (Stuttgart, 1977), Dieter Dorn (Munich, 1987) and Peter Stein (Hanover, 2000).'[16]

No one who has watched Gustaf Gründgens's depiction of Mephistopheles in Gorski's film version will ever be able to get the performance out of their head. Only occasionally, as at the very beginning, when in Heaven conversing with 'the Lord', does he register an emotion. (In this case, when 'the Lord' asks him, 'Kennst du den Faust?' and Mephistopheles replies, 'Den Doktor?' there is a chilling complicity. You feel they are two old queens in a bar somewhere in Hamburg, planning the seduction of an under-age boy.)

When he intrudes himself into Faust's study, Gründgens is arrayed like a Pierrot, with white make-up, and the scarlet lip-gloss emphasizing the yellowing, smoker's teeth, so redolent of the era. There are so many unsatisfactory things about this production, not least its utter lack of psychological plausibility. When he says (line 1646) 'Ich bin dein Geselle', the scene surely demands that Faust will believe him, or at least half *want* to believe that he has found a new friend who will break the bounds of the normal 'striving' of the human race by the release of magic, demonic power. Never for a second would we believe that Faust, as played by Will Quadflieg, a solid-looking, humourless, beefy figure, will want to associate with this prancing, sinister embodiment of 1930s high camp.

Yet we remember Gründgens. He disgusts and haunts us. He manages to remove from the production all the ingredients which make *Faust*, as written by Goethe, bearable – namely, the fact that Faust is a divided soul. Even when he is behaving with truly reckless lack of pity, we cannot dismiss 'the Lord's' idea that

A good man, [*ein guter Mensch*] even in darkest stress,
Is yet aware of the right way. [17]

For the 'guter Mensch' Faust to be seduced by Mephistopheles's cynicism, we have to believe, for at least some of the time, that the mage believes it is worth cutting moral corners to achieve a higher good, or at least a higher degree of consciousness. And there should be an element of playfulness in the relationship he forms with the devil – the playfulness which characterized the relationship between the young Goethe and Merck, as with Jacobi and some of the other chums of the Strasbourg era.

Gründgens alarmingly and unforgettably brings with him a completely different weight of moral, rather, amoral, baggage. It is not merely the high camp of the 1930s which he brings. It is the reading of the play which so many Germans, not merely the party propagandists of that era, wished to believe. Osman Durrani, in a magnificent survey of the modern reception of *Faust*, sees it as the equation of Faust himself with 'the wayward genius of Germany'.[18] It is well known that this is the core of Thomas Mann's slightly ponderous novel *Doktor Faustus*. What some readers will have missed is that Mann was inspired to write his novel by his son Klaus's much sprightlier fiction *Mephisto* based on his close knowledge of Gründgens. They had been actors together in Hamburg as young men, when both were far to the left politically in the Revolutionary Players. They were lovers for a time, and the analysis of Gründgen's (Höfgen in the book) descent into Nazism, his toadying to Goering, his utter ruthlessness to his former friends, is quite devastating. 'But the novel is not just a hatchet job on an ex-lover. Klaus Mann would later explain that the book was not aimed at a particular person, but at the careerist, the German intellectual who sold and betrayed the German mind and spirit.'[19]

Klaus Mann felt – and this is certainly one reading which can be made of *Faust* – that the actor shared with Faust the knowledge that what he was doing was morally wrong. The high-minded liberal Protestants of the nineteenth century who had wanted to see Faust as a fundamentally good man in a bad world, 'striving' towards enlightenment, were challenged by the truly terrifying reading which became popular in Germany during the 1920s and until 1945.

Which is more disturbing? To think that Goethe was distorted and betrayed by such a reading, or to believe that these qualities and strands of thought were existent in the piece? What if they explain *Faust*'s power as a great work of literature? Is it the ultimate exploration of the world Beyond Good and Evil, to use the title of one of Nietzsche's books? Never mind for the moment whether, or how far, Elisabeth Förster-Nietzsche distorted the brother's work. What if *Faust* was, as the Nazis believed, a foreshadowing of their own diseased worship of death and power?

The end of the Second World War in Thuringia provided the most extreme demonstration of the fact that Goethe's works could, like the Bible, become the possession of any ideologue who was prepared to lay claim to them. When the US air raids began, Hans Wahl, director of the National Goethe Museum, vice-president of the German Goethe Society and, from 1928, director of the Schiller-Goethe Archive in Weimar, arranged for the coffins of Goethe and – they supposed – Schiller to be taken to Jena for safe-keeping and kept in hiding. When the Americans arrived in Thuringia, William M. Brown was appointed Commandant of the town of Weimar. This US army major was, in civilian life, a Germanist professor at Columbia University in New York. Photographs show him bare-headed in the ruined, recently bombed church of St Peter and St Paul, at the grave of Herder. And, in time to commemorate (three days late) the anniversary of Schiller's death, Brown arranged for the sarcophagi to be returned to the ducal vaults. Professor Hans Wahl, who had laboured so arduously to assure Gauleiter Ziegler of his National Socialist credentials, attended the ceremony, his gangling figure towering over the other people around the tombs – including Major Brown. Wahl would remain in post when the Russians came to pay their respects to Goethe's grave, and during the DDR years would make at least a plausible showing of his belief that *Faust* anticipated the collapse of capitalism and the triumph of the People. During all these years, Goethe's rooms in the Frauenplan were closed to public view, though the apartments occupied by his wife, Christiane Vulpius, supposedly a proletarian heroine, were sometimes shown to interested visitors.

Satire can smile at such self-serving, but smiles die when one visits Weimar and considers the journey from the Goethe-time to our own: the Light (whether or not he called for it at his end) dying to three great darknesses: the Wilhelmine militaristic horror story; the Third Reich; and the era when so many minds and bodies were imprisoned in the Soviet satellite of the DDR. Through all these eras, German

341

students were given *Faust* to read, and the different messages they read in it were in part owing to the historical circumstances in which they were unlucky to find themselves, in part to the protean character of the poem itself.

When he was about fifty, Goethe doodled a fragment of verse about *Faust*.

Our human life is not unlike this poem.
It has a start, all right, it has an end.
Only a finished whole – that it is not.[20]

Is it too ambitious on the part of our generation to suppose that this might make us better qualified to read it than those who were shackled by an ideology? Those of us who are post- even the post-modern, and who look back with a mixture of bafflement and pity at the mid-twentieth-century need for ideology ... are we the readers that Goethe has been waiting for since he completed the poem sometime during his eighty-third year of life?

17

SOON, PEACE

The same stream of life that runs through my veins night and day
runs through the world and dances in rhythmic measures.
It is the same life that shoots in joy through the dust of the earth
in numberless blades of grass and breaks into tumultuous waves
of leaves and flowers.

Rabindranath Tagore, 'Stream of Life'

It so happened that, on the ship which contained the last consignment of the so-called Elgin Marbles, being transported from Athens to London, was the poet Lord Byron.

> When they carry away three or four shiploads of the most valuable and massy relics that time and barbarism have left to the most injured and most celebrated of cities, when they destroy, in a vain attempt to tear down those works which have been the admiration of ages, I know no motive which can excuse, no name which can designate, the perpetrators of this dastardly devastation.[1]

His words resonate because the issue remains a matter of such bitter dispute to this day.

Should the Parthenon Marbles, the glory of the British Museum, remain in London, or should they be returned to Athens whence, with some clumsiness, they were gouged out in the early nineteenth century by Lord Elgin, and bought from the then governors of Athens, the Ottoman Turks? The sculptures of Phidias give plastic form to the Greek notion of civilization itself: its struggles between Lapiths and Centaurs is a struggle between enlightenment and savagery. The worship of Athene was not simply the cult of a city-state's favourite mythological female; she was the symbol of intellectual light, of philosophy, of a sane politics – as conceived by the Greeks of Athens's glory period, a period which continues both to influence and to reproach our societies today.

The return of the Marbles is a question which occupies us now, since the whole phenomenon of the museum – of one country possessing the artefacts and sacred objects of another culture and civilization – has undergone such radical rethinking in our time. When Leonard Woolley (1880–1960) dug up Ur of the Chaldees in Mesopotamia, from 1922 onwards, financed largely by the University of Pennsylvania, few, if any, questioned his right to possess these treasures for the West – half going to the British Museum, half to Philadelphia – where the astounded visitor can enjoy them to this hour. For Woolley's generation it was axiomatic that the Western academics had the know-how and the skill and the money to find these objects, saw their significance, probably, more deeply than most of the economically challenged indigenous population and were saving the artefacts for the world. Out of Mesopotamia came the beginnings of what we call civilization in the West.

Now, if some archaeologist makes a discovery in Mesopotamia, the excavated object is seen by everyone to belong in Iraq, and it would be an act of piracy to take it to the United States or anywhere else. Likewise, in Greek archaeological sites, Greece is the place where Greek vases, stones, statues and seals must stay, if found.

The case of the Parthenon Marbles is special, not just for the British Museum, and for the successive Greek governments who demand their return, but for all of us, because of the central role played in world consciousness by the Greeks from archaic times to the decline of Athens. Homer gave to the world not simply two great poems, but a way of looking at the world which influenced an entire culture. The three great tragedians of the fifth-century BCE derive nearly all their dramas from Homer. If comparisons can be made, he occupied a position vis-à-vis the Greek world more like Moses to the Hebrew culture than like Shakespeare to the British. That is to say, Homer's poems are key religious texts. The tragic last duel between Achilles and Hector at the end of the *Iliad* is 'the great fight of Hellenism against barbarism'.[2] It is all the more heroic, splendid, appalling, because Homer's Hector is himself every bit as noble and brave as his Hellenic opponent; and the means of overthrowing the Trojans, the combined brutality of the Greeks and their gods, are so utterly ruthless.

After the French Revolution, and perhaps even more after the collapse of Napoleon's ambition to conquer Europe, this conflict, seemingly an everlasting one, was revived. This is why the Greek War of Independence against the Ottoman Empire was of such key symbolic importance, just as, in the 1930s, the civil war in Spain was much more than a battle about who occupied the seat of power in Madrid. It was the fight between Fascism and Communism which led men and women from so many other countries in the world to enlist to fight. It was not merely sympathy with Spain which made them join up. It was a war about what kind of Europe, what kind of world, the combatants wanted to live in.

Goethe's *Faust Part Two* came to its conclusion while the Greek War was being fought, and one of the catalystic events, for the poet, which led to the final shaping and flowering of *Faust*, was the death of Lord Byron in that conflict. Helen of Troy: a symbol, not merely of the erotic power of woman over the poetic imagination, but also, as her name implies, of Hellenism, of the ideals and philosophy of ancient Greece. Faust: the old German intellectual, coming to birth at the time of the Reformation, still steeped in all the witchy superstitions of old Germany which were being unearthed, as Goethe grew old, by the Brothers Grimm; Faust the man of the Reformation, the man of science, evolving into Enlightenment man. And then, the concept of the daimonic. The forceful energy embodied in Napoleon, also in Goethe himself, and in Byron. All these were coming together in Goethe's brain, and forming themselves into *Faust Part Two*. And a key ingredient was the decision by Byron to fight in the Greek War of Independence, his falling ill – a tick-bite at Missolonghi poisoning his system – and the doctors finishing him off by excessive bleeding.

Byron and Shelley read the first part of *Faust*, and Goethe was displeased by some of their comments, not least by Byron's suggestion that it was unoriginal. The German poet said that he had not even read some of the supposed 'sources' for passages in his *Faust*. 'Byron is only great as a poet. As soon as he makes reflections, he is childish.'[3]

When Professor Riemer raised the matter of Byron's recent death, in 1824, Goethe said that although Byron had died young, literature had not suffered significantly, since he had already 'peaked'. 'He had reached the summit of his creative power, and whatever he might have achieved in the future he would have been unable to extend the limits of his talent.'[4]

Nevertheless, Byron had the *dämonisch*[5] in his nature to the highest degree. This is where he was to be a key figure in stimulating the development of the finished *Faust*. Byron was an apt symbol to seize upon since 'Byron is not antique and he is not romantic, but he is like the present day itself. This is the sort of man I needed.'[6] Goethe saw him as 'undoubtedly the greatest genius of our century'.[7] When you consider Goethe's admiration for Napoleon and the Humboldt brothers, when you consider the greatness of Goethe himself, when you remember that he was a contemporary of Hegel and Beethoven, it's quite a claim.

But, he needed Byron. And what he needed him for, in *Faust*, was something completely revolutionary in literature. *Faust Part Two* is a complex literary construction.

> They come and ask what idea I meant to embody in my *Faust*; as if I knew myself, and could inform them. From heaven, through the world, to hell, would indeed be something. But this is no idea, only a course of action. And further: that the devil loses the wager, and that a man continually struggling from difficult errors towards something better, should be redeemed, is an effective – and to many a good, an enlightening – thought; but it is no idea at the foundation of the whole, and of every individual scene. It would have been a fine thing indeed if I had strung so rich, varied, and highly diversified a life as I have brought to view in *Faust* upon the slender string of one pervading idea.[8]

One of the most astonishing innovations which he pulled off, as an old man, was to create, in the second and third acts of the play, an onion layer of consciousness, so that, within each level, you are not always sure who is experiencing, who is receiving, the representations which we find on the page. Page, note well, not stage. Though gallant – and sometimes frankly silly – efforts have been made to stage it, the piece actually defies presentation.

Mephistopheles summons up for the Emperor and his court a vision or pageant of Helen of Troy, with her lover Paris, and at the end of this scene there is an explosion, and Faust passes out into a kind of trance. Like 'The Mousetrap' in *Hamlet*, what we have here is a play within a play; but it is also, like the theatrical show put on for Prince Ferdinand and Miranda in *The Tempest*, a masque of spirits. 'These our actors/As I foretold you, were all spirits/Are melted into air, into thin air.' The pageant of 'The Rape of Helen' at the end of Act I prepares us for the Classical Walpurgis Night in Act II, but the complexity of the multi-layered onion doesn't end here. We are taken back to Faust's old study in the university, where we began. Faust's harmless drudge, his colleague Wagner, now occupies his professorial chair. Like Frankenstein, Goethe's contemporary, this backroom boffin, this dullard, has managed to pull off the technological feat of creating a human being in a test tube – the Homunculus. And like modern Artificial Intelligence, the Homunculus would appear to have an independent capacity of its own to take possession of another person's consciousness.

The readers might, by this stage of *Faust Part Two*, feel that they have had enough pageants, but what the Homunculus is going to provide is something much more extraordinary. What he will allow us to see is what is going on inside Faust's head. We are going to see ancient Greece as envisaged by Faust, Hellenism as conceived by the generation of Byron. Faust has long left behind his study in an early modern university. The spiders have multiplied, the papers are yellowing, the very quill with which Faust signed his 'pact' with the devil is dry and dusty.

We are going inside the head, not of a scholar of the 1520s, but of a modern man of the 1820s. This is both Goethe's supreme homage to the art of theatre – namely that so much is here expected from, extracted from, a dramatic form – and a renunciatory creation. The spirit actors melt into 'air, into thin air'. Cinema would perhaps be capable of conveying what is going on here, but how could it plausibly be staged? Among its many, many paradoxes, Goethe's last and greatest play is a renunciation of theatre itself. He was self-consciously following Shakespeare/Prospero.

No wonder Freud loved Goethe so much – he who tried to plumb the mysteries of the subconscious mind, to discover in the depths of our being, in our childhood memories, in our compulsions and phobias, those sinister re-enactments of the Greek myths – Oedipus slaying his father, Electra her mother. Goethe, who had been meditating on the meaning of the Greek Experience since his teens, since Adam Friedrich Oeser introduced him to the ideas of Winckelmann, now takes us to the heart of why Greece is of such importance, in all time, and at this particular moment of time.

It is something much, much more than a simple switch in decorative taste to Greek Revival buildings. Rather, these buildings took the shape they did in the European capitals because of just such thoughts and impressions and imaginative responses to Greece as were passing through Faust's head. We are concerned here with what we mean by civilization. A good question, after the American Revolution had recast it in political terms, and revived that old Greek word and concept – democracy; after the French Revolution had caused the most gigantic laboratory explosion with their republican experiment.

Hugh Trevor-Roper entitled his appreciative essay on the great Swiss scholar of the Renaissance, Jacob Burckhardt, 'The Faustian Historian'. Many would be surprised at the epithet, if they consider Burckhardt's quiet sanity, and if they think *Faust* to be the drama of the diabolic, or even of the daimonic … But Faust in Goethe is *not* daimonic. He is tormented and eventually his endeavours are shown to be vain; but Trevor-Roper's analysis of Burckhardt's philosophy would come close to that of Goethe in his maturity:

> his deep prophetic pessimism, his profound distrust of the masses. Like his great contemporary Alexis de Tocqueville, he saw more clearly the price of democracy by being himself, in his family tradition and intellectual outlook, one of its victims: an aristocrat.
>
> For if one looks at Burckhardt's philosophy, it always comes back to this: civilisation is a delicate and precarious thing which only an educated and perhaps unscrupulously self-preserving hierarchy

can protect against the numerical revolt of the masses with their materialism, their indifference to liberty; their ready surrender to demagogic power; and the crises of civilisation consist in precisely that revolt of the masses which, however, can never prevail against the strength of conservative institutions unless it is aided within by moral and intellectual decay.[9]

Goethe's views entirely. (And Burckhardt, together with his Basle colleague Nietzsche, was steeped in Goethe.) To which one should add, however, a double belief, one of which makes him alien from our century, and another which makes him very close to us. The second – the thing which makes him very close – is his holistic science, his sense of humanity being part of the natural world and the necessity if we are to survive, and to understand more about the nature of life itself, that we should all be better informed about natural science and more and more attuned to our kinship with the natural world.

The first, which alienates him from us, is his belief in the destiny of the German-speaking peoples – Burckhardt would have agreed with him in this – his wish that Weimar, Jena, Tübingen, Heidelberg could produce something of what Florence gave to Europe during the Renaissance, and what Athens gave the world in the fifth-century BCE. His uncompromising belief in a higher culture.

The Greeks, who had puzzled over the nature of Being, who had been the pioneers of modern science, mathematics, medicine, philosophy, were, in the 1820s, coming back to life. Greek Revival meant very much more than simply delighting in Doric arches, though such delight implied an adherence to a whole new/ancient way of viewing the universe – with intellectual curiosity unshackled by superstition; intelligence embodied in symbol; mythology defining and tracing the life of the mind. Greece as a nation was fighting for its new political life, independence from the Islamic Ottomans.

So, we are back in Faust's old study, and the moment that Mephistopheles shakes Faust's academic gown, creating a cloud of dust, the insects hop out of it, exclaiming, 'You old boss, welcome! Welcome!' Who could ever hope to bring this scene of animated insects to life? The answer which supplies itself is surprising at first; for it is surely not one of Goethe's contemporaries, and not a theatrical director, but one of the greatest *maestri* of twentieth-century cinema.

The two-hour-long musical extravaganza *Fantasia* began, in the fertile brain of Walt Disney (1901–66), as a much more modest affair than the film we see today. He had merely conceived of animating Goethe's 'Sorcerer's Apprentice' as part of a 'Silly Symphonies' series. This would enable his most celebrated cartoon character – 'that damned mouse', as King George V of England had called him – to make a comeback to the silver screen. The idea grew, however. In 1937, the year of *Snow White and the Seven Dwarfs*, his animated version of the Grimm fairy story, Disney walked into a restaurant in Los Angeles and met Leopold Stokowski, star conductor of the Philadelphia Orchestra, who agreed to conduct Paul Dukas's 1897 score of 'Scherzo after a Ballad by Goethe'. As the two men discussed the matter, they began to see that other scores might lend themselves to being performed as accompaniments to Disney animations. Igor Stravinsky's *The Rite of Spring*, for example, became a vehicle for expounding the current scientific view of how life itself had emerged from single-cell organisms living under water, and progressing through the 200 million years when dinosaurs were the Lords of Creation.

For many of us, growing up in the era after the Second World War, Disney's film must occupy some part of the brain which in earlier generations was programmed by the Bible. And there can be no doubt, when we view the film again with adult eyes, that this was part of its intention, with the alternative evolutionary biology replacing the Creation myth of Genesis. As for little Mickey, half able to turn a broomstick into his obedient vassal, but unwittingly engulfing the Sorcerer's home into a flood which he is powerless to control – is he an emblem of his times? Is he the German voter who unwittingly chose to make a maniac his Chancellor? Or is he that Maniac-Chancellor himself, thinking at first to bring control, efficiency, full employment and harmony, and ending in catastrophe? In 1940, the American audiences could not have guessed the answer, nor the ending to the horror story which was contemporaneously being enacted in Goethe's homeland.

Fantasia must be one of the strangest films ever made. Mickey Mouse and Goethe do not easily sit together, but the whole conception, in which thematic meditations on the natural world mingle with pageants whose meaning works at a subliminal, rather than an obvious rational level, in which the political undercurrents are swept up into a reawakening of the creatures of classical mythology – centaurs, fauns and nymphs – is as close an aesthetic experience as I know to what is the strangest reading experience so far known to me – namely reading Goethe's *Faust* in both its parts.

The finished movie was a commercial flop. One reason for this was that, by the time it was released, in 1940, Europe was at war. American audiences alone could not recoup the enormous expense which had gone into the making of this extraordinary piece of cinema. How to describe it? It is a playlist of European music, conducted by Stokowski, and taking in, as well as the Dukas interpretation of 'The Sorcerer's Apprentice', J. S. Bach's Toccata and Fugue, played in a lush, schmaltzy full-blown-modern American hurdy-gurdy which would make any music lover wince, Beethoven's Sixth Symphony, and Stravinsky's *The Rite of Spring*. Some sequences – such as the scene during the Pastoral Symphony in which a crudely racist depiction of 'Sunflower', an African American girl, obediently shines the shoes of one of the preening cutie all-American Centaurettes – must have struck the original audiences as crass, and have now been edited out of any version of the piece you will find on DVD or online.

Nevertheless, for all its pink, candyfloss gaudiness, and its vulgar sentimentality, *Fantasia* is, at the same time, a work of genius. More than this, it is, surely deliberately, a tribute to the poet who inspired the original Mickey Mouse scene – Johann Wolfgang Goethe.

Fantasia did not really reach Europe until after the Second World War. The canny Disney distributed it over and over in cinemas in the 1950s and 1960s, eventually making his money back and more – not least, towards the close of the 1960s, when hallucinogenic drugs became fashionable. The film then developed a cult status. Its psychedelic inconsequentiality met the mood of a generation that was as far from the spirit of 1940 as it was possible to be. The Hollywood versions of the Great Wave off Kanagawa and the explosions of flowers, insects, balletic fungi and prehistoric monsters with roguish, flirtatious facial expressions have an effect on the sober viewer not unlike the narcotic effect on a drug user's mind of dropping acid or puffing on the most potent marijuana.

The original audiences, however, seeing the film in New York or Philadelphia while the European war entered its most tragic shadows – Paris falling to the Nazis, Stalin and Hitler still in triumphant alliance as they carved up Poland, Spain and Portugal neutral but pro-Fascist – must have had very different mental impressions from those which played their fantastical magic-lantern show in the brains of the hippy generation a quarter of a century later. In 1940, what had been conceived as a Silly Symphony, a Scherzo after a Ballad by Goethe, must have seemed to some in the audience like a requiem for a lost Europe.

It is difficult to imagine that Thomas Mann was a devotee of Mickey Mouse, but he surely recognized *Fantasia* as (in part) a tribute to Goethe – about whom, in fiction and non-fiction, he wrote with such perspicacity. Mann, who, with his wife and family, had emigrated to the United States in 1939, was just beginning his German-language broadcasts via the BBC, in which he condemned Hitler and his 'paladins' as crude philistines completely out of touch with European culture. In one noted speech he said, 'The war is horrible, but it has the advantage of keeping Hitler from making speeches about culture.'[10]

Mann's own version of the *Faust* legend, the novel he wrote in America during the war, chose, like Disney, to retell Goethean material via musical means. His imagined composer, Adrian Leverkühn, sells his soul to the devil, while being a composer of genius who deliberately devalues the 'culture' which had been Germany's most cherished possession since the so-called Goethe-time – *Die Goethezeit*, when his country's sky shone with the Weimar constellation, when Schiller and Goethe could spend evenings in the company of Wilhelm and Alexander von Humboldt, when Hegel and Fichte and Novalis and Hölderlin were all to be found in the same lecture halls or drawing rooms at nearby Jena, when Schlegel, Georg Forster, Voss, Heyne, were all at work, when classical learning went hand in hand with modern scientific discovery, and when Beethoven was composing incidental music for Goethe's play *Egmont*. Those with any consciousness of what that generation of Germans had given to the world – as poets, as dramatists, as botanists, as geologists, as composers, as painters, as archaeologists, as philosophers and theologians, as the nurses of culture in its highest form, and as midwives of the Enlightenment, the

Modern, the conception of the world which educated humanity now had in its head the world over – were now, in 1940, living through an era where it all appeared to have been destroyed.

Of course, you could say that Walt Disney and popular American culture were in their presumably well-intentioned way doing as much damage to 'culture', in the sense just described, as did the coarse brutalities and mumbo jumbo of the Nazis and the Communists. But that would be a cynical, snobbish viewpoint which it would not take long to demolish. Little as Goethe and his contemporaries would have enjoyed the 'popular culture' of the twentieth century, they would have seen the literature, the science, the music and the art which was contemporaneous with *Fantasia* as part of their gift to the world; Einstein and Mann and Stravinsky as their heirs and friends, whose work was being drowned out by the brash, cruel nonsense blared from loudhailers at Nuremberg,

I like to think that in the first audiences of *Fantasia* there were those who were reminded, not only of 'The Sorcerer's Apprentice', but of Goethe's masterpiece *Faust*. The story of 'The Sorcerer's Apprentice' is well known, and stretches back to ancient Greece. Goethe read it in one of his favourites, the satirist Lucian (120–185 CE),[11] an author discovered in his adolescence. In the absence of his master, the sorcerer's apprentice, to save himself the trouble of fetching buckets of water to fill the bath, performs one of his master's magic spells. He commands an inanimate broom to fetch the pails of water on his behalf. One problem. He has forgotten, or never known, the formula to stop the obedient broom filling the house with water, and by the time the sorcerer returns the place is awash.

In the Disney version, the apprentice is played by Mickey. In the German ballad version of Goethe, written in 1797 for Schiller's *Musen Almanach für das Jahr 1798*, the story had implications too obvious to be pointed out. Goethe, the Privy Councillor in a small principality – Saxe-Weimar – ruled over by an enlightened Prince – Carl August – and dependent for its very existence on the ancient hierarchies of the creaking, moribund, Holy Roman Empire, had, during the previous decade, witnessed the French Revolution, the invasion of Germany by the Revolutionary Armies, the decapitation of the French Queen (sister of the Holy Roman Emperor) and the threatened dissolution of the entire social framework. The heedless apprentice began by teaching a broom to carry a bucket, and ended by causing an unstoppable deluge. When the sorcerer returns, his apprentice cries out:

> The spirits I have summoned,
> I cannot now dispel.[12]

As a small c-conservative in a small provincial princedom, Goethe was understandably horrified by the collapse of social order represented by the revolution. On the other hand, he was far from being a maintainer of the status quo. In his personal life, he had scandalized small-town Weimar by openly living with a woman of a lower social class, without marrying her. He made no secret of the fact that he was not a Christian. He was at the forefront of scientific experiment, not merely as a follower of the scientists, but as their colleague: he had made a breakthrough discovery in human anatomy, and engaged in experiment and debate in matters as varied as geology and optics. As the son of republican burghers in the independent city-state of Frankfurt, he was not, in his gut, a royalist toady, even though the Duke of Saxe-Weimar was a lifelong friend and patron. Worried as he might have been by the Revolution, he was light-hearted enough to buy his son a toy guillotine. When Napoleon appeared on the scene, Goethe – much to many Germans' horror – was an enthusiast – even though the French Emperor had by then massacred tens of thousands of Germans, burned and harried their cities (including Frankfurt, where Goethe's mother was still living, and Weimar and Jena). When the tide of the war turned, and German forces joined with the allies to drive Napoleon to his ultimate defeat at Waterloo, Goethe refused to allow his son to join them, and he continued proudly to wear the *Légion d'honneur* which had been bestowed upon him by Napoleon during their meeting at Erfurt in 1806.

Moreover, 'The Sorcerer's Apprentice' represented only one strand of Goethe's delicately complex and in many ways rather cynical view of this life. Yes, it was terrifying when human beings summoned up spirits which they could not control. On the other hand, as he was to write in one of his most powerful lyrics, it is only those who live dangerously who achieve anything in this world.

> You will be no more than a dismal guest
> On the dark earth,

For as long as you have not grasped this truth:
Die and become something![13]

Goethe would have said that his horror at social anarchy and his manifesto in that lyric were not incompatible. Most people, he would be unashamedly elitist enough to say, are incapable of living dangerously and should not be encouraged to do so. It is the few who will achieve greatness, see into the life of things, advance culture and civilization.

Such exclusivity would not be to anyone's taste in today's world. It could be said that by placing himself so far above us in intellectual achievement and aspiration, Goethe deserves his current status as the Great Unread – revered and known among the German-speakers, but in the English-speaking world known only by very few readers. This is partly because his best work was all in poetry, and this is notoriously difficult to translate. It is also because he could be windy, nebulous, in his aim to be all-inclusive. He wanted to write about *everything*. Equally, he was an egomaniac, a great proportion of whose voluminous works are either direct works of autobiography, or records of his brilliant conversations.

If Walt Disney's *Fantasia* failed to be a box-office success when it first appeared, this was because it was in part highly comparable to *Faust*. Those who know the Faust story tend to do so via Christopher Marlowe's English play of the late sixteenth century, in which a scholar-mage makes a covenant with the devil, in exchange for secret power and knowledge. He is damned. The devil exacts his revenge.

Goethe, as we shall see in our remaining pages, was fascinated by this story, but when he came to write his own version he shifted its emphasis fundamentally. Again, many of us are unaware of this, since we become aware of 'Goethe's *Faust*', not by reading it, but by going to see the operatic version of Gounod. Goethe added a strand to the Faust story, namely the seduction of an innocent young woman called Gretchen (Margaret), who is sentenced to death for killing the child she begets with Faust. For his appalling behaviour to her, Gounod's Faust is condemned to damnation; so is the Faust of Berlioz.

But Goethe's Faust is not damned. Gretchen dies at the end of *Part One*, and by the time we meet Faust again, in the *Part Two* that occupied Goethe's old age, Gretchen has either been forgotten, or subsumed into a figure of the Eternal Feminine, after whom Faust and his readers yearn eternally.

In the course of our, or Faust's, journey to this vision of the Feminine Ideal (best known, perhaps, through Mahler's interpretation in his Eighth Symphony) we have taken in a lifetime of imaginative experience: an assessment of what has happened to Europe since the rise and fall of Napoleon; we have explored the limitless ambitions of modern science; we have reflected on modern economics, with the arrival of paper currency, credit capitalism and industry based on mining; we have seen in the Greek Revival, and the discovery of modern Greek Independence, something much more than a mere 'aesthetic' appreciation of Homeric hexameters or of the statues of antiquity collected in museums and great houses. We have revisited Hellenistic culture with the eagerness of ex-Christians who want to return to pre-Christian European roots and learn once more at the fountainhead of mathematics, philosophy, physics, biology, what the Greeks had to teach the human race before it was distracted by the pointless sexual guilt and incomprehensible redemption theology of St Paul.

A big journey! And one, moreover, which anyone patient enough to revisit the works of Goethe will discover to be a strangely prophetic one. Goethe anticipates the Modern Age. This was partly because he was a natural post-Christian, whose sexual morals, scientific outlook and belief in reasonableness as well as reason simply bypass the burden of the Christian centuries and speak directly to the post-Christian time in which we (whether or not we are Christians) now live.

Unlike so many younger Germans – Hölderlin, Feuerbach, Strauss – who underwent such agonies as they wrestled with their doubts and felt their faith in Christ draining away – and whose writings had such an effect on the nineteenth-century honest doubters – Goethe never believed in Christianity to begin with. He had spent a few months, perhaps, at most, as an adolescent recovering from illness, in the company of a pious female friend of his mother, and he would seem, for this very brief period, to have been a believer, or sort of believer, in her brand of evangelical faith. But it did not last, and his tribute to her – Fräulein Klettenberg – simply became, as did everything else, especially when women were concerned, grist for his literary mill – she became the long chapter (Book Six) in his rambling novel *Wilhelm Meister*, 'The Confessions of a Beautiful Soul'. Thereafter, the worries of the Tübingen School of theology, which George Eliot translated into English and which transformed Victorian England into a nation of honest doubters, tearfully listening to the Sea of Faith clawing the shingle as it ebbed away, were matters which troubled Goethe not in the very least. And one reason for this, as one of his wisest twentieth-century readers winkled out,[14] was obvious: despite his idolatrous love of Sophocles and Shakespeare, Goethe had no tragic sense. It is in this, I think, that he most seems our contemporary. We have a sense of disgust sometimes, and of shock at cruelty. We wallow in horror and sadness in our films, histories of the Second World War, we buy, and write, misery memoirs; but this is not *tragedy*. It is pathos or sentimentality or simply bad taste. Goethe had more in common with Walt Disney than he did with Thomas Mann who was possessed of a profound tragic sense.

It is also because, in so many of Goethe's concerns, he seems to be interested in what interests us – more than it interested our parents and grandparents. The most obvious example of this is in his science, which immediately anticipated what was wrong with a purely materialistic or reductionist outlook, and saw that an imaginative or poetic understanding of the environment, and a scientific knowledge of botany and geology point to the kind of relationship with the planet which more and more of us, taught by a younger generation than our own, feel to be truthful and productive.

The last five years of his life were devoted to patching together the bits of *Faust* which had already been written, and composing the rest. Not that it was easy to find the time, since his life as a famous genius meant almost daily visits from strangers and pilgrims; his life as a courtier could not be neglected either.

'I turned the conversation,' Eckermann tells us, 'to the second part of *Faust*, especially the Classical Walpurgis Night, which existed as yet only as a sketch, and which Goethe has told me he meant to print in that form. I had tried to advise him not to do so; for if it were once printed it would always be left in this unfinished state. Goethe must have thought that over in the meantime, for he now told me that he had resolved not to print the sketch ... "It might be finished in three months", said he, "but when am I to find time for it? The day has too many claims on me; it is difficult to isolate myself sufficiently. This morning the hereditary Grand Duke was with me; tomorrow at noon the Grand Duchess proposes visiting me. I must prize such visits as a high favour; they embellish my life, but they occupy my mind. I am obliged to think what I have new to offer to such dignified personages, and how I can worthily entertain them."[15]

The scene which these distinguished visitors prevented Goethe from completing was, when he had managed to do so, something without parallel, both for oddity and brilliance. First comes the scene in Faust's study, in which the Homunculus reveals to us the inside of Faust's imagination. This was written in late 1829, when he was eighty years old. The Classical Walpurgis Night, in some respects the most remarkable thing he ever wrote, belongs to the following year. It is difficult to think of any work of art with a longer period of gestation and completion, though an obvious, and mysterious, comparison could be made between the inception of Bach's B Minor Mass – when he wrote, and conducted, the Sanctus – in 1724, and then, a quarter of a century later, was putting the finishing touches to the full Latin Mass (as a Lutheran, he had never written such a thing before) in his very last years. (The first public performance was not until 1859!)

The obscurity, the 'incommensurable' quality of Faust, was of a piece with the careful editing, both of his work and of his self-image, to which the last years were devoted. Since 1824, Cotta the publisher had wanted him to produce the Final Edition – Ausgabe letzter Hand – and in the final years, no fewer than three helpers were engaged upon the task – Riemer, Eckermann and the philologist Karl Wilhelm Göttling.

One of Goethe's modern biographers[16] wittily recalled the passage in Poetry and Truth when Goethe was a student in Strasbourg when they cleared the streets of the disabled beggars, so that nothing unsightly could disturb the happiness of the Archduchess Maria Antonia, as she passed through the town from her home in Austria to become Marie Antoinette, Queen of France. Whereas the young Goethe had regarded it as absurd, and offensive, to try to tidy away these human evidences of imperfection and dirt in this dirty and imperfect world, the old poet of Weimar considered the cleaning-up operation to be entirely reasonable.[17]

The three editors of the Final Edition were therefore entrusted with the task of discarding and destroying anything which damaged the reputation of the poet. When Goethe, in 1794, had told Schiller that there were 'hundreds' of his Venetian Epigrams, some of which were unsuitable for publication, they printed 103. Today, of the hundreds omitted, only fifty-three survive. In 1822, there was a collection of material entitled 'What cannot be told in the Chronicles'. He wrote a note to explain: 'There is a significant amount of surviving poems which it is probably inadvisable to publish. They are to be put secretly into the hands of my son, and future counsellors can decide whether to destroy or to publish.'[18] Boisserée noted that there were a lot of papers in which Goethe had expressed intemperately about the politics of the day – that is, in extremely reactionary terms – and that these – both poems and prose works – had all been destroyed.

The questionable poems – presumably many of them in the erotic manner of the Venetian Epigrams and Roman Elegies – could not, in the final days, be placed into the hands of his son, because August predeceased him. The failure of the son's marriage and the constant noise of drunken rows coming from the upstairs apartment were a source of misery to the aged Goethe. Alcohol was having a catastrophic effect on August's physical and mental health. As he expressed it in a sad letter to Ottilie, 'The greatest necessity compels me to try to save myself, right now.'[19]

The letter was sent on the first leg of August's journey to Italy. He was accompanied by the faithful Eckermann, and the attempt to follow in his father's footsteps only emphasized the pathetic gulf between the two men. In his depleted state, he contracted meningitis. He died in Rome on 27 October 1830, and the news reached Weimar on 10 November. Goethe suffered from a pulmonary haemorrhage, and it looked for a while as if the news had killed him.[20] A few days later, however, he could write to Zelter, 'The individual is still in one piece and in his right mind!'[21]

The son had died. Carl August had died in Berlin, back in 1828. The Grand Duchess Luise died in 1830. All the old links with the past were going, or gone, and it was now his task, as the old Sage of Weimar, to edit the past, and to keep the routines of daily life. He slept with the key to the woodshed under his pillow. Up to this point, he had entrusted the day-to-day running to the young couple, but now the domestic burden must be resumed. It suited him that way. He retained control.

Almost every day, visitors came. In 1794, the royal menagerie in Paris had been transferred to the Jardin des Plantes; 1828 would see the opening of the first scientific zoo – the Zoological Society of London. It was the live equivalent of a museum, and would be followed by many others all over the world. In Paris, and in Regent's Park in London, the scientists peered at the animals. The house in the Frauenplan was a zoo with a difference – the wild beasts came to peer at the scientist.

An American in 1825 observed, 'His attitude and expression, as I entered, were those of an expectant naturalist, eagerly awaiting the transatlantic phenomenon.' Goethe had noted five years before that scarcely a day passed without some visit from a stranger. When he was in a good mood, the succession of strangers appeased the sense of chilly loneliness which engulfed him.[22]

George Bancroft, later American Navy Minister, but at the time a student at Göttingen, noted the stiff formality of the aged figure.[23] In May 1829, Princess Zenaide Aleksandrovna Volkonskaya – a relation of the future novelist Tolstoy – came to call, bringing with her the Russian translator of *Werther*, Nikolai Mikailovich Roshalin. 'He stands in the middle of his salon,' wrote the young Russian, 'with the dignified bearing of a government minister, but, while he granted the whole troop of us an audience, he was also horrified by it, and it required all the art of my Princess Volkonskaya to restore his equilibrium.'[24]

We began our journey, at the start of this book, with the disastrous delegation to the Frauenplan, to tell Goethe of the scheme to perform *Faust* in his honour at the Court Theatre in 1829. We noted that he did not attend, spending his eightieth birthday entirely alone with his thoughts in the old house. It was only one of many instances where anger was either scarcely held in check, or where it burst forth. Even new scientific discoveries had begun to rile him, since he had, in effect, closed down, as he approached death.

The old controversy between Vulcanists and Neptunists resurfaced. Goethe was entrenched in the view that the geological evidence suggested that mountains and rock formations had built up gradually as a result of the movement of waters. In November 1829, Alexander von Humboldt believed he had proved the exact opposite and, from his researches in Russia, felt confident that volcanic eruption caused the formations we see today. 'The Paris Academy has sanctioned this fancy,' wrote Goethe testily. 'Montblanc arose from the abyss with a fully formed rocky surface. So this utter nonsense rises up and it's going to become the superstitious belief both of the common herd and of the academic community, just as in the darkest ages of superstition, people believed in devils, witches and their works, even though one advanced against them with the most hideous torments.'[25] He complained that nowadays people could not rid themselves of mechanical and atomistic ideas.[26] Stuart Atkins pertinently noted that the 'point' of the Anaxagoras/Thales debate here is not so much whether the Neptunists or the Vulcanists were 'right' as that the reader should understand the nature of science and scientific language. All this is happening within the known universe. There is no outward divinity or controller, there's no Paley's watchmaker, no Jehovah. Anaxagoras looks to the three-fold chaste goddess Hecate/Diana/Luna and says, in the Atkins translation,

> Have I been rashly heeded?
> Has my appeal
> To higher beings
> Caused Nature's laws to be suspended?[27]

NO! is the answer. The answers to all scientific conundrums are to be found in the world 'which is the world of us'. Modern environmentalism has discarded the Mythos of a new Heaven and a new Earth coming into being when the old planet has been fried by God. We must reverence Great Creating Nature, *Deus sive Natura*, here a divine immanence.[28]

The Classical Walpurgis Night is *both* a Disneyan phantasmagoria *and* the most wonderful meditation on the different ways science (on the one hand) and Mythos (on the other) have to bear on our perceptions of reality – the reality of Nature, of natural phenomena hitherto only dimly understood, of human understanding, character, perception: in short, of *Poetry*. For Goethe, this is what poetry *is*. This is what a poet is, and what he has been set apart, as a poet, to do: to hold up a glass to the very life of things. It has been given to only very, very few human beings to have this degree of perceptivity. Atkins writes, 'The great water-pageant which concludes the Classical Walpurgis-night is, by virtue of its tolerant irony and healthy gaiety, the most convincing expression of Goethe's sympathetic understanding of the universal harmony of Nature, of his sense of man's proper place within that harmonious order.'[29] All those months in Italy, seeing the Renaissance Neoplatonic reinterpretations of Greek mythology in the paintings of the Old Masters is here bearing fruit. The triumphal conclusion is his unconditional profession of faith in the inexhaustible creative force which makes life and matter one. With themes and motifs furnished by the misguided fuddy-duddy Wagner and the uncreating anarch Mephistopheles, and by an interpretative poetic mirroring of his own experiences and insights, he has composed a masquerade whose rising scale of being this time expresses successfully his affirmative vision of the dignity of man and the meaningfulness of the cosmos in which man has his being.[30] To this degree, we find Goethe infinitely more optimistic about the planet than the twenty-first-century Greens, who of course are surveying a planet which has been all but wrecked, but whose rhetoric draws, often unconsciously, on the more spine-chilling passages of the Apocalypse of John.

Although he wanted to wade into the debate between Cuvier and Saint-Hilaire, Goethe in fact ploughed his thoughts into *Faust*. The Parisian debate of summer 1830 became, in the Classical Walpurgis Night, the dispute between Anaxagoras and Thales – a very serious joke (*sehr ernste Scherze*) indeed. The historical Anaxagoras, a friend of Pericles in the mid-fifth-century BCE, developed a philosophy of Nature as a constantly shifting system of material units, atoms, motivated by an all-encompassing divine mind (*Nous*). Goethe makes him the spokesman for the Vulcanist position in 1830. Thales, a pre-Socratic philosopher who lived a century earlier than Anaxagoras, was one of the first cosmologists in Greek culture. In *Faust* he is made to represent Goethe's own doctrine of natural creation, Neptunism. 'It is in moisture that life came into being' – 'Im Feuchten ist Lebendiges erstanden.'[31]

In some ways, Goethe's Critique of Plotinus foreshadowed or suggested Nietzsche's criticism of Socrates in *The Birth of Tragedy*.

Namely, the insistence on the One (in Plotinus's *Enneads*), the Good in Plato's version of Socrates, leads in the end to the extinction of what Nietzsche called the Dionysian, which fed on polytheistic mythology. The frenzy of human, natural, divine energy – this we feel in the *Iliad* and in the early tragedians. When Plato/Socrates began to demolish the Homeric theogony, leaving us with a monotheistic narrowness, much else would go – including, as Nietzsche openly stated and Goethe half feared, the idea of God Himself.

Goethe tried, therefore, to cling imaginatively to a sort of polytheistic mysticism, to a pantheistic Nature-worship.

> I do not ask whether this Highest of Beings is conscious, or reason, but I feel: it is consciousness, reason itself. All Creation is shot through with it: and humanity has this capacity to recognize itself as a part of the Most High.[32]

Most of the Classical Walpurgis Night was written from late 1829 to the end of 1830, when he was over eighty. He was moving towards the conclusion of the drama, also written at this time (the choruses after Faust's death), in which it is asserted that all our perceptions of truth are allegorical/metaphorical, and that we are led upwards by our aspirations to the Eternal Feminine. Helena herself, in Goethe's final version, does not realize that she is only a spirit, summoned up by the human imagination from her quasi-existence in the Underworld. It is difficult to decide (and probably it does not matter much) whether the whole drama of Act III – Faust's love affair with Helen of Troy, their begetting of Euphorion, the spirit of poetic genius/ Byron figure, and the tragic death/fading of Helen and her son – are merely the dreams passing through Faust's mind, or a fantasy staged by the Master of Ceremonies Mephistopheles, who, disguised as the Phorkyas throughout, steps forward at the end of the sequence, and is found sitting in front of the proscenium curtain and removes his mask. We perceive reality, including scientific reality, through onion layers of meaning, some of which are imposed by art, some of which are received as knowledge.

The great pageant in the closing scenes of Act II reveal this, and we are able to see Goethe's creative process at work as the verses, like the waves of the sea which they depict, roll forwards. Goethe uses as his template Raphael's wall painting of *The Triumph of Galatea* in the Villa Farnesina[33] which he came to know well during his Roman sojourn. Goethe had, for years, worked intermittently on a translation of the *Eikones* or Images/Paintings by Philostratus, a third-century CE Greek commentary on the wall paintings in Naples. Art historians are divided about whether Raphael himself used Philostratus in his depiction of the Galatea myth. Goethe utilizes the imagery of the Raphael picture to recast his original plan. He had been going to make Faust go down into the Underworld and draw Helen out, like Herakles rescuing Alcestis, or Orpheus charming Eurydice from the grip of Hades. As a very old man, he switched plans, and created this huge marine pageant, of Galatea, the water nymph, sweeping across the Mediterranean, drawing Helen in her train. In Ovid's version of the story (*Metamorphoses*) Galatea is beloved of the giant Cyclops, Polyphemus, who kills Acis, the youth whom the nymph loves. In Goethe's version, Galatea alights on the little test-tube baby, the Homunculus, and she is in thrall not to a giant but to her father the Old Man of the Sea, Nereus.

There is so much going on in this superb pageant that it is no surprise to find commentaries on it which are ten times longer than the poem itself. We find, as we read it and reread it, that we are in the exciting position of being inside Goethe's own eighty-year-old imagination. Guiding us through the layer upon layer of meaning, the philosopher Thales explains that the test-tube experiment of the Homunculus, like the images of classical mythology themselves, the figures of Galatea and Helen, will eventually be discarded. Humanity has been evolving for thousands of years – 'Durch tausend abertausend Formen'[34] – but, mysteriously, the evolutionary buck stops with humanity. Humanity is not going to evolve beyond itself. The only imaginable thing we have, at present, is the fact that we are human; the only means we have of understanding ourselves, science, the mystery of the universe, is human brainpower and imagination.

The distinction made by scholars between the youthful, Storm and Stress Goethe and the Classical Weimar implies, as he liked to imply himself, that in age he had moved to a more sober, more rational way of picturing the world of experience through Greek mythology. But, as Mephistopheles is quick to discuss, at the beginning of the

Classical Walpurgis Night, the division Goethe wanted to make (in his conversations with Eckermann) – Classical healthy, Romantic sick – won't really do.

Goethe in his extreme old age anticipated a rereading of the classical world which was made in 1951 by E. R. Dodds in his pioneering book *The Greeks and the Irrational*. What Goethe was writing in his old age was not 'mad', as some early readers believed;[35] it was controlled; but he saw that the mythology expressed in the vases, reliefs, statues and dramas from 700 to 400 BCE in the Hellenic world were as 'irrational' as the old witches and werewolves and ghosties of the Teutonic mythology. Goethe's perusal, in the Frauenplan, of the innumerable prints of Renaissance pictures, and of classical sculpture, revealed the bubbling frenzy, the infinitude of suggestiveness and suggestibility, in the war of the cranes and the pygmies, in the sharing of an eye and a tooth by the Graiae (Phorkyads), in the shriek of Sirens, in the destructive hate of the Sphinxes with their great lion claws, in the erotic dances of the Lamia, the enticements of the Nereids. The external natural world with which poetry and science try to come to terms is teeming with completely amoral energy. The clear perceptions of this eighty-year-old human brain – surely the most interesting brain which ever inhabited a human skull – dwells on the clash between the earthquake Seismos, the fiery Vulcanism of Anaxagoras, the tsunami, water-bearing gush of Thales, being both an accurate vision of the violent, eruptive power of observed geology and a metaphor for the political violence and military slaughters of the Napoleonic era.

When his son died, it looked very much, in the late autumn of 1830, as if Goethe aged eighty was going to die, too, with *Faust* incomplete. In the final week of November, during the night, he was seized with a violent haemorrhage, which – such was the savage cruelty of contemporary medicine – the doctors, Hofrat Vogel and colleagues, treated by further bleeding. By the time they had opened a vein, the old man had lost six pounds of blood.

Goethe trusted Vogel – maybe that had something to do with the fact he recovered. Vogel had been the only minister in the little Weimar

Cabinet who had supported Goethe in opposing any extension of press freedom.[36] An arch-reactionary, Vogel also opposed the allowing of any mitigating circumstances, from a medical viewpoint, in criminal behaviour, and he had been firm – Goethe thoroughly supporting him – over a case where a young woman, prosecuted for killing her own child, had put in a plea of diminished responsibility on the grounds of mental instability.[37] Yet more evidence that the author of *Faust Part One*, while acutely conscious of the pathos of Gretchen's prison plight, nevertheless felt her crime to have been correctly punished.

It was not, however, Vogel's support which brought Goethe back to life – still less, his use of that bleeding technique which killed so many in the past, including Byron at Missolonghi. It was, surely, the thought of the unfinished masterpiece. As soon as he was strong enough to hold a pencil, and when he was still forbidden by the doctors to attempt speech, he scribbled: 'Have the goodness, my dear Doctor, to go through these poems, which you already know, and rearrange the others which will be new to you, so as to make them fit into the whole collection. *Faust* follows shortly!'[38] The work continued.

Eckermann's pages, for the first part of 1831, witness the completion of the two complementary works – *Poetry and Truth*, the autobiography, and *Faust* itself.

It is often remarked that the fourth act shows signs of the poet's failing powers, and there can be no doubt that it is the weak link in the whole piece. *Part Two* took Faust and Mephistopheles from the private drama of their crimes against Gretchen and her family into the wide sphere of world politics. They present themselves as the solution to the Empire's economic problems, with a double scheme for enrichment – the extraction of minerals and fossil fuels from the earth, and the invention of global capitalism with the printing of paper money and the extension of government loans via the banking system. But Goethe had so much to say in this second part, and his prime interest was not solely with the world in which he was writing the piece – the post-Napoleonic era – but also with the huge imaginative legacy of the classical world. Look around at any great American or European city of this period, the 1820s to the 1830s – and what do you see? Greek Revival architecture. But Greek Revival was not simply a matter of having public buildings which delighted the eye, with porticos, caryatids and the formalities of classical order. The return to the Greeks – coinciding with the Greek War of Independence and the philosophical challenges to Christianity posed by science, by the disruptions post-war in the class system, by the disruption of the Holy Roman Empire – was a return to the very *fons et origo* of the human intellectual and imaginative journey in the West. It had been a return to science, to a complete rethink of what constituted a good city, to the question of whether democracy, as celebrated in the great oration of Pericles was a possibility in the post-revolutionary world. It was all these things, but it was also, for Goethe as for many contemporary artists, architects and poets, a revisit to classical mythology. So the great myth of the Trojan War, of Helen – the divinely hatched child of Zeus disguised as a swan – is milked for all its richness.

Where does the Faust drama go from here? We have already explored the ending which Goethe had completed (more or less) by 1830. Faust, far from being damned, as in the earlier versions of the play and in Goethe's own *Urfaust*, will be led onwards, after death, into a glimpse of the Eternal Feminine. The technical problem for Goethe as he recovered from his near-death experience at the end of 1830 was how to cast a bridge over the Classical Walpurgis Night and the Helena drama, so as to reconnect Faust's journey with his earlier appearance at the Court of the Emperor. Another way of saying this is: how to connect all the multifarious concerns, which had been so dazzlingly mythologized in Acts II and III, when Goethe was at the height of his powers, with the contemporary world, implied by the world of the Two Emperors? And in so doing, how to mythologize what had happened to Europe, when the old Empire, the world of the Holy Roman Empire, was displaced by a world of revolutions; the rivalry between Napoleon and the Old Regimes; the restoration after he – Goethe's 'mon empereur' – had been sent into exile on the island of St Helena? Goethe was not writing an allegory. He was, however, mythologizing his own times, the contemporary concerns of science, religion, politics as the new world of the nineteenth century emerged from the turmoils of thirty years of warfare.

Act IV – the Bridge between Faust the economist and political fixer to Faust the belated and completed flawed philanthropist – is the story of the military restoration of the old order, and the claims of the old religion who try to re-establish throne and altar. As our allusions to the reactionary views of Goethe's doctor made clear – Goethe's agreement with Vogel wishing to suppress press freedom and to hang unmarried mothers – Goethe wanted to return, if possible, to the pre-revolutionary stabilities. But he knew that this wish was illusory and impossible. He makes the military victory over the Rival Emperor (a sort of Napoleonic figure, but also a personification of revolution) a matter of magic. Mephistopheles summons up the Three Mighty Men, mythological figures from the Book of Samuel 2, 23.8–13 who rose up to fight against the Philistines and secure victory for King David, and from Isaiah 8.1–3 (the latter names the monsters Raubebald, Habebald and Eilebeute).

It is possible that, had he been younger, and on form, Goethe could have pulled off the feat of using this trope – the Three Mighty Men – as a shorthand emblem of the capricious fates of the battlefield. In *Part Two* Act IV, however, there are gross structural flaws. The build-up to the battle is painfully boring. Goethe takes twelve pages to lay out a scene which Shakespeare, in his history plays, would have managed in about twelve lines. But then, having erred by long-windedness, he then rounds off the battle, and the whole crisis of the threat to the Empire, in a completely perfunctory way. We see scarcely anything of the Rival Emperor, and what we do see is painfully lacking in the Napoleon 'demonic' which would have made this section of the drama interesting.

Nevertheless, the gift which so beautifully and mysteriously remained in the old poet was the capacity now and then to write poetry which is unsurpassed, as when the Emperor, straining his eyes, cannot really understand what is happening down on the battlefield, and Faust tells him

Have you not heard of the misty bands[39]
Which along the coast of Sicily?
There, hovering clear in daylight,
Lifted up towards the middle air.
Mirrored in a special fragrance
That strange face/appearance is seen[40]

and the old gooseflesh effect returns to the reader.

The point is that, however unsatisfactory Act IV may be, it was finished. No work of art which had been composed over sixty years and which, by the time of its completion, aspired to include more or less *everything* could possibly be polished and finished like a tragedy of Racine or the marbled glossy, sometimes soulless work of Canova. Goethe was never that kind of artist; though some of his lyrics have a perfection, they are not of a crystalline perfection.

In 1831, he was anxious, if possible, to avoid the celebration of his birthday in Weimar which would now be without his son, without his Duke. Two days before that event, on Friday 26 August 1831, he had the horses harnessed up, and with summer mist still filling the meadows around Weimar – soon to break into glorious sunshine – he set off. He was accompanied by his servant Krause, and the two grandsons, Wolf, aged twelve (born 1818) and Walther, aged ten (born 1820).

Both children, as we have seen, were to grow up as figures of pathos, unable to carry the burden of their great surname and their grandfather's fame. 'A remnant of the house of Tantalus'[41] was how one of them described himself.

But on that day, as children accompanying their grandfather to Ilmenau, the boys knew nothing of the lonely future, nor of the ending of their dynasty – as Shakespeare's dynasty was doomed to die out, and Milton's, in nonentity.

They were heading up into the hills, to visit the mines of Ilmenau, the region so often visited by Goethe with Duke Carl August when he was little more than a boy; a place where Goethe had frequently been alone, and which had inspired some of his most enduring poetry.

They left Ottilie behind. This was a journey into the past. He had not visited Ilmenau for thirty years. Here, as the young director of the mines, he had urged Carl August to reopen the mines – rather as Mephistopheles urged the Emperor to do so in *Faust*. He used to come here with old von Stein, and Charlotte had visited him here when he had loved her so intensely. The cave in the Hermannstein, a bluff on the north-west slope of the Kickelhahn, was a symbol of their covert happiness.[42] It was here that he had developed his passion for mineralogy. Here he had written the fourth act of *Iphigenia*.

The second part of *Faust* has the chief character standing on a hillside, at the very beginning of the drama, dazzled by the sunrise, an image, for him, of how the will, believing it has achieved the highest possible of its aims, is confounded: from the eternal depths, flash bursts of sun, excess of flame, engulfing us with light brighter than we can imagine, fire-blasting any satisfied sense that one has achieved the summit of one's potential. It is one of the most powerful of all Goethe's poems, and like so much of his greatest work, it is shot through with ambiguity. The Nature-painting is without parallel, more vivid than photography or film, it places us there – with that sounding cataract, that blazing dawn. Moreover, it is one of his keenest expressions of mysticism, his consciousness that the human psyche both is and is not utterly alone in the realm of Nature, since the force which drives Nature is at one, is the same as the eternal force within ourselves, making us aware of this inherent life in Nature. Rabindranath Tagore, twentieth-century mystic-poet-philosopher, wrote in 'Stream of Life', 'The same stream of life that runs through my veins night and day runs through the world and dances in rhythmic measures.'

A local official, Johann Christian Mahr, acted as his guide, and on the Saturday morning – the day before the birthday – they left the boys in the care of Krause and headed up the Kickelhahn. When they reached the crest of the hill, Goethe exclaimed, 'Ah! I wish my dear Duke Carl August could have seen all this beauty once more.' Mahr recalled how the man who would be eighty-two years old the next morning strode vigorously through the blueberry bushes to the crest of the hill.

There was a two-storey hunting lodge here. Mahr offered to help him, as they entered it and ascended the staircase, but Goethe brushed help aside. 'Don't think I can't climb those stairs – I'm quite capable!'

He told Mahr that years ago he had spent eight days immured in this upper room, with its superb views out across the treetops and the valley. 'I wrote a little poem on the wall. I'd like to have a look at it again.'

Sure enough, there were the words, which – though they are now perhaps the most famous poem in the German language – had not yet been printed in any of the collected versions of his work.[43]

To whom had he at first addressed the lines? Who was the 'Du'? Whoever it had been when first composed, on 6 September 1780, to the old man reading his own lines in the late summer of 1831, there could be no doubt that the words were addressed to himself, and that the peace which was soon to be his, the stillness as on the peak of the mountain the birds have flown to the silence of the wood, was none other than his own death.

Ruhest Du auch ...

A month later, Goethe would write, in a letter to Zelter, in which he had worked up the experience, edited it for posterity:

> In a lonely wooden house on the highest peak in the fir forest, I recognized the inscription ... After so many years, I could then survey what lasts, what has disappeared. Successes stood out and cheered me, failures were forgotten, over and done with. People all continued to live as is their custom, from the charcoal burner to the porcelain manufacturer. Iron was being smelted, brown coal dug from the crevices ... pitch boiled ... and so it went, like ancient granite. In general, a remarkable exploitation of the manifold surfaces and depths of the earth and mountains prevails.[44]

The conclusion of Richard Wagner's Ring cycle brings with it a miraculously expressed calm, when all the power striving of men and gods is seen to be less powerful than the enduring existence of Nature itself, and as the Ring of Power is reclaimed by the Rhine-maidens and the water of the river.

Goethe's Message to the Planet is comparable. As he wrote in another letter to Zelter, 'Nature is eternally alive and active, superfluous and extravagant in order that what is eternal may be continuously present because nothing can persist.'[45] In the eternity of that present moment, he felt the truth of Plotinus's knowledge: that whatever is, is eternal, and what is not eternal, but ephemeral, does not matter. Nature is not God, but Nature is riven with the eternal creative power which human beings feel within themselves, both when they fall in love, and when they are in communion with Nature and its mysterious force.

He ends this letter to Zelter, which is a self-consciously crafted testament, 'since you ask about *Faust*, I can tell you that the Second Part is at last complete. I've known, for so many years, exactly what I wanted, but only lately been able to work out the passages which interested me at the moment. In consequence, the gaps became evident, and they had to be filled up. I was absolutely determined to do this before my birthday. And so it was done. The whole work lies before me.'

ACKNOWLEDGEMENTS

Nicholas Boyle, Jonathan Gaisman, Anthony O'Hear, Angelika Tasler and Judith Wolfe all read chapters while they were in preparation and I am very grateful for their comments. Alex Mortimore, at a later stage, read it all and my debt to him is enormous. As so often before, Tamsin Shelton was a punctilious copy editor. Dennis Chang and John Gilhooly have been an enormous encouragement, as have Gina Thomas and Dr Susanne Frane. Robin Baird-Smith had the courage to commission this book in the full knowledge that many anglophone readers would take some persuading before they opened a book about the greatest writer they had never read. Octavia Stocker, my editor, has been beyond words helpful in preparing the book for the press. Fahmida Ahmed helped spare me from many an error (those remaining are my own). Grateful thanks for the faith of Tomasz Hoskins in this project, and to his wife, Dr Olenka Horbatsch, for sparing the time to show us Rembrandt's marvellous engraving called A Scholar in His Study ('Faust') and other Goethean treasures in the Print Room at the British Museum. Grateful thanks, too, to Jack Chauncy for his expertise in chemistry. Thanks too to my agent Matthew Hamilton for his encouragement and support.

BIBLIOGRAPHY

The Collected Works of Goethe on my own shelves are found in *Goethes Saemtliche* [*sic*] *Werke*, in seventeen volumes (Insel Verlag, Leipzig, 1932). When quoting from poems, scientific works and from some of the prose works, I have given a reference to this edition. So XIV.4 would mean Volume XIV of this edition, page 4. This edition does not contain his Letters and Diaries, which can be found in *Johann Wolfgang Goethe, Gedenkausgabe Der Werke, Briefe und Gespräche*, edited by Ernst Beutler in twenty-four volumes (Artemis-Verlag, Zürich, 1948–71).

Most learned books about Goethe refer to one of the huge Collected editions by a simple abbreviation – the Beutler edition is usually abbreviated as GA.

The trouble with this, from the point of view of a reader without access to a large library, is that the reference is all but useless. In as many cases as possible, therefore, I have aimed for a simpler method of reference. In the case of letters and diaries, whether letters to or from Goethe, I have supplied their date. I have done the same in the case of conversations. In the case of quotations from the major works, I have referred to chapter numbers, or, in the case of *Faust*, line numbers. The reason is obvious. If you want to look up, say, a particular conversation with Eckermann, it will be no use to you simply to have a reference to a huge collected edition. With the date, you can find it in either a German or a translated one-volume edition.

Consider the item in the Bibliography by Robert Steiger – eight huge volumes, together with a ninth heavy volume of index: *Goethe's Life from Day to Day. A Documentary Chronicle*. This mighty reference work began in 1982 and was completed in 2011. From really quite early in Goethe's life it is possible to see where he was, who he was with, what he wrote, on a daily basis; often on an hourly basis. No wonder his great English biographer Nicholas Boyle began his masterwork with the words, 'More must be known, or at any rate there must be more to know, about Goethe, than about almost any other human being.'[1]

That makes the task of writing about him, as of reading about him, formidable. Vast amounts have to be omitted, even from Professor Boyle's huge biography which, at the time of writing, consists of two volumes, ending in 1803, when the poet was still in his early fifties, and the completion of *Faust* lay decades in the future. When Nicholas Boyle finishes his task, it will be many times longer than the masterpiece of one of Goethe's most fervent British admirers, Thomas Carlyle's multi-volume *Life of Frederick the Great*.

The old Ovidian adage, that Life is Short and Art is Long, is quoted more than once in the opening scenes of *Faust*. One of the problems for the biographer of Goethe is that we know too much to be able to contain it all in manageable volumes.

I have tried to limit my book to the story of how *Faust* evolved. That inevitably involves considering much else besides, since Goethe, over the years, put so many of his vast range of interests into this single work. Although the Bibliography contains more volumes than the general reader will wish to consult, it represents only a tiny fragment of the number of books written about Goethe or touching upon Goethean themes.

My initial aim, when I began to draft an outline of my book, was to consult only two sources: Trunz's one-volume edition of *Faust* (Christian Wegner Verlag, Hamburg, 1963), which contains an abundance of information about the chronology of the work's composition, and about its interpretation, both by Goethe himself, his contemporaries and subsequent generations of readers; and secondly the invaluable six-volume *Goethe Handbuch* (Verlag J. B. Metzler, Stuttgart/Weimar, 1996–8). Any reader who knows these two sources will know that most of my book is culled, one way or another, from them. For any reader of my book wishing to read more, I recommend starting with those two.

For the reader with no German, I recommend Bayard Taylor, the nineteenth-century American poet, not least because he reproduced with great skill the multiplicity of verse forms in *Faust*. It is easily obtainable, but the handiest edition is the old, pocket-sized World's Classics (Oxford University Press, reprinted 1954). Much the best translation in modern

English is the version by Louis MacNeice (Faber & Faber, 1961). He was not a Germanist, but he relied heavily on the literal translation by his colleague E. L. Stahl. It was designed to be broadcast on radio, and MacNeice shortened the play considerably – to good effect.

Stuart Atkins owes much to MacNeice. His translation (Princeton University Press, 1984) is also good, and so is his *Goethe's Faust: A Literary Analysis* (Harvard University Press, 1958). Philip Wayne in the old Penguin edition did an admirable job (1949). The Norton edition of *Faust*, with a poorish translation by Walter Arndt, has a superb apparatus by Cyrus Hamlin, with a commentary on the entire poem and extracts from many of the more helpful commentaries and exegesis. This paperback (W. W. Norton, second edition, 2001) is highly recommended.

Learning languages has been a pastime of mine all my life, though I would never claim to be especially gifted in this regard. The thrill comes when you start to be able to get the feel of poetry in the language concerned. It was about ten years after my rudimentary attempts to master Italian that I felt myself beginning to 'get' Dante. Pushkin seemed easier when I tried to learn Russian, but once, at a very drunken party, when I tried to quote *Evgeny Onegin* and talk about it, a Russian furiously told me I was kidding myself, and she was probably right. I could have no idea, she said – and at this point I feared she would break her vodka glass in my face – no idea at all – of the nuances and subtleties of her great poet. The next morning, I was grateful to my furious interlocutor. She had alerted me to something which was so obvious that it was difficult to appreciate or remember when reading the comments of outsiders on any national literature. How many French, German, Russian readers of Shakespeare, however sophisticated, 'get' him, in the way that even an averagely intelligent schoolchild whose first language was English would automatically 'get' him? Does this not explain Tolstoy's quite extraordinary denunciation of *King Lear* which, quite simply, he had clearly failed to understand? His English was not good enough. However fluent you might be in a foreign language, and however easy you might find it to read a newspaper or work of modern prose, how confident are you, when reading the great poets, that you have really 'got' them?

Whether I have similarly 'got' Goethe, I do not know. What I do know is that his poetry is fiendishly difficult, not merely to translate, but to convey to a reader with no German. None of the translations of *Faust* are really adequate. That is why I would urge the English reader, even if, as with me and Pushkin, you are 'kidding yourself', to try to read Goethe in German, even if with an English translation at your elbow. Like Shakespeare and Dante, he was a poet who enormously enriched and expanded the capabilities of his own language and there are innumerable neologisms or enhanced usages of old words which it would take a lifetime to appreciate, even for one for whom German is the mother tongue. I do not claim to have reached the end of my Goethean journey; I am in the foothills, and the snowy peaks are only visible on the far horizon, but I do feel quite enormously enriched by the experience of reading him, each time I read a few pages of *Faust* being an expansion not only of linguistic appreciation but of something more. There are few authors outside the canon of Dante, Shakespeare, Homer and the three great Greek tragedians who have such titanic and universal power to speak to people of all ages and backgrounds. President Xi Jinping professes to know *Faust* by heart. He told Angela Merkel that in his youth he was sent to a remote part of China for re-education, and the only book for many miles around was *Faust*. He read it again and again.[2] Readers who have not yet begun their experience of immersion in *Faust* might, from this anecdote, realize that this extraordinary poem about power and its abuses is not necessarily to be approached without a 'trigger warning'.

Allen, James Smith, *A Civil Society: The Public Space of Freemason Women in France, 1744–1944*, Lincoln, NE, University of Nebraska Press, 2001

Alten, Friedrich von, *Aus Tischbeins Leben und Briefwechsel*, Leipzig, 1872

Ameriks, Karl, ed., *The Cambridge Companion to German Idealism*, Cambridge, Cambridge University Press, 2000

Andrews, William Page, *Goethe's Key to Faust: A Scientific Basis for Religion and Morality and for a Solution of the Enigma of Evil*, Boston/New York, Houghton Mifflin, 1913

Armstrong, Karen, *Sacred Nature: How We Can Recover Our Bond with the Natural World*, London, Bodley Head, 2022

Arndt, Walter and Hamlin, Cyrus, *Faust: A Norton Critical Edition*, 2nd edition, New York, W. W. Norton, 2001

Atkins, Stuart Pratt, *Goethe's Faust: A Literary Analysis*, Cambridge, MA, Harvard University Press, 1958

—— ed. and trans., *Faust Parts One and Two*, Princeton, Princeton University Press, 2014

Barth, Karl, *Protestant Thought from Rousseau to Ritschl*, New York, Harper and Brothers, 1959

Bellin, Klaus, *Das Weimar des Harry Graf Kessler*, Berlin, A. B. Fischer, 2013

Berlin, Isaiah, *The Crooked Timber of Humanity: Chapters in the History of Ideas*, London, John Murray, 1990

―― *The Roots of Romanticism*, Princeton, Princeton University Press, 1999

Biedermann, Floddard, Freiherr von, *Goethes Gespräche ohne die Gespräche mit Eckermann*, Leipzig, Insel Verlag, 1909 (abbreviated as *GG*)

Bishop, Paul, *Analytical Psychology and German Classical Aesthetics: Goethe, Schiller, Jung*, Hove, Routledge, 2008

Bloom, Harold, *The Western Canon: The Books and School of the Ages*, New York, Harcourt Brace, 1994

Bode, Wilhelm, *Charlotte von Stein*, Berlin, Mittler, 1920

―― *Goethe in vertraulichen Briefen seiner Zeitgenossen, auch eine Lebensgeschichte*, edited by Regine von Otto and Paul-Gerhard Wenzlaff, 3 volumes, Berlin/Weimar, Aufbau Verlag, 1979

Bortoft, Henri, *The Wholeness of Nature: Goethe's Way of Science*, Edinburgh, Floris Books, Sixth Printing, 2018

Bowie, Andrew, *Schelling and Modern European Philosophy*, London and New York, Routledge, 1993

―― *Aesthetics and Subjectivity: From Kant to Nietzsche*, Manchester, Manchester University Press, 1990

Boyle, Nicholas, *Goethe: The Poet and the Age*, Volume I, *The Poetry of Desire (1749–1790)*, Oxford, Clarendon Press, 1992

―― *Goethe: The Poet and the Age*, Volume II, *Revolution and Renunciation (1790–1803)*, Oxford, Clarendon Press, 2000

―― 'The Composition of *Die Wahlverwandtschaften*', *Publications of the English Goethe Society*, 84:2, pp. 93–137

Brewster, David, *The Kaleidoscope: Its History, Theory and Construction*, London, 2nd edition, John Murray, 1858

Brown, Hume, *The Youth of Goethe*, London, John Murray, 1913

Buchwald, Jed Z., *The Rose of the Wave Theory of Light: Optical Theory and Experiment in the Early Nineteenth Century*, Chicago, University of Chicago Press, 1989

Butler, E. M., *The Fortunes of Faust*, Cambridge, Cambridge University Press, 1952

―― *The Myth of the Magus*, Cambridge, Cambridge University Press, 1948

―― *Ritual Magic*, Cambridge, Cambridge University Press, 1949

―― *The Tyranny of Greece over Germany*, Cambridge, Cambridge University Press, 1935

―― *Goethe and Byron: Analysis of a Passion*, London, Bowes and Bowes, 1956

Camus, Albert, *Le Mythe de Sisyphe*, English translation by Justin O'Brien, *The Myth of Sisyphus*, London, Hamish Hamilton, 1955

Carlyle, Thomas, *Complete Works*, Edinburgh Edition, New York, Charles Scribner, 1904

Citati, Pietro, *Goethe*, English translation by Raymond Rosenthal, New York, The Dial Press, 1974

Clark, Robert T. Jnr, *Herder, His Life and Thought*, Berkeley and Los Angeles, University of California Press, 1955

Coleridge, Samuel Taylor, *Faustus from the German of Goethe*, edited by Frederick Burwick and James C. McKusick, Oxford, Clarendon Press, 2007

Colson, Bruno and Mikaberidze, Alexander, *The Cambridge History of the Napoleonic Wars*, Volume II: *Fighting the Napoleonic Wars*, Cambridge, Cambridge University Press, 2023

Conrady, Karl Otto, *Goethe und die Französische Revolution*, Frankfurt am Main, Insel Verlag, 1988

Critchley, Simon, *Tragedy, the Greeks and Us*, London, Profile Books, 2019

Damm, Sigrid, *Sommerregen der Liebe: Goethe und Frau von Stein*, Berlin, Insel Verlag, 2015

Davidson, Thomas, *The Philosophy of Goethe's Faust*, Boston/New York/Chicago/London, Ginn & Company, 1906

Dilthey, Wilhelm, *Das Erlebnis und die Dichtung*, Leipzig, B. G. Teubner, 1910

Dodds, E. R., *The Greeks and the Irrational*, Berkeley, University of California Press, 1951

Durrani, Osman, *Faust: Icon of Modern Culture*, Robertsbridge, Helm Information, 2004

Eastlake, Charles Lock, *Goethe's Theory of Colours. Translated from the German*, John Murray, 1840

Eckermann, Johann Peter, *Gespräche mit Goethe in den letzten Jahren seines Lebens*, Herausgegeben von Christopher Michel unter Mitwirkung von Hans Grüters, Berlin, Deutscher Klassiker Verlag, 2011

Eissler, Kurt R., *Goethe: A Psychoanalytic Study, 1775–1786*, Detroit, Wayne State University, 1963

Epstein, Klaus, *The Genesis of German Conservatism*, Princeton, Princeton University Press, 1966

Fairley, Barker, *A Study of Goethe*, Oxford, Clarendon Press, 1947

Friedenthal, Richard, *Goethe: His Life and Times*, Weidenfeld & Nicolson, 1965, reissued by Transaction Publishers with an Introduction by Martha Friedenthal-Haase, 2010

Gasset, José Ortega y, *The Dehumanization of Art and Other Essays on Art, Culture and Literature*, translated by Willard K. Trask, Princeton, Princeton University Press, 1968 (reprint of first edition 1948)

Gay, Peter, *The Enlightenment, An Interpretation*, New York, Alfred A. Knopf, 1967

—— *The Enlightenment: An Interpretation*, Volume Two, *The Science of Freedom*, New York, Alfred A. Knopf, 1969

Geary, John, *Goethe's Other Faust. The Drama of Faust Part Two*, Toronto, University of Toronto Press, 1992

—— *Wallenstein*, Toronto, University of Toronto Press, 1992

Ghibellino, Ettore, *Goethe und Anna Amalia. Eine verbotene Liebe*, Denkena Verlag, Weimar, 2003

Goethe, Johann Wolfgang, *Gedenkausgabe Der Werke, Briefe und Gespräche*, edited by Ernst Beutler, 24 volumes, Zürich, Artemis-Verlag, 1948–71

—— *Goethes Faust, Kommentiert von Erich Trunz*, Hamburg, Christian Wegner Verlag, 1963

Goodden, Angelica, *Miss Angel: The Art and World of Angelica Kauffman*, London, Pimlico, 2023

Hall, Edith, *Adventures with Iphigenia in Tauris: A Cultural History of Euripides's Black Sea Tragedy*, Oxford/New York, Oxford University Press, 2013

Hamlin, Cyrus, ed., *Faust. A Norton Critical Edition*, with the translation of Walter Arndt, New York, 2nd edition, W. W. Norton and Company, 2001

Hartmann, Gerhard and Schnith, Karl, eds, *Die Kaiser, 1200 Jahre europäische Geschichte*, Wiesbaden, Marix Verlag, 2006

Hawking, Stephen, *A Brief History of Time*, Toronto/London, Bantam, 1988

Hayward, A., revised and with an introduction by C. A. Buchheim, *The First Part of Goethe's Faust together with the prose translation, notes and appendices of A. Hayward*, London, Bohn's Collegiate Series, 1892

Hein, Karsten, 'Ottilie von Goethe. Einsichten in das Haus am Frauenplan', in Andreas Remmel and Paul Remmel (Hrsg.), *Goethe-Blätter. Schriftenreihe der Goethe-Gesellschaft Siegburg e. V.*, Band IV, Bonn, Bernstein Verlag, 2008

Heller, Erich, *The Disinherited Mind: Essays in Modern German Literature and Thought*, London, Bowes and Bowes, 1952

—— *The Artist's Journey into the Interior, and Other Essays*, London, Secker & Warburg, 1965

Hermann Brauning, Oktavia, *Johann Heinrich Merck und Herder. Die Geschichte einer Freundschaft*, Darmstadt, Justus von Liebig Verlag, 1969

Herzen, Alexander, *My Past and Thoughts: The Memoirs of Alexander Herzen*, 4 volumes, translated by Constance Garnett, London, Chatto & Windus, 1968

Hill, W. C. Osman, *Man as an Animal*, London, Hutchinson, 1957

Hind, Arthur, *A Catalogue of Rembrandt's Etchings*, London, Methuen, 1923

Hölscher-Lohmeyer, Dorothea, *Faust und die Welt. Zur Deutung des 2. Teiles der Dichtung*, Potsdam, Athenaion, 1940

—— *Faust und die Welt. Der zweite Teil der Dichtung. Eine Anleitung zum Lesen des Textes*. München, C. H. Beck, 1975

—— *Johann Wolfgang Goethe*, München, C. H. Beck, 1992, 2. Auflage 1999, 3. Auflage 2007

Houben, H. H., *J. P. Eckermann. Sein Leben für Goethe*, Leipzig, H. Hässel Verlag, 1925

Hume Brown, P., *The Youth of Goethe*, London, John Murray, 1913

Inge, W. R., *The Philosophy of Plotinus*, 2 volumes, London, Longmans, Green, 1918

Jaeger, Hans, 'The Problem of Faust's Salvation', *Goethe Bicentennial Studies*, Bloomington, Indiana University Publications, 1950

Janetzki, Ulrich (Hrsg.), *Ottilie von Goethe, Goethes Schwiegertochter. Ein Porträt*, Frankfurt, Ullstein, 1982

Jantz, Hartold, *Goethe's Faust as a Renaissance Man: Parallels and Prototypes*, Princeton, Princeton University Press, 1951

Jenkins, Ian and Sloan, Kim, *Vases and Volcanoes: Sir William Hamilton and His Collection*, London, British Museum Press, 1996

Kemp, Friedhelm, *Goethe, Leben und Welt in Briefen*, München/Wien, Hanser, 1978

Keuchel, G., *Goethe's Religion und Goethe's Faust*, Riga, Verlag von Jonck und Poliewsky, 1899

Klessmann, Eckhart, *Christiane: Goethes Geliebte und Gefährin*, Zürich, Artemis & Winkler, 1992

Kuéss, Gustav and Scheichelbauer, Bernhard, *200 Jahre Freimaurerei in Österreich*, Wien, Verlag O. Kerry, 1959

Lamport, F. J., *Goethe, The Natural Daughter and Schiller, The Bride of Messina, MHRA New Translations*, Volume 13, Cambridge, Modern Humanities Research Association, 2018

Lewes, George Henry, *The Life and Works of Goethe*, London, J. M. Dent [Everyman Library], 1959, first published 1863

Lichtenbergs, G. Chr., *Ausgewählte Schriften*, hrsg. von E. Reichel, Leipzig, 1879

Luke, David and Pick, Robert, eds, *Goethe: Conversations and Encounters*, London, Oswald Woolf Books, 1966

Luke, David, *Goethe: Selected Verse with an Introduction*, Harmondsworth, Penguin, 1964

Luttwak, Edward, 'Goethe in China', *London Review of Books*, 3 June 2021

MacCarthy, Fiona, *Byron: Life and Legend*, London, John Murray, 2002

MacNeice, Louis, *Goethe's Faust: An abridged version*, London, Faber & Faber, 1961

Maertz, Gregory, *Literature and the Cult of Personality: Essays on Goethe and His Influence*, Stuttgart, ibidem-Verlag, 2017

Magnus, Rudolf, *Goethe as a Scientist*, New York, Collier, 1961

Mann, Thomas, *Doktor Faustus*, Frankfurt, Fischer Verlag, 2020, first published 1947

—— *Lotte in Weimar*, London, Vintage Classics, translated by H. T. Lowe-Porter, 2019, translation first published 1940

Marchand, Suzanne, *Down From Olympus: Archaeology and Philhellenism in Germany, 1750–1970*, Princeton, Princeton University Press, 1996

Marshall Miller, David and Jalobeanu, Dana (eds), *The Cambridge History of Philosophy of the Scientific Revolution*, Cambridge, Cambridge University Press, 2022

Mason, Eudo C., *Goethe's Faust: Its Genesis and Purport*, Berkeley/Los Angeles, University of California Press, 1967

—— *Hölderlin and Goethe*, Bern/Frankfurt, Verlag Herbert Lang & Cie AG, 1975

Matthaei, Rupprecht, ed., *Goethe's Colour Theory*, London, Studio Vista, 1971

McGilchrist, Iain, *The Master and His Emissary: The Divided Brain and the Making of the Western World*, New Haven/London, Yale University Press, revised edition 2019

McGrath, William J., *German Freedom and the Greek Ideal*, New York, Palgrave Macmillan, 2013

Meakin, Annette, *Goethe and Schiller: 1785–1805. The Story of a Friendship*, 3 volumes, London, Francis Griffiths, 1932

Merchant, Carolyn, *The Death of Nature: Women, Ecology and the Scientific Revolution*, London, Wildwood House, 1982

Merseburger, Peter, *Mythos Weimar. Zwischen Geist und Macht*, Stuttgart, Pantheon, 1998

Messner, Paul, *Das Deutsche Nationaltheater Weimar. Ein Abriss seiner Geschichte*, Weimar, Satstmuseum Weimar, 1985

Miller, Douglas, *Goethe: Scientific Studies*, New York, Suhrkamp, 1988

Mommsen, Katharina, 'Faust II als politisches Vermächtnis des Staatsmannes Goethe', *Jahrbuch des Freien Deutschen Hochschifts*, Frankfurt am Main, Freies Deutsches Hochstift, 1989

Müller, Olaf L., *Mehr Licht. Goethe mit Newton im Streit um die Farben*, Frankfurt am Main, S. Fischer Verlag, 2015

Müllner, Ludwig, *Goethes Faust im Lichte seiner Naturförschung*, Stuttgart, Orient-Occident Verlag, 1981

Nevinson, Henry, *A Sketch of Herder and His Times*, London, Chapman and Hall, 1884

Nicholls, Angus and Liebscher, Martin, eds, *Thinking the Unconscious: Nineteenth-Century German Thought*, Cambridge, Cambridge University Press, 2010

Nicolai, Heinz, *Goethe und Jacobi. Studien zur Geschichte ihrer Freundschaft*, Stuttgart, J. B. Metzlersche Verlagsbuchhandlung, 1965

Nisbet, H. B., *Goethe and the Scientific Tradition*, University of London, Institute of Germanic Studies, 1972

Noyes, John K., *Herder: Aesthetics Against Imperialism*, Toronto/Buffalo/London, University of Toronto Press, 2015

Obenauer, Karl Justus, *Der faustische Mensch*, Jena, Eugen Diederichs, 1922

—— *Goethe in seinem Verhältnis zur Religion*, Jena, Verlegt bei Eugen Diederichs, 1921

Otto, Regine, Witte, Bernd et al., eds, *Goethe Handbuch*, 6 volumes, Stuttgart/Weimar, Verlag J. B. Metzler, 1996–98

Patterson, Michael, *The First German Theatre: Schiller, Goethe, Kleist, and Büchner in performance*, London, Routledge, 1990

Pelikan, Jaroslav, *Faust the Theologian*, New Haven/London, Yale University Press, 1995

Piper, Andrew, 'Egologies: Goethe, Entoptics, and the Instruments of Writing Life', in Richter and Block, 2013

Powys, John Cowper, *The Pleasures of Literature*, London, Cassell and Company Ltd, 1938

Prokhoris, Sabine, *La Cuisine de la sorcière*, Paris, Aubier, 1988

Proskauer, Heinrich O., *The Rediscovery of Color*, Spring Valley, NY, Anthroposophic Press, 1986

Pruys, Karl Hugo, *Die Liebkosungen des Tigers*, Berlin, Verlags-GmbH, 1997

Quetel, Claude, *History of Syphilis*, translated by Judith Braddock and Brian Pike, Cambridge, Polity Press, 1990

Reed, T. J., *Classical Centre: Goethe and Weimar, 1775–1832*, London, Croom Helm, 1980

Richter, Simon and Block, Richard (eds), *Goethe's Ghosts: Reading and the Persistence of Literature*, Rochester, NY, Camden House, 2013

Ridley, Jasper, *A Brief History of the Freemasons*, London, Constable, 1999

Robertson, Ritchie, *The Enlightenment: The Pursuit of Happiness, 1680–1790*, London, Penguin Books, 2020

—— 'Goethe's Faust II. The Redemption of an Enlightened Despot', *Publications of the English Goethe Society*, 23 March 2022

Safranski, Rüdiger, *Goethe: Kunstwerk des Lebens*, München, Karl Hanser Verlag, 2013, English translation by David Dollenmeyer, New York, Liveright, W. W. Norton, New York, 2017

—— *Romantik. Eine deutsche Affäre*, München, Karl Hanser, 2007

Salm, Peter, *The Poem as Plant: A Biological View of Goethe's Faust*, Cleveland/London, The Press of Case Western Reserve University, 1971

Saltner, Lutz, 'Hier Nicht'. *Goethes letzte Tage*, Berlin, Anthea Verlag, 2020

Schiller, Friedrich, *Schillers Werke*, Frankfurt am Main, Insel Verlag, 1966, 4 Voklumes

Schmidt, Irmgard, 'Angelika Kauffmann – Goethes Freundin in Rom. Ein Lebensbild nach ihren Briefen und nach Berichten ihrer Zeitgenossen', in *Goethe Jahrbuch*, Wien, 67 (1963)

Schmitz, Hermann, *Goethes Altersdenken im problemgeschichtlichen Zusammenhang*, Bonn, H. Bouvier und Co. Verlag, 1959

Schöne, Albrecht, *Der Briefschreiber Goethe*, München, C. H. Beck, 2015

Schulz, Karlheinz, *Goethe. Eine Biographie in 16 Kapiteln*, Stuttgart, Philip Reclam jun., 1999

Schweitzer, Albert, *Goethe*, London, Adam and Charles Black, 1949

Seidel, Renate, *Charlotte von Stein und Johann Wolfgang Goethe, Die Geschichte einer grossen Liebe*, München, nymphenburger, 1993

Sepper, Dennis L., *Goethe contra Newton: Polemics and the Project for a New Science of Color*, Cambridge, Cambridge University Press, 1988

BIBLIOGRAPHY

—— 'Goethe, Newton and the Imagination of Modern Science', *Revue internationale de philosophie*, 2009/3, no. 249

Sherrington, Charles, *Goethe on Nature and on Science*, Cambridge, Cambridge University Press, 1942

Smeed, J.W., *Faust in Literature*, London/New York/Toronto, Oxford University Press, 1975

Stammen, Theo, *Goethe und die Französische Revolution*, München, C. H. Beck, 1966

Stawell, F. and Lowes Dickinson, G., *Goethe and Faust: An Interpretation*, London, G. Bell and Sons, 1928

Steiger, Robert, *Goethes Leben von Tag zu Tag. Eine dokumentarische Chronik*, 9 volumes, Berlin, De Gruyter, 2011

Stephenson, R. T. H., *Goethe's Conception of Knowledge and Science*, 1995

Stollberg-Rilinger, Barbara, *Maria Theresa: The Habsburg Empress in Her Time*, Princeton, Princeton University Press, 2022

Tillette, Xavier, *Schelling. Biographie*, Paris, Calmann-Lévy, 1999

Trevelyan, Humphrey, *Goethe and the Greeks*, Cambridge, Cambridge University Press, 1941, with an introduction by Hugh Lloyd Jones, 1981

Trevor-Roper, H. R., *Historical Essays*, London, Macmillan & Co., 1957

Trunz – see Goethe, Johann Wolfgang, *Goethes Faust*

Tümmler, Hans, *Carl August von Weimar, Goethes Freund: Eine vorweigend politische Biographie*, Stuttgart, Klett-Cotta, 1978

Valdez, Damian, *German Philhellenism: The Pathos of the Historical Imagination, from Winckelmann to Goethe*, New York, Palgrave Macmillan, 2014

Van Abbé, Derek, 'On Correcting Eckermann's Perspectives', *Publications of the English Goethe Society*, NS Vol. XXIII, 1954

Van der Laan, J. M., *Seeking Meaning for Goethe's Faust*, London/New York, Continuum, 2007

Vietor-Engländer, Deborah, *Faust in der DDR*, Frankfurt am Main, Peter Lang, 1987

Vogel, Julius, *Aus Goethe's Römischen Tagen*, Leipzig, Verlag von E. U. Seemann, 1905

Wells, George A., 'Goethe and the Intermaxillary Bone', *British Journal for the History of Science*, December, Vol. 3, No. 4, 1967

Wilkinson, Elizabeth, 'The Theological Basis of Faust's Credo', *German Life and Letters*, 10, 1957, pp. 229–39

Williams, John R., *The Life of Goethe*, Oxford, Blackwell, 1998

Williamson, George S., 'What Killed August von Kotzebue? The Temptations of Virtue and the Political Theology of German Nationalism, 1789–1819', *Journal of Modern History*, Vol. 72, No. 4, December 2000, pp. 890–943

Wilson, W. Daniel, *Der Faustische Pakt*, München, dtv, 2018

—— 'Goethe and his Duke and Infanticide: New Documents and Reflections on a Controversial Execution', *German Life and Letters*, Vol. 61, Issue 1, July 2008, pp. 7–32

—— *Geheimräte gegen Geheimbünde*, Stuttgart, Metzler, 1991

Wulf, Andrea, *Magnificent Rebels: The First Romantics and the Invention of the Self*, London, John Murray, 2022

Wutrich, Timothy Richard, *Prometheus and Faust*, Westport, CT, Greenwood Press, 1995

Yates, Frances, *Giordano Bruno and the Hermetic Tradition*, London, Routledge and Kegan Paul, 1964

—— *The Art of Memory*, London, Routledge and Kegan Paul, 1966

Zapperi, Roberto, *Incognito*, Roma, Bollati Boringhieri, 1999

NOTES

CHAPTER 1 – THESE VERY SERIOUS JOKES

1 F 32 43–4.
2 C. S. Lewis, *The Abolition of Man*, p. 46.
3 F 1112.
4 Eckermann, 27 March 1825.
5 See *Goethe Handbuch*, Band 2, p. 522.
6 Ibid.
7 Ibid., p. 523.
8 Nicholas Boyle, *Goethe: The Poet and the Age*, Vol. I, p. 286.
9 Eckermann, 1 April 1827.
10 W. Daniel Wilson, *Der Faustische Pakt*, p. 241.
11 It was Hitler.
12 Wordsworth, 'The French Revolution as It Appeared to Enthusiasts at Its Commencement'.
13 Eckermann, 7 October 1827.
14 I owe these insights, and much of my understanding of *Faust*, to an all-day seminar held by Professor Paul Bishop, 22 October 2016, at the Unitarian Church in Kensington, entitled 'Reading Goethe at Midlife'.
15 F 6272.
16 Bertrand Vergely, *The Dialectic of the Secret*.
17 Quoted by Butler, *The Myth of the Magus*, p. 143.
18 13 November 1925, quoted in Robert Hass's selection of Rilke, Picador, p. 316.
19 A profound, wide-ranging and stimulating survey of the whole question is found in Iain McGilchrist, *The Master and His Emissary: The Divided Brain and the Making of the Western World*.
20 Isaiah Berlin, *The Roots of Romanticism*, pp. 21–2.
21 Contemporary scholarship has shied away from considering the Enlightenment as a purely rational, or left-hemisphere phenomenon. Ritchie Robertson, for example, in his latest book *The Enlightenment: The Pursuit of Happiness, 1680–1790*, argues that the Enlightenment was a philosophical development which emphasized the role of emotion, or sensibility, as well as reason. It was not solely about cold, mechanical rationalism.
22 David Luke, *Goethe: Selected Verse with an Introduction*, p. xxv.
23 XIV.538.
24 Quoted Karen Armstrong, *Sacred Nature*, p. 39. The translation is that of Stephen Addiss and Stanley Lombardo, Indianapolis, 1992.
25 F 328–9.
26 Erich Heller, *The Disinherited Mind*.

27 Stuart Atkins, *Goethe and Faust*, p. 274.
28 Ibid., p. 275.
29 Letter to Wilhelm von Humboldt, 17 March 1832.

CHAPTER 2 – TURNING LIFE INTO A PICTURE

1 F 18, 1840–41, 'Das Beste was du Wissen kannst,/Darfst du den Buben doch nicht sagen' – 'the best you know, you dare not tell the boys' (i.e. Faust's pupils).
2 Rüdiger Safranski, *Goethe: Kunstwerk des Lebens*, p. 96.
3 Samuel Taylor Coleridge, *Faustus from the German of Goethe*, p. 7.
4 XV.74. 'Und in seiner Trauten Kreise,/Sorgenfrei und unterhaltend,/Eine Welt nach seiner Weise,/Nah und fern umher gestaltend' [1815]
5 F 357.
6 F 3454.
7 *Poetry and Truth*, Part One, Book One.
8 *Wilhelm Meisters Theatralische Sendung*, reworked as *Wilhelm Meisters Lehrjahre*.
9 Book One, Chapter One, 1. 126.
10 E. M. Butler, *The Myth of the Magus*, pp. 122–31.
11 Genesis 3.4–5.
12 E. M. Butler, *The Fortunes of Faust*, pp. 94–5.
13 Eckermann, 26 September 1827.
14 Barbara Stollberg-Rilinger, *Maria Theresa*, p. 82.
15 *Dichtung und Wahrheit*, III.422.
16 Ibid., I.3.
17 'Goethe as the Sage', in T. S. Eliot, *On Poetry and Poets*, London, Faber & Faber, 1957, p. 220.
18 *Dichtung und Wahrheit*, Part Two, Book VII, III.302.

CHAPTER 3 – THE SPIRIT OF NATURE – WHERE ARE YOU, FAUST?

1 Boyle, Vol. I, p. 63.
2 *Dichtung und Wahrheit*, Part Two, Book Eight, III.330.
3 Ibid., Part Two, Book Eight, III.350.
4 *Wilhelm Meisters Lehrjahre* (Sixth Book), II, 361.
5 Ibid., II, 387.
6 Boyle, Vol. 1, p. 75.
7 F 377.
8 F 434–8.
9 26 August 1770.
10 W. R. Inge, *The Philosophy of Plotinus*, Vol. I, p. 269.
11 *Dichtung und Wahrheit*, Part Three, Book Fourteen, III.665.
12 Letter to Ludwig Julius Friedrich Höpfner, April/May 1773.
13 *Dichtung und Wahrheit*, Part Two, Book 9, III.385. Exactly the same thing happened in Windsor, on the eve of the marriage of Meghan Markle to Prince Harry. The vagrants, beggars and unfortunates were cleared from the streets near the castle, so as not to 'spoil' the princess's day.
14 *Oeuvres de Frédéric le Grand*, ed. J. D. E. Preuss, 31 volumes, 1846–57, Vol. VII, p. 125.
15 Trunz, p. 641.

16 Arthur Hind, *A Catalogue of Rembrandt's Etchings*, p. 107.
17 See Stephen Clucas, 'Astrology, Natural Magic and the Scientific Revolution', in David Marshall Miller and Diana Jalobeanu, eds, *The Cambridge History of Philosophy of the Scientific Revolution*, p. 167.
18 Frances Yates, *Giordano Bruno and the Hermetic Tradition* (1964) and *The Art of Memory* (1966).
19 F 446–50.
20 *Urfaust*, 102.
21 Unless otherwise stated, all the observations about *Faust* in this book derive from the notes in Trunz.
22 F 1746.
23 *Urfaust*, 150.
24 P. Hume Brown, *The Youth of Goethe*, p. 290.
25 *Urfaust*, 477.
26 Ibid., 565.
27 Ibid., 1157.

Chapter 4 – Some Notes on Suicide

1 Center of Disease Control and Prevention, 'Suicide Prevention'; UK Census of 2021, supplied by the Office for National Statistics; Zero Suicide Alliance.
2 Boyle, Vol. I, p. 131.
3 James Boswell, *Life of Johnson*, 118, AD 1750.
4 *Dichtung und Wahrheit*, Part Three, Book Thirteen, III.603.
5 G.Ch. Lichtenbergs, *Ausgewaehlte Schriften*, p. 499.
6 Friedhelm Kemp, *Goethe, Leben und Welt in Briefen*, p. 526.
7 Albrecht Schöne, *Der Briefschreiber Goethe*, pp. 98, 114–15.
8 *Dichtung und Wahrheit*, Part Three, Book Eleven, III, 521.
9 Ibid., III.521.
10 Lucretius, *De Rerum Natura*, III, 91ff.
11 20 February 1821.
12 Armstrong, p. 11.
13 24 December 1771.
14 Hans Mayer, *Goethe im Zwanzigste Jahrhundert: Spiegelungen und Deutungen*, Frankfurt, Insel Verlag, 1987, p. 24.
15 George Henry Lewes, *The Life and Works of Goethe*, p. 127.
16 20 November 1772.
17 25 September 1772.
18 Martin van Creveld, *Command in War*, Cambridge, MA, Harvard University Press, 1985, p. 96.
19 *Goethe Handbuch*, Band 4/2, p. 746.
20 Ibid., p. 747.
21 Eckermann, 11 March 1828.
22 Ibid.
23 Goethe said it to Riemer, *Goethe Handbuch*, Band 4/2, p. 746.
24 Albert Camus, *The Myth of Sisyphus*, p. 3.
25 Office for National Statistics website.
26 Eckermann, 17 March 1830.
27 F 734–5.
28 III.338.
29 'Freuden des Jungen Werthers', XIV, 158–9.

30 Letter to Herder, 5 December 1772.
31 G. H. Lewes, *The Life and Works of Goethe*, p. 10.

Chapter 5 – Bildung

1 *Wilhelm Meisters theatralische Sendung, Wilhelm Meisters Lehrjahre* and *Wilhelm Meisters Wanderjahre oder die Entsagenden.*
2 Lavater, February 1773, quoted Kemp, p. 78.
3 Boyle, Vol. I, p. 188, Lichtenberg Aphorismen E69, written July 1775.
4 Inge, Vol. II, p. 32.
5 Boyle, Vol. I, p. 141.
6 Safranski, *Goethe: Kunstwerk des Lebens*, p. 367.
7 Karl Hugo Pruys, *Die Liebkosungen des Tigers*, p. 33.
8 Heinz Nicolai, *Goethe und Jacobi*, p. 71.
9 Pruys, p. 36.
10 Karl Robert Mandelkow, ed., *Briefe an Goethe*, 3rd edn, 2 vols, München, Beck, 1988, 28 December 1812.
11 Jason Josephson-Storm, *The Myth of Disenchantment: Magic, Modernity, and the Birth of the Human Sciences*, Chicago, University of Chicago Press, 2017, p. 69.
12 Karl Ameriks, ed., *The Cambridge Companion to German Idealism*, p. 96.
13 Ibid., p. 98.
14 Frederick Beiser, 'The Enlightenment and Idealism', in Ameriks, ed., p. 26.
15 Tennyson, in *In Memoriam*.
16 Inge, Vol. II, p. 27.
17 Beiser, in Ameriks, ed., p. 27.
18 Boyle, Vol. I, p. 242.
19 Hans Tümmler, *Carl August von Weimar, Goethes Freund*, p. 18.
20 Boyle, 202HA Br i. 182–3, ie Briefe Hamburg Munich 1988.
21 Eckermann, 10 August 1824.
22 Ibid., 5 March 1830.
23 Letter to Auguste, in Lewes, p. 187.
24 30 October 1775.
25 *Dichtung und Wahrheit*, ii. 304, Part Four, Book 20, III.820.

Chapter 6 – Weimar

1 Thomas Mann, *Lotte in Weimar*, translated by H. T. Lowe-Porter, p. 103.
2 Ibid., p. 105.
3 Ibid., p. 190.
4 Ibid., p. 191.
5 Boyle, Vol. I, p. 148.
6 Peter Merseburger, *Mythos Weimar*, p. 9.
7 Great-grandfather of Prince Albert of Saxe-Coburg-Gotha.
8 Etore Ghibellino, *Goethe und Anna Amalia*, p. 14.
9 Merseburger, p. 65. Maria Pavlovna was the daughter of Tsar Paul I, and became Grand Duchess of Saxe-Weimar-Eisenach by her marriage to Karl Friedrich of Saxe-Weimar.
10 Merseburger, p. 53.
11 Peter Gay, *The Enlightenment: An Interpretation*, Volume Two, *The Science of Freedom*, p. 20, quoting Kant Werke IV, 174, 'Was Ist Äufklaerung?'.
12 Many times great-aunt of Philip, Duke of Edinburgh.

13 Safranski, *Goethe: Kunstwerk des Lebens*, p. 167.
14 Richard Friedenthal, *Goethe: His Life and Times*, pp. 176–7.
15 8 August 1776, from Ilmenau.
16 F 26.
17 Andre Wakefield, *The Disordered Police State: German Cameralism as Science and Practice*, Chicago, University of Chicago Press, 2009, p. 24.
18 Sebastian Ferlten, 'The history of science and the history of knowledge: Saxon mining circa, 1770', *The History of Science*, 2018, Vol. 56, No. 4, pp. 403–31.
19 Walter Herrmann, 'Goethe und Trebra. Freundschaft und Austausch zwischen Weimar und Freiberg', in *Freiberger Forschungshefte*, ser. D. no. 9, 1955.
20 Letter to Charlotte von Stein, 8 August 1776.
21 15 June 1779.
22 Boyle, Vol. I, p. 137.
23 Wilhelm Bode, *Charlotte von Stein*, p. 61.
24 GG, 1. 397.
25 Bode, *Charlotte von Stein*, p. 5.
26 26 January 1775.
27 Says Boyle, Vol. I, p. 265, quoting Karl Robert Mandelkow, ed., *Briefe an Goethe*, i. 408, Letter to Lavater, 20 September 1780.
28 William Wordsworth, *The Prelude*, IV. 334.
29 F 3956.
30 F 4692–3.
31 F 4727.
32 *Farbenlehre*, First Part, 'Physiologische Farben', section 75, XVII.62.
33 Boyle, Vol. I, p. 259.
34 Ibid., p. 260.
35 Ibid., p. 304.
36 Ibid., p. 339.
37 Boyle, Vol. I, p. 266.

Chapter 7 – Archbishop of Titipu

1 'Toil, Envy, Want, the Patron or the Gaol', *The Vanity of Human Wishes*, line 160.
2 Boyle, Vol. I, p. 244.
3 For this and all previous paragraph, Henry Nevinson, *A Sketch of Herder and His Times*, pp. 237–78.
4 Ibid., p. 241.
5 The Wettin family divided into those descended through the Ernestine line and those who came through the Albertine line.
6 Boyle, Vol. I, p. 342.
7 30 June 1780.
8 F Part Two, 4866–76.
9 Ibid., 4892–3.
10 Safranski, *Goethe: Kunstwerk des Lebens*, p. 267.
11 F Part One, 3462–5.
12 But it was not exclusively male. It has been argued that Freemason women, embracing the ideals of brotherly love and classlessness, helped to create a more humane and open society in post-Revolutionary French Republics. See James Smith Allen, *A Civil Society: The Public Space of Freemason Women in France, 1744–1944*, University of Nebraska Press, 2001.

13 Kipling, 'The Mother-Lodge', 1895.
14 Quoted Boyle, Vol. I, p. 274.
15 Gustav Kuéss and Bernhard Scheichelbauer, *200 Jahre Freimaurerei in Österreich*.
16 Boyle, Vol. I, p. 353.
17 W. Daniel Wilson, *Geheimräte gegen Geheimbünde*, pp. 12–13.
18 22 June 1781.
19 See Klaus Epstein, *The Genesis of German Conservatism*, p. 503.
20 Jasper Ridley, *The Freemasons*, p. 117.
21 Freemasonry Matters (online site), 17 January 2019.
22 'Symbolum'. See 'Goethe Freemason. Short Talk Bulletin', Vol. X, September 1932, No. 9.
23 F Part One, 1972 ff.
24 W. Daniel Wilson, 'Goethe, His Duke and Infanticide', p. 9.
25 Wilson, 'Goethe, His Duke and Infanticide', pp. 7–32.
26 Kemp, p. 235.
27 11 February 1782, quoted Safranski, *Goethe: Kunstwerk des Lebens*, p. 272. (It's from Gôchhausen's copy of pages from his early version that we have *Urfaust*.)
28 Boyle, Vol. I, p. 349.
29 George A. Wells, 'Goethe and the Intermaxillary Bone', p. 319.
30 W. C. Osman Hill, *Man as an Animal*, p. 52.
31 Wells, p. 327.
32 Ideen 2nd Buch Kap 4. Quoted Boyle, Vol. I, p. 713.
33 'Was war ein Gott, der nun von aussen stiesse,/Im Kreis das All am Finger laufen liesse?'
34 Rudolf Magnus, *Goethe as a Scientist*, p. 22.
35 Safranski, *Goethe: Kunstwerk des Lebens*, p. 253.
36 Ghibellino, p. 105.
37 Book I, Chapter 7.
38 John R. Williams, *The Life of Goethe*, p. 161.
39 Act V, Scene 2,VIII, 348–9.
40 9/10 July 1786.
41 *Italian Journey*, 12 October 1786.

CHAPTER 8 – ITALY

1 He arrived in Italy in 1779, studied for two years in Florence, then went to Switzerland and arrived in Rome in January 1783. Julius Vogel, *Aus Goethe's Römischen Tagen*, p. 100.
2 Ibid., p. 99.
3 Friedrich von Alten, *Aus Tischbein's Leben und Briefwechsel*.
4 *Dichtung und Wahrheit*, Part 4, Book 20.
5 F 2342.
6 F 2604.
7 Zapperi, p. 142.
8 Epigram 10, 'Knaben liebt ich wohl auch ...' XIV.660.
9 Claude Quetel, *History of Syphilis*, p. 96.
10 XIV.660.
11 Foreword to his *Deutsche Grammatik*, Part 1, p. vi.
12 Boyle, Vol. I, p. 393.
13 Eckermann, 7 April 1829.

14 Irmgard Schmidt, 'Angelika Kauffmann – Goethes Freundin in Rom. Ein Lebensbild nach ihren Briefen und nach Berichten ihrer Zeitgenossen', pp. 101–23.

15 *Italian Journey*, British Library copy 408, 23 July 1787.

16 Angelika Goodden, *Miss Angel*, p. 236.

17 Pliny the Younger (61–113 CE) was a naturalist who famously described the eruption of Vesuvius which had engulfed the region in October 79, during which his uncle, Pliny the Elder, died. Pliny's combination of farming, living the life of a country gentleman, connoisseurship and scholarship made him the natural role model for eighteenth-century gentlemen scholars.

18 John Thackray, '"The Modern Pliny": Hamilton and Vesuvius', in Ian Jenkins and Kim Sloan, *Vases and Volcanoes*, p. 72.

19 *Italian Journey*, 27 February 1787.

20 Paul Bishop, 'The unconscious from the Storm and Stress to Weimar Classicism. The dialectic of time and pleasure', in Angus Nicholls and Martin Liebscher, eds, *Thinking the Unconscious*, p. 26. See also Hans Dahnke, 'Italian', *Goethe Handbuch*, Band 4/1. XV1.9.

21 Sabine Prokhoris, *La Cuisine de la sorcière*, pp. 7–13.

22 K. M. Kraus, February–March 1775, David Luke and Robert Pick, eds, *Goethe: Conversations and Encounters*, p. 42.

23 Prokhoris, p. 2.

24 Ibid., p. 122.

25 *Italian Journey*, IV, 584.

26 I am being deliberately anachronistic in introducing the concept of the *Dämonisch* at this early stage. He only fully developed it in the early nineteenth century when he had renewed his study of the Neoplatonists, especially Plotinus. But the concept of the *Dämonisch* had surely, in embryo, been with him from a very early stage, and is central to the idea of *Faust* from the beginning.

27 Trunz, p. 517.

28 Prokhoris, p. 140.

29 Ibid., p. 2.

30 F 24.

CHAPTER 9 – VULPIUS

1 F 10 235.

2 Eckhart Klessmann, *Christiane: Goethes Geliebte und Gefährin*, p. 96.

3 Ibid.

4 Venetian Epigrams 17. XIV, 661.

5 Klessmann, p. 145.

6 Ibid., p. 139.

7 XIV, 282.

8 XIV, 651.

9 XIV, 284.

10 Klessmann, p. 50.

11 Ibid.

12 28 June 1784.

13 Friedenthal, p. 328.

14 *Optice: Sive de Reflexionibus, Refractionibus, Inflexionibus et Coloribus Lucis*, 1740.

15 'Confessions of the Author' 5, in Rupprecht Matthaei, *Goethe's Colour Theory*, p. 199.
16 'Confessions of the Author' 7, in ibid.
17 Dennis L. Sepper, *Goethe contra Newton*, pp. 271–2.
18 Charles Lock Eastlake, *Goethe's Theory of Colours*, p. 79.
19 Ibid., Introduction. Facsimile reproduced in Matthaei, p. 215.
20 Matthaei, p. 197.
21 Herder to Karoline, 11 October 1788, Kemp, p. 346.
22 Karoline to Herder, 18 August 1788.
23 8 March 1789, Kemp, p. 351.
24 29 May 1789, Kemp, p. 352.
25 Epigramme, 54 Venedig, 1790. XIV.312.

Chapter 10 – War

1 Quoted Gerhard Hartmann and Karl Schnith, eds, *Die Kaiser, 1200 Jahre europäische Geschichte*, p. 642.
2 IV.642.
3 Safranski, *Goethe: Kunstwerk des Lebens*, p. 320.
4 XIV.326.
5 Karlheinz Schulz, *Goethe*, p. 264.
6 Hermann Schmitz, *Goethes Altersdenken im problemgeschichtlichen Zusammenhang*, p. vi.
7 30 August 1792, Schmitz, p. 90.
8 12 September 1792, ibid., p. 123.
9 26 September 1792.
10 All described in my novel *Resolution*.
11 Quoted Friedenthal, p. 327.
12 Annette Meakin, *Goethe and Schiller*, Vol. I, p. 268.

Chapter 11 – The Friendship with Schiller

1 Meakin, Vol. I, p. 31.
2 T. S. Eliot, *The Complete Prose*: Vol. I, *Apprentice Years, 1905–1918*, eds Jewel Spears Brooker and Ronald Schuchard, Baltimore, Johns Hopkins University Press, 2014, p. 259. It is from Chapter 2 of his PhD Thesis 'Knowledge and Experience in the Philosophy of F. H. Bradley'.
3 1 March 1787.
4 8 June 1787.
5 And his utter distance from the kind of materialist reductionism into which Charles Darwin would slide in the second half of his life when, as he tells us, he lost all taste for literature, music, or the imaginative side of life.
6 Peter Salm, *The Poem as Plant*, p. 105.
7 F 382.
8 See 'Goethe as Philosopher' by Eckhart Förster, in *Goethe's Wilhelm Meister's Apprenticeship and Philosophy*, ed. Sarah Vandegrift Eldridge and C. Allen Speight, New York, Oxford University Press, p. 25.
9 19 December 1788, Meakin, Vol. I, p. 107.
10 Peter Lahnstein, *Schillers Leben*, München, List Verlag, 1981, p. 306.
11 Meakin, Vol. I, p. 149.
12 Ibid., Vol. II, p. 211.

13 Letter to Carl August, 5 July 1789.
14 Meakin, Vol. I, p. 177.
15 Ibid., p. 179.
16 Ibid., p. 187.
17 F 22.
18 Ibid., Vol. II, p. 135.
19 Lewes, p. 242.
20 *Lover's Vows* was Elizabeth Inchbald's adaptation of Kotzebue's play *Child of Love*.
21 Michael Patterson, *The First German Theatre*, p. 114.
22 Lewes, p. 454.
23 Ibid., p. 439.
24 Meakin, Vol. I, p. 342.
25 Ibid., p. 287.
26 23 August 1794.
27 Ibid., p. 800.
28 27 October 1800, Meakin, Vol. II, p. 217.
29 *GG*, i. 644.
30 Letter to Schiller, 7 February 1798.
31 *GG*, 1. 906.
32 Bode, ed., *Goethe in vertraulichen Briefen seiner Zeitgenossen*, Vol. II, p. 146.
33 Meakin, Vol. I, p. 279.
34 Lewis, *The Abolition of Man*, p. 46.
35 F 1675.
36 F 1676.
37 F 1851–67.

Chapter 12 – The Parades of Death

1 F 286.
2 F 328.
3 F 327.
4 F 339.
5 F 353.
6 F 104–7.
7 F 3440.
8 Thomas Carlyle, *The Life of Friedrich Schiller*, in *Complete Works*, Vol. XXV, p. 110.
9 Michael Inwood, *A Commentary on Hegel's Philosophy of Mind*, Oxford, Oxford University Press, 2010, pp. 64, 246. See *Enzyklopedie der philosophiscen Wissenschaften*, 3 vols, I.242, 'A great spirit has great experiences, and discerns in the motley play of appearance the point of significance.' Hegel is here directly referencing Goethe.
10 They are all wonderfully brought to life in Andrea Wulf's *Magnificent Rebels*.
11 28 August 1788.
12 2 May 1798.
13 *GG*, i. 952.
14 1 January 1799, *Briefwechsel mit Friedrich Schiller*, p. 675.
15 Christmas Day 1797.
16 Lewes, p. 421.
17 John Geary, *Wallenstein*.

18 See Walter Hinderer, *Der Mensch in der Geschichte*, Königstein, Athenäum Taschenbücher, 1980.
19 Friedrich Schiller, *Schillers Werke*, p. 720.
20 Ibid., p. 761.
21 Ibid., p. 715.
22 Friedenthal, p. 373.
23 Safranski, *Goethe: Kunstwerk des Lebens*, p. 383.
24 F 765.
25 Safranski, *Goethe: Kunstwerk des Lebens*, p. 384.
26 Ibid.

CHAPTER 13 – DEMONS

1   Matthaei, p. 210.
2   Schmitz, p. 27.
3   Robert Steiger, *Goethes Leben von Tag zu Tag*, Vol. I, p. 145.
4   Ibid., Vol. IV, p. 627.
5   1 September 1805.
6   Ibid.
7   Letter to Friedrich August Wolf, 9 August 1805. See also *Maximen und Reflexionen*, pp. 642–4, 'Eine geistige Form wird aber keineswegs verkürzt, wenn sie wahre Zeugnung, eine wahre Fortpflanzung sei. Das Gezeugte ist nicht geringer als das Zeugende, ja es ist der Vortheil lebendiger Zeugung, dass das Gezeugte vortrefflicher sein kann als der Zeugende.'
8   It is perhaps worth saying that, while Goethe was inspired by his excursus into the *Enneads*, it is hard to imagine the somewhat puritanical and austere Plotinus finding much common ground with Goethe, or with Byron or, come to that, with Napoleon.
9   XIV.540.
10 Flodoard Freiherr von Biedermann, *Goethes Gespraeche ohne die Gespraeche mit Eckermann*, Leipzig, Insel Verlag, pp. 185–8, no date to publication. Date of conversation 1 August 1805.
11 Ibid., p. 381.
12 F 3040–44.
13 Grateful thanks to Andrew Roberts for recommending me to walk across the battlefield, which I did on a frosty morning in spring 2023. I passed a solitary local exercising his dog, who told me that almost every week a farmer would find a human bone, often a skull, in the soil.
14 Bruno Colson and Alexander Mikaberidze, *The Cambridge History of the Napoleonic Wars*. Volume II, Fighting *the Napoleonic Wars*, p. 393.
15 10 August 1806, Luke and Pick, p. 61.
16 F. Stawell and G. Lowes Dickinson, *Goethe and Faust: An Interpretation*, p. 2.
17 Katharina Mommsen, 'Faust II als politisches Vermächtnis des Staatsmannes Goethe', pp. 24–5.
18 Safranski, *Goethe: Kunstwerk des Lebens*, p. 407.
19 Klessmann, p. 81.
20 Safranski, *Goethe: Kunstwerk des Lebens*, p. 451.
21 Ibid., p. 399.
22 Ibid., p. 400.
23 First Part, Chapter Nine. I.833.
24 Chapter 4.

25 Nicholas Boyle, 'The Composition of *Die Wahlverwandtschaften*', p. 98.
26 Ibid., p. 231.
27 In a paper printed in *The German Quarterly*, Vol. 89, Issue 3, pp. 298–312.
28 *Goethe Handbuch*, Band 2, p. 391.
29 F 8488–93.
30 Boyle, Vol. II, p. 662.
31 GG, 501, 30 August 1827, F. V. Müller.
32 Eckermann, 13 December 1826.
33 XV.45.
34 Williams, p. 272.
35 XV.263.
36 *Goethes Sämtliche Werke*, Band XVI, p. 144, 'Epochen der Wissenschaften'.
37 XV.71.
38 Safranski, *Goethe: Kunstwerk des Lebens*, p. 471.
39 *Goethe Handbuch*, Band 4/2, p. 1156.
40 Klessmann, p. 78.
41 Ibid., p. 171.
42 *Venetian Elegies*.
43 Klessmann, p. 184.
44 Ibid., p. 167.
45 Ibid., p. 174.
46 Hume Brown, *The Youth of Goethe*, p. 294.
47 *Goethe Handbuch*, Band 4/1, p. 396.
48 Inge, Vol. II, p. 173.
49 *Farbenlehre*, quoted Olaf F. Müller, *Mehr Licht*, p. 23, XVII.43.
50 Henri Bortoft, *The Wholeness of Nature*, pp. 195ff.
51 Galileo, *Il Saggiatore* (The Assayer), quoted Bortoft, p. 196.
52 Stephen Hawking, *A Brief History of Time*, p. 175.
53 Sepper, pp. 27–38.
54 Heinrich O. Proskauer, *The Rediscovery of Color*, p. 25.
55 Bortoft, p. 225.
56 Sepper, p. 262.
57 That is, the ultimately Platonist idea that there is the true world, that of Reason, where the Forms or Ideas exist in some ethereal plane, and the world of matter where natural phenomena are mere shadows or images of the Ideas. Bortoft and other Goethean scientists believe that Galileo, Locke, Hume, Newton et al. believed ultimately in the power of reason, especially mathematical law, to be the ultimate test of reality, and that they imposed this view on their examination of Nature. They were retaining the Platonist mind/matter, Idea/Shadow idea in a different guise.
58 Bortoft, p. 233.
59 Quoted Miller p. 39, Douglas Miller, *Goethe: Scientific Studies*, p. 175ff.
60 Carolyn Merchant, *The Death of Nature*, p. 168.
61 F 675–7.
62 F 382–3.
63 F 4679.
64 Müller, p. 127.
65 Ibid., pp. 441–51.
66 Ibid., p. 385.
67 Safranski, *Goethe: Kunstwerk des Lebens*, p. 390.
68 Ibid., p. 542.

Chapter 14 – Ottilie

1 Andrew Piper, 'Egologies: Goethe, Entoptics, and the Instruments of Writing Life', p. 21.
2 XVI.123.
3 2 September 1812.
4 F 11,572.
5 IV.208 (9 March 1787, Naples).
6 20 October 1817, Luke and Pick, p. 101.
7 *Lotte in Weimar*, Chapter Five.
8 XIV.358.
9 XV.245.
10 Merseburger, p. 164.
11 XV.181.
12 George S. Williamson, 'What Killed August von Kotzebue? The Temptations of Virtue and the Political Theology of German Nationalism, 1789–1819'.
13 Boyle, Vol. II, p. 792.
14 Ibid., p. 780.
15 Paul Messner, *Das Deutsche Nationaltheater Weimar*, S.41.
16 *Goethe Handbuch*, Band 2, p. 40.
17 Eckermann, 2 May 1824.
18 See Piper.
19 Jed Z. Buchwald, *The Rose of the Wave Theory of Light*, pp. 41–110.
20 Simon Richter and Richard Block, eds, *Goethe's Ghosts*, pp. 17–36.
21 Friedenthal, p. 451.
22 He was in fact seventy-two.
23 Luke and Pick, p. 113.
24 Quoted Friedenthal, p. 412.
25 Friedenthal, p. 412.
26 Humphrey Trevelyan, *Goethe and the Greeks*, p. 284.
27 Friedenthal, p. 413.
28 Ibid.
29 F 765.
30 The recollection is that of Friedrich von Müller, quoted Luke and Pick, p. 125.
31 XV, 181.
32 Quoted Friedenthal, p. 456.
33 Friedenthal, p. 451.
34 Piper, p. 28.
35 Piper, p. 27.
36 David Brewster, *The Kaleidoscope*, p. 18.
37 Piper, p. 27.
38 F 12,082.
39 Erich Heller, *The Artist's Journey into the Interior*, p. 29.
40 Thomas Davidson, *The Philosophy of Goethe's Faust*, p. 155.
41 Ibid., p. 157.
42 J. M. van der Laan, *Seeking Meaning for Goethe's Faust*, p. 148.
43 Ibid., pp. 148–9.
44 F Part Two, 12,094.
45 F. Weitze, 19 August, 1805. In Flodoard Freiherr von Biedermann, *Goethes Gespraeche ohne die Gespraeche mit Eckermann*, p. 185.
46 F 12,104.

47 Van der Laan, p. 138.
48 F 317.

Chapter 15 – Eckermann

1 F 328–9.
2 H. H. Houben, *J. P. Eckermann*, p. 100.
3 Ibid., p. 23.
4 Eckermann, p. 28.
5 Houben, p. 23.
6 Ludwig Müllner, *Goethes Faust im Lichte seiner Naturförschung*, p. 137.
7 John Bayley made a comparable point about the death of John Keats in a celebrated British Academy lecture, 'Keats and Reality', *Proceedings of the British Academy*, 1962.
8 Eckermann, 6 December 1829.
9 Van Abbé, p. 12.
10 Safranski, *Goethe: Kunstwerk des Lebens*, p. 315.
11 28 April 1820.
12 *Goethe Handbuch*, Band 4, p. 659.
13 Safranski, *Goethe: Kunstwerk des Lebens*, p. 510.
14 See, e.g. C. S. Lewis: *The Allegory of Love*, which perversely argues that falling in love is a literary construct, a trope invented by the troubadours.
15 XV.288.
16 My allusion is to Thomas Hardy's perfect lyric, describing the same phenomenon of an old man's capacity to feel the pains of love – 'I look into my glass/And view my wasting skin/And think, "Would God it came to pass, My heart had shrunk as thin!"'
17 Eckermann, 27 January 1824.
18 Ibid., 16 November 1823.
19 Ibid., 24 February 1824.
20 Ibid., 26 February 1824.
21 Ibid., 18 January 1825.
22 Ibid., 24 February 1825.
23 Ibid.
24 Ibid.
25 Ibid., 22 March 1825.
26 Julius Petersen, *Die Entstehung der Eckermannschen Gespräche und ihre Glaubwürdigkeit*, Berlin, 1924, p. 80.
27 Derek van Abbé, 'On Correcting Eckermann's Perspectives', p. 5.
28 Ibid.
29 Eckermann, 11 December 1826.
30 Ibid., 21 February 1827.
31 Ibid., 22 October 1828.

Chapter 16 – The Myth of Weimar

1 'Wanderer's Night Song' I.184.
2 Eckermann, 9 July 1827.
3 Bertrand Russell, *A History of Western Philosophy*, p. 764, London, George Allen & Unwin, 1946. Chillingly, given the date when Russell wrote his book, he adds, 'This is a very superfine brand of freedom. It does not mean that you will be able

to keep out of a concentration camp. It does not imply democracy, or a free press, or any of the usual Liberal watchwords, which Hegel rejects with contempt.' It is understandable that a book published by an Englishman, one year after the Second World War, should have included the mention of concentration camps; but it would have been fairer of Russell to have added, first, that no such things existed in the days of Hegel and Goethe; and secondly, that concentration camps were invented by the British, in their South African wars.

4 Quoted Merseburger, p. 356.
5 Especially Julius Petersen – see Derek van Abbé, op. cit. in the last chapter.
6 Eckermann, 11 March 1832.
7 T. S. Eliot, *The Complete Prose*: Vol. VIII, *Still and Still Moving, 1954–1965*, eds Jewel Spears Brooker and Ronald Schuchard, Baltimore, Johns Hopkins University Press, 2019, p. 64.
8 Ibid., p. 74.
9 Ibid, p. 80.
10 Lutz Saltner, '*Hier Nicht*'. *Goethes letzte Tage*, p. 57.
11 Eckermann, no date, Vol. II, last page.
12 *Goethe Handbuch*, Band 4/1, p. 410.
13 Klaus Bellin, *Das Weimar des Harry Graf Kessler*, p. 3.
14 Wilson, *Der Faustische Pakt*, p. 98.
15 Merseburger, p. 345.
16 Osman Durrani, *Faust*, p. 226.
17 F 328–9.
18 Durrani, p. 172.
19 Ibid., p. 175.
20 Safranski, *Goethe: Kunstwerk des Lebens*, p. 555.

Chapter 17 – Soon, Peace

1 Fiona MacCarthy, *Byron: Life and Legend*, p. 151.
2 W. Leaf and M. A. Bayfield, *Iliad*, Vol. II, London, Macmillan, 1898, p. 521.
3 Eckermann, 18 January 1825.
4 Ibid., 18 May 1824.
5 Ibid., 8 March 1831.
6 Ibid., 5 July 1827.
7 Ibid.
8 Ibid., 6 May 1827.
9 H. R. Trevor-Roper, *Historical Essays*, pp. 274–5.
10 Thomas Mann, *Deutsche Hörer! 25 Radiosendungen nach Deutschland*, Insel Verlag, Leipzig, 1970.
11 *Goethe Handbuch*, Band 1, p. 293.
12 XIV, 441.
13 The lyric 'Selige Sehnsucht', *Gesammelte Werke*, XV, p. 55.
14 Heller, *The Disinherited Mind*.
15 Eckermann, 15 January 1827.
16 Schulz, p. 199.
17 Ibid., p. 452.
18 Hans Rudolf Vaget, Introduction to David Luke, *Goethe Erotic Poems*, p. xxxiii, Oxford, Oxford World's Classics, 1999.
19 August 1830.

20 *Goethe Handbuch*, Band 4/1, p. 392.
21 1 December 1830.
22 Letter to C. F. von Reinhard, 15 September 1820, Luke and Pick, p. 136
23 Heller, *The Disinherited Mind*, p. 234.
24 Schulz, p. 445, *GG*, 3/2, 411.
25 Letter to Zelter, 9 November 1829.
26 Ibid.
27 Stuart Atkins, *Faust Parts One and Two*, p. 201.
28 F 7935.
29 Atkins, *Faust Parts One and Two*, p. 183.
30 Ibid., p. 190.
31 F 7856.
32 Eckermann, 23 February 1831.
33 Vogel, p. 222.
34 F 8325.
35 Friedrich Theodor Vischer, for example, a leading scholar, proclaimed, upon the publication of *Faust Part Two* in 1832, that Goethe had become senile and lost his poetic powers; and that these symbolic-mythological sections of the drama constituted a reduction of meaning and a loss of control. Cyrus Hamlin, *Faust*, p. 421.
36 Eckermann, 27 March 1831
37 Ibid., 9 February 1831.
38 Ibid., 30 November 1830.
39 The reference is to the so-called Fata Morgana.
40 F 10,584–9.
41 Quoted Friedenthal, p. 449.
42 Safranski, *Goethe: Kunstwerk des Lebens*, p. 557.
43 He had copied it and read it to friends, and it soon became famous: a pirated version had been published in *The Monthly Magazine*, 1803 and again it appeared, pirated, in Kotzebue's periodical *Der Freimüthige, oder Berlinische Zeitung für gebildete unbefangene Leser* (1815).
44 4 September 1831.
45 Briefe die Jahre 1814–1832, p. 1,000, Band 19, Artemis Verlag, Zürich.

BIBLIOGRAPHY

1 Boyle, Vol. I, p. vii.
2 Edward Luttwak, 'Goethe in China', *London Review of Books*, 3 June 2021, quoted by Ritchie Robertson in 'Goethe's Faust II. The Redemption of an Enlightened Despot', a paper for the English Goethe Society, *Publications of the English Goethe Society*, March 2022.

INDEX